BLAISE CENDRARS

BLAISE CENDRARS
THE INVENTION OF LIFE

ERIC ROBERTSON

REAKTION BOOKS

For my parents

Published by
REAKTION BOOKS LTD
Unit 32, Waterside
44–48 Wharf Road
London N1 7UX, UK
www.reaktionbooks.co.uk

First published 2022

Printed and bound in Great Britain by TJ Books Ltd, Padstow, Cornwall

A catalogue record for this book is available from the British Library

ISBN 978 1 78914 520 5

CONTENTS

Introduction

> My hero is Blaise Cendrars, do you see? He's my hero in every respect: as a man, as a personality, as a writer, the style of writing and everything that he did in his life to me is marvellous.
>
> HENRY MILLER

Blaise Cendrars is an extraordinary figure. The events of his life resemble an adventure story, and his writings are packed with wisdom, insight and the experience of a life lived to the full. He left us a very sizeable literary oeuvre that encompasses poems, novels, travel narratives, film scripts, short stories, critical essays and radio plays. These works bear witness to one of the most distinctive and unique voices in twentieth-century European literature. His writings offer the reader a seismographic record of a distinctly modern, inventive, erudite sensibility; they afford valuable insights into the time and places he inhabited, as well as communicating shrewd observations on human nature that are as true today as they were when they were written. And in the process, they take literature in startling new directions. Cendrars is a visionary in the tradition of Coleridge or Rimbaud, a free spirit, a global traveller and a dowser of life's secrets in their messy, multiform reality. Henry Miller wrote this about him: 'Worshipping life and the truth of life, he comes closer than any author of our time to revealing the common source of word and deed. He restores to contemporary life the elements of the heroic, the imaginative and the fabulous.'[1] For literary scholar Richard Sieburth, Cendrars is 'a Whitmanesque citizen of the cosmos'.[2] The contemporary French author Philippe Forest selected Cendrars's

Le Lotissement du ciel as the most important book of the twentieth century.[3] All of Cendrars's books carry distinct traces of his own lived experience, but without ever becoming a straightforward record of it, since they rely on observation and invention. This is as true of the poems he wrote in the first two decades of the twentieth century as it is of the novels and other works of prose that began to appear in the 1920s, the autobiographical and fictional writings of the post-war years, and the books he was still planning until his death in 1961.

The emphasis of the present study rests on his literary output and the nature and implications of his many innovations in the fields of poetry, prose fiction and life-writing. It will also consider some of his creative collaborations with painters, cinematographers and photographers and will assess their impact on his writing as well as considering the influence of other writers on his work. It is instructive to comment on his life to the extent that it can help to shed light on his methods and practice as a writer; this is all the more pertinent given how full and varied a life Cendrars had, and how much of his experience feeds into his work. His practice of writing in the guise of characters called Blaise, and his frequent references to the places, people and events that he encountered, make it tempting to read much of his work as autobiographical, but we should beware of interpreting even his most overtly personal life-writing through this lens. Admittedly, much of his life flows into his writing, but in turn, his writing tends to take on a life of its own; as a result, even those texts that could be assumed to be autobiographical accounts are often embellished with imaginative digressions. His heavily autobiographical narratives published in the years following the Second World War are much more than straightforward accounts of factual events; they include myriad digressions, disruptions of chronology, invented passages and embedded narratives that are the fruit of his imagination. In his later years, Cendrars became known as a somewhat loquacious storyteller, and in radio interviews conducted in the 1950s, we can detect a measure of disbelief in the interviewers' voices, and a defiant insistence in his, when he recounts anecdotes from his past. The conversations recorded for French radio with fellow poet Michel Manoll are exemplary in this regard.

Accusations of mythomania have been levelled at Cendrars over the years. While he unquestionably embellished some facts and altered some dates, it is important not to exaggerate his fondness for inventing stories, since this would be to miss the point; much of what he wrote was indeed based on his life and on his rich and wide knowledge of the world. Whether he ran away from his family home as a teenager, as he claimed to have done, or left with his parents' accord, matters little; the fact remains that he did travel far and frequently at an early age, and he also read widely and voraciously. These two kinds of travels – journeys on foot, by car, train and boat, and journeys through the world of literature – provide an extremely fertile basis for his impressive body of work consisting of poetry, novels, literary essays and reportage. Cendrars's unique style of writing is a product of these two influences, and he deserves to be hailed as a pioneer of a distinctive form of literature that is heavily indebted to real-life experiences but not bound by recourse to their pedantic recounting. Claude Louis-Combet's term '(auto)mythobiography' is helpful, since it does not regard autobiography and dream as absolutely incompatible but envisages a literary space in which they may coexist and nurture one another.[4]

From his early days as an experimental poet to his mature years as a writer of autobiographically inflected prose, his literary output seems concerned in equal measure with what it means to live and what it means to write. He repeatedly expressed impatience at the demands of being a writer, preferring life spent outdoors, travelling or in the company of others to the solitary confinement of the writing desk. Cendrars was widely photographed, most famously by Robert Doisneau, but never at a writing desk. The closest we get to that is a well-known photographic portrait by Doisneau depicting the writer in front of his notes, pen in hand, seated at the kitchen table of his home in Aix-en-Provence.[5] In an interview with Michel Manoll, Cendrars derides the hackneyed image of a writer sitting in a study, whistling nonchalantly as he casually bashes out another book on his typewriter.[6] Writing, for Cendrars, entails hardship: not the suffering of the tortured Romantic, but the sacrifice of an individual who would rather be outside, in the street, speaking with people, travelling, doing things. Henry Miller, who ranked Cendrars as one of his five most important influences, summed up the mutually imbricated pressures of living and writing that made him unique. For him, Cendrars is '[t]he most gregarious of men and yet a solitary. "O mes solitudes!" A man of deep intuition and invincible logic. The logic of life. Life first and foremost. Life always with a capital L.'[7]

In his childhood, Cendrars lived in Switzerland, Italy and Germany. While still a teenager, he went to work in St Petersburg; as a young man he spent time in New York and London; and in the interwar years he became acquainted with Brazil. But it was in Paris that he made his name as a writer, and indeed it was there that he assumed his literary identity, shedding his legal name, Frédéric-Louis Sauser, to become the writer Blaise Cendrars. His arrival in Paris in the summer of 1912 brought his work to the attention of Guillaume Apollinaire, who must have seen in him a kindred spirit. Apollinaire, who was already engaged in his own pursuit of poetic innovation, was spurred on by Cendrars's radical and ultra-modern approach to poetry. Much has been written about the impact that Cendrars's inaugural poem *Les Pâques* is thought to have had on Apollinaire; the latter retrieved the galley proofs of his own volume *Alcools* from the publishers in order to make substantial amendments to his poems so that they might compete with the sheer innovation of the new arrival on the scene. Apollinaire took an interest in Cendrars's welfare, recruiting him to help copy incunabula at the Bibliothèque Mazarine; it was not long before Cendrars was celebrated as a poet in his own right and admired by other writers as well as artists on the Parisian avant-garde scene. He went on to befriend Henry Miller and John Dos Passos, who were both heavily influenced by his work. Dos Passos famously nicknamed him 'the Homer of the Transsiberian' in 1926.

A footnote in an article published in the *French Review* in 1941 points out an apparent contradiction regarding the biographical fact of Cendrars's place of birth: 'The *Dictionnaire historique et biographique de la Suisse* gives La Chaux-de-Fonds, in French-speaking Switzerland, as his birthplace; but in his own autobiographical sketch, published in Kunitz's *Authors Today and Yesterday*, Cendrars states that he was born in Paris.'[8] It tells us much about Cendrars, and what makes him special, that both of these statements are true and contribute to the mythology surrounding him. Even those close to the writer have, in different ways, contributed to the confusion: the back cover of *Blaise Cendrars: l'or d'un poète*, written by Miriam Cendrars, the writer's daughter, reads: 'Blaise Cendrars naît à New York le 6 avril 1912. Il a 24 ans.' (Blaise Cendrars was born in New York on 6 April 1912. He was 24 years old.)[9] Cendrars scholarship has often commented on the writer's prolific self-mythologizing, on his creation of a persona, Cendrars the *bourlingueur* – a globetrotting, genial author of prose fiction and travel writing. While this does indeed describe one aspect of Cendrars's literary identity, it does not even come close to capturing the sheer originality and diversity of his creative writing. As Christine Le Quellec Cottier put it in her eponymous book,

Cendrars is 'un homme en partance' (a man leaving) – constantly on the move, almost pathologically incapable of standing still.[10] As a writer, he seems to play a game of hide and seek with his reader, offering snippets of information that bring us closer to him, but only to retreat into the fictional space of his writing and shake us off his scent. Throughout his entire literary oeuvre, we encounter tantalizing references to 'Blaise', to his family, to experiences that are close or even identical to those we know he underwent in his life. The seeming proximity of the narrating 'I' to the real Blaise Cendrars is accentuated by his frequent use of the first-person narrative voice, but even at its most heavily autobiographical, his writing is never a straightforward reflection of his identity. Rather, it seems that writing the self, or writing *around* the self, is a strategy that Cendrars employs both to chart new literary paths and to reinvent himself repeatedly. Any attempt to sum him up is bound to produce a snapshot of a blur, yet the cumulative effect of reading his work leaves the reader with a powerful sense of an identity that is concomitant with the literary work and is shaped by the act of writing it. Across its very considerable breadth, Cendrars's literary oeuvre is surprisingly homogeneous; it has myriad facets and employs many different literary modes, but it does so with a single, unmistakable voice.

The aims of this book are to explore Cendrars's literary work against the backdrop of his extraordinary life, to assess whether an underlying consistency can be found in his work across its multifaceted stylistic and thematic plurality, to pay particular attention to those aspects of his writing that brought him into close contact with his literary, artistic and social environment and to reflect on the consequences of those interactions for our understanding of Cendrars as a writer. The book asks to what extent it is possible to consider Cendrars's extensive literary output as a continuous whole. It encompasses more than five decades of activity and a plethora of literary genres; indeed, it is easy to see Cendrars as an elusive writer, never staying in the same place long enough for us to get the measure of him. Certainly, with his invented name, his abhorrence of stasis and his repeated excursions in new literary directions, he shaped his career around reinvention and flux. While this is all true, and makes Cendrars a fascinating subject, this book will argue that a strong continuity underpins his literary oeuvre.

Another question that this book examines is to what extent Cendrars should be considered an avant-garde writer. Many of his early poems were published by small presses on the margins rather than in the mainstream;

he was acquainted with numerous members of the international avant-garde scene and engaged in an array of collaborations with pioneers of experimental and abstract art; he wrote about cinema, and for a time was directly involved in the making of films; and his poetry and other writings broke new ground by importing techniques of collage, montage and cinematic effects into literature. Yet for most of his career he worked alone, and throughout his long career he never became a member of any group, movement or -ism. In light of this paradoxical situation, the book also aims to ascertain in which ways and to what extent Cendrars's extraordinary achievements in the field of literature call for a reappraisal of his importance in the context of twentieth-century European literature and his continuing relevance in the twenty-first century.

The intention of this book is not to provide an exhaustive or comprehensive account of Cendrars's writings, but to provide readings of a selection of his works and situate them against the background of key events in his life and the times through which he lived. Given his very extensive collaborations with artists, film-makers, musicians and photographers, this book will consider the place within his oeuvre of the works that emerged from such creative exchanges.

Existing Literature on Cendrars

Acclaimed in his lifetime as an important and influential writer, Cendrars is again the subject of renewed scholarly interest in France, thanks in part to the recent appearance of his work in the French school curriculum. In the early years of the twenty-first century, a number of critical studies appeared in France with a school-age readership in mind. For the serious scholar, the re-edition of a special number of the journal *Europe* devoted to Cendrars originally published in 1976 testifies to the lasting value of the essays it contains. Books by Jay Bochner, Yvette Bozon-Scalzitti, Miriam Cendrars, Monique Chefdor, Jean-Carlo Flückiger, Christine Le Quellec Cottier, Claude Leroy, David Martens, Michèle Touret and others have shed much light on his work and life. Georgiana Colvile's monograph *Blaise Cendrars, écrivain protéiforme* deals expertly with Cendrars's poetry, novels, essays and his intertextual connections to John Hawkes.[11] Francis Boder's *La Phrase poétique de Blaise Cendrars* provides a detailed stylistic analysis of his use of language in the prose fiction.[12] Jean-Pierre Goldenstein's excellent study of *Dix-neuf poèmes élastiques* brings a wealth of contextual information to bear on individual readings of the poems.

Collective publications focusing on Cendrars in relation to Brazil, the First World War, European Modernism and the visual arts have helped to bring these specific aspects of his life and work into sharper focus.[13]

The single most notable event for research on Cendrars since his death has been the publication of a multi-volume scholarly re-edition of his collected works. Compiled by a team of experts under the leadership of Claude Leroy, the new editions contain a wealth of valuable documentation and annotations for the serious researcher.[14] The inclusion of Cendrars's complete poems, novels and autobiographical writings in the highly prestigious Bibliothèque de la Pléiade surely confirms, belatedly but definitively, his entry into the pantheon of great French writers.[15] The four tomes that contain the entire corpus of Cendrars's published works, along with various previously unpublished drafts and associated writings, are an extraordinary resource for scholarship. The extensive bibliographical, biographical and critical apparatus within them offers insights of unrivalled breadth and depth that enhance our understanding of Cendrars, his working methods and the relationship between his writings and events in his life.

Translations by Esther Allen, Alan Brown, Monique Chefdor, John Dos Passos, Ron Padgett, Nina Rootes and others have made the poetry and some novels and essays accessible to anglophone readers; Jay Bochner's *Blaise Cendrars: Discovery and Re-Creation* (1978) and Monique Chefdor's *Blaise Cendrars* (1980) are essential critical studies in English. In *The Futurist Moment: Avant-Garde, Avant Guerre, and the Language of Rupture* (1986), Marjorie Perloff situates Cendrars at the very core of the European pre-war avant-garde, and at the start of an itinerary that takes in Cubist collage, avant-garde manifestos, Russian Futurist books and Ezra Pound's rhythmic prose, before identifying Futurist legacies in the 'earthworks' and 'earthwords' of Robert Smithson. The book correctly identifies the *Prose du Transsibérien*, with its extraordinary hybrid format, its spectral colours and its bold use of language, as an emblematic and pioneering instance of experimentation. Clive Scott's *Reading the Rhythm: The Poetics of French Free Verse, 1910–1930* (1993) analyses Cendrars's poetry in depth and produces brilliant close readings that shed much light on the capacity of rhythm not only to structure his poetry but to contribute to the creation of often multiple meanings. Christopher Butler's *Early Modernism* (1994) relates Cendrars's pre-war poetry to the wider artistic and musical experimentation of the period, both in France and beyond. Mikhail

Iampolski's excellent book *The Memory of Tirésias: Intertextuality and Film* (1998) examines Cendrars's interactions with Gance, Léger and Survage, and brings to light some fascinating insights, but since the book is a wider-ranging study of intertextuality, the case of Cendrars understandably accounts for just a single chapter. In *Poetry at Stake: Lyric Aesthetics and the Challenge of Technology* (1999), Carrie Noland explores Cendrars as an exemplary instance of a lyricist (Noland's case studies range from Rimbaud to Patti Smith) whose work engages creatively with industrialization, mechanization and consumerism. Christophe Wall-Romana's *Cinepoetry: Imaginary Cinemas in French Poetry* (2013) states perceptively the importance of cinematography in shaping Cendrars's distinctive literary style. These studies allude to some of the myriad ways in which Cendrars's writing foregrounds visuality and ocular perception. This book aims to build on their findings while working towards a more comprehensive understanding of Cendrars in light of recent critical and theoretical writings.

One respect in which this book seeks to enhance existing scholarship is by considering Cendrars's creative and radically experimental approach to established literary genres, which often entails their partial or complete undoing. This seems particularly germane to Cendrars's oeuvre, and for several reasons. First, as we have noted, throughout his career he produced an exceptionally broad range of types of work, which included poems, essays, play and film scripts, novels, reportage, biographies of remarkable figures and autobiographical works in prose. In doing so, he experimented with the parameters of all of these categories: as a poet, from an early stage he broke with traditional approaches to versification, rhyme, punctuation and style. He chose to work in free verse and employed irregular stanza lengths and unconventional literary effects. The subject-matter of his poetry reflects a heterogeneous and innovative understanding of the 'poetic' and emphatically rejects hierarchical distinctions between 'high' and 'low' cultural forms. As early as the 1910s, he also wrote poems that embraced the notion of the ready-made and pioneered copy-and-paste techniques several decades before William Burroughs and others adopted such methods.[16]

As a novelist, Cendrars produced works that ranged dramatically in scope, style and degrees of complexity; to the uninitiated it must be hard to believe that the same author could have produced novels as dramatically divergent in length, structure and narrative voice as *L'Or* and *Moravagine*, and moreover to have published them within a year of each other. In his journalistic work, he broke with some of the accepted conventions of the genre in order to write in a more literary voice and employed syntax with the kind of elasticity that we also find in his poetry and prose fiction. His writing style juxtaposes concise utterances with sentences that run for an entire page or more, and it alternates between everyday subjects and extraordinary, oneiric flights of fancy.

Across this diverse array of types of text, a certain ethical position is perceptible too, and here, without equating the author with any of his protagonists, we can cautiously identify character traits that reflect aspects of Cendrars's own personality. In the various literary forms we have enumerated, it is striking how often the reader encounters a first-person narrator, who usually identifies himself as 'Blaise' and who refers to incidents from Cendrars's life; this is true of the modern epic poems such as *Les Pâques à New York*, *Prose du Transsibérien* and *Panama*, but also of the circumstantial poems of *Dix-neuf poèmes élastiques* and *Feuilles de route*, in all of which we are brought closer to events that the poet experienced. The protagonists of his novels and other prose writings of the 1920s and '30s are, for the most part, male; whether invented or real, they are often either troubled anti-heroes in the style of Moravagine or Dan Yack, or heroic figures who fell victim to circumstance such as August Suter or Jean Galmot (female characters are scarcer in Cendrars's oeuvre, and his relationships with women were complicated). It is easy to detect sympathy and even self-identification in Cendrars's accounts of these doomed adventurers. In the expansive, autobiographically inflected writings of the years following the Second World War, he frequently focuses on the lives and preoccupations of ordinary people or those living on the margins of society rather than members of the social or cultural elite. Without adopting a specific political or moral agenda, his works often address social issues such as poverty and the uneven distribution of wealth, topics that were close to his heart. In these and other ways, Cendrars's work is about life in its messy, contradictory, frustrating, inexplicable and sometimes marvellous totality.

ENGAGING WITH CENDRARS CAN be an overwhelming task; indeed, at times it seems implausible that a single individual could live as eventful a life as he did and somehow find the time to document it so extensively in writing. This is all the more astonishing in light of the serious injury that he sustained in the First World War, which could easily have brought his literary career, and even his life, to a premature end. The sheer volume of writing that he produced is dauntingly vast, and so too is the scholarly criticism that his works have generated over the nearly six decades since his death, a small portion of which has been acknowledged above. The two dense volumes of poems and novels and two further volumes of autobiographical writings constituting the Pléiade edition total over 5,000 pages of small, tightly arranged print; a significant portion of this consists of the detailed introductions, annotations, chronologies, variants, notes and other critical resources that accompany them. This scholarly apparatus alone, the result of years of work by Cendrars's most knowledgeable and dedicated scholars, testifies to a breathtaking level of knowledge of Cendrars's work and a depth of insight into his working methods for which future generations of his readers will be grateful. The present book, enhanced as it is by the existence of these resources, can do little more than dip a tentative toe into this ocean of material; it will focus on a selection of Cendrars's work across its many literary forms. This will be charted in the following chapters.

one

Birth of a Poet: From Sauser to Cendrars

The boy who would become the French writer Blaise Cendrars was born Frédéric-Louis Sauser in the Swiss town of La Chaux-de-Fonds on 1 September 1887, the son of Georges-Frédéric Sauser, an unsuccessful businessman, and Marie-Louise Dorner, whose influence on Cendrars is perceptible throughout his work. Frédéric, known at home as Freddy, was the youngest child: his sister, Marie-Elise, and his brother, Jean-Georges, were five and three years his senior respectively. Their father was a descendant of winemakers from Sigriswil in the Bernese Oberland, but the family business had fallen on hard times as a result of a pest that destroyed the crop at the end of the eighteenth century. Georges-Frédéric Sauser set up in business working as a salesman for a watchmaker. In September 1894, he took the family to Naples as he attempted to export German beer to Italy; poor storage and transport meant that the initiative failed, so in the face of financial ruin, the family returned to Switzerland. In March 1896, they made their home in Neuchâtel, where they stayed for a year. The sojourn in Naples had lasted only eighteen months, but it had a lasting impact on Freddy's character. Cendrars later wrote about this chapter of his life, and the peripatetic lifestyle more broadly, in his first overtly autobiographical book, *Vol à voiles* (1932), and again in *Bourlinguer* (1948), which focuses on European ports.

By August 1897, the family had moved to Basel, and Freddy was sent to a boarding school in Germany to improve his language skills in preparation for pursuing his schooling in German-speaking Switzerland. In the academic year 1898–9 he made the acquaintance of August Suter, who would remain a lifelong friend. While Freddy was an athletic child and a talented sportsman, it was at this stage in his life that he began to cultivate his mind in a more sustained way: his readings of Erasmus nurtured his intellect and his imagination, while piano lessons revealed his musical abilities. In 1900, the Sauser family visited Paris to see the Exposition Universelle; in its Russian pavilions they experienced a simulated journey on the Trans-Siberian express, complete with moving backdrop depicting scenery between Moscow and Beijing.[1] The exhibit also contained nine painted scrolls by artist Pavel Piasetsky measuring a total of nearly a kilometre in length and depicting the Trans-Siberian route.[2]

The family moved again in 1902, this time back to Neuchâtel, and Freddy's relationship with his family worsened dramatically, as too did his performance at school. In *Vol à voiles*, Cendrars admits that his school report from 1903–4 recorded some 374 unjustified hours of absence from class. The fifteen-year-old, who had spent more time yachting on the lake than in the classroom, resolved to leave home. Indeed, in September 1904, he embarked on a three-month work placement in Moscow, after which he obtained a three-year contract in St Petersburg working as a trainee for jeweller and watchmaker Henri Albert Leuba.[3] One of his colleagues there was Grigori Alexandrovich Rogovin, a Jewish travelling jeweller from Warsaw, who probably inspired the unnamed 'voyageur en bijouterie qui se rendait à Kharbine' (travelling jewel merchant on his way to Harbin) mentioned in *Prose du Transsibérien*.[4] Sauser's arrival in January 1905 coincided with the beginnings of revolution: only days after his arrival in St Petersburg, 'Bloody Sunday' broke out, resulting in the death of hundreds of demonstrators at the hands of the tsar's cavalry.[5] This new phase of his life saw him coming into contact with anarchist circles; according to Miriam Cendrars, a female acquaintance who initiated this contact was sentenced to death by hanging.[6]

Against this backdrop of social unrest, and dissatisfied with his work, Sauser frequented the Imperial Library, where he was able to indulge his passion for literature. There he befriended a librarian to whom he refers only as R. R. With the latter's encouragement, Sauser began to write: the first outlet for his expressive energy was a diary in which he documented his extensive and wide-ranging reading.[7] In parallel, he kept another notebook in which he wrote about paintings he had seen on visits to the Hermitage Museum.

Freddy's first love was Hélène Kleinmann, then sixteen years of age, a Russian of aristocratic descent whom he met in April 1906 in St Petersburg. Despite their blossoming romantic friendship, Sauser's guilt

Frédéric-Louis Sauser, *c.* 1907.

towards abandoning his mother, who was seriously ill, prompted him at the end of that year to request leave of absence, which was granted for the end of February 1907.[8] On Freddy's arrival in Basel in April, his brother Georges failed to recognize him when he stepped off the train, so profoundly had his appearance changed during his time in Russia.[9] His reunion with his parents in Neuchâtel was painful, as it came to light that his father had been leading a double life while his mother was suffering from physical and mental illnesses.[10] That June, still in Neuchâtel, Sauser learned that Hélène had died in a freak accident after she knocked over an oil lamp in her home. This tragedy doubtless has its part to play in Sauser's adoption of the nom de plume Blaise Cendrars: *braise* is French for embers, and Cendrars evokes *cendres* (cinders), so his chosen name has connotations of a blazing fire that leads to regeneration and phoenix-like rebirth from the embers. This trope runs throughout Cendrars's entire literary oeuvre.

In the inventories of his own publications that Cendrars compiled at various times in his life – a symptom of his fondness for lists – he gives 1907 as the year of his first poem, 'The Legend of Novgorod', claiming that it was written that year and translated into Russian in 1909 by the friend known as R. R. under whose aegis the book allegedly appeared in a print run of fourteen. Long assumed to be one of the many 'ghost' publications that never progressed beyond a title, the book was thought to have been discovered in 1995, when a copy was unearthed in the city of Sofia. Serious doubt reigns over the authenticity of this book, now in private hands.[11] Its status, though, is assured as part of the Cendrars myth; Claude Leroy suggests that the title, if reduced to the initials LN, may be interpreted as a reference to Hélène, whose name it imitates phonetically.

In February 1908, only months after Hélène's fatal accident, Freddy's mother died. In April, his brother married and adopted his wife's surname, becoming Georges Sauser-Hall. Freddy had embarked on medical studies at the University of Bern, but grief over his mother's death may have forced him to spend time in a clinic.[12] He signed up for philosophy lectures, but by spring 1909 he was diagnosed with cyclothymia and dissociative identity disorder. As part of his studies in medicine, he took a work placement at the Waldau clinic, near Bern, where the schizophrenic patient Adolf Wölfli had been interned for some fourteen years. Wölfli, a prodigious and highly prolific artist, is thought to have inspired the character of Moravagine, and similarly, the Waldau clinic reappears in the novel lightly disguised as 'Waldensee'.[13]

Blaise Cendrars as a student at the University of Bern, 1907.

In Bern in the spring of 1909, Freddy met a Polish woman, Félicie (Féla) Poznanska, with whom he struck up a relationship. That autumn, his father, who had shown little interest in the family for some years, remarried; he and his new wife had a child the following year and a second in 1914. Freddy distanced himself from them; arguably the most significant event for him in 1909 was discovering the work of writer Remy de Gourmont, who became his lifelong literary hero and whose influence can be felt at regular intervals throughout Cendrars's oeuvre.[14]

Sauser's restlessness and health worries continued throughout 1910: he moved to Brussels in February and found occasional work there, including bit part acting at the Théâtre de la Monnaie and juggling in a music hall. He briefly returned to Bern in May, but, suffering from neuralgia and dizziness, spent time at a spa in La Panne near Ostend in June. In August, he took detailed notes on the works of Gourmont and wrote an article on him that was published two years later.[15] By the autumn he was in Paris, where he met his old school friend August Suter, by then a sculptor. Cendrars believed mistakenly that his friend was related to General Johann August Suter, whose extraordinary life as a pioneer of the Californian Gold Rush he would turn into his most successful book, *L'Or* (*Sutter's Gold*), in 1925.

In April 1911, Féla left for New York, where her sister was living, and gave classes at the Ferrer School. Freddy left for St Petersburg, where he stayed with Hélène's family. There, he continued to read extensively and embarked on *Aléa*, an autobiographical novel, as well as a volume of poems, *Séquences*, which he later dismissed and removed from lists of his works. Reluctant to return to Switzerland, he tried to find a job in Russia, but ended up accepting Féla's invitation to join her in New York. In November he boarded the SS *Birma*, a vessel belonging to the Russian East Asiatic Company, and arrived three weeks later. The year ended on a momentous note: he wrote a text called *Hic, Haec, Hoc* and signed it Blaise Cendrart. On the advice of his brother, he changed the final 't' to an 's', arriving at the name that would accompany him through the rest of his life.[16]

Having arrived in New York in December 1911, he managed to find some casual work, spending one hour per week as a pianist in a cinema screening silent films and as a butcher in the abattoir in the Jewish quarter; six months later, after spotting an advertisement from a dressmaker looking for a tailor, he presented himself as a Parisian dressmaker and was briefly taken on until it became clear that he was not even remotely qualified to do the job. That experience lasted just one week, but Sauser managed to take his first pay cheque with him and live off that for a while.[17] When the money ran out, he started to take refuge from the cold in the New York Public Library.

In May 1912, he wrote to his old schoolfriend Suter; apart from his poverty and constant hunger, he mentions just one thing – his burning desire to write:

> Je n'ai qu'une pensée: écrire! Je suis malade. Mon crâne se fend comme une grenade trop mûre, un sang chaud m'obstrue les yeux, tombe sur mes mains. J'écris et mes pensées pâlissent, se

> tordent comme dans une fournaise. J'ai trop de fièvre. Je viens de terminer un petit drame. J'en rédige un deuxième et je veux en composer un troisième jusqu'à la fin de la semaine.
>
> (I have only one thought: to write! I am ill. My skull is splitting like an over-ripe pomegranate, a hot rush of blood is obstructing my eyes, falling onto my hands. I write and my thoughts go pale, twisting like in a furnace. I've got too much of a fever. I just finished a small play. I'm writing a second one and I want to write a third one by the end of the week.)[18]

The febrile urge to write propelled Sauser/Cendrars to draft a poem that would prove to be both career-making and groundbreaking. The circumstances of its creation, emerging from a state of hunger and nervous exhaustion, are no less extraordinary than the poem itself, and, at least in retrospect, cast the young poet in a distinctly Rimbaldian light, even if such comparisons were probably far from Sauser's mind at the time.

Les Pâques: An Easter Rebirth

The largely unhappy experience of living in New York served as a catalyst for one of Cendrars's most significant creative successes, the long poem to which he initially gave the title *Les Pâques* (Easter), and which he would later rename *Les Pâques à New York* (Easter in New York). It is a modern-day epic written in rhyming couplets in which the marginal figures of the city, its drunks, prostitutes and gangsters, provide the cast for a meditation on faith in the modern city.

Les Pâques is a landmark in terms both of Cendrars's life and his poetic development. Even more compellingly, it represents a key moment in the creation of the mythology around the persona of Blaise Cendrars. The poem publicly heralded the demise of Freddie Sauser and the birth of his new name and his new identity as a poet. By Cendrars's own account, it was written in a single night, 6–7 April 1912, during his stay in New York.[19] More recent studies have suggested that the writing took rather longer than this, and that he may have continued to make changes to the poem after his arrival in Paris at the end of June 1912.[20] In its frank and at times brutal treatment of life's hardships and suffering, the poem was bound to stir even the least progressive-minded. Its modern treatment of a biblical theme was perfectly suited to the mood of the times in which the canon of

Blaise Cendrars, *Les Pâques à New York*, with illustrations by Frans Masereel (1926).

western European heritage was being questioned and undone. The poem foreshadows a defining aspect of Cendrars's work across the decades, namely the imbrication of his own subjectivity in the writing; with its themes of suffering, death and rebirth, the theme of Easter had particular resonance for Freddy Sauser. The poem was inspired by a chance encounter on Easter Sunday 1912 with a performance of Haydn's *Creation* in a presbyterian church. Sauser walked out during the performance because a member of the church harangued him several times to make a donation.[21] By his own account, he walked home, ate some dry bread and went to bed, only to wake up in the middle of the night and write the poem in a single draft and in a state of virtual hallucination.[22]

Having failed to find a job in New York or with the Swiss legation in Washington, he spent $5 on a boat ticket and, intent on embarking on a new career in the old continent, left Féla behind and set off on 6 June on the SS *Volturno*, bound for Rotterdam. (Shortly before midnight on Sunday 14 April 1912, just one week after he wrote *Les Pâques*, the SS *Birma*, on which he had travelled to New York, received a distress signal from the *Titanic*, which had hit an iceberg. The *Birma*'s captain changed course and sped towards it, only to discover that the stricken ship had announced its map position incorrectly.)[23] His travelling companions on the *Volturno* included over four hundred convicts. The ship completed the crossing safely, but on 2 October of the following year, it set sail from Rotterdam with over six hundred passengers on board, chiefly Jewish emigrants from Austria, Hungary, Galicia and Russia. One week later, while it was crossing the Atlantic Ocean, a fire broke out towards the bow. An intensive rescue operation ensued, saving over five hundred passengers and crew, but 135 of those onboard, mostly women and children, lost their lives.[24]

Blaise Cendrars, Untitled drawing (self-portrait), New York, 1912.

On arriving in Europe, he lived briefly in Geneva at the home of his brother Georges, who, not for the first time, lent him money.[25] His desire to live in Paris was granted when Georges's father-in-law, the artist Richard Hall, lent him his studio in the 16th arrondissement of the capital.[26] Very quickly relations soured, with Sauser accused of keeping the wrong company. He moved into a hotel in the 5th arrondissement and took an attic room next to the Hungarian writer and anarchist Emil Szittya. Cendrars's initiation into the Parisian literary scene was neither immediate nor straightforward. His financial situation meant that his first priority was to find work, and he did this by conducting research at the Bibliothèque Mazarine and the Bibliothèque Sainte-Geneviève, a job sub-contracted to him by Guillaume Apollinaire, who in turn was writing for the Swiss literary critic, translator and writer Pierre-Paul Plan; Cendrars recalls that this was a collection of Chrétien de Troyes' *Romans de la table ronde* that Plan was editing.[27] He also mentions writing pornographic books for Apollinaire, who did this to earn a living.

In that summer of 1912, he delivered his poem to *Mercure de France*, where Apollinaire worked as a journalist and art critic. The manuscript was returned to him without comment three months later, whereupon Cendrars published it himself under the imprint of *Les Hommes nouveaux*, a Franco-German journal that he had set up with Szittya and another anarchist, Marius Hanot. He then sent the poem directly to Apollinaire, who expressed surprise that it had not been accepted by *Mercure de France* despite his enthusiastic recommendation. This is significant, as it confirms that Apollinaire had indeed read Cendrars's poem in its manuscript stage at a time when he himself was preparing a volume of his own poems to be called *Eau de vie*. In October 1912, Apollinaire read a new unfinished poem, 'Cri' (Cry), to some of his friends; in its length, its lack of punctuation, its use of rhyming couplets, its bold imagery and its combination of spiritually charged references with depictions of society's marginal figures, the poem offers clear parallels with *Les Pâques*. Apollinaire inserted his new poem, by now renamed 'Zone', into his collection, which also bore a new title, *Alcools*, shortly before the book appeared in print in April 1913. Over a century later, our knowledge that Apollinaire had read *Les Pâques* before he began writing 'Zone' compels us to see Cendrars as a significant and perhaps decisive influence on Apollinaire's move towards a more radical form of stylistic experimentation.[28]

Visions of New York

Les Pâques creates a blueprint for Cendrars's pre-war poetry, since it establishes some defining traits of his early poetic output. Its substantial length, its openly subjective first-person poetic voice and its invocation of biblical themes relocated to the world's most archetypally modern city are just some of the ways in which this poem sets the tone for Cendrars's subsequent poems. Structured in rhyming couplets, and with a heavy predominance of alexandrines, it takes the form of a direct address to Christ; indeed, much of it reads like an extended prayer. The title announces both a point in the calendar and the poem's central trope of death and rebirth, themes that recur in a number of further instances throughout Cendrars's literary career.

Drafted in a febrile state in the circumstances outlined above, the poem paints a vivid picture of the city's poor, destitute and marginal figures. The theme is a parable of its time and astonishingly prescient of the shape this still-young century would take: modern society, infatuated with corporate greed and intent on worshipping Mammon, has become detached from the symbolism of Easter and the compassion once associated with Christ. The poem is a cry of anger on behalf of the poor, the marginalized and the displaced; it bemoans the plight of numerous disadvantaged communities in the city:

> Il y a des Italiens, des Grecs, des Espagnols,
> Des Russes, des Bulgares, des Persans, des Mongols.
>
> Ce sont des bêtes de cirque qui sautent les méridiens.
> On leur jette un morceau de viande noire, comme à des chiens.
>
> (There are Italians, Greeks, Bulgarians,
> Spaniards, Persians, Russians and Mongolians.
>
> They're circus animals that leap meridians.
> They're thrown a piece of rotten meat, like dogs.)[29]

In strident rhyming couplets the narrator urges Christ to protect the city's community of Jewish refugees, while expressing sympathy for other marginalized groups such as prostitutes, petty thieves and the homeless.

During his stay in New York, Cendrars was impoverished and spent much of his time in the city's Central Library, where he could keep warm. The poem recounts the testimony of a first-hand witness who could relate to the hardship of those mentioned in its lines.

As we have seen, the poem bridges biblical antiquity with contemporary urban life, establishing a parallel between the suffering of its modern-day protagonists and that of Christ. A parallel can be drawn in this respect with Gourmont's 1906 novel *Une Nuit au Luxembourg*, in which a spiritual encounter takes place after the protagonist walks off the street into Saint-Sulpice church in Paris.[30] Cendrars's depictions of the city's social underclasses are interspersed with references to well-known artistic representations of religious themes, including the Veil of Veronica and ecclesiastical scenes by Eugène Carrière and others. Such examples are part of a wider array of references in the poem to visual, textual and musical modes of representation: these include allusions to Rembrandt and Hokusai, but also the gold lettering in which the 'moine d'un vieux temps' transcribes the Bible, and the lyrics of a German hymn sung aloud. These examples are juxtaposed with real-life experiences, as if the poet is consciously drawing our attention to the relationship between reality and its mediation through art. Moreover, the poem implies that not even the most realistic likeness or the most sacred effigy can replace experience. Of the Veil of Veronica, the speaker notes:

> C'est la meilleure relique promenée par les champs,
> Elle guérit tous les malades, tous les méchants.
>
> Elle fait encore mille et mille autres miracles,
> Mais je n'ai jamais assisté à ce spectacle.
>
> (It's the best relic carried in procession
> It cures every illness and transgression.
>
> It does thousands and thousands of other miracles,
> But I've never seen any of those spectacles.)[31]

In numerous instances the poem collapses time so as to conflate the moment of writing with the biblical era depicted. It depicts Christ's actions in graphic realism and endows him with a physical presence that stresses his humanity:

C'est à cette heure-ci, c'est vers la neuvième heure,
Que votre Tête, Seigneur, tomba sur votre Coeur.

(It was the same time as now, around the ninth hour,
When your Head, Lord, dropped onto your Heart.)[32]

These lines call to mind the ink line drawing that Cendrars produced as the design for the original 1912 edition of the poem, depicting a man standing with his head bowed and his hands clasped. According to Claude Leroy, the figure is depicted in the act of masturbating; but an interpretation of the image as a portrayal of Christ gains validity when we consider the head and neck of the drawn figure. These details, while not conforming to conventional depictions of Christ on the cross, do nevertheless hint at physical pain and emotional suffering. We do not see the figure's face, since it is downturned, but the pose, in its particular visual rendering, suggests the possibility of a scene of violence. Adopting a more extreme interpretation, one might argue that the bowed head appears to be detached from the body, as if caught in the fleeting moment of decapitation. Indeed, only a few lines above these, we find a couplet that prefigures an allusion, if not to decapitation, then at least to mutilation:

Votre flanc grand ouvert est comme un grand soleil
Et vos mains tout autour palpitent d'étincelles.

(Your wide-open side is like a big sun
And your hands throb with sparks all around.)[33]

In these lines, the vivid conflation of Christ's wounded body with the sun foreshadows the concluding image of Apollinaire's 'Zone':

Tu marches vers Auteuil tu veux aller chez toi à pied
Dormir parmi tes fétiches d'Océanie et de Guinée
Ils sont des Christ d'une autre forme et d'une autre croyance
Ce sont les Christ inférieurs des obscures espérances

Adieu Adieu

Soleil cou coupé

(You head for Auteuil you want to walk home
Sleep among your fetishes from Guinea and the South Seas
They're other Christs of other faiths
Lesser Christs of obscure hopes

Farewell Farewell

Sun sundered head)[34]

Not only does *Les Pâques* suggest intertextual links with the work of other poets such as Apollinaire, but it resonates intriguingly with other instances of Cendrars's own literary and poetic oeuvre. In many respects the poem anticipates motifs and thematic concerns that characterize his later poems. The confessional character of the direct address to Christ returns in 'Journal' (Newspaper), the first of his *Dix-neuf poèmes élastiques*, which refers explicitly to *Les Pâques* in its opening lines:

Christ
Voici plus d'un an que je n'ai plus pensé à Vous
Depuis que j'ai écrit mon avant-dernier poème Pâques

(Christ
It's been more than a year now since I stopped thinking about
    You
Since I wrote my next-to-last poem 'Easter')[35]

Line 5 of *Les Pâques*, 'Un moine d'un vieux temps me parle de votre mort' (An old-time monk tells me about your death), prefigures a line from near the beginning of *Prose du Transsibérien*, in which the speaker tells us, 'Un vieux moine me lisait la légende de Novgorode' (An old monk was reading me the legend of Novgorod).[36]

The speaker's story, mediated by a monk from earlier times, sets in place a series of oppositions between antiquity and modernity, organized religion and individual faith. On his own admission, even as a child he never prayed, and nor does he do so in adulthood. The speaker acknowledges that his faith is flawed: 'Mon âme est une veuve en deuil au pied de votre Croix' (My soul is a grieving widow at the foot of your Cross).[37] The speaker's voice is rooted in the modern world and located within the underclasses that constitute the underbelly of the modern metropolis:

he feels an affinity with poorly paid immigrants arriving in New York by boat, prostitutes, thieves, street musicians and associated waifs and strays. The humanity of this poem is readable in the poet's sympathetic treatment of these normally invisible citizens, here raised to the status of serious poetic personae.

The alignment of religious faith with modern life recurs in 'Journal'. The entire poem is an address to Jesus and questions the place of spirituality and the human sensibility in the modern world. The lines 'Christ/ Vie crucifiée dans le journal grand ouvert que je tiens les bras tendus' (Christ/ Life crucified in the wide-open paper I hold at arm's length) sum up its imbrication of spirituality and everyday life, whereby the seated poet, reading news of world events, unknowingly mimics the posture of Christ on the cross.[38]

If one aspect of *Les Pâques à New York* prevails over all others, then it is its bold reinterpretation of biblical subject-matter, relocated to the streets of the modern city. In the rawness of its language and its unflinching confrontation with poverty and social inequality in the most modern city of the world, this work signals the poet's intention to shake up poetry and perhaps even to redefine it. It is easy to see why Cendrars's arrival into the Parisian pre-war scene caused a stir. This impetus would continue in his next poem, which became one of his best-known publications and remains a landmark to this day.

La Prose du Transsibérien et de la petite Jehanne de France

After he arrived in Paris in 1912, Cendrars very soon made contact with the large and heterogeneous community of artists based in a building known colloquially as La Ruche (The Beehive) in the Passage de Danzig. Originally designed by Gustave Eiffel as a pavilion for the Exposition Universelle of 1889, the building was subsequently converted into studios for young artists in 1902, since which time it had served as a refuge for a large number of impecunious artists living in the city. The list of those who either lived in or frequented La Ruche in the early years of the twentieth century reads like a *Who's Who* of modern art and poetry at the time: their number included Guillaume Apollinaire, Alexander Archipenko, Constantin Brancusi, Marc Chagall, Robert Delaunay, Max Jacob, Amedeo Modigliani, Diego Rivera, Chaim Soutine, Ossip Zadkine and others. Cendrars met Chagall there in late 1912 or early 1913. He had already met the artist Fernand Léger in the previous autumn at the Salon de la Section d'or.[39]

Reminiscing about the pre-war years in Paris, Cendrars comments on the close proximity of artists and poets:

> A cette époque, les peintres et les écrivains, c'était pareil. On vivait mélangés avec probablement les mêmes soucis; on peut même dire que chaque écrivain avait son peintre. Moi, j'avais Delaunay et Léger, Picasso avait Max Jacob, Reverdy, Braque, et Apollinaire, tout le monde.
>
> (At that time, painters and writers were one and the same. We lived with one another and probably shared the same concerns; you might even say that every writer had his painter. I had Delaunay and Léger, Picasso had Max Jacob, Reverdy had Braque, and Apollinaire had everyone.)[40]

The Delaunays, Robert and Sonia, and Léger were Cendrars's closest contacts at the time, but it is clear that his artistic aquaintances were far more extensive than those figures alone. A French television programme made in 1953 shows Cendrars retracing his steps to La Ruche, which, long since vacated by its artists, now appears empty and forlorn. He reminisces about his erstwhile friend, the artist Amedeo Modigliani, whose studio was so spartan that he used to sleep on a pile of newspapers. The Delaunays, by contrast, were affluent, and their flat in Paris became a frequent refuge for Cendrars after Apollinaire introduced them.[41]

Much critical attention has been devoted to Cendrars's modernizing influence on Apollinaire, particularly on his elimination of punctuation in *Alcools*. Rather less has been written on the possible sources of Cendrars's stylistic modernity, a phenomenon often accepted unquestioningly as a natural corollary of the poet's archetypally 'modern' transatlantic nomadism. Admittedly, *Les Pâques à New York* is more adventurous in its provocative content than in its style, which still adheres to conventional punctuation and a regular scheme of rhyming couplets. In the two years between his return from New York to Paris and the outbreak of war, his poetry underwent a radical stylistic development. Without yet departing from the epic form of *Les Pâques à New York*, the *Prose du Transsibérien et de la petite Jehanne de France* (1913) employs free verse and intersperses grammatically complete lines with passages that telescope syntax and disrupt chronological sequence. This in turn points ahead to the fragmented, telegraphic style of the *Dix-neuf poèmes élastiques* (Nineteen Elastic Poems), circumstantial poems written mainly between the summers of 1913 and 1914 but not published as a collection until 1919. This progression from an essentially sequential narrative mode towards more complex and multi-perspectival poetic forms may have stemmed in part from his encounter with the artistic community and perhaps especially his close acquaintance with the Delaunays, who at the time were moving away from figuration and striving towards a new aesthetic based on colour contrasts and devoid of reference to the natural world.

For Cendrars and the Delaunays, as for so many of their peers in the avant-garde, Paris was the source of inspiration and the subject of their most memorable work. Robert Delaunay's art is so inextricably associated with the capital and its landmarks that in 1916 the German writer Theodor Däubler termed the Eiffel Tower 'Delaunay's father'.[42] Significantly, the city always appears in his work as the starting point of formal experimentation rather than a subject to be reproduced in all its naturalistic detail. In her excellent book on Orphism, Virginia Spate reveals that the series of paintings of the Eiffel Tower was executed in the country from memory, a process that freed the artist to concentrate on formal and compositional considerations rather than labouring over realistic minutiae.[43]

In his volume of essays *Aujourd'hui*, Cendrars recounts the fortuitous circumstances that enabled him to witness at first hand Robert Delaunay's struggle to capture the Eiffel Tower pictorially. Cendrars had broken his leg and was obliged to spend a month bedridden in a Paris hotel. He recalls that Delaunay visited him nearly every day and often did sketches or paintings of the tower, which was visible through the window.[44] (Cendrars dates this to 1910–11, but he first met the Delaunays at the end of January 1913 and his accident happened in June of that year.)[45] In the same essay, Cendrars describes how Delaunay would close himself off from the external world in order to work in a darkened room, allowing a single ray of light to filter through a small gap in the shutters so he could study its refracted colours as a subject in its own right free of distractions from the outside world.[46]

Delaunay, aware that he was departing from the figurative tradition, found a term to describe what he was doing: 'Poésie pure – et plastique – lyrisme – en opposition au successif et monodique ancien.' (Pure – and plastic – poetry – lyricism – in opposition to the successive and monodic ways of old.)[47] The possibility of attaining 'pure poetry', and of overcoming a sequential mode of representation within a *poetic* framework, preoccupied Cendrars. This interest was most vividly borne out by the publication of *La Prose du Transsibérien et de la Petite Jehanne de France*, with 'simultaneous colours' provided by Sonia Delaunay. While Cendrars acknowledges his lengthy discussions with Sonia's husband Robert, the two men never worked together on an artistic or poetic project, whereas the friendship with Sonia was immediate and highly fruitful. Born in Odessa, Ukraine, she spent most of her childhood in St Petersburg, so she almost certainly felt a particular affinity with the poet. In a radio interview, she recalls first meeting Cendrars at Apollinaire's flat in the boulevard Saint-Germain; alongside the physically imposing and dominant figure of Apollinaire, whom she describes as 'decorative', Cendrars struck her as 'a small, quite physically insignificant young man'; the following day, Cendrars returned with a copy of 'Pâques', which she, more literary-minded than Robert, pounced on straight away. She instantly knew it was an exceptional piece of work. The poem so enthused her that she rushed out to buy the materials to make a multicoloured collaged cover for it. Cendrars, who lived nearby in the rue de Savoie, started eating lunch at their home nearly every day. She recalls that the young poet, who was 'very poor', told her that he had inherited 3,000 francs from an aunt and wanted to spend this on producing a fine edition of his new poem, 'The Trans-Siberian'; this poem would become *Prose du Transsibérien et de la petite Jehanne de France*.[48] In truth, the money had come from Cendrars's girlfriend Féla, who had returned from New York in May to join him in Paris. Sonia took Féla under her wing and helped her to adjust to life in Paris.[49] It was Sonia's idea to give the poem its now famous polychrome appearance with the words and abstract colours unfolding vertically down its 2-metre length. It is easy to understand why a collaborative work based on the Trans-Siberian Railway would appeal to her, but few can have predicted that the project would produce such a staggeringly audacious, radically experimental and ravishingly beautiful work of art.

The poem's publication in the autumn of 1913 was accompanied by a hail of publicity, including a programmatic letter-cum-manifesto published in the leading Berlin expressionist journal *Der Sturm*, in which Cendrars was keen to flaunt his affinity with the Delaunays' simultaneous art: 'j'ai la fièvre. Et c'est pourquoi j'aime la peinture des Delaunay, pleine de soleils, de ruts, de violences. Mme Delaunay a fait un si beau livre de couleurs, que mon poème est plus trempé de lumière que ma vie.

Voilà ce qui me rend heureux.' (I have a fever. And that's why I love the Delaunays' paintings, full of suns, ruts, violence. Mme Delaunay has made such a beautiful book of colours that my poem is more soaked in light than my life. That's what makes me happy.)[50] Even if Cendrars in his work appears to have been much more firmly bound than Delaunay to the mimetic representation of the real world, they must have had highly compatible views with regard to the practice of incorporating popular and folk elements into their creative work. The idea for its vertical design was Delaunay's, and the poem inspired her to create 'une harmonie de couleurs qui se déroulait parallèllement au poème' (a harmony of colours that unfolded in tandem with the poem).[51]

Billed audaciously by Cendrars as 'le premier livre simultané' (the first simultaneous book), *La Prose du Transsibérien* might at first sight appear to be a mere transposition of the Delaunays' theories into a verbal and visual medium. Published in November 1913 under the imprint of Les Hommes nouveaux, the work bears the influence of the Delaunays' work exploring what they termed 'simultaneous contrasts': not only is it intended to be read and viewed simultaneously, but indeed the text itself is built upon a series of spatial, temporal and stylistic juxtapositions. The book embroiled its authors in a fierce and high-profile dispute with poet Henri-Martin Barzun, who contested their use of the term 'simultané' in his journal *Poème et drame* and other publications.[52] Such avant-garde polemics belie the fact that, for all its modernity, the poem looks to the past as well as the future, and refers implicitly to an age-old heritage of oral narrative in its epic length and even its title. The archaic spelling of Jehanne's name points to this conscious historicizing intent: Joan of Arc spelt her name that way, and the name appears with this spelling in *Le Testament* by Cendrars's literary hero François Villon.[53] In a letter to Alexander Smirnov, Cendrars explains his choice of 'prose' rather than 'poem' for the title of this work in verse: 'Pour le mot Prose; je l'ai employé dans le Transsibérien dans un sens bas-latin de "prosa", "dictu". Poème me semblait trop prétentieux, trop fermé. Prose est plus ouvert, populaire.' (As for the word 'prose', I used it in the Trans-Siberian in the Low-Latin sense of 'prosa', 'dictum'. Poem seemed too pretentious, too closed, Prose is more open, popular).[54] And in a letter to his brother Cendrars announces his wish to write an accessible form of everyday poetry encompassing 'tout le monde d'aujourd'hui, la vie de tous les jours, les annonces des journaux, les étiquettes des boîtes de conserves, les marques de fabrique, les horaires [. . .], en un mot nos richesses' (the whole of today's world, everyday life, newspaper adverts, the labels on jars, brand names, timetables [. . .], in a word, our treasures).[55]

The poem is based on recollections of a train journey eastwards from Moscow on the Trans-Siberian railway. Its narrative construction is symptomatic of the poet's tendency to blur factual and fictional forms of discourse: the protagonist, called Blaise, tells us he went with a travelling jewel salesman bound for Harbin, and itemizes details with photographic accuracy: 'Nous avions deux coupés dans l'express et 34 coffres de joaillerie de Pforzheim/De la camelote allemande "Made in Germany"' (We had two compartments on the express and 34 boxes of jewellery from Pforzheim/German junk 'Made in Germany').[56] He adds that he slept on the jewels and enjoyed playing with the nickel-plated Browning pistol the salesman had given him.[57] Yet shortly afterwards the text dispels any assumption that this is a straightforward narration of factual events by invoking Jules Verne and 'Ali Baba and the Forty Thieves'.[58]

His travelling companion is Jeanne, a sick young prostitute, who in a feverish state asks Blaise repeatedly: 'Sommes-nous bien loin de Montmartre?' (Are we really a long way from Montmartre?)[59] As if to soothe her, Blaise tells her stories of earlier journeys. The poem jumps abruptly – one might say cinematically – across locations and time levels: Blaise recollects his earlier journeys, which alternate with observations from the train and more abstract sequences such as the transcription of the 'clickety-clack' of the wheels, a kind of sound poetry that has a visual equivalent in the mesmerizing place names encountered en route and reeled off like a mantra: 'Tomsk Tchéliabinsk Kaïnsk Obi Taïchet Verkné Oudinsk Kourgane Samara Pensa-Touloune' (Tomsk Chelyabinsk Kansk Ob' Tayshet Verkne-Udinsk Kurgan Samara Penza-Tulun).[60] The geographic itinerary offers a prism through which to reflect upon other kinds of journey, primarily life itself, and our complex, subjective and often unreliable memory of it. The poem begins with the narrator reflecting on this: 'En ce temps-là j'étais en mon adolescence/ J'avais à peine seize ans et je ne me souvenais déjà plus de mon enfance' (Back then I was still young/ I was barely sixteen but my childhood memories were gone).[61] Another important theme is the creative process, specifically poetry: the narrator repeatedly claims 'Et j'étais déjà si mauvais poète/ Que je ne savais pas aller jusqu'au bout' (And I was already such a bad poet/ That I didn't know how to take it all the way).[62]

This meeting of minds at the point of contact between fine art and applied art – and between high literature and popular discursive forms

– is most palpably evident in the extraordinary material form of the *Prose* in its original edition. Its highly striking and unusual design deserves detailed consideration, as arguably this, more than the poetic text or the artwork in isolation, accounts for the enduring acclaim that it commands even today. Opening out into a single composite sheet measuring 2 metres long by 36 centimetres wide, this is an artefact that calls to mind comparisons with various non-literary objects but refuses to elide neatly with any of them. Folded once centrally down its entire length, and several times horizontally to fit into its neat cardboard sleeve, it resembles a map intended to be removed for use and replaced as required. Upon opening it, our first impressions are confounded, both by its heterogeneous appearance and its patchwork of textual and visual elements. Questions as to its generic identity abound. In his pre-publication announcement, Cendrars exclaimed that the book would reach the height of the Eiffel Tower; this hyperbole did contain a grain of truth, since a height of 300 metres would indeed be reached if the intended 150 copies were placed end-to-end.[63]

The original cover sleeve, made of card and adorned with Sonia Delaunay's geometric colour washes, is attached to the top right-hand side in such a way that it covers the uppermost rectangle on the right side of the main sheet containing the *Prose*.[64] If we lift the flap, we discover a route map partly hidden away underneath it. Closer inspection reveals that it is a Michelin map indicating the train journey from Moscow to Harbin; we will later discover that this is the route taken by the two protagonists of the *Prose*. Not only does the map thus announce the very raison d'être of the poem, even before the title hints at it, but its combination of iconic, indexical and symbolic signs anticipates metonymically the various signifying elements that the reader will encounter in the body of the text and its accompanying blocks of colour. We also find the inscription of the year 1913 at the head and foot of the sheet. These elements point towards the identity of the *Prose* as a utilitarian object rather than a piece of fine art: consequently, distinctions between documentary and fiction, fine art and industrial design, experimental typography, free verse and prose all dissolve into a blur. Such was the intention of Cendrars, who rejected all schools of thought and defined his work with the audacity of a Rimbaldian *voyant*: 'Je ne suis pas poète. Je suis libertin. Je n'ai aucune méthode de travail. J'ai un sexe. Je suis par trop sensible.' (I am not a poet. I am a libertine. I have no working method. I have a sex. I am too sensitive.)[65]

Extant documents relating to the genesis of the *Prose* suggest that the process from conception to publication of the final draft was much more arduous than the author's words might suggest.[66] Just as Robert Delaunay's series of *Fenêtres* paintings or Sonia Delaunay's *Prismes électriques* derive their visual power from the constant interplay of figurative and abstract forms, so the *Prose* defines its modernity by virtue of the tension between its opposing poles: the unifying thread of the poem is the train journey from Moscow to Harbin, and yet this journey is interrupted by other real and imaginary excurses. As it shifts with cinematic regularity between different temporal and spatial levels, the poem fuses the everyday with the esoteric, alternating images of childhood innocence and exuberance with those of corruption, violence and despair. The train's last stop is Harbin, but the poem terminates in Paris: the abrupt, quasi-cinematic change of location prompts us to question whether the journey has taken place at all. At this point the entire journey is revealed as an exercise in memory recall on the part of the narrator-poet, the purpose of which is to help him understand his own past and in turn point him towards a new poetic goal. At first sight, both quests seem to have failed: the end result of the voyage appears not to be greater knowledge and self-understanding, but alienation and despair:

Maintenant, j'ai fait courir tous les trains derrière moi
Bâle–Tombouctou
J'ai aussi joué aux courses à Auteuil et à Longchamp
Paris–New York
Maintenant, j'ai fait courir tous les trains tout le long de ma vie
Madrid–Stockholm
Et j'ai perdu tous mes paris
Il n'y a plus que la Patagonie, la Patagonie, qui convienne à mon immense tristesse, la Patagonie, et un voyage dans les mers du Sud

(Now I've made the trains follow me
Basel–Timbuktu
I've played the horses at tracks like Auteuil and Longchamps
Paris–New York
Now the trains run alongside me
Madrid–Stockholm
Lost it all at the gay pari-mutuel

> Patagonia is what's left, Patagonia, which befits my immense
> sadness, Patagonia and a trip to the South Seas)[67]

With characteristic economy, Cendrars creates an insistent rhythm through the counterpoint structure that alternates between past and present as it cuts from one city and continent to another. His extended play on place names serves a variety of functions. First, the hyphenated couplings 'Basel–Timbuktu' and 'Madrid–Stockholm' convey the cosmopolitan simultaneity of a world undergoing rapid internationalization; the syntactic compression of these lines reflects the idea that they express, accentuating the rapidity with which it is possible to travel between countries and even across continents. In this respect they call to mind the advertising hoarding that inhabits Robert Delaunay's *L'Equipe de Cardiff FC* of 1913, in which the names 'New York–Paris' are prominently displayed. Cendrars creates wordplay from the place names 'Paris' and 'Patagonie': by replacing the uppercase initial P with lowercase p, he overlays the name of France's capital city with the French word for bets ('paris'), thereby producing a neat connection with the references to the well-known racetracks at Auteuil and Longchamp. As for 'Patagonie', the act of repeating this line situates it in a particular geographic location while also imitating the repetitive rhythm of the train moving on its tracks: ('la/ Pa/ta/go/nie,/ la/ Pa/ta/go/nie'). In these ways, Cendrars hints overtly at the poem's self-referentiality, whereby the train journey is a metaphor of the poet's tortuous search for a new poetic medium.

Towards the end of the journey, the narrator again strays from his account of the train's progress to betray Cendrars's doubts and uncertainty regarding his function as a poet in an era that has rendered traditional poetic values obsolete and stripped him of his monopoly as social documenter:

> 'Pardonnez-moi mon ignorance
> 'Pardonnez-moi de ne plus connaître l'ancien jeu des vers'
> Comme dit Guillaume Apollinaire
> Tout ce qui concerne la guerre on peut le lire dans les *Mémoires* de Kouropatkine
> Ou dans les journaux japonais qui sont aussi cruellement illustrés
>
> ('Forgive my ignorance
> 'Pardon my forgetting how to play the ancient game of Verse'

As Guillaume Apollinaire says
If you want to know anything about the war read Kuropotkin's
Memoirs
Or the Japanese newspapers with their ghastly illustrations)[68]

As the momentum of the train carries the poem forward at breakneck speed, the narrator is overwhelmed by the frantic stream of images, both visual and imagined, which assail him and defy his attempts to assimilate them. Painting 'like my friend Chagall', he speculates, might offer the only means of registering this mass of information, but he is inadequately prepared for such a task. Overwhelmed by this barrage of sensations and images, the poet is on the point of giving up altogether, but realizes that recording the involuntary jolts of his past experience will offer the key to his salvation and the source of his creative voice:

J'ai déchiffré tous les textes confus des roues et j'ai rassemblé les
éléments épars d'une violente beauté
Que je possède
Et qui me force.

(I deciphered all the garbled texts of the wheels and united the
scattered elements of a violent beauty
Which I possess
And which drives me.)[69]

By harnessing his memory, the poet may better understand his past and in turn face the present, if not with hope or happiness, then at least with lucidity.

The poem, then, is both the document of a search for better self-understanding and tangible proof of its success. Paris, that 'Grand foyer chaleureux' (great warm hearth) and ever-present backdrop to the journey, is the catalyst of the narrator's realization: only after rediscovering the city and its associations with his past is he able to retrieve his lost youth and in turn confront the void of the present through the act of writing. The thematic importance of memory also reminds us that the poem itself, with its metadiegetic structure and multiple time levels, is sequential and relies on our perception of time. Cendrars's 'simultaneous' poetry still works within a temporal framework.

The final, tripartite image of Paris as 'Ville de la Tour unique du grand Gibet et de la Roue' (City of the incomparable Tower the great Gibbet and the Wheel) is physical and symbolic, temporal and timeless.[70] The tower, an embodiment of the city's modernity, has the silhouette of an enormous scaffold, creating an elision between the first two elements of the line. According to an alternative reading, the 'grand Gibet' may refer to the city's past and specifically to the Gibet de Montfaucon, the site of executions from the eleventh century until its demolition in 1760.[71] From this perspective, the Tower and great Gibbet can be understood as evoking respectively present-day Paris and its history. The final noun, the Wheel, is multi-referential: in a first, literal sense it almost certainly refers to the Grande Roue de Paris, a 100-metre-high Ferris wheel that had graced the city's skyline since its construction for the Exposition Universelle in 1900.[72] More symbolically, it could be taken to suggest a wheel of fortune, or the cycle of life, continually regenerating itself. As John Harding observes, the image of the wheel links the mechanical movement of the train's wheels with the spiritual implications of circularity and cyclical regeneration.[73] This semantic indeterminacy is quite apposite to Cendrars's Simultanist vision and contrasts with the syntactic closure of the tripartite final line.

Ultimately, both the painter and the poet typify the very contrary of the 'dehumanization' that José Ortega y Gasset identified as the 'superior algebra of metaphors':[74] Cendrars's search for the 'first poem without metaphors' locates him in diametric opposition to the abstraction that such an 'algebra' might entail. Cendrars insisted that his work was no abstraction but derived directly from real experience, just as Robert Delaunay defended his art vigorously as stemming from his sensibility and reacted angrily when German artist August Macke praised its underlying 'geometry'.[75] Delaunay's assertion of instinct over calculation calls to mind the specific terms in which Henri Bergson analyses the respective characteristics of the vital and the geometrical orders in *L'Evolution créatrice* (*Creative Evolution*): he establishes a hierarchy of values, at the top of which is the vital order. The geometrical order is inferior to it, but still superior to chaos, which is tantamount to a complete absence of order.[76]

However close to abstraction Robert Delaunay may have ventured, his words suggest that his intention was never to abandon figuration altogether. He conceived his *Fenêtres* paintings not as barriers isolating him from the external world but as links with it, which stop his work short of full abstraction. If we are to understand his aims fully, we must imagine Robert Delaunay's windows to be 'wide open onto the boulevards', like the kind of poetry that Cendrars announces in the opening line of 'Contrastes', the second of his *Dix-Neuf poèmes élastiques*.[77] In contrast, Sonia Delaunay's luminescent colours accompanying the text of the *Prose du Transsibérien* would be entirely abstract were it not for two broadly geometric forms at its lower edge that tease the work back towards the represenational subject: these sketch a radically simplified red silhouette of the Eiffel Tower enlacing an orange circle that could depict the Ferris wheel, the sun or both. The poem's text and its painted forms engender a whole series of tensions between viewing and reading, between form in its pure state and form as representation, that encapsulate perfectly the visionary and lasting brilliance of this multimedia work.

THE CLOSE PERSONAL FRIENDSHIP between the Delaunays and Cendrars that gave rise to the collaborations, influences and meetings of ideas outlined above came to a premature and sudden end, prompted by the hostilities of 1914–18 that changed so many lives. The Great War had life-changing consequences for Cendrars, and arguably it shaped the entirety of his subsequent work as a writer. For the Delaunays, by contrast, the outbreak of war merely marked a brief caesura in an otherwise relatively untroubled creative itinerary. Robert obtained a declaration that he was unfit for service and thereby enabled the couple to travel to Portugal for the duration of the war.

Writing decades later in *Le Lotissement du ciel*, Cendrars recalled his friendship with Robert Delaunay in the years before the war and his close creative collaboration with Sonia Delaunay at that time; he also reflected on the circumstances that had caused their paths to separate. More than the fact of Robert Delaunay's non-involvement in the war *per se*, what angered Cendrars was the posturing – and, implicitly, the dishonesty – that characterized the painter's return to Paris when peace had been restored.[78]

The Poem as Isthmus: *Le Panama, ou les aventures de mes sept oncles*

Published in 1918, but written before the Great War, *Le Panama, ou les aventures de mes sept oncles* is a long poem that deserves to be regarded, both thematically and compositionally, as a companion piece to *Les Pâques* and *Prose du Transsibérien*. Indeed, Claude Leroy has no hesitation in describing *Le Panama* alongside these other poems as the final element in the trilogy of Cendrars's 'poèmes d'apprentissage' (poems of apprenticeship).[79] While the author himself appended to the poem the dates June 1913 to June 1914, we owe to Charles-Ferdinand Sunier the revelation that its writing began as early as October 1912.[80] As Leroy observes, this striking revelation makes *Le Panama* contemporaneous with the writing of *Prose du Transsibérien*; moreover, the close kinship of these last two long poems is borne out by the fact that the first manuscript bore the title *Prose du Canal de Panama et de mes sept oncles*.[81]

The chronological overlap of their composition should come as no surprise, given how much the two poems have in common. Indeed, while *Prose du Transsibérien* and *Le Panama* are looser in structure, freeing themselves of the rhyming couplets of *Les Pâques*, all three poems share their first-person narrative voice and their confessional tone. The significant stylistic development that separates *Prose* and *Le Panama* from *Les Pâques* hints at Cendrars's growing maturity and confidence as a poet, but it also tells us something about the impact that a specific place and time can have on the creative process: the much greater degree of experimentation in the two poems written in Paris surely has much to do with the transition that Cendrars underwent from his isolated existence in New York to the avant-garde community on his arrival in the French capital. His contacts with visual artists seem to have been particularly influential in liberating his approach to poetry at that time.

The textual content of *Le Panama* relates fascinatingly to the broad themes of *Prose du Transsibérien* and *Les Pâques*. Not only do they relate to one another, but, moreover, from the very outset, *Le Panama* presents itself as a meditation on storytelling and reading more generally, in which respect it once again ties in with the fabular quality of *Prose du Transsibérien*. Tellingly, *Le Panama* begins with a reference to various forms of reading matter:

> Des livres
> Il y a des livres qui parlent du Canal de Panama
> Je ne sais pas ce que disent les catalogues des bibliothèques
> Et je n'écoute pas les journaux financiers
> Quoique les bulletins de la Bourse soient notre prière quotidienne
>
> (Books
> There are books that talk about the Panama Canal

I don't know what the card catalogues say
And I don't pay any attention to the financial pages
Although the Stock Market quotations are our daily prayers)

As the speaker then acknowledges, the Panama Canal is intimately connected to his childhood. Significantly, though, the explanation of this revelation is deferred, as the narrator recalls the pleasure of listening as his mother used to recount the adventures of her seven brothers:

Ma mère me racontait les aventures de ses sept frères
De mes sept oncles
Et quand elle recevait des lettres
Eblouissement!
Ces lettres avec les beaux timbres exotiques qui portent les vers
de Rimbaud en exergue
Elle ne me racontait rien ce jour-là
Et je restais triste sous ma table

(My mother used to tell me about the adventures of her seven
brothers
My seven uncles
And when she got letters
Dazzlement!
Those letters with beautiful exotic stamps inscribed with lines
from Rimbaud
She didn't tell me any stories on those days
And I stayed sad under my table)[82]

The precise significance of Panama in the narrator's life remains to be elucidated, but these opening lines already announce one of the important themes of the poem, namely, the narrator's love of listening to stories; it shares this feature with *Prose du Transsibérien*, which opened with the narrator listening as 'an old monk was reading the Legend of Novgorod to me'. Indeed, in *Le Panama*, the negative association that Panama held in his boyhood mind was connected to the fact that it interfered with his favourite ritual of listening to his mother's daily storytelling.

Rather than being primarily concerned with the specific adventures of any of the narrator's seven uncles, the fundamental point that this poem seems to be making is intimately bound to its mobility, its insistence on experience as flux, as a necessarily multifaceted, eternally ongoing process: the poem shifts without warning between present and past tenses, which stand in an inconsistent relationship with linear time. Lines relating the narrator's recollections of childhood appear alternately in the past and present tenses – 'Comment voulez-vous que je prépare des examens/ Quand une lettre est sous la porte/ J'ai vu/ La belle pédagogie!' (How am I supposed to study for my tests/ When a letter slides under the door/ I saw/ This beautiful pedagogy!)[83] – and are interspersed with reflections that appear to stem from the narrator's, or the poet's, adult self: 'Je voudrais lire *la Feuille d'Avis de Neuchâtel* ou *le Courrier de Pampelune*/ Au milieu de l'Atlantique on n'est pas plus à l'aise que dans une salle de rédaction/ Je tourne dans la cage des méridiens comme un écureuil dans la sienne' (I feel like reading the *Neuchâtel Tattler* or the *Pamplona Courier*/ In the middle of the Atlantic you're no more comfortable than in an editorial office/ I go round in the cage of meridians like a squirrel in his).[84] The poem is no more respectful of the unity of space, moving effortlessly across locations, time zones and even continents. It mixes first-person and third-person narrative voices, and blurs the distinction between the two: even the first person is multiplied, since it conveys not only the narrator's point of view but those of his uncles, mediated through their letters, which appear without speech marks, as if to level out direct and indirect speech, reported speech and other forms of discourse. On many occasions, the narrative voice comes remarkably close to articulating the voice of the real Blaise Cendrars, such as the autobiographical line, 'Je reviens d'Amérique à bord du *Volturno*, pour 35 francs de New York à Rotterdam' (I come back from America on board the *Volturno* for 35 francs from New York to Rotterdam), the reference to the people of Solothurn in his native Switzerland, or the allusion to 'mon vieil ami Perl', an abbreviation for Joseph Perlberg, a friend and fellow student of the young Sauser from his university days in Bern.[85]

Ultimately, though, it matters little that elements of the poem come close to the poet's real experience. What is particularly noteworthy is the poem's ecstatic ubiquity, its evocation of life as an incessant flow of present moments:

> Je connais tous les horaires
> Tous les trains et leurs correspondances
> L'heure d'arrivée l'heure du départ

Tous les paquebots tous les tarifs et toutes les taxes
Ça m'est égal

(I know all the timetables
All the trains and the connections
Time of arrival time of departure
All the steamers all the fares all the taxes
It's all the same to me)[86]

The powerfully articulated sense of immediacy and immersion in the present is accentuated by the profusion of monolexical lines, some of which are brand names. The impression is of colour billboards whose names are recorded at speed, without time for further contemplation. Cendrars's approach calls to mind the Cubists' practice of pasting labels ('Bass', 'Suze' and so on) alongside cut-out newspaper headlines, articles, wallpaper and other ready-made fragments alluding to contemporary life and consumer society. Cendrars's words appear in their raw form as fragments of reality, neither analysed nor explained, and it is down to the reader to absorb them and draw any conclusions as to how they might relate to the surrounding lines. We read the names 'Maggi/ Byrrh/ *Daily Chronicle*',[87] and they evoke a shorthand impression of an urban everyday milieu, of kiosks and billboard posters glimpsed at speed, as if from the window of a bus or train. The first of these names, Maggi, is the manufacturer of the 'Bouillon Kub', a product that lends itself especially well to Cendrars's Cubist-inspired poetry: not only was this a household name in France – in 1912, some 1.2 million advertisements for the Bouillon Kub were to be found throughout the streets of France[88] – but the nature of this foodstuff, with its modern, cubic form, makes it a culinary equivalent of Cendrars's syntactically compressed, compact form of poetry. Picasso had deftly exploited the ubiquity of the Kub brand and the convenience of its name in his *Paysage aux affiches* of 1912, where the name 'Kub' is depicted against a fragment of a cube shape resembling a perspective diagram. The Bouillon Kub, Cendrars seems to suggest, is a metaphor for the poetry of modernity, readily available, practical, within reach of everybody and available for speedy consumption:

J'ai du pain du fromage
Un col propre
La poésie date d'aujourd'hui

(I have some bread and cheese
A clean collar
Poetry dates from today)[89]

Like the *Prose*, with its recurrent refrain in which the narrator professes his inability to 'go all the way', the first-person narrator of this poem repeats lines that convey a similar sense of despondency:

Et il y avait encore quelque chose
La tristesse
Et le mal du pays.

(And there was still something else
Sadness
And homesickness.)[90]

Echoing the principle of variations on a theme that applies to the different permutations of the route maps, these words are applied in turn to each of the narrator's seven uncles, providing the poem with a narrative continuity that links their various adventures, and endowing it with an effect of modulation.

Panama shares with the *Prose* the breakneck pace that threatens to leave everyone, even its narrator, in its wake. As we saw, the narrator of the *Prose* battled against the frenetic rhythm of the image-associations that exceeded his capacity to absorb them; analogously, the narration of *Le Panama*, with its strings of single-word lines and its ultra-rapid jumps across space and time, is constantly at risk of leaving the reader lagging behind, unable to process the images but conscious of a blurred kaleidoscopic image of the myriad places, moments and situations experienced whose names remain as indexical traces. For Jay Bochner, the rapidity of the poem is such that notions of sequence give way to an intensely felt experience of simultaneity: 'In *Panama*, we meet, we leave, then we blend, in our minds, the places we visit so quickly that the idea of a voyage recedes leaving in its place the sense of all places coexisting simultaneously.'[91]

Le Panama, then, is a poem that employs its various textual, paratextual, typographic and graphic elements to great effect. Cendrars combines them to create a multilayered web in which our reading activity is necessarily accompanied by reflections on the role of the various visual elements

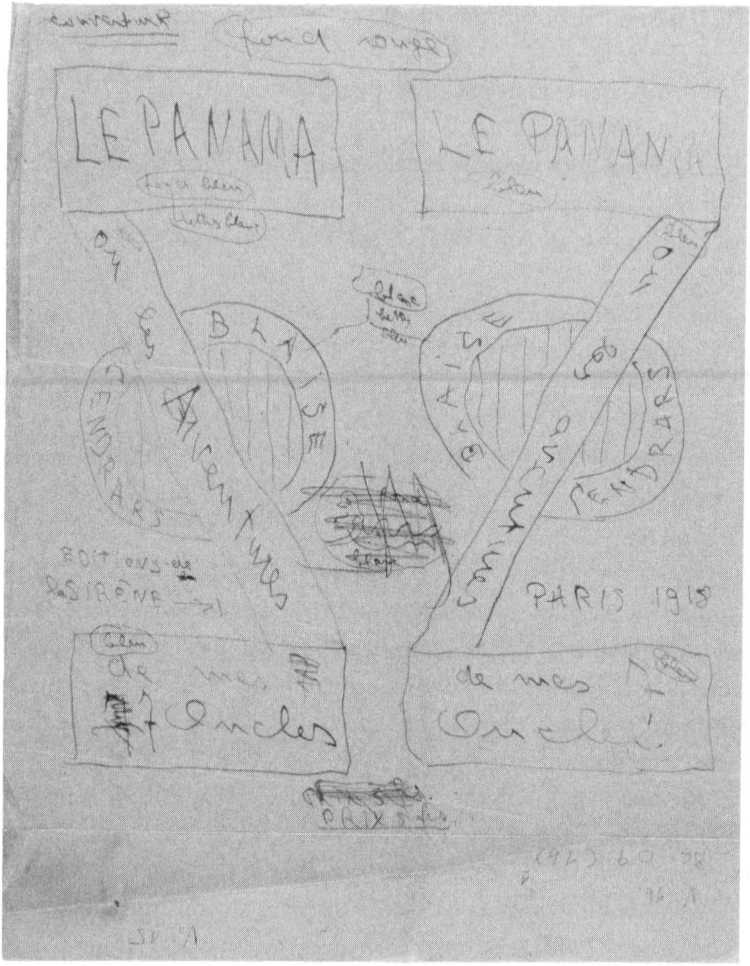

Blaise Cendrars, draft design for the cover of *Le Panama, ou les aventures de mes sept oncles* (1918), ink on paper.

that enclose and punctuate the body of the text. The particular typography and layout of the original edition, with its intersecting lines and folds, makes it a ludic object that derives a series of effects from the trope of the isthmus that has provided the very starting point of the poem. The striking original edition was published in 1918 by the Editions de la Sirène, for which Cendrars had worked as literary adviser alongside its director Paul Laffitte since the previous year.[92] Even if its retention of the book format makes it arguably less daring and certainly less ostentatious than the poster/map layout of the *Prose*, it is no less original in its conception.

Cover design of Blaise Cendrars, *Le Panama, ou les aventures de mes sept oncles* (1918), realized by Raoul Dufy.

Indeed, as we shall see, *Le Panama* possesses many features that make it a worthy successor to the *Prose* in terms of its experimentation with the printed medium and the interaction of its textual and graphic elements.

One aspect of *Le Panama* that deserves mention is its negotiation of the spaces that normally separate fine art and poetry from applied art and other creative forms that are often unjustly considered to be of lesser aesthetic value. A firm resistance to such elitist attitudes is a characteristic that this poem shares with many of Cendrars's other works; indeed, as we shall see, the poem vouches for the lack of preciousness in his attitude to

Cover of the Union Pacific Railroad timetable, 1917.

the literary world, an attitude that in turn points towards his strong conviction that poetry should belong to the masses and not just to the social elite. As he would express it in 1924, 'Jusqu'à présent, la poésie nouvelle est la meilleure illustration de cette science nouvelle appelée à bouleverser toutes les vieilles habitudes de l'histoire et de la critique littéraires.' (To this day, modern poetry is the best illustration of this new science destined to upset all the old habits of literary criticism and history.)[93] As noted earlier, the *Prose du Transsibérien*, in its conception and realization alike, rejects notions of the straightforwardly 'literary' and replaces them with a hybrid aesthetic that seeks to bring together literary and non-literary elements, as well as 'high' and 'low' cultural forms (poetry, fine art, poster design, applied art) without hierarchical distinction. In many respects, *Le Panama* embraces the same aesthetic of the everyday, and this is just as much the result of Cendrars's radically experimental approach to the material presentation of his poem as it is a reflection of the textual content itself.

That this is no straightforward book is already evident from a cursory glance at its cover, designed by Cendrars and realized by Raoul Dufy. The personal input of Cendrars the inveterate traveller is immediately apparent in the cover design, which he himself drafted.[94] Borrowing its shape and format from a train timetable, *Le Panama* features a vertical fold that runs down the centre of its red, blue and white cover. The graphic design that adorns the cover is based around this fold, with two identical halves on either side of it; these become matching front and back covers if the book is folded down its long side. As Jay Bochner puts it, this is a format that 'invites casual pocketing', a fact that already tells us much about Cendrars's anti-elitist intentions.[95]

As can be seen from the cover of the 1917 Union Pacific railroad schedule, the duplicate image and folding cover were already in use at that time, and these provided the inspiration for Cendrars's design. Anticipating the subject-matter of the poem, and underscoring its affinity both with the *Prose* and with Cendrars's autobiography, the lifebelt already alludes to the trope of the voyage, connoting the routes of ocean liners such as the *Volpurno*, which had brought him from the USA to France in 1912, and to which a line of the poem refers explicitly. Another striking visual feature of Cendrars's book – one that not only reinforces the railway theme of the book's cover design, but underscores the thematic affinity between *Le Panama* and *Prose du Transsibérien* – are the 25 extracts of railway maps that intersperse the lines of verse at regular intervals. Like the cover motif, these are taken from genuine printed North American railway timetables; both textual and visual in nature, the extracts relate to the poetic text and to the overall conception of this book in a variety of ways. First, they emphasize the metaphorical importance of the poem as a journey: one 'itinerary' – that of the poem's lines of verse – is echoed and extended graphically and geographically by another, indicated on the page by the routes on the maps. The latter function metonymically as fragments signifying travel, but rather than relating to any specific journey mentioned in the text, they have associations with the *idea* of travel more broadly. They also serve to draw our attention to the displacement and movement of the reading process, in which our eyes constantly scan the text, our hand turns the pages and we engage bodily with the book we are holding.

The relationship of these maps to the specific history of the Panama Canal, its catastrophic construction projects and its financial failures, is thus somewhat indirect and tangential; but no less marginally related to the canal is the poem itself, which refers to it in a much less sustained way than the title might lead us to expect. Admittedly, the poem does allude to the financial crash of 1892 that caused the funding of the canal's building project to collapse. Yet rather than providing the central thrust of what follows, this acts as the starting point for a series of digressions that radiate concentrically between the central hub of the narrator and the seven narrative threads that lead us to their original sources, the narrator's seven uncles. As the narrator explains,

> C'est aussi vers cette époque que j'ai lu l'histoire du tremblement
> de terre de Lisbonne
> Mais je crois bien
> Que le crach du Panama est d'une importance plus universelle
> Car il a bouleversé mon enfance.
> [. . .]
> Banquier
> Mon père perdit les trois quarts de sa fortune
> Comme nombre d'honnêtes gens qui perdirent leur argent dans
> ce crach,
> Mon père
> Moins bête
> Perdit celui des autres,
> [. . .]
> C'est le crach du Panama qui fit de moi un poète!
>
> (It was also around that time that I read the story of the Lisbon
> earthquake
> But I really believe
> That the Panama crash had a much wider effect
> Because it turned my childhood upside down.
> [. . .]
> As a banker
> My father lost three-fourths of his fortune
> Like a number of upright people who lost their money in that
> crash,
> My father
> Less stupid
> Lost other people's money,
> [. . .]
> It was the Panama crash that made me a poet!)[96]

It is worth reflecting on the relationship that brings the graphic elements that adorn this book into contact with the poem's linguistic contents. The map fragments all share a similar format: their principal characteristic is a long horizontal line indicating the route of the railroad, with place names emanating on either side. Upon closer inspection, we see that they offer three variants of railway lines connecting San Francisco and the Pacific coast to Chicago and St Louis, and one from Chicago north to Wisconsin. This fact relates well to the structure of the poem, which also tells a story that is divided into a series of interrelated episodes corresponding to the narrator's seven uncles. The route maps carry out the typographical function of dividing the poem into smaller sections; significantly, they also invite our interaction both as readers and as viewers, and this semiotic versatility opens up various interpretative possibilities. On one level, the maps offer a series of broadly accurate, if somewhat schematic images of real geographic locations: their *effet de*

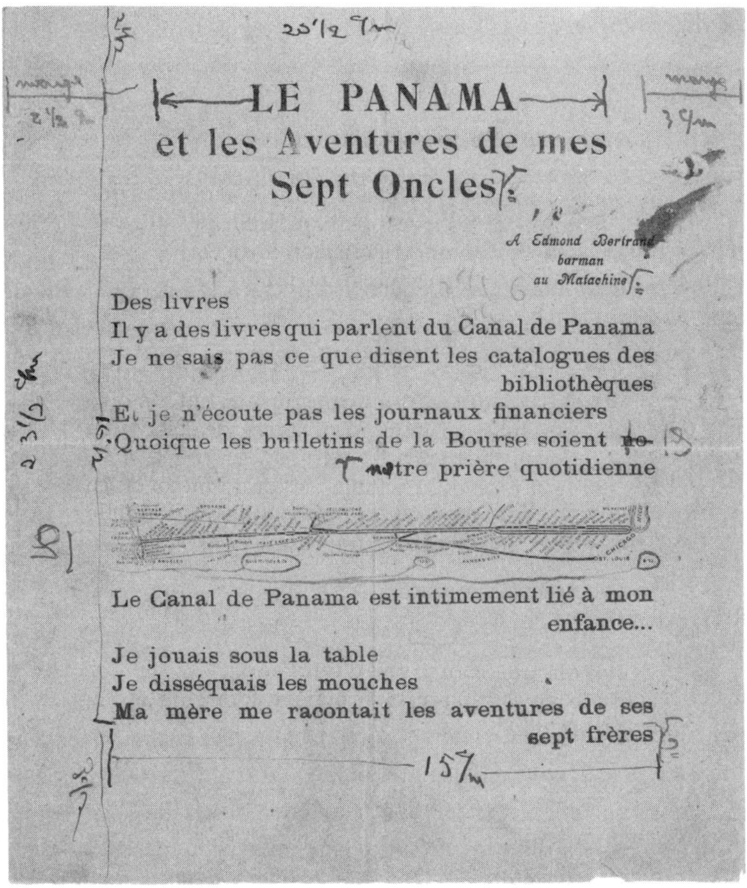
LE PANAMA
et les Aventures de mes
Sept Oncles

A Edmond Bertrand
barman
au Matachine

Des livres
Il y a des livres qui parlent du Canal de Panama
Je ne sais pas ce que disent les catalogues des bibliothèques
Et je n'écoute pas les journaux financiers
Quoique les bulletins de la Bourse soient notre prière quotidienne

Le Canal de Panama est intimement lié à mon enfance...
Je jouais sous la table
Je disséquais les mouches
Ma mère me racontait les aventures de ses sept frères

Proof page of *Le Panama, ou les aventures de mes sept oncles* (1918), with Blaise Cendrars's handwritten annotations.

réel vouchsafes the factual status of the events narrated. In this light, they constitute a documentary element further substantiating the veracity of the poet's tales. The place names that the narrator enumerates are, as it were, countersigned, and doubly at that, by their repetition as a linguistic signifier and as a schematic icon (a dot on a line) on the railroad map. This overdetermination has an effect not dissimilar to that of a photograph, in that it affirms what Roland Barthes describes as the 'emergence of the referent', the 'ça a été' (that has been) that he sees as the preserve of photography.[97]

But why should Cendrars have chosen railway maps? Unlike the *Prose du Transsibérien*, this poem is not specifically about a journey, and even less a journey by train. One answer, presumably, may lie in the visual appearance of the maps: their long, narrow, linear form has a similarity to the shape of the Panama Canal. In other words, each one of the 25 map extracts resembles a tiny isthmus; but instead of narrow areas of land separating two stretches of sea, these are iconic signifiers on either side of which are expanses of paper populated by place names. Rather more tenuously, we might also argue that the 25 railroad extracts also link *Le Panama* intertextually and intermedially to the *Prose du Transsibérien* in the sense that they resemble its elongated form with its central spine.

A similar property can be identified in the fold line that splits the book vertically down the middle. If the reader carries out the author's intended actions and folds it along that central spine, then it, too, becomes an isthmus of sorts. And if we consider another paratextual element – an important one, given the privileged place it occupies – namely, the poem's title on the front and back covers, we note that the key element, the name of the country itself, is hyphenated:

LE PA-

NAMA

The effect of this typographic detail is not as insignificant as it may seem: without eliminating the semantic function of the place name, the hyphen (in French, *trait d'union*), like the fold, could stand for the geological hyphen connecting North and South America which the canal divides, uncoupling the two continents. It thus anticipates graphically and typographically the central theme and geographic focus of the poem. In these diverse ways, then, this poem is replete with references to the isthmus that is its thematic starting point.

The dedication at the head of the poem, 'A Edmond Bertrand barman au Matachine' (To Edmond Bertrand, barman of the Matachine), suggests a further layer of meaning that relates to the choice of illustrations. First, the specificity of the dedicatee's name and place of work helps to situate the poem firmly in the real world, in the quotidian reality of drinking establishments, and thereby establish the author's credentials as a man of the people. Moreover, as Yvette Bozon-Scalzitti has pointed out, the name 'Matachine' may contain a clue to help us understand the relationship between the railroad map and the narrator's anecdotes. In Spanish, 'Matachino' would translate as a 'killer of Chinese', and so the dedication may be a discreet allusion to the construction of the North American railroad, an undertaking that led to the enlisting of thousands of Chinese labourers, many of whom lost their lives on the construction project. This, then, could help to explain the inclusion of the railway maps: the story of the construction of the Panama Canal is just one aspect of the poem's historical narratives; another, more implicit strand is the no less troubled saga of the construction of the North American railroads.

Before we leave the poem behind, another extraordinary typographic feature of the book requires consideration. Nestling between two pages of verse located just over two-thirds of the way through the poem, from which it emerges to meet our gaze entirely without warning, is a full-page advertisement for Denver.[98] Like the railroad maps, but in an even more forceful way, this extra-textual device brings us into contact with the real world, and prompts us to reflect on the possible reasons for its inclusion, the nature of its relationship to the fiction that surrounds it, and how and to what extent these two different forms of discourse affect one another by virtue of their being thrust together in such an unorthodox way. Here, Cendrars is offering us another instance of a reality effect that causes us to reconsider the relationship between experience and representation and the borderline between factual and fictional modes of representation.

The advertisement compels us to question, first, its semiotic status: is it an integral part of the poem? To what extent is it supposed to relate to the adventures of the narrator's seven uncles? We sense that any such connection must be a very tenuous one. Of the many place names that the poem's narrator cites, Denver is not one; it does, however, appear on the railroad map and, moreover, it marks the approximate mid-point between the map's end points, San Francisco and Chicago. Both of these locations, as well as the Sacramento Valley, do appear in the anecdotes of

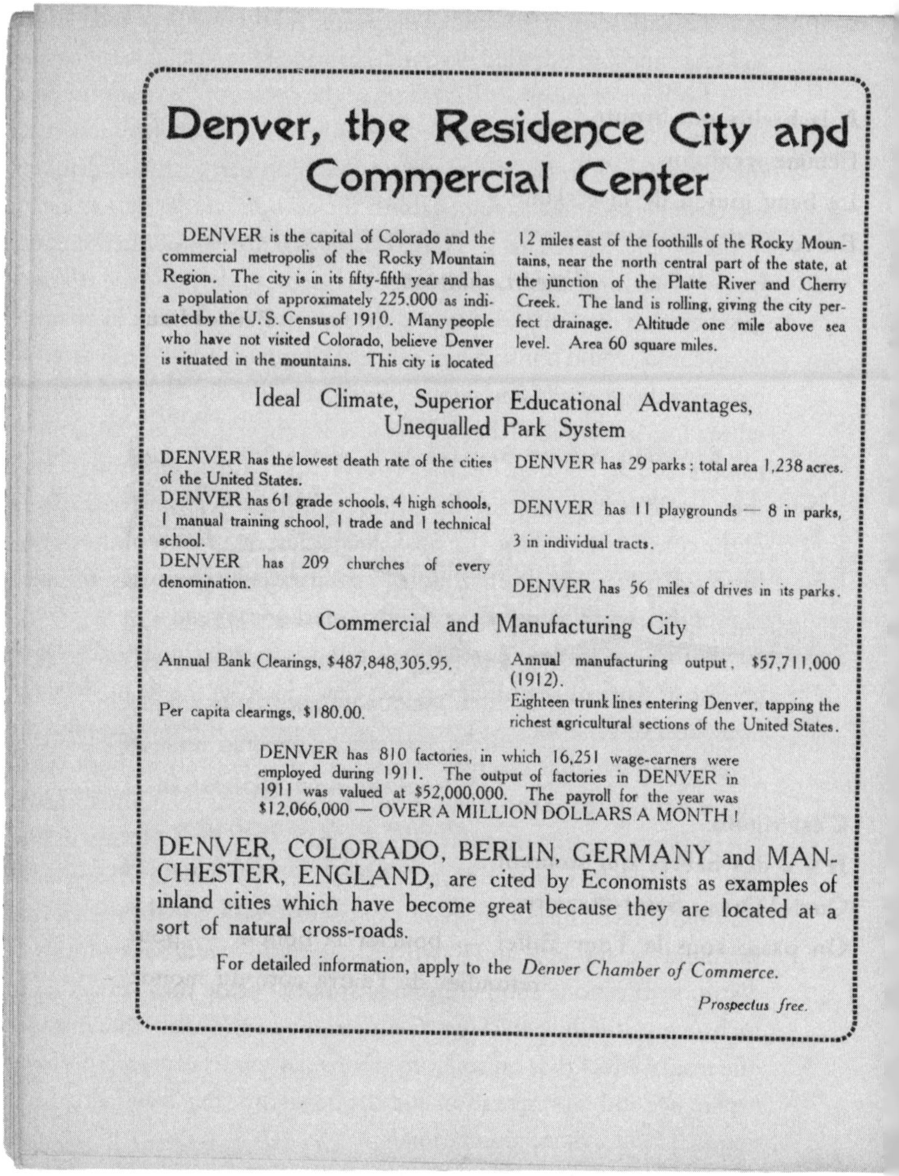

Denver, the Residence City and Commercial Center

DENVER is the capital of Colorado and the commercial metropolis of the Rocky Mountain Region. The city is in its fifty-fifth year and has a population of approximately 225,000 as indicated by the U. S. Census of 1910. Many people who have not visited Colorado, believe Denver is situated in the mountains. This city is located 12 miles east of the foothills of the Rocky Mountains, near the north central part of the state, at the junction of the Platte River and Cherry Creek. The land is rolling, giving the city perfect drainage. Altitude one mile above sea level. Area 60 square miles.

Ideal Climate, Superior Educational Advantages, Unequalled Park System

DENVER has the lowest death rate of the cities of the United States.

DENVER has 61 grade schools, 4 high schools, 1 manual training school, 1 trade and 1 technical school.

DENVER has 209 churches of every denomination.

DENVER has 29 parks: total area 1,238 acres.

DENVER has 11 playgrounds — 8 in parks, 3 in individual tracts.

DENVER has 56 miles of drives in its parks.

Commercial and Manufacturing City

Annual Bank Clearings, $487,848,305.95.

Per capita clearings, $180.00.

Annual manufacturing output, $57,711,000 (1912).

Eighteen trunk lines entering Denver, tapping the richest agricultural sections of the United States.

DENVER has 810 factories, in which 16,251 wage-earners were employed during 1911. The output of factories in DENVER in 1911 was valued at $52,000,000. The payroll for the year was $12,066,000 — OVER A MILLION DOLLARS A MONTH!

DENVER, COLORADO, BERLIN, GERMANY and MANCHESTER, ENGLAND, are cited by Economists as examples of inland cities which have become great because they are located at a sort of natural cross-roads.

For detailed information, apply to the *Denver Chamber of Commerce.*

Prospectus free.

the narrator's uncles.[99] But is it at least connected to the broad themes of the poem? True, Denver is in the same continent as Panama, if not exactly close to it. For a French reader reading the published poem in 1918, the name would connote an air of exoticism and alterity, but little by way of a specific mental image. But, while the geographical connection to Panama is only tenuous, the short history of Denver offers a more credible basis for establishing connections with the poem's themes. For

Puis on continue

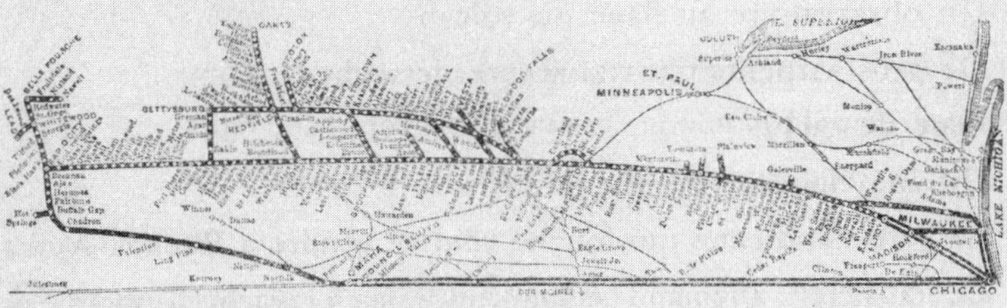

Les catapultes du soleil assiègent les tropiques irascibles
Riche Péruvien propriétaire d'une exploitation de guano
d'Angamos
On lance l'Acaraguan Bananan
A l'ombre
Les mulâtres hospitaliers
J'ai passé plus d'un hiver dans ces îles fortunées
L'oiseau-secrétaire est un éblouissement
Belles dames plantureuses
On boit des boissons glacées sur la terrasse
Un torpilleur brûle comme un cigare
Une partie de polo dans le champ d'ananas
Et les palétuviers éventent les jeunes filles studieuses

Double page from *Le Panama, ou les aventures de mes sept oncles* (1918).

instance, Denver's creation was a direct consequence of the gold strike of 1858, which brought prospectors flooding into the town, hopeful of a repeat of the great Californian Gold Rush that had begun eight years earlier. Denver's rapid growth gave way to an equally sudden decline when a huge gold strike in the nearby town of Central City left Denver nearly deserted. From this perspective, then, a parallel can be established between the histories of the Panama Canal and Denver.

What do the specific textual contents of the Denver advertisement reveal about the city? At the bottom of the page, the final declaration suggests another possible connection with the themes of the poem:

> DENVER, COLORADO, BERLIN, GERMANY and MANCHESTER, ENGLAND, are cited by Economists as examples of inland cities which have become great because they are located at a sort of natural cross-roads.[100]

These last words suggest that the selection of this advertisement may have been much less random than initially appears to be the case. The reference to 'a sort of natural cross-roads' is particularly evocative; after all, the Isthmus of Panama is a narrow strip of land that connects two larger landmasses across large expanses of sea, and the Panama Canal is a thoroughfare that cuts across one of its narrowest points at a right angle. The isthmus itself, and the canal, can both be regarded as types of 'crossroads', the former a natural one and the latter a construction. Seen in this light, the Denver advertisement leaps into focus as being thematically congruent within the poem; moreover, its typographic composition, arranged in two vertical columns bisected by headings and subheadings, means that we can even consider the advertisement to have a metonymic function, its bipartite construction standing for the entire poem and for the idea of the isthmus. Of course, we cannot be sure that Cendrars wished to grant the advertisement any particular symbolic meaning; but a reading of that sort certainly gains credence when we take into account the specific point in the poem at which it occurs, immediately after a line that transports us without warning back to Paris, before moving onwards again:

> Paris-adieux
> C'est rigolo
> Il y a des heures qui sonnent
> Quai d'Orsay – Saint-Nazaire!
> On passe sous la Tour Eiffel – boucler la boucle – pour retomber
> de l'autre côté du monde
> Puis on continue

(Paris good-bye
It's a riot
There are hours that chime
Quai-d'Orsay – Saint-Nazaire!
You go under the Eiffel Tower – looping the loop – to come
down on the other side of the world
Then you go on)[101]

The insertion of the Denver advertisement in the space between these lines seems significant: this is the first mention of Paris in a poem that covers huge expanses, but remains mostly rooted in the continent of America, with occasional excurses to Africa and Asia. The only other occurrences of allusions to the French capital are a reference to the address of Cendrars's hero, Remy de Gourmont, and again, in the closing lines of the poem, where the speaker alludes discreetly to the café on the boulevard Montparnasse where Cendrars and his acquaintances from the literary and artistic circles would spend time:

Tout bas
A la Rotonde
Comme tout au fond d'un verre

J'attends

(Very low
At the Rotonde
As if at the very bottom of a glass

I'm waiting)[102]

These lines display a clear similarity with the closing lines of *Prose du Transsibérien*, whose narration suddenly breaks off when the protagonists have reached Harbin, the final stop on the Trans-Siberian Express line, only to shift abruptly to Paris, where the narrator intends to drown his sorrows nostalgically in the Lapin Agile before returning home alone.[103] This similarity, however, is attenuated by their respective closing lines: we have seen how the *Prose* conveys a strong degree of resolution in its tripartite expression, describing the French capital as 'Ville de la Tour unique du grand Gibet et de la Roue' (City of the incomparable Tower the great Gibbet and the Wheel).[104] Even if this finality is undermined by the absence of a full stop, the fact that it is accompanied by Sonia Delaunay's visual representation of the tower and the Ferris wheel helps to accentuate these lines as a privileged moment in the poem. By contrast, *Le Panama* usurps and undermines the geographic specificity of its allusion to Paris with a cluster of short lines which seem to suggest that the poet's or at least the speaker's true place is in perpetual movement, or a state of simultaneity that defies notions of spatio-temporal singularity:

Je voudrais être la cinquième roue du char
Orage
Midi à quatorze heures
Rien et partout

(I'd like to be a fifth wheel
Storm
Noon at 2 p.m.
Nothing and everywhere)[105]

The qualitative shift from the finality and singularity of the *Prose* to the multiplicity of *Le Panama* is underlined by their respective inscriptions of the place and time of their writing. For the *Prose* ends with 'Paris, 1913', whereas *Le Panama* concludes with a long list of place names that appears to be a deliberately expansive riposte to the earlier poem:

PARIS ET SA BANLIEUE.
Saint-Cloud, Sèvres, Montmorency, Courbevoie, Bougival, Rueil, Montrouge, Saint-Denis, Vincennes, Etampes, Melun, Saint-Martin, Méréville, Barbizon, Forges-en-Bière.

Juin 1913–juin 1914

(PARIS AND ITS SUBURBS:
Saint-Cloud, Sèvres, Montmorency, Courbevoie, Bougival, Rueil, Montrouge, Saint-Denis, Vincennes, Etampes, Melun, Saint-Martin, Méréville, Barbizon, Forges-en-Bière.

June 1913–June 1914)[106]

The experimental practices that Cendrars adopts here, employing a fragmented construction, everyday materials and readymade visual and textual elements, remind us of his close familiarity with contemporaneous tendencies in the visual arts, and the important role that the painters played in fuelling his creativity. With astonishing modernity and uncompromising boldness, Cendrars's poem foregrounds its various textual and extra-textual sources without attempting to explain them, or minimize the differences between them, or adjust them to create a perfectly smooth fit. If the technique represents a form of textual collage, then it is a collage that is happy to leave the glue (*colle*) plainly visible. He entrusts the reader with the task of interpretation and allows us to negotiate our way around the poem. It is a form of poetry that borrows from several semiotic systems but refuses to remain in any single one. Its visual and textual structures accentuate repetition and difference, the logic of variations on a theme, the constant to-ing and fro-ing of signifiers and signifieds that allows meanings to proliferate rather than come to rest into a single semantic field. The maps on the page are thus a reminder of the task that lies before us, since our reading process will necessarily entail the processes of mapping and orientation, and the risk of losing our way. The poem's deliberate refusal to provide neat explanations for the discrepancies it contains makes it tempting to see it as a form of rhizome, which, as Gilles Deleuze and Félix Guattari remind us, 'has no beginning or end; it is always in the middle, between things, interbeing, *intermezzo*'.[107] This seems particularly well attuned to the poetic structure that Cendrars has created, with its rhizomatic character, its eschewal of a singular narrative in favour of a succession of byways that intersect and bifurcate endlessly, folding into one another and weaving new associations and meanings.

What, then, of the Panama Canal? The failed construction project under the leadership of Ferdinand de Lesseps resulted not only in the collapse of his company, but in the financial ruin of its investors and a huge political debacle that blighted the Third Republic. The saga of the canal had a sequel: in 1903, the USA took over the construction project, and work began in May of the following year. By a strange twist of fate, the canal was completed on 3 August 1914, coinciding exactly with the declaration of the First World War. This meant that, instead of attending the official opening of the canal as he had planned, Cendrars found himself drafting his 'Appeal to Foreign Writers', in which he implored them to join him in fighting for France. As we know, this decision would have profound and lasting consequences for Cendrars, both as an individual and as a writer.

It is worth considering one final aspect of this complex kaleidoscopic poem, an aspect that remained hidden for decades but which came to light when the original manuscript was unearthed. As Claude Leroy notes, Cendrars had sold the manuscript in 1919, but when Charles-Ferdinand Sunier located it, it was discovered that it contained Cendrars's handwritten annotations and amendments written with his right and left hands, before and after his amputation. This is a poem that is marked by time in so many ways: the four-year lapse that separates its writing and its publication is the most profoundly significant period in Cendrars's life. The poem, with its fold lines, its borders and its timetables that are so many markers of shifts in time and space, is also the tangible proof of Cendrars's own painful negotiation of the passage from the heady optimism of the pre-war period to the sober reality of the interwar years, the passage from the young avant-garde poet of the pre-war years to the *mutilé de guerre* and poet of the left hand, *la main amie*.

The three long poems were published in 1919 as a single volume under the title *Du Monde entier* (which can be translated as *About the Whole World* or *From the Whole World*) under the imprint of the prestigious Editions de la Nouvelle Revue française. For the poet, whose work until then had appeared in small presses and partly at his own expense, this constituted a very significant step towards a broader readership, even if the new edition stripped the poems of their experimental visual and typographic form. Leroy's notes in the Pléiade edition allude to a particularly prestigious reader whose own literary work Cendrars coincidentally revered: this was none other than Marcel Proust, who wrote a fourteen-page letter to the author of *Du Monde entier* in 1920 expressing his gratitude and enthusiasm for the book.[108] Cendrars stopped writing poems only a few years later in order to devote his energies to other forms of writing, but before that, he produced some volumes of poetry that take the genre in new experimental directions. The next chapter will consider these and the possible factors behind his departure into new expressive realms.

two

Profound Today: Poetry Before and After the Great War

The year 1914 began promisingly for Cendrars as some of his recent poems were published in literary journals in France and Germany.[1] Meanwhile, the *Prose du Transsibérien* continued to create a stir in avant-garde circles, its renown reaching as far as St Petersburg, where Sonia Delaunay's acquaintance Alexander Smirnov gave a talk about it at the Chien errant, a well-known artistic haunt. Such literary success was not matched by financial rewards, though, and to save what little money they had, Cendrars and Féla had left their rented room in Paris in late 1913 for the more peaceful but spartan setting of a farmworker's cottage near Barbizon, the village that had given its name to the artistic movement in the previous century. In April, Féla gave birth to their first child, a boy whom they named Odilon after the Symbolist artist Odilon Redon. They moved briefly to Saint-Martin-en-Bière before returning to Forges-par-Barbizon, where regular payments from Cendrars's childhood friend August Suter kept them afloat. Cendrars made a little money by teaming up with a local beekeeper and selling the honey via upmarket shops in Paris.[2] Around this time, he and his friend the Italian film theorist Ricciotto Canudo hatched the idea of making a series of films about nature. Canudo's connections with the production company Pathé helped to broker a deal whereby Cendrars would write the scripts.[3] Then dramatic world events intervened.

After the assassination of Archduke Franz Ferdinand in Sarajevo on 27 June, international tensions escalated throughout Europe, and in July, Cendrars felt compelled to return to Paris to be close to the international community of writers and artists in whose midst he had lived when he first arrived in France. On 29 July 1914, Cendrars and Canudo published an article under the title 'Appel à tous les étrangers' (Call to All Foreigners), which was widely published in the French press. It begins: 'Des étrangers amis de la France, qui pendant leur séjour en France ont appris à l'aimer et à la chérir comme une seconde patrie, sentent le besoin impérieux de lui offrir leurs bras.' (Foreigners loyal to France, who during their stay in France have learnt to love and cherish it like a second homeland, feel the imperious need to offer their arms for it.)[4] As a Swiss national, Cendrars was under no obligation to fight for France, but on 3 August, the day after Germany declared war on France, he and Canudo registered their intention to fight in the French army. Cendrars received a few weeks of training, initially hoping to be taken on by the French air force, but was assigned to the First Foreign Battalion, which was merged into the Foreign Legion a year later.

The alacrity of this call to arms may suggest that Cendrars had been convinced of the need for a war for some time, but Giselle Bienne notes that the reality was much less clear-cut. Cendrars was one of many writers who had signed a petition in 1913 calling for peace in Europe; in fact, he signed it twice under different names.[5] There is much to suggest that Cendrars's decision to fight in the war had little to do with any innate antipathy towards the Germans. He had, after all, lived in Germany and German-speaking Switzerland, had learnt to speak and write the language fluently, and in the pre-war years had been in contact with members of the German avant-garde and published in *Der Sturm*, the journal that Herwarth Walden had founded in Berlin in 1910. As well as publishing progressive literature by German authors, the journal was international in outlook and did much to foster closer cultural and artistic links between Berlin and Paris in the pre-war years; its gallery, founded in 1912 to mark the hundredth number of the publication, also exhibited works by the Fauves and other French artists. Along with Cendrars, other French-language poets including Apollinaire had poems published in the journal. 'Crépitements' (Crackling), the ninth of the *Dix-neuf poèmes élastiques*, written in September 1913, ends with a dedication to the German Expressionist poet Ludwig Rubiner, with whom Cendrars had become friends.[6]

Cendrars's decision to fight almost certainly had something to do with his precarious situation as a foreigner living in France. When mobilization was declared, the French transport network shut down and Cendrars was trapped in Paris. Meanwhile, Féla tried to care for Odilon in Forges with dwindling resources, and her situation became all the more precarious when she was subjected to xenophobic abuse. Cendrars's sudden disappearance from the village on the eve of war and his foreign accent had led many of the locals to suspect that he was a German spy.[7] He and Féla married on 16 September 1914, a decision prompted by the urgent need for a measure of stability in those febrile times.

For Cendrars, then, the war offered the opportunity to prove his love of his adopted nation once and for all and to resolve some of these issues affecting his status in France. Less noble reasons may also have lain behind the decision to enlist; indeed, Cendrars wrote to his friend Suter at the start of September that the war was 'une douloureuse délivrance pour accoucher de la liberté. Cela me va comme un gant.' (a painful deliverance to give birth to freedom. This fits me like a glove.)[8] Giselle Bienne goes further, suggesting that the war provided Cendrars with an outlet for violent tendencies that he had been harbouring for some time.[9]

The First World War was devastating for Cendrars, but it proved defining, too. On 28 September 1915, during the Battle of Champagne, his right arm was shot to pieces in machine-gun fire. Thereafter nicknamed 'l'écrivain de la main gauche' (the left-handed writer), he would be haunted by his 'phantom hand' for the rest of his life, but avoided addressing the specific circumstances of his wound for some thirty years.[10] In *La Ferme de Navarin*, Bienne recounts the events that led to Cendrars's devastating injury in the battle of Champagne in September 1915. The tenth division of the colonial infantry joined forces with the Foreign Legion to launch an attack on the Navarin Farm. Rain flooded munitions stores, caused heavy artillery to malfunction and delayed supplies reaching the front. Yet the French army made some initial gains that instilled confidence in the commanding officers. They decided to send thousands of men towards the German lines, but failed to reckon with the Germans' reserve position, which picked off the attackers by the thousand. Cendrars's regiment launched an attack under heavy rainfall at 7.30 p.m. on Tuesday 28 September. As he was running approximately 200 metres from the ruins of the farm, German machine-gun fire struck him above the elbow on his right arm, leaving it dangling by the skin. He asked one of his comrades to remove it, but nobody dared to do so, and instead he was taken to the makeshift military hospital in Châlons-sur-Marne for emergency treatment. His act of bravery earned him military honours, and in February 1916, he was granted French citizenship.[11]

Blaise Cendrars in the French Foreign Legion uniform, a few months after the amputation of his right arm, 1916.

The wound affected Cendrars for the rest of his life and certainly had an effect on his subsequent career as a writer. As he recuperated, he taught himself to write with his left hand; his manuscripts dating from this era show how challenging this must have been. He also became deeply immersed in cinema: in the summer of 1918, he began working alongside Abel Gance on *J'Accuse*, and again two years later on *La Roue*. Thanks to the intervention of Jean Cocteau, with whom he had worked at the Editions de La Sirène publishing house in Paris, Cendrars was recruited as a film director by the Rinascimento film production company in Rome in 1921.[12] Additionally, he wrote scripts that adopted the concise language and abbreviated structure of film notations while still functioning as literary texts in their own right. The move towards cinema, and a concomitant shift from the manual activity of writing to the visual undertaking of film directing, might seem to fit a certain assumption about Cendrars's psyche in the wake of his war wound and the loss of his writing hand. Yet we should not simply assume that the war was the sole catalyst for this shift. Cendrars acknowledged years later that fighting and writing were two very separate things for him, and that he could never belong to the combat writers. 'On est combattant ou l'on est écrivain. Quand on écrit, on ne combat pas à coups de fusil et quand on tire des coups de fusil, on n'écrit pas, on écrit après. On aurait bien mieux fait d'écrire avant et d'empêcher tout ça . . . ' (You are either a combattant or a writer. When you're writing, you're not fighting with a rifle and when you're firing a rifle, you're not writing, you do the writing afterwards. We'd have done much better to write first and prevent all that . . .)[13] Decades would pass before he engaged with his own war experience in any significant detail.

His collection of *Dix-neuf poèmes élastiques* (Nineteen Elastic Poems), mostly written before the war but published after it, already signals his growing fascination with the modern city in its heterogeneous forms and his sense that poetry needs to adapt to the new era. In contrast to *Les Pâques*, the *Prose* and *Panama*, the elastic poems are all short and treat explicitly quotidian subjects with no claim to any larger thematic significance. The poems reflect the diversity of the modern world and celebrate everyday life; they also reassert the mutual dependence of creativity and experience. As Cendrars states in various instances, the act of writing depends on being engaged with the world and open to all that it has to offer. Yet the *poèmes élastiques* hint that the creative act can also entail recycling and remediating the words and experiences of others:

the tenth poem, 'Dernière Heure' (Newsflash), is a verbal collage taken almost word-for-word from a newspaper article, which it transforms by means of lineation. Written some two years before Tristan Tzara's 'How to Make a Dadaist Poem', this foreshadows the Dada group's experimentations with chance, T. S. Eliot's use of cut-and-paste techniques in *The Waste Land* and the cut-up techniques popularized by William S. Burroughs in the 1950s and '60s. In all of these respects, the *poèmes élastiques* anticipate some of Cendrars's writings of the interwar years, including the readymade poetic collages of *Documentaires*, the short texts on advertising and his forays into reportage in the 1930s; these will be examined in later chapters.

Eighteen of the nineteen *poèmes élastiques* were written between August 1913 and July 1914 and published in avant-garde journals; the final poem was written in February 1919, and the collection appeared in print that year.[14] Cendrars points out wryly in a brief note at the end of the volume that neither the French literary establishment nor even that country's 'so-called avant-garde' took an interest in the poems, which had instead appeared in foreign publications. As Claude Leroy observes, this account is economical with the truth: while seven of the poems had indeed appeared in journals in Belgium, Germany, Italy, Sweden and Switzerland, no fewer than nine had been published in France, and five of these in *Les Soirées de Paris*.[15] Cendrars's words are nevertheless telling, since they hint at his antipathy towards all groups and suggest that he preferred to cultivate the status of an outsider, even in relation to the avant-gardes.

In their subject-matter, these 'circumstantial poems' are a natural sequel to *Prose du Transsibérien* in their express wish to bear out their author's dictum that 'La Littérature fait partie de la vie. Ce n'est pas quelque chose "a part".' (Literature is part of life. It is not something 'separate'.)[16] Yet in stylistic and structural terms these poems inhabit a realm far removed from the trio of modern epics with their ambitious scale and digressive narrative threads. The *poèmes élastiques* are much briefer, explicitly topical and focus on a range of contemporary subjects such as art and artists, current affairs, news items and issues of cultural interest. They are consciously popular, rejecting grand, timeless poetic tropes in favour of the ephemeral. They show Cendrars working in an opaque, multireferential, abstract idiom, without however abandoning all of the formal norms associated with the genre; elastic though they may be, these are still poems and present themselves as such.

In his letter announcing *Prose du Transsibérien*, Cendrars had claimed to have no working method and surmised that his poetic vocation had arisen 'peut-être par instinct; peut-être par spiritualité' (perhaps out of instinct; perhaps out of spirituality).[17] Here, too, he asserts the spontaneity of this collection by situating it within the category of 'circumstantial' poetry. Closer scrutiny reveals echos, structural layering and resonances both within individual poems and across the collection that suggest that the poet's methods were more systematic than he admits. Jean-Carlo Flückiger has shown how 'Journal' (Newspaper), the opening poem of the collection, generates an impression of radiating concentric movement in the seven-line clusters that follow the repeated invocation of Christ. Another means by which the sensation of concentric movement is generated is by contrasting long and short lines, many of the latter being monolexical. As Clive Scott observes, these have at once the ambivalent status of an exclamation and that of a mere item on a list, a kind of zero degree of rhythm.[18] The resultant effect of these techniques is the sensation of depth through simultaneous realization of two distinct perspectives, an effect akin to that created by Robert Delaunay's series of highly experimental paintings of 1912–13 with collective titles *Windows* and *Solar Discs*, in which overlapping layers of transparent colour invite a variety of different readings, both figurative and abstract. The eye flits incessantly from one reading to another, settling in neither, and as a result perceives in the canvas a sensation of movement.

Both *Prose du Transsibérien* and *Dix-neuf poèmes élastiques*, in their own ways, deal with this confrontation between the medium in its pure state and the medium as a conveyor of meaning; there is, however, a difference in the way they deal with this confrontation. Where the *Prose* allows the reader a degree of insight into the poetic processes that are at play, the *poèmes élastiques* can be defined to a large extent as an enactment of those processes. As a result, the reader is at times denied the possibility of interpretation, as any controlling poetic voice has been all but eliminated by the momentum of language. In 'Ma Danse', a rhythmic sequence culminates in the utterance 'Paritatitata/ Je tout-tourne' (Paritatitata/ I all-turn).[19] Here, the extreme reduction of syntax rids words of their signifying ballast so that they become a textual approximation of the sheer, unmediated sensation of movement. Only minimal vestiges of grammatical form hold this frenetic motion tenuously in check, keeping the work together as a 'poem'. Many of the *poèmes élastiques* explore the expressive potential of strings of disparate images devoid of connecting phrases or any obvious unifying semantic field: 'Gong tam-tam zanzibar bête de la jungle rayons X express bistouri symphonie' (Gong tom-tom Zanzibar jungle animal X-rays express scalpel symphony); or 'Des cosaques le Christ un soleil en décomposition' (Cossacks Christ a shattered sun); or, more obscure still, 'L'hélice des gemmes des foires des menstrues' (The propellor of gems of the runs of menses).[20]

Lines such as these defy the reader's attempts to gain a degree of coherent interpretative purchase. Instead, they leave us with a powerful impression of the dizzying opacity of language when it lacks the safety ropes of context, punctuation and syntactical markers. Devoid of the caesuras and pauses for breath that texts normally offer the reader, these lines require us to either add or omit them as we see fit. If we read the lines aloud as they are printed, with no concessions to punctuation, our reading process acquires such frenetic momentum that the strings of words remain beyond the reach of our processing capacity. We strive to develop them into meaningful, coherent images; but before we can do so, the next line is already emerging, and it in turn will sweep us up and carry us along in the wash of its rhythm. Such a relentless pace makes a serious impact on our reading process: we find ourselves forced to abandon the search for any stable meaning, and instead we are left with the raw acoustic traces of isolated elements of language. Words appear as momentary sensations that refuse to coalesce into a clear mental image, rather like colours that flash before our eyes on a screen or that we glimpse fleetingly from a fast-moving vehicle.

A comparison of this sort that implies a tidy correlation between word and image is, of course, flawed. Full abstraction in poetry is impossible without breaking words down into sound fragments or resorting to neologisms, and Cendrars was strongly opposed to what he saw as the gimmickry of Futurist words-in-freedom. His work is bound to the notion that the word is a syntactic unit charged with some semantic function; he does not practise the sort of chance-based lexical fragmentation that poets associated with Dada such as Kurt Schwitters and Raoul Hausmann would explore in their sound poems.[21] So, even in the most obscure of the *poèmes élastiques*, such as 'Titres' (Titles), where it is difficult to form a coherent overall picture from the poem as a whole, its individual words in isolation still undeniably have a signifying function. As we read the poem, we notice that some words are divested of any clear signification and experienced as pure sound, while others articulate some kind of meaning; the coexistence of these two modes of interaction with language creates a 'depth' that unites them on a single plane. By stripping syntax and omitting punctuation, Cendrars places the onus on the readers to apply their own interpretative skills to the reading process with no guarantee of ascertaining a single, clear meaning.

If the experimentation with concentric movement in the *Poèmes élastiques* offers a close analogy with Robert Delaunay's disc paintings and Sonia Delaunay's *Prismes électriques* of 1914, then it may also be seen to anticipate a new form of poetic discourse, characterized by syntactic compression, brevity and the predominant use of the present tense. This is a form of writing that derives its brevity and immediacy from the aesthetics of the billboard, the telegram or cinema. In poem 3, 'Contrastes' (Contrasts), we read:

> Il pleut les globes électriques
> Montrouge Gare de l'Est Métro Nord-Sud bateaux-mouches
>   monde
> Tout est halo
> Profondeur
>
> (It's raining electric lightbulbs
> Montrouge Gare de l'Est Métro Nord-Sud
> Seine omnibus people
> One big halo
> Depth)[22]

Like the rings of water that it evokes, this section creates concentric circular movement, both in the contrast of long and short lines and in its phonetic patterns. In the original French, the longest of these lines creates subtle phonetic and typographic effects that multiply its possible meanings. It creates a phonetic circularity or echoing in that the first syllable ('*Mon*t-') returns at the end of the line ('*mon*de'); moreover, there is a simultaneous outward movement from the specific ('Montrouge', 'Gare de l'Est' and so on) to the global and even cosmic ('monde', meaning 'world'). The 'depth' to which the poem refers stems from the use of multi-referential words, which radiate 'simultaneous contrasts': Montrouge contains the colour red ('rouge'), Nord-Sud is both a compass marking and the name of a metro line, while, taken literally, 'bateau-mouche' conflates the idea of a boat with that of a fly.[23] Phonetically, 'Tout est halo' can be understood as 'Everything is a halo' and 'Everything is in the water' (Tout est *à l'eau*), and therefore echoes the line 'It's raining light bulbs'. The syntactic reduction of the line, which has removed all articles, means that even the final word is capable of generating more than one mental image, since it can be understood as meaning either 'world' ([le] monde) or 'people' ([du] monde). Forced to choose one or other option, Ron Padgett in his published translation plumps for the latter, thereby conveying the impression of throngs of people. While this satisfactorily renders the impression of the bustling city and introduces a human element into the line, the translation loses the cosmic, planetary dimension conveyed by 'monde'. He compensates for this brilliantly by translating 'bateaux-mouches' as 'Seine omnibus'; the first of these terms inserts the specificity of place while the gently archaic second endows the passenger boat, and the scene, with the expansiveness and totality of 'omni', 'for all'.[24]

In its montage of disparate images without causal links, and in the emphasis it places on motion and on electricity, the above extract may be interpreted as having a particularly cinematic character. Such a reading gains credence by virtue of the fact, affirmed by Deleuze, that film-makers such as L'Herbier, Epstein, Renoir, Vigo and Grémillon all exploited water as a means to shift from the referential to the abstract, 'to endow movements with an irreversible duration independently of their figurative character'.[25] Alongside this use of imagery favoured by film-makers, Cendrars's elliptical syntax repeatedly suggests a peculiarly cinematographic effect of movement. 'Contrasts' ends with an apposition that functions like a fade:

Les hommes sont
Longs
Noirs
Tristes
Et fument, cheminées d'usine

(The men are
Tall
Dark
Sad
And smoking, factory stacks)[26]

By the addition of 'like', the final line would have become a straightforward simile drawing a clear analogy between the men, smoking their cigarettes and clad in dark clothes, and factory chimneys. By omitting any such explicit term of comparison, Cendrars allows the image of the chimneys to superimpose itself onto that of the men smoking, but leaves the latter image intact. As a result, the two 'shots' coexist in the reader's mind in a single composite image, creating a poetic equivalent of a cinematographic fade or a double exposure. It is devices such as this that remind us of Cendrars's close affiliations with cinema and his absorption of its discursive forms.[27]

Poem eighteen, entitled 'La Tête' (The Head), takes its inspiration from Alexander Archipenko's eponymous sculpture of 1913. The first three lines are taken wholesale from Cendrars's earlier poem, *Le Panama*; and, as if to underline their status as a poetic readymade, cut out and spliced in, they foreground the notion of the cut, albeit a rather less innocuous one, that of the guillotine:

La guillotine est le chef-d'œuvre de l'art plastique
Son déclic
Crée le mouvement perpétuel

(The guillotine is the masterpiece of visual art
Its click
Creates perpetual motion)[28]

Again, here – rather fittingly in an image of decapitation – the cutting room seems to be raising its head. Archipenko's eponymous sculpture is likened to 'a motionless top/ On its spinning point'. Some months after this poem was published in the review *De Stijl*, the same journal printed an essay by Theo van Doesburg on the abstract film experiments of Viking Eggeling and Hans Richter. Van Doesburg cites exactly this combination of stasis and mobility, 'uniting aesthetically the dynamic with the static', as the very basis of abstract film.[29]

The closing poem of the collection, the only one written after the war, focuses on Fernand Léger, who would become Cendrars's closest and most lasting artist friend and artistic collaborator. Their friendship was sealed by their shared experience of the war, in which both suffered serious injury; the contrasting experience of Cendrars's erstwhile ally Robert Delaunay will be discussed later.[30] 'Construction' adopts a simple syntax and a minimalist structure that creates rhythmic tensions between its long and short lines and between images of stasis and movement. The industrial imagery and geometric forms of Léger's work appear modern yet as old as the Earth itself:

De la couleur, de la couleur et des couleurs . . .
Voici Léger qui grandit comme le soleil de l'époque tertiaire
Et qui durcit
Et qui fixe
La nature morte
La croûte terrestre
Le liquide
Le brumeux
Tout ce qui se ternit
La géométrie nuageuse
Le fil à plomb qui se résorbe

(Colour, colour, and more colours . . .
Here's Léger who grows like the sun in the tertiary epoch
And who hardens
And who fixes
The still life
The earth's crust
The liquid
The steamy
Everything that grows dim
The cloudy geometry
The plumb line that retracts itself)[31]

Some lines consist of a single noun, with or without an article ('Ossification/ Locomotion'). Only in its closing lines does the poem shift from the natural realm to that of manufactured artefacts:

Tout grouille
L'esprit s'anime soudain et s'habille à son tour comme les
animaux et les plantes
Prodigieusement
Et voici
La peinture devient cette chose énorme qui bouge

La roue
La vie
La machine
L'âme humaine
Une culasse de 75
Mon portrait

(Everything is teeming
The mind suddenly comes alive and gets dressed in its turn like
    the plants and animals
Prodigiously
And now
Painting becomes this great thing that moves
The wheel
Life
The machine
The human soul
A 75 mm breech
My portrait)[32]

This final line, which avoids resolution by omitting a full stop, brings us back to the first poem in the collection, 'Journal' (Newspaper), with its confessional tone and its similarity to a diary entry. Fittingly, the preceding five lines construct a web of resonances that connect with Cendrars's own life and his work. 'The wheel' recalls the closing line of *Prose du Transsibérien* and anticipates the definitive title, *La Roue*, that he gave to the film on which he worked alongside Abel Gance and which the latter had provisionally entitled 'La Rose des roues' (The Rose of the Wheels).[33] The poem's next lines, 'La vie/ La machine/ L'âme humaine' (Life/ The machine/ The human soul), conflate human and mechanical elements in a way that anticipates the montages of Léger's film *Ballet mécanique* (1924), while the poem's reference to the breech of a 75 mm cannon hints at Léger's many paintings of soldiers and the machinery of modern warfare.

During the war, Cendrars did his best to avoid writing poems. Interviewed by Michel Manoll in 1950, he expressed astonishment at Apollinaire's capacity to write beautiful lines of verse against a background of such violence and horror. It seems fair to conclude that for Cendrars, the war was a time for action, not poetic reflection. Yet such a version of events does not convey the full significance of the war years for Cendrars's life, still less his literary career. He may have largely refrained from writing during his time serving in the French Foreign Legion, but many years later he recalled his wartime experiences in literary and partly mythologized form; the war makes its presence felt in works ranging from the short stories 'J'ai tué' (I Have Killed) and 'J'ai saigné' (I Have Bled) to the post-war tetralogy of heavily autobiographical novels, especially *La Main coupée*. But as we will see, the most profoundly traumatic experience of Cendrars's war, namely the mutilation and loss of his right arm, remains surprisingly absent from even these most direct accounts of his wartime activities.

'La Guerre au Luxembourg'

The sheer scarcity of poems written by Cendrars during the war makes 'La Guerre au Luxembourg' particularly important. This is heightened by the fact that he wrote it in 1916, only months after the attack which required the amputation of his right arm. The poem is thought to be the first ever complete text that he wrote with his left hand, so on this basis alone, it occupies an important place within his work. It is prefaced by a dedication to three of his comrades from the Foreign Legion who had lost their lives; their names are listed, as too are the places where they were killed. This foreshadows the post-war memoir *La Main coupée*, which is structured around individual chapters, each devoted to a legionnaire who lost his life.[34]

Perhaps surprisingly, Cendrars avoids any personal identification with the poem's subject-matter. Instead, it adopts the perspective of small children playing in the Jardin du Luxembourg; their innocent remarks can be understood as a wry comment on the poet's part about the naivety of those adults who viewed the war as a positive or necessary catalyst for social renewal, or possibly poets such as Apollinaire, whom Cendrars criticized for writing 'sweet little poems' at the front:[35]

Il n'y a que les petits enfants qui jouent à la guerre
La Somme Verdun
Mon grand frère est aux Dardanelles
Comme c'est beau
Un fusil

(Only little children play at war
La Somme Verdun
My big brother is in the Dardanelles
Look how beautiful
A rifle is)[36]

Yet the reality of war seeps into their playful enactment of battle, and alongside the tricolour 'ROUGE BLANC BLEU' (RED WHITE BLUE) which appears in the right margin, the lines of verse acquire a darker tone:

Puis on relève les morts
Tout le monde veut en être
Ou tout au moins blessé
Coupe coupe
Coupe le bras coupe la tête

(Then they raise the dead
Everyone wants to be dead
Or at least wounded
Cut cut
Cut off the arm cut off the head)[37]

Here is an early instance of Cendrars's compulsive tendency to allude to his war wound in circuitous terms: it is a recurrent presence in his writing, overshadowing everything he wrote after 28 September 1915, but it always appears at some remove, taking shape by means of displacement, deferral or projection. This recalls Freud's theory of 'repetition compulsion', which derived from his observations of survivors of war. He noted the uncanny way in which traumatic events repeat themselves in their consciousness, often in a displaced form. He notes that 'dreams occurring in traumatic neuroses have the characteristic of repeatedly bringing the patient back into the situation of his accident.'[38] Freud cites the literary example of Tasso's *Gerusalemme Liberata*, in which the protagonist Tancred, having unwittingly killed his beloved Clorinda, is haunted by her voice. As Cathy Caruth argues, 'Tancred's story thus represents traumatic experience not only as the enigma of a human agent's repeated and unknowing acts but also as the enigma of the otherness of a human voice that cries out from the wound, a voice that witnesses a truth that Tancred himself cannot fully know.'[39] Another image from 'La Guerre au Luxembourg' will recur later in Cendrars's work: the line 'La place de l'Etoile montera au ciel' (The place de l'Etoile will rise up into the sky) foreshadows the instances in which he imagines his severed right hand rising into the sky and forming the constellation Orion.[40]

A curious omission from Cendrars's literary oeuvre is information relating to his wife and family. This absence is all the more frustrating given his penchant for writing anecdotes about the many characters he encountered throughout his life, a tendency that comes to the fore in autobiographical stories such as *Vol à voiles* and even more so in the post-war novels. Féla gave birth to their second second son, Rémy, in 1916, and a daughter, Miriam, was born in December 1919. In truth, there is much to suggest that family life occupied a low priority in Cendrars's plans, and indeed, domestic stability is highly incompatible with the lifestyle of an itinerant writer. The correspondence between Cendrars and Féla testifies to her repeated pleas for him to take responsibility for their children, and his insistent and uncompromising rejection of any paternal duty. When Rémy was born, Cendrars did not stay around long enough to declare his son's birth to the registrar, leaving this task to some friends. He was already in a relationship with a young artist's model called Gabrielle, more commonly known as Gaby.[41] Remarkably, she even lived with Féla for a time in early 1917. By the autumn of that year, Cendrars had already fallen for another woman, the actress Raymone Duchâteau, who became his idealized, idolized companion for the rest of his life and eventually his second wife. That relationship too was complex and unorthodox, characterized by long periods apart, and never consummated. The love that Cendrars felt for Raymone was largely unrequited, or at least was not matched by a comparable degree of sentiment; she described him as nothing other than a friend.[42] In 1921, Cendrars encouraged Féla to live her own life, and she duly left France with their children and settled in San Remo, Italy, where they lived until 1929. Cendrars and Féla divorced in 1937, and she died in 1943 in a clinic in Montpellier.

Profond aujourd'hui

Cendrars returned to writing in a more regular way in 1917, some two years after his amputation. This was an extraordinarily productive period as he recovered from his mutilation and learned to write again, this time with his left hand. In late 1916, he was no longer in need of regular hospital visits and was allowed to recuperate at home. He, Féla and their two children had been living in a farmhouse near Méréville, but he was allocated a flat in Cannes to assist with his recuperation. Féla and the children spent the autumn and winter of 1916–17 there while Cendrars returned to Paris, ostensibly to be closer to the artistic and literary scene, but also to spend time with Gaby.[43] In 1916, he had also made the acquaintance of Eugenia Errázuriz, a wealthy Chilean who was heiress to a family fortune gained through silver mining. In the interwar years, she would frequently receive him at La Mimoseraie, her home in Biarritz, and welcome him into her high-society life. Along with Picasso and Stravinsky, Cendrars received her patronage, which came with a degree of possessiveness that the naturally itinerant poet must have endured with some difficulty.

The year 1917 was one of extremes for Cendrars: as the year began, he was in Cannes with his family; by the springtime, he had returned to Paris and met with Apollinaire, who introduced him to Philippe Soupault. In May, he mingled with Jean Cocteau, Erik Satie and Serge

Igor Stravinsky and Blaise Cendrars, Biarritz, August 1932.

Diaghilev at the Théâtre du Châtelet as they created the Cubist opera *Parade*; it is possible that he attended the première of Apollinaire's play *Les Mamelles de Tirésias* in Paris a month later. Amid all the creative fervour, he was beset by alcoholism and suicidal thoughts.[44] That year also heralded some of his most inventive and ambitious literary plans: it gave rise to the vast novel project *La Fin du monde*; this never saw the light of day, but it did spawn *Moravagine*, *Profond aujourd'hui*, 'Les Armoires chinoises', *L'Eubage* and *La Fin du monde filmée par l'Ange N.-D.*, the last of which was written in a single feverish burst of inspiration on the night of his thirtieth birthday, an event he recalls in detail in *Une Nuit dans la forêt*.[45] The interconnectedness of these various writings is underlined by a title page, which Cendrars penned with his left hand and dated 1918, announcing the publication of *La Fin du Monde Filmée par l'Ange N.-D.*, which flaunts the auspicious and ambitious generic label 'Grand Roman Cinéma' (Great Cinema Novel).

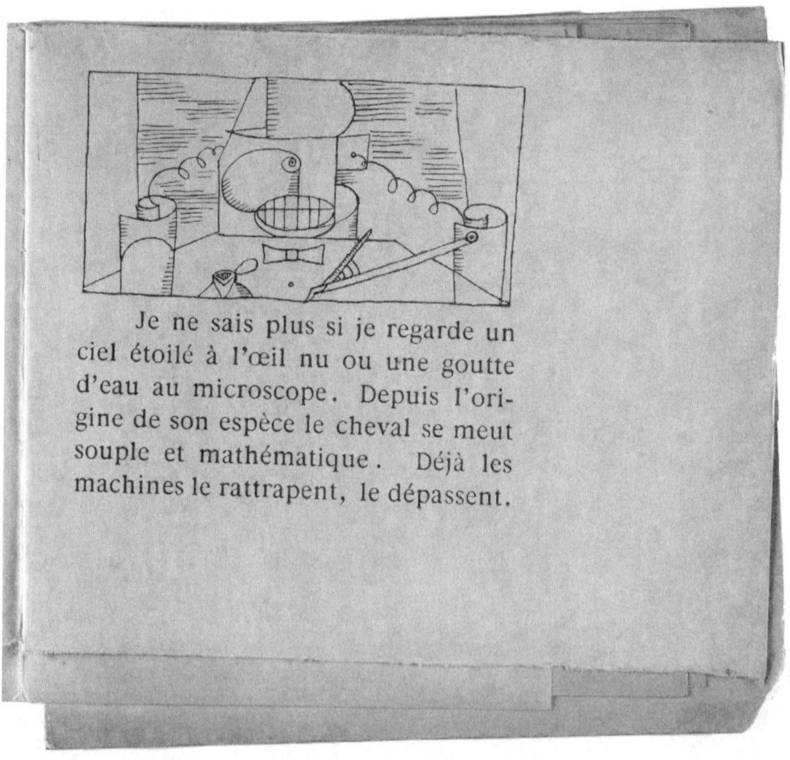

Page from Blaise Cendrars, *Profond aujourd'hui* (1917), with illustration by Ángel Zárraga.

The short poetic prose text *Profond aujourd'hui* is a life-affirming literary roar from a writer who had stared death in the face and risen again, more determined than ever to live life to the full. Written in Cannes in February 1917, it was originally intended to be the preface of *La Fin du monde*, but was published in its own right under the imprint of à la Belle Edition as a small book in September 1918, accompanied by five illustrations by the Mexican artist Ángel Zárraga.[46] Its genesis accompanies a drift in Cendrars's writing towards the aesthetics of cinema. Although it is not explicitly about film, the flickering, shadowy forms of that medium can be felt both in the paratactic structure of Cendrars's text and in its rapid montage of fragmentary ideas. Presented in a single unbroken stream devoid of paragraph breaks, the text unfolds in a breathless sequence. Narrated almost exclusively in the present tense, it employs a daring form of discourse that treats syntax as highly elastic, comprising sentences ranging from page-long strings of clauses to single words. Despite its ostensibly loose narrative structure, the text deals with some clearly identifiable themes that communicate his vision of modernity and meditate on what it is to be a writer amid it. As we shall see, *Profond aujourd'hui* also relates in different ways to Cendrars's situation at the time of its writing.

As its title suggests, the text begins with a meditation on the nature of the modern world and the implications it holds for the individual. More than a century later, it is difficult for us to have a sense of the scale and speed of developments in science, engineering and technology that had accompanied the end of the nineteenth century and ushered in the twentieth. The sheer rapidity of scientific and technological progress and sociocultural change, and their giddying impact on the mind and the senses, are powerfully felt in his text. The opening line already hints at the ambivalent impact of optical technologies on our perception, at once illuminating our vision and provoking an extreme sense of disorientation: 'Je ne sais plus si je regarde un ciel étoilé à l'oeil nu ou une goutte d'eau au microscope.' (I no longer know if I'm looking with my naked eye at a starry sky or at a drop of water through a microscope.)[47] As Claude Leroy has observed, this opening sentence alludes to Pascal's meditation in *Pensées* on the existence of two infinites, while also implicitly pointing towards a new sense of disorientation provoked by Cendrars's mutilation.[48] The close proximity in the text of the natural act of seeing and the mechanically enhanced 'eye' of the microscope also calls to mind Bergson, who, in *Creative Evolution*, considers human physiology and the relationship between the brain and the eye. He observes the striking contrast between the act of seeing and the nature of the organ of vision:

> La machine qu'est l'oeil est donc composée d'une infinité de machines, toutes d'une complexité extrême. Pourtant la vision est un fait simple. Dès que l'oeil s'ouvre, la vision s'opère. [. . .] C'est ce contraste entre la complexité de l'organe et l'unité de la fonction qui déconcerte l'esprit.
>
> (The mechanism of the eye is, in short, composed of an infinity of mechanisms, all of extreme complexity. Yet vision is one simple fact. As soon as the eye opens, the visual act is effected. [. . .] This contrast between the infinite complexity of the organ and the unity of the function is what gives us pause.)[49]

The 'machine' in Bergson's text is a figurative one, since he is concerned with two different types of process, both of which are intrinsic to human beings; the machine of which Cendrars writes, by contrast, is very literal, and he is more interested in the impact it may have on the human senses. His text proceeds to reflect upon the fact that machines have elbowed their way into the Darwinian struggle that pitted human against animal; the arrival of this new element has clearly had a powerful impact on the very fabric of society. More than this, the text conveys the sense that all points of reference that were once held to be reliable have been thrown into question, and this extends even to the known universe: 'Depuis l'origine de son espèce, le cheval se meut souple et mathématique. Déjà les machines le rattrapent, le dépassent. Les locomotives se cabrent et les paquebots hennissent sur l'eau.' (Since the origin of the species, the horse moves, supple and mathematical. Machines are already catching up, moving ahead. Locomotives rear and steamships whinny on the water.)[50] The two verbs in this last sentence recall the third and central line of Apollinaire's calligramme, 'Il pleut' (It is raining): 'Et ces nuages cabrés se prennent à hennir un univers de villes auriculaires' (And those clouds rear and begin to whinny a universe of auricular cities).[51] Apollinaire's attribution of the act of rearing up and whinnying to the forces of nature – the clouds – places him at some remove from Cendrars, who instead imagines the machines of modern transport enacting this role. But in sharing this combination of verbs, the two writers also converge in their conflation of the natural world, both animate and inanimate, with the new world of enhanced transport infrastructures and fast travel. As we shall see presently, Cendrars exploits the scope for expansiveness that continuous prose offers in order to extend and develop the animal metaphors more fully than the concise poetic framework can allow Apollinaire.

In *Profond aujourd'hui*, the location depicted is not identified with any specific geographic location – at least not initially – but it is an unmistakably urban and industrial milieu, peppered as it is with references to trams, trolley buses and railway stations, advertising posters, shops and cafés. The text, with its rapid-fire succession of short sentences and its paratactic syntax, radiates with a dynamism that celebrates and even mimics the chromatic explosion of colour, the constant noise and the bustling energy of the modern city. Significantly, though, as noted above, Cendrars chooses to situate this scene within the semantic field of wild animals, nature and natural phenomena, as if to assert the identity of the modern metropolis as an urban jungle. He evokes locomotives rearing up like horses, barges whinnying on the water and trams climbing the city streets like noisy monkeys holding on to each other by the tail. The urban trope is accompanied by a series of references to industry: the opening lines allude to inexhaustible coalmines, brand names and steam-operated machinery. The implicit message here is that this new urban environment is as unsullied and new as a virgin forest.

Another aspect of the modern city that figures prominently here is that of the human sensibility and its reaction to the encounter with the multifarious stimuli of the city: 'Tout se sensibilise. Est à la portée des yeux. Se touche presque. Où est l'homme?' (Everything is sensitized. It is all within range of the eye. You can almost touch it. Where is man?)[52] Recurring like a refrain throughout the text is this suggestion that the human psyche can feel intimately in touch with the world while simultaneously inhabiting an otherworldly realm. A symptom of the modern condition that fascinates and unsettles Cendrars is the growth of consumerism in the large cities and its effect on the individual. In this respect, we can observe a close parallel between Cendrars and Dada, the group whose very name functioned like a registered brand and whose textual and visual output frequently satirized the workings and the manifestations of mass consumerism. (Indeed, the very name 'Dada', often explained away by former group members as an entirely fictitious neologism, was in all probability derived from the hair tonic of the same name manufactured in Zurich, the city in which Dada was formed in 1916.) Using an image that would not look out of place in a Dada journal, Cendrars suggests a scandalous complicity of spiritual faith, modern consumerism and physical well-being: 'Comme une religion, une pilule mystérieuse active ta digestion' (Like a religion, a mysterious pill activates your digestion).[53] This expresses similar sentiments to the admittedly more vulgarly worded slogan that appeared in Francis Picabia's Dada journal *391* in 1920: 'Dieu nous aide et fait pousser le caca' (God helps us and makes poo grow).[54]

The theme of consumerism is a symptom of modern urban life about which Cendrars would write in numerous instances with varying degrees of enthusiasm. In this respect he has much in common with Apollinaire, who in 'Zone' noted the impact of the posters and signposts that adorned the city streets in ever-growing numbers: 'Les inscriptions des enseignes et des murailles/ Les plaques les avis à la façon des perroquets criaillent' (Billboards signs and murals/ Shriek like parakeets).[55] Cendrars too acknowledges the irresistible seduction of advertising: 'Tu fumes avec Mr Book le havane à 25 sous qui est sur l'affiche.' (With Mr Book you smoke the 25-cent Havana featured in the advertisement.)[56] While it celebrates the exuberance and vibrant colours of the posters, *Profond aujourd'hui* also articulates his wariness towards the pernicious effect of consumer culture on our individuality: 'Tu te perds dans le labyrinthe des magasins où tu renonces à toi pour devenir tout le monde.' (You get lost in the labyrinth of stores where you renounce yourself to become everyone.)[57] And it seems that it is not only consumerism that holds this risk; the very nature of the city itself, huge, imposing, alienating, threatens to undermine our sense of selfhood. If the melting pot offers scope for us to shed our inhibitions, then it also carries the threat of dissolving our sense of self: 'Tu fais partie de ce grand corps anonyme qu'est un café. Je ne me reconnais plus dans la glace, l'alcool a effacé mes traits.' (You are part of the great anonymous body of a café. I no longer recognize myself in the mirror, alcohol has blurred my features.)[58] From this it is clear that Cendrars saw the relationship of the individual to the city as one of conflicting forces: the city sets the individual free, but in so doing, it also cuts the ropes that bind us to a stable sense of place. In this respect, his vision of the phenomenon of urban modernity is indebted to *The Metropolis and Mental Life* written in 1903 by the German sociologist Georg Simmel, and foreshadows the work of Walter Benjamin, who in his *Arcades Project* would identify the city as a site of spectacle but also as one of alienation.[59]

The powerful sense of a decentring of the self is conveyed in images such as those cited above and enacted at a textual level. Cendrars

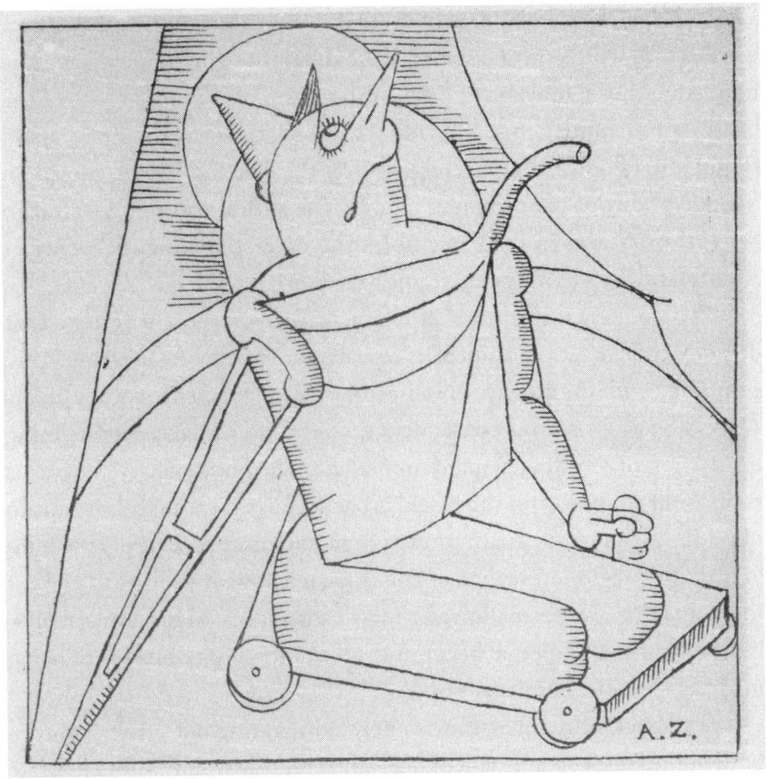

Ángel Zárraga, illustration for *Profond aujourd'hui* (1917).

manipulates language in such a way that the reader's understanding of the message is overlaid with a sensation that at times borders on the physical. Following on from the allusions to the unsettling effects of alcohol cited above, we find a string of sentences, each one of which employs a different personal pronoun: 'Il épouse comme le premier venu le magasin des nouveautés. Nous sommes tous l'heure qui sonne. Vous vous ruez à la ménagerie des gares pour dompter la bête de votre impatience. Ils partent.' (He espouses the novelty shop as he would the first passer-by. Every one of us is the hour sounding on the clock. To control the beast of your impatience you rush into the menagerie of railway stations. They leave.)[60]

This proliferation of voices and perspectives is effective in various ways: first, the accelerated cadence of these sentences generates a kaleidoscopic impression of reality that goes some way towards conveying a sensation of the incessant, pulsating rhythms of the modern city. This draws on themes that appear in *Dix-neuf poèmes élastiques* but replaces the aereated feel of those poems with intense, densely packed prose. On a lexical level, Cendrars intensifies further the impression of dynamism by selecting words from a semantic field emphasizing immediacy ('the hour sounding'), movement ('you rush', 'They leave') and urgency ('the beast of your impatience'). Cendrars refuses to allow the first-person singular to establish any sovereignty over the text and insists instead on the polyphony of metropolitan babble. The author too seems to forego his authority and instead assembles the diverse fragments, rather as Apollinaire does in his poem 'Lundi rue Christine'.[61]

This sequence illustrates a characteristic of the entire text that deserves consideration, namely its repeated use of the present tense. This, combined with the absence of indicators of sequence, chronology or any suggestion of cause and consequence, contributes to an overwhelming impression of simultaneity and immediacy. The phrase, 'Every one of us is the hour sounding on the clock' is particularly meaningful: it calls to mind Bergson's conceptualization of time, and more specifically the individual's perception of reality, as the constant flow of transitory present moments that are never allowed to settle into stasis: in his terms, reality is perceived as a perpetual becoming, constantly in the process of being made or unmade, but never finished.[62]

The shock of the new is extremely exhilarating but unsettling too; both of these aspects are evident here, and Cendrars establishes a delicate tension between them. The sensitization of everything, from the large factories and newly expanded transport infrastructures to the tiniest piece of cloth or jar of preserves, means that human beings can no longer confidently assert themselves as the indisputable centre of a stable universe. On the contrary, the overriding impression is one of dislocation, as the spiritual and physical points of reference once taken for granted have lost their reliability and become unstable: 'Tout change de proportion, d'angle, d'aspect. Tout s'éloigne, se rapproche, cumule, manque, rit, s'affirme et s'exaspère.' (The proportion, angle, appearance of everything is changing. Everything moves away, comes closer, cumulates, misses the point, laughs, asserts itself, and gets aggravated.)[63] The impression conveyed here, of objects that no longer appear static but appear to be in a state of constant flux, calls to mind Bergson's definition of duration in *Creative Evolution*:

> Prenons le plus stable des états internes, la perception visuelle d'un objet extérieur immobile. L'objet a beau rester le même, j'ai beau le regarder du même côté, sous le même angle, au même jour; la vision que j'ai n'en diffère pas moins de celle que je viens

> d'avoir, quand ce ne serait que parce qu'elle a vieilli d'un instant. Ma mémoire est là, qui pousse quelque chose de ce passé dans ce présent.
>
> (Let us take the most stable of internal states, the visual perception of a motionless external object. The object may remain the same, I may look at it from the same side, at the same angle, in the same light; nevertheless the vision I now have of it differs from that which I have just had, even if only because the one is an instant older than the other. My memory is there, which conveys something of the past into the present.)[64]

The atmosphere that Cendrars's text evokes seems to have much in common with Bergson's understanding of the ways in which our perception of the present moment is continually coloured and modulated by past recollections. Cendrars's descriptions of the familiar sights adorning the Paris skyline render them unstable and susceptible to movement and flux:

> La tour Eiffel va et vient du sommet. Le soleil, un nuage, un rien suffit pour l'allonger, la raccourcir. Les ponts métalliques sont tout aussi mystérieux et sensibles. Les montres se mettent à l'heure. De tous les côtés les transatlantiques s'avancent vers leurs correspondances. Alors le sémaphore fait un signe. Un oeil bleu s'ouvre. Le rouge se ferme. Tout n'est bientôt que couleurs. Compénétration. Disque. Rythme. Danse. Un orangé et un violet se mangent.
>
> (The Eiffel Tower sways on the horizon. The sun, a cloud, anything is enough to stretch it or shrink it. The metal bridges are just as mysterious and sensitive. Watches set themselves. From every direction ocean liners move toward their connections. Then the semaphore signals. A blue eye opens. The red one closes. Soon there is nothing but colour. Interpenetration. Disk. Rhythm. Dance. Orange and violet hues devour each other.)[65]

Of the many echoes that these lines summon up, some of the most vivid are those that call to mind the pre-war paintings of Robert Delaunay, especially his numerous pencil studies and oil paintings of the Eiffel

Tower. Not only that, but Cendrars's words are remarkably similar to the description of this series that Delaunay provides in *Du Cubisme à l'art abstrait*. He refers to the series as a product of his destructive phase; but rather than 'destroying' his subject, he is recreating it as a tottering, unstable structure undermined by nothing more solid than the air that surrounds and penetrates it. This is an artistic practice that builds by means of successive dismantlings: the resultant edifice in paint on canvas can only be achieved by undoing the laws of single-point perspective and replacing them with an understanding of space and time as plural and shifting. The visual impact of this on the pictorial subject is evocative of so many shards of solid and empty space captured in mid-collapse.

These lines enact a fluctuation between discrete elements of an identifiably real world of modern engineering – the Eiffel Tower, metal bridges, transatlantic liners, the operation of semaphore signals – and a sensation of colours in motion that detaches itself from any broader context. The effect is akin to that of a film camera closing in on a scene to such an extreme extent that the viewer loses any clear sense of the identity of individual objects and instead confronts a mass consisting entirely of colours and forms. Simultaneously, in these lines we witness the dissolution of conventional syntax as the familiar sentence structure of subject, verb and object is broken down, first into shorter sentences and then into single-word utterances. Here, as in so many other instances in Cendrars's oeuvre, the mode of narration adopted forms a close bond with the nature of the subject tackled: his writing dismisses the rules of grammar and conventions of syntax as it rejects the notion that the external world is the only viable point of reference for literature. The contexts of transatlantic communication, industrial manufacture and long-distance travel – embodied by the Eiffel Tower with its radio transmitting function, the metal bridges, ocean liners and different time zones – disappear into the pure sensation of light, colour and movement.

Appropriately, this shift from the material to the immaterial is triggered by the reference to semaphore: contiguous with the semantic field of transatlantic travel, this evocation of an alternative system of signs creates a *mise en abyme* of the very processes that Cendrars is exploring at a textual level. By compressing his own text into the isolated signifiers 'Compénétration. Disque. Rythme. Danse', Cendrars is producing something akin to a textual equivalent of semaphore, that most concise form of communication, while at the same time conveying a literary awareness of the capacity of even such syntactically reduced signs to resonate with myriad meanings. The interpenetration (*compénétration*) to which he refers is a brilliantly versatile word, and one that reflects extremely well the processes at play in his text. First, it may allude to the actual movements of the coloured railway semaphore signals, which, as early as 1868, used gas lights fitted with blue and red lenses.[66] Indeed, by 1918, the Lafayette station near Bordeaux possessed the world's most powerful arc transmitter, using 1000 kW of signalling power to ensure good communications between the Allied governments and the American Expeditionary Force. According to Ken Beauchamp, it was the world's most powerful transmitter for a time, and its signals could be received all over the world with unrivalled clarity.[67]

Besides this primary sense, the term 'interpenetration' also hints at the processes at play in Cendrars's text: it could allude to the overlapping of meanings in the words that immediately follow it: 'Disque. Rythme. Danse.' The first of these terms, while possibly referring to the circular shape of a semaphore light, also connotes the disc of a gramophone record. This, in turn, collocates logically with the words 'rythme' and 'danse', suggesting that these visual, gestural and auditory experiences are intimately connected. The implications of this combination of sensory impressions merit further consideration, and not least in view of Cendrars's friendship with Fernand Léger: the movements of the coloured signals, Cendrars implies, have become a kind of 'ballet mécanique'. From this perspective, his text foreshadows by some seven years the eponymous film by Fernand Léger, Dudley Murphy and Georges Antheil in which the 'ballet' in question combines repeated shots of predominantly circular forms in motion with a repetitive, insistent rhythmic musical score.

The evocation of rhythm and dance, immediately followed by a reference to orange and violet devouring each other, skilfully overlays the theme of semaphore signals with the trope of the animal world that we have observed in the opening lines of the text. This conflation of industrial technology and animal imagery recurs shortly afterwards, but transported to a cosmic dimension, in the sentence: 'Tout fait la roue sur les quais alors que le lion du ciel étrangle les vaches du crépuscule.' (Everything turns cartwheels along the docks while the lion of the sky strangles the cows of twilight.)[68] At this point, the focus shifts from the bustling activity of a port, the loading and unloading of goods, to the interior of a large cruise ship. Without departing from the theme of nautical travel, the text cuts almost imperceptibly, and without any explicit typographical pause or break in its rhythm, to the scene of passengers dining aboard a liner. At this point, the cinematographic model appears to have informed Cendrars's writing style, as the text seamlessly edits together related but disparate settings without warning; it transports us from the bustle of a large port to the interior of a cruise ship via a single poetic sentence that has an effect akin to that of a voiceover in a film, albeit a somewhat surreal one: 'Les femmes européennes sont comme des fleurs sous-marines devant le travail farouche des débardeurs et l'apothéose rouge sombre des machines.' (European women are like subaqueous flowers confronting the stern labouring of longshoremen and the dark red apotheosis of machines.)[69] The text now cuts to a scene in the dining hall of the ship, where the voices of passengers are partly obscured by the orchestra and other background sounds. Isolated by this sonic interference, the writing 'I' becomes further detached from his surroundings by the cloud of cigar smoke that engulfs him. At this point the text develops the idea further, transporting the reader into an underwater realm: 'Scaphandrier, dans la fumée de mon cigare, seul, j'entends mourir la musique de la sentimentalité qui fait résonner mon casque.' (A deep-sea diver, submerged in the smoke from my cigar, alone, I listen to the dying music of sentimentality that resonates in my helmet.)[70] The trope of nature that accompanied the opening lines of the text thus reappears here, but we have moved from the terrestrial to the subaquatic realm. Now, as then, the natural world is present essentially as a complement to the realm of the machine, but the precise nature of the relationship has shifted to a degree. The text began with the suggestion that the new technologies of the time are threatening to overtake the animal world, whereas now, the focus rests on the natural realm. But this is no bucolic scene of repose and tranquillity; the sea, replete with life, is portrayed as a powerful machine that operates with extreme precision and on the industrial scale of a factory: 'J'entends le moteur des eaux, la sidérurgie des ventouses. Mille pores à succion fonctionnent, sécrètent de l'iode.' (I hear the engine of the waters, the steel forge of leeches. A thousand suction pores function, secreting iodine.)[71]

The feeling of shock and sensory overload that characterizes the individual's experience of the modern urban space is again articulated in the closing lines of the text. Not only is our perception of our surroundings affected, but the text suggests the self is fragmented and fissured by the collision:

> Des centres de sensibilité se polarisent. Indépendance de toutes les fonctions. L'oeil tend à toucher; le dos mange; le doigt voit. [. . .] L'être se rassemble difficilement. [. . .] L'esprit partout épars se concentre dans la cocarde de la conscience. [. . .] Le minéral respire, le végétal mange, l'animal s'émeut, l'homme se cristallise.
>
> (Nerve centres are polarized. All functions are independent. Eyes reach to touch; backs eat; fingers see. [. . .] The being reassembles itself with difficulty. [. . .] The spirit, scattered everywhere, concentrates in the rosette of consciousness. [. . .] Minerals breathe, vegetables eat, animals emote, man crystallizes.)[72]

Lines such as these suggest a troubling slippage of matter in which nothing is as it seems, or as it used to be. A similar phenomenon is perceptible in the text at a linguistic level. Cendrars exploits the capacity of the written word to become what Walter Benjamin, discussing the visual art of

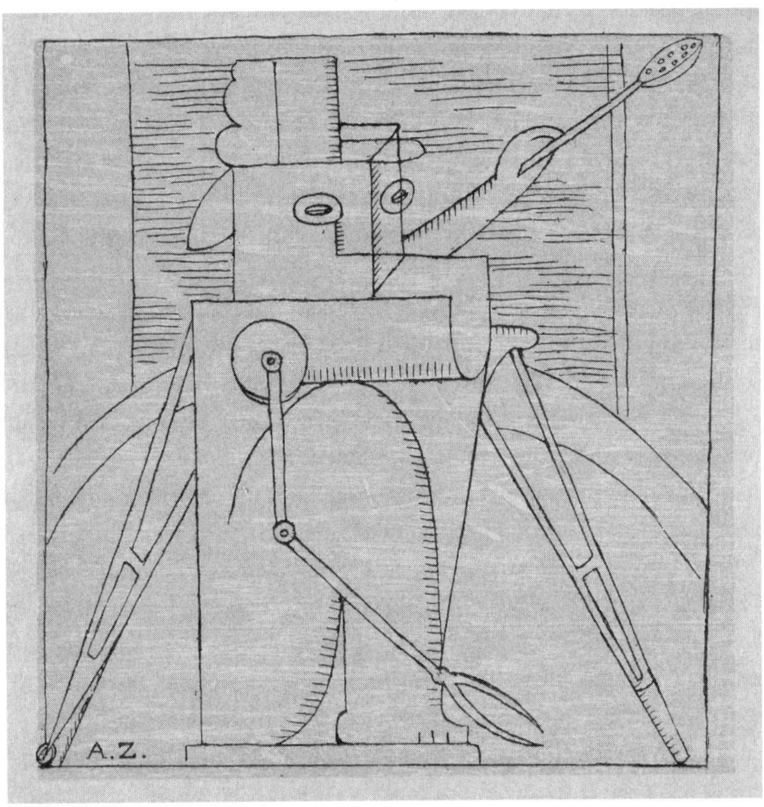

Ángel Zárraga, illustration for *Profond aujourd'hui* (1917).

Dada, described as a 'bullet'.[73] The projectile quality of his words is as much the result of their style as of their subject-matter, for the text not only describes an experience, but becomes one of its tangible symptoms, too: under the onslaught of the external world, the grammatical structures and conventions that normally hold language in place lose their grip and start to slide. The consequences of this can be felt particularly vividly in a few key instances of linguistic inventiveness: 'Ton œil, cheval marin, vibre, virgule et passe.' (Your eye, sea horse, vibrates, commas, and passes.)[74] Esther Allen's English translation of the second verb as 'marks a comma' is an idiomatic and grammatically accurate rendering, but it lacks both the brevity and the impact of the original French term, which gives the noun 'virgule' (comma) a highly unusual verbal form, 'virguler' (to comma).[75] This word is brilliantly concise and multi-referential: it suggests, first, the curved physical shape of the seahorse, but also the rapid arc of the creature's eye as it moves through water. As if to further underline the relationship of the textual and paralinguistic signifiers to the signified, the three commas that punctuate this short sentence (four in the English translation) not only draw attention to the syllabic balance of this near-perfect alexandrine but mirror graphically the bobbing movement of the sea horse. Cendrars's structuring of language in this text has already implied that conventional syntax offers an inadequate framework for the authentic expression of multidimensional reality, and here he makes a similar point with regard to lexis. A world of ever-increasing intensity, speed and diversity requires forms of expression that are sufficiently flexible and direct to rise to the challenge, even if this means employing new or unfamiliar linguistic forms. We are reminded of the Futurists' declaration of a new 'telegraphic lyricism' which led Apollinaire to proclaim the demise of syntax and punctuation in his manifesto-synthesis, 'L'Antitradition futuriste'.[76]

The full significance of the earlier reference to semaphore signals has now become clear: as that image hinted, one of the key ideas that this text articulates is the possibility of a radically new system of communication. Cendrars's writing, with its breathless tempo, its elastic syntax, startling connections and vivid imagery, offers a manifesto of what language can do when it adopts the rapidity and boldness of semaphore. However else we might define this short text, what is certainly clear is that it articulates a response to the vastly expanded network of communications that emerged in the early twentieth century: it is not so much a meditation on the subject as a demonstration of it in action. This is nowhere clearer than in the concluding lines, where spatial and temporal coordinates have been swept up in the maelstrom of modernity, a powerful spiralling movement that embraces all matter:

> Prodigieux aujourd'hui. Sonde. Antenne. Porte-visage-tourbillon. Tu vis. Excentrique. Dans la solitude intégrale. Dans la communion anonyme. Avec tout ce qui est racine et cime, et qui palpite, jouit et s'extasie. Phénomènes de cette hallucination congénitale qu'est la vie dans toutes ses manifestations et l'activité continue de la conscience. Le moteur tourne en spirale. Le rythme parle. Chimisme. Tu es.
>
> (Prodigious today. Wave. Antenna. Door-face-whirlwind. You live. Off-centre. In integral solitude. In anonymous communion. With everything that is root and summit and that throbs, revels, jubilates. Phenomena of this congenital hallucination which is life in all its manifestations and the continual activity of consciousness. The motor spirals. The rhythm speaks. Chemistry. You are.)[77]

Again here, Cendrars's innovative use of language is in evidence. Like his highly unusual verbal form, 'virguler', the composite noun 'Porte-visage-tourbillon' (Door-face-whirlwind) finds him bending rules of syntax and combining lexical units into unfamiliar shapes that deny easy interpretation. The compression of syntax into such a reduced form means that the reader's task must consist in loosening the individual words from their syntactic wrapping, allowing the meanings contained within them to unfold, or, to adopt another analogy, to infuse like a stock cube dissolving in water.[78] At moments such as this, the reading or listening activity can fall out of synchronization with the text's speed. As our eyes scan the text with the rapidity that such a syntactically reduced form of discourse invites, we encounter a cluster of words such as 'Porte-visage-tourbillon' and promptly trip up: the inherent ambiguity of such a word-cluster thwarts rapid comprehension, with the effect that the brain lags behind the eye or ear and our interpretative process struggles to keep up with the insistent rhythm of the text. The problem has nothing to do with complicated lexis or sophisticated structures; the meaning of the individual lexemes 'porte', 'visage' and 'tourbillon' will be clear to readers familiar with French. On the other hand, the particular combination of these three words in the form of a hyphenated compound noun poses problems of interpretation that cannot be resolved in an instant, at least not without some loss of meaning. The problem lies in the individual elements of the triad and in the ways each relates to the other two: should 'Porte-visage-tourbillon' be understood as a proto-surreal version of a portmanteau word? Or should we attribute a nominal function to each of the three elements? And, if 'porte' is to be translated as 'door', is the 'tourbillon' equal in status to the other two nouns, or does it qualify and describe the relationship between 'porte' and 'visage'? The latter interpretation seems to correspond most closely to Esther Allen's published translation of the French text: the resultant rendering, 'Door-face-whirlwind', suggests that the first two elements are seen in the blur of fast motion, and that the 'whirlwind' is used figuratively to convey the impression that the sheer speed of movement has made all but the most basic actions imperceptible to the eye. But this 'tourbillon', coming as it does so close to the end of the text, can also be understood as relating to its themes more broadly. The image of a whirlwind not only relates metonymically to the atmosphere of the entire text, summing up its frenetic rhythm and vertiginous spatio-temporal leaps, but foreshadows the allusion to the spiralling motor in the closing lines. The French term 'tourbillon' is most typically used to describe the interaction of air and water currents, so it lends itself well both to the image of the Eiffel Tower swaying on the horizon and to the passages describing the undulating, teeming marine realm. The allusion to a whirlwind also points discreetly to the history of science, and more specifically to Descartes, whose theory of the *mécanique des tourbillons* maintained that planetary movements were governed and kept in check by vortexes (*tourbillons*) of ether. An avid and eclectic reader, Cendrars may have been familiar with Henri Poincaré's *Théorie des tourbillons* (Theory of Whirlwinds), which had appeared in print in 1893.[79] Cendrars's reference to the 'continual activity of consciousness' suggests that he was familiar with Bergson's belief that the human being was in a state of constant reinvention.[80]

Cendrars's text not only evokes, but provokes in the reader, a sense of displacement, a loss of bearings, as the first-person narration that opens the text shifts to the second, via the third, by the end. Instability and constant flux are reflected on a linguistic level as verbs and nouns start to lose their identity. As the text draws to an end, the material world retreats, to be eclipsed by the sensation of pure colour in movement. The kind of writing we have seen here has the visual acuity of the minimalist poems by Pierre Reverdy in *Les Ardoises du toit* or Pierre-Albert Birot's poster-poems and signpost-poems, while additionally possessing the sort of dynamism that the Futurists craved, but without the bombast that weighs down much of their work.[81] The next chapter will examine some of the other works that Cendrars produced as he became a left-handed writer and started to come to terms with his amputation. As we will see, the late 1910s and early '20s found him exploring other expressive forms, especially photography and cinema, but also advertising, in all of which he found the means to expand the parameters of literature and tap into the *profond aujourd'hui*.

three

Through the Lens: Writing, Photography, Cinema

As we have seen, the slow process of recuperation from the amputation of Cendrars's right arm was followed by a twofold rebirth in 1917: while his phantom arm would haunt him for the rest of his life, he learned to deal with the loss by learning to write with his left hand. (He is said to have been issued with a prosthetic arm, which he promptly removed and left in a locker at the Gare St Lazare, never to retrieve it.) It was also a significant year in his affective life: he had already drifted away from Féla, a process that seems to have been merely accelerated by the birth of their two sons and the attendant prospect of assuming paternal and familial responsibilities that would hamper his writing. His encounter with the actress Raymone Duchâteau was also decisive, although arguably her presence is more significant in his writing than in his day-to-day existence: their itinerant lifestyles kept them apart for very long periods, and yet aspects of her appear in fictionalized and mythologized form at various points throughout his oeuvre.

Another significant watershed of this period was his encounter with cinema, which shaped his career in numerous ways. First and foremost, it offered him a means to occupy his creative impulse during his readjustment to life after the traumatic war experience. Cinema also affected him as a writer; it exposed him to a different creative form and instilled in him the confidence to write for the screen. As we will see, a number of his scripts (or *scenarios*) did not become the basis of films, but the style in which they are written makes them interesting early examples of a hybrid, cinematographic form of writing. A photographic idiom had also appeared in his poetry from an early stage: the short, often single-word lines that appear in *Prose du Transsibérien* can be understood as verbal snapshots, a technique that the *Dix-neuf poèmes élastiques* develop more extensively. An implicit understanding of a certain kind of minimalist free verse as being related to photography will reappear in a different form in his collection *Kodak (Documentaire)* of 1924.

Since being invalided out of the war, he began to keep himself at some remove from the literary scene in Paris; much later, writing in *L'Homme foudroyé*, Cendrars dated his 'decisive break with the world of literature' to October 1917, stating that 'la poésie qui prenait vogue à Paris me semblait devenir la base d'un malentendu spirituel et d'une confusion mentale' (the poetry that was becoming fashionable in Paris seemed to me to be becoming the basis of spiritual misunderstanding and mental confusion).[1] He later attributed his departure from the literary scene to his encounter with Raymone.[2] Once peace was restored, his erstwhile involvement in the pre-war avant-garde community was replaced with forms of creativity that kept him at a distance from the future Surrealists and other writers who frequented the Café Certa and the capital's other fashionable literary haunts. He had a low opinion of the Parisian literary scene more generally. While he professed his admiration for Rimbaud, Baudelaire and Mallarmé, he was less impressed by the more recent generation of poets: 'Paul Valéry, cet épigone qui a eu tous les honneurs dus à son maître, et jusqu'à des funérailles nationales, et les surréalistes n'ont pas protesté!' (Paul Valéry, that epigone who has had all the honours that his master deserved, even a state burial, and the Surrealists didn't protest!)[3] Valéry is not the only target of his cynicism: 'Cette vieille toupie de Mauriac m'ennuie. Il n'a donc pas d'ami pour lui conseiller de ne plus parler du bon Dieu dans les journaux à quinze francs ? C'est une véritable pie grièche qui saute sur tout ce qui brille.' (That old crone Mauriac bores me. Hasn't he got a friend who can advise him to stop talking about God's greatness in the fifteen-franc papers? He's a real magpie who jumps on everything that shines.)[4]

Cendrars's increasingly individualist stance marked a significant shift from the pre-war years, when he was in frequent contact with the artists living in La Ruche as well as Apollinaire and other writers based in Paris. This is not to say that Cendrars ceased to be an avant-garde writer in the interwar years; on the contrary, he continued to push the boundaries of the literary genres in which he was active and began in earnest to explore new forms of creativity. As he continued to recover from his war wound, he became more involved in cinema, graduating from working as Abel Gance's assistant and playing a minor role in *J'Accuse* in 1918 to working as a technical assistant on *La Roue* in 1920, and directing a film of his own,

La Venere nera (Black Venus), the following year at the Rinascimento Studios in Rome. This film, starring Raymone and the dancer Dourga, met with a negative reaction when it was released in 1923, and is now lost; Cendrars claimed to have destroyed the master copy himself. The script of the film was, however, published as *La Perle fiévreuse* in 1922 in the journal *Signaux de France et de Belgique*. We will discuss it shortly.

One of the overriding impressions that strikes the reader in his texts from 1917 is the powerful way in which the act of writing becomes itself an extension of the experience: the immediacy of style dissolves the spatio-temporal gap between event and its narration. In ways similar to *Profond aujourd'hui*, the short texts *J'ai tué* (I Have Killed) and *L'ABC du cinéma* (The ABCs of Cinema) dispense with paragraph breaks and adopt an extremely elastic syntax incorporating everything from the single-word sentence to huge, sprawling lists. The influence of cinema is powerfully felt in the narrative voice, which flits without warning between the first, second and third person and from an impersonal, generalized, panoramic point of view to an intimate, subjective voice with the speed of a cinematic jump cut. In *L'ABC du cinéma*, he reflects upon the dizzying effect of the close-up:

> A l'accéléré la vie des fleurs est shakespearienne ; tout le classicisme est donné dans le développement d'un biceps au ralenti. Sur l'écran le moindre effort devient douloureux, musical, et les insectes et les microbes ressemblent à nos plus illustres contemporains. Eternité de l'éphémère. Gigantisme. On lui attribue une valeur esthétique qu'il ne s'était jamais connue.
>
> (At high speed the life of flowers is Shakespearean; all of classicism is present in the slow-motion flexing of a biceps [*sic*]. On screen the slightest effort becomes painful, musical, and insects and microbes look like our most illustrious contemporaries. Eternity in the ephemeral. Gigantism. It is granted an aesthetic value which it has never had before.)[5]

Fernand Léger, writing about his film *Ballet mécanique* in 1924, relates how he conducted an experiment by filming a polished fingernail in extreme close-up and projecting the magnified image: 'Le public étonné a cru reconnaître une photo astronomique.' (The astonished audience thought they were looking at a photo of the stars.)[6] Like Cendrars, he is struck by the power of the cinema screen to amplify reality; rather than simply making the subject clearer or more easily discernable, the enlarging process has the capacity to transform it into something unfamiliar. Léger's and Cendrars's remarks anticipate Walter Benjamin's famous observation of film's shock effect, and its power to reveal an 'unconscious optics' that would remain imperceptible to the naked eye.

On 8 November 1918, a mere three days before the armistice, *J'ai tué* was published as a visually stunning illustrated book with colour lithographs that Léger produced while recovering from his own war wounds, having been poisoned and nearly killed by mustard gas at Verdun in 1916. Cendrars, forever keenly interested in typography, was closely involved alongside the publisher François Bernouard in overseeing the typesetting and printing process at the latter's publishing house, à la Belle Edition. The text was printed in red ink, while Léger's illustrations are in red and

Cover of Blaise Cendrars, *J'ai tué*, with illustration by Fernand Léger (1918).

blue. In their fragmentation and so-called 'tubist' style, the illustrations reflect the same principle of montage that characterizes the structure of Cendrars's text, which presents a fast succession of juxtaposed points of view. These contrasts offer the reader a series of radically diverse perspectives on the action, rather like the mobile eye of the camera. Richard Abel has commented on the effective use Gance makes in *J'Accuse* of just such a 'rhythmic montage' based on the constant interplay of similarities and differences and on the film's extensive use of rhetorical images.[7] Canudo defines *J'Accuse* in terms of 'the collective body acting as a single individual'.[8] In *J'ai tué*, Cendrars conveys a similar impression through a panoramic, anonymous narrative voice: 'Respiration d'un million d'hommes. [. . .] Embrasement général. Mille éclatements.' (A million men breathing. [. . .] Everything ablaze. A thousand explosions.)[9] This is disrupted violently by the sudden incursion of the first-person voice: 'Des membres volent en l'air. Je reçois du sang plein le visage.' (Limbs fly through the air. A gob of blood hits me right in my face.)[10] The text ends with a graphic account of hand-to-hand combat, which is also a battle between two kinds of warfare: the distant, remote, technologically enhanced modern version, and the age-old struggle of one man against another: 'J'ai bravé la torpille, le canon, les mines, le feu, les gaz, les mitrailleuses, toute la machinerie anonyme, démoniaque, systématique, aveugle. Je vais braver l'homme. Mon semblable. Un singe. Œil pour œil, dent pour dent.' (I've braved torpedoes, cannon, mines, fire, gas, guns, the whole blind, systematic, demoniac, anonymous machinery. I'm going to brave man. My counterpart. An ape. Eye for eye, tooth for tooth.)[11] *J'ai tué* is a remarkable text, all the more so in view of its uniqueness: none of Cendrars's other texts of that period engages as bluntly with the experience of war. That said, an apocalyptic tone certainly is present in the other texts written around the same time.

L'ABC du cinéma, for instance, presents the medium of film in terms of an eternal revolution in which 'the good fight of black and white is going to begin on all the screens in the world.'[12] The text ends with the image of crowds all over the world rushing out of cinemas into the street 'comme un sang noir, qui comme une bête puissante allonge ses mille tentacules et d'un tout petit effort écrase les palais, les prisons.' (like a black stream of blood spreading its thousand tentacles like a powerful beast and crushing palaces and prisons with the slightest effort.)[13] In this text we find his boldest pronouncement on cinema's potential to turn the upheaval of the times to creative ends:

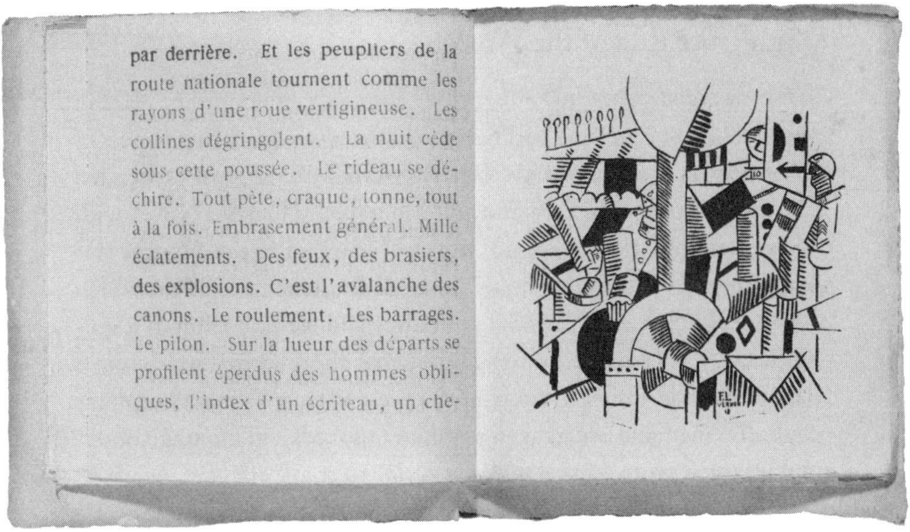

par derrière. Et les peupliers de la route nationale tournent comme les rayons d'une roue vertigineuse. Les collines dégringolent. La nuit cède sous cette poussée. Le rideau se déchire. Tout pète, craque, tonne, tout à la fois. Embrasement général. Mille éclatements. Des feux, des brasiers, des explosions. C'est l'avalanche des canons. Le roulement. Les barrages. Le pilon. Sur la lueur des départs se profilent éperdus des hommes obliques, l'index d'un écriteau, un che-

Double page from Blaise Cendrars, *J'ai tué*, with illustration by Fernand Léger (1918).

> Les derniers aboutissements des sciences précises, la guerre mondiale, la conception de la relativité, les convulsions politiques, tout fait prévoir que nous nous acheminons vers une nouvelle synthèse de l'esprit humain, vers une nouvelle humanité et qu'une race d'hommes nouveaux va paraître. Leur langage sera le cinéma.
>
> (The latest achievements of the exact sciences, world war, the conception of relativity, political convulsions, all this makes us predict that we are heading towards a new synthesis of the human spirit, towards a new humanity and that a race of new men will appear. Their language will be cinema.)[14]

As these quotations suggest, film, with its violent immediacy and its disruption of spatio-temporal unity, is the ideal medium in which to express this brave new mechanized world. As Carrie Noland has argued, the machine is 'a fully dialectical entity for Cendrars: it threatens to obliterate certain forms of experience while simultaneously providing humans with visual and verbal languages they would not otherwise have at their disposal.'[15] Noland concurs with Jay Bochner, who has observed an ambivalence in Cendrars's attitude to machines, which can be liberating but also oppressive.[16]

Filming the End of the World

La Fin du monde filmée par l'Ange N.-D. occupies an important place in Cendrars's oeuvre, in large part because of the mythical circumstances of its creation on the night of his thirtieth birthday.[17] Originally intended to be just one part of his vast and ambitious 'Great Cinema Novel' with the overarching title 'La Fin du Monde' (The End of the World), this short text still calls itself a 'novel'. It drops the 'cinema' epithet, which is strange, since it embraces the structures and forms of film in a very obvious way. It is divided into 55 numbered short scenes, written in a telegraphic style almost entirely in the present tense. The text explores peculiarly cinematic effects such as different speeds and montage, and it employs some proto-surreal *mises en abyme* to comic effect.

Like *J'ai tué*, this story conveys a vision of war; this one is comically exaggerated but has serious undertones. The main character, as we might expect of a tale of the apocalypse, is God, cast as a Hollywood-style director complete with fat cigar and green sun shield; the Angel of Notre-Dame is his cameraman. God has made a huge profit from nearly a century of war – a billion souls to put to rest at 1 franc 25 apiece – but realizes that he will need to raise the stakes if he wants to maximize his return.

He accepts a telegrammed invitation to visit Mars, where he unwittingly starts another war and is forced into hiding. In an attempt to make this war pay too, he sends a telegram to 'quelques vieux coquins de l'Ancien Testament' (some old rascals from the Old Testament) requesting them to carry out the prophecies. The Angel of Notre-Dame blows his horn and the earth goes into meltdown. So too, literally, does the roll of film that is figuratively showing us all this action. A technical assistant sets fire to the projector, and we then witness the entire film rewinding, sequence by sequence, to the starting point. We return to the opening scene with God as film director at his desk; this time, however, he is bankrupt.

The implications of all this are curious. The chapter in which the Angel brings about the end of the world is called 'L'Ange N.-D. Opérateur': in the twentieth century, the term *opérateur* came to denote a camera operator or cameraman, but also a telegraph operator and typesetter. In this sense, the Angel as 'opérateur' is the perfect symbol for Cendrars at a time when his writing straddled literature and cinema. But the word 'opérateur' also retained more archaic meanings, ranging from

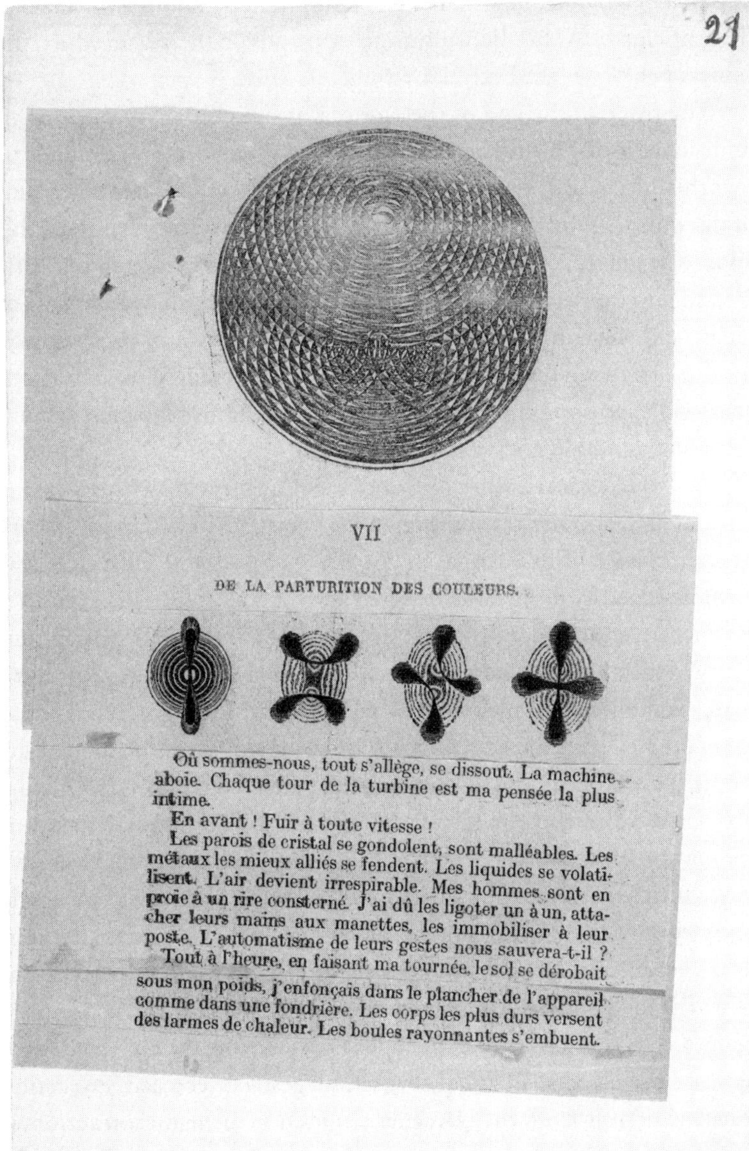

21

VII

DE LA PARTURITION DES COULEURS.

Où sommes-nous, tout s'allège, se dissout. La machine aboie. Chaque tour de la turbine est ma pensée la plus intime.

En avant ! Fuir à toute vitesse !

Les parois de cristal se gondolent, sont malléables. Les métaux les mieux alliés se fendent. Les liquides se volatilisent. L'air devient irrespirable. Mes hommes sont en proie à un rire consterné. J'ai dû les ligoter un à un, attacher leurs mains aux manettes, les immobiliser à leur poste. L'automatisme de leurs gestes nous sauvera-t-il ?

Tout à l'heure, en faisant ma tournée, le sol se dérobait sous mon poids, j'enfonçais dans le plancher de l'appareil comme dans une fondrière. Les corps les plus durs versent des larmes de chaleur. Les boules rayonnantes s'embuent.

Blaise Cendrars, proof page from Chapter VII of *L'Eubage*, with illustrations taken from Camille Flammarion, *Astronomie populaire* (1880). The book was written in 1917, and this page was from a complete set of proofs destined for publication in 1922 under the imprint of the journal *L'Esprit Nouveau*. This version of the book was never realized for reasons that remain unknown. The book was eventually published with illustrations by Joseph Hecht as *L'Eubage* (1926).

a charlatan to someone who conducts surgical operations – an analogy that anticipates Walter Benjamin's observations on the way in which the camera penetrates the body like a surgeon's knife.

The trope of the end of the world is also highly significant for an understanding of Cendrars's particular views on cinema: it reminds us that this 'machine of vision' has a tremendous power to create new forms of discourse.[18] We might even go so far as to say that for Cendrars, this 'mutilé de guerre', cinema for a time offered a prosthetic limb that enabled him to transcend the loss of his right arm and open up new ways of seeing and engaging with the world. But as *La Fin du monde* suggests, he also saw that cinema contains a destructive potential, in that it can enact violence upon more traditionally lyrical forms of expression and the world view that goes with them.

The paradoxical nature of Cendrars's involvement with cinema is illustrated in another text written in 1917 entitled *L'Eubage: aux antipodes de l'Unité* (The Eubage; or, At the Antipodes of Unity). It was commissioned by the fashion designer and art collector Jacques Doucet, to whom Cendrars sent the text in monthly installments throughout 1917. While circumstances prevented it from appearing in print until 1926, extant drafts from 1917–18 provide a valuable insight into its creation. The story recounts an intergalactic voyage 'in the hinterland of the Milky Way'. Some of the most vivid scenes described in this fascinating text derived directly from Cendrars's first-hand observation of so-called colour rhythms, a series of illustrations that were to be the basis of a never-realized abstract film by Léopold Survage, a Russian avant-garde artist working in Paris.[19] Cendrars's beautiful and highly evocative visions bear witness to the expansive imagination that cinema opened up for him. Taking their inspiration from mysticism, alchemy and astronomy, many scenes develop series of metaphors connecting the eye, the camera lens and the planets. The final chapter, suggestively entitled 'Projection Powder', derives from the elements required in alchemical transmutation, but the term also contains very clear allusions to cinema. Like *La Fin du monde filmée par l'ange N.-D.*, this story too concludes apocalyptically: 'Il n'y a même pas une tête de mort pour ricaner. Nous allons être agglomérés, digérés, anéantis, jetés aux murènes, derrière le ciel. [. . .] Maintenant, rien ne peut arrêter notre course; nous retournons à notre origine.' (There isn't even a skull to snicker. We will be agglomerated, digested, annihilated, thrown to the moray eels behind the sky. [. . .] Nothing can stop us now; we are returning to our origin.)[20]

These destructive visions foreshadow with uncanny prescience Cendrars's own short-lived career as a cineast. We must be thankful, then, that he wrote his imaginary films, films that were probably never intended to be made but which confirm beyond doubt his prediction in *L'ABC du cinéma* that, for a time at least, cinema would provide an exciting and radically new discourse for writers. Some lines from that essay, written in response to cinema, are equally relevant to his writing as he tries to make sense of a world turned on its head: 'Remue-ménage d'images. L'unité tragique se déplace. Nous apprenons. Nous buvons. Ivresse. Le réel n'a plus aucun sens. Aucune signification. Tout est rythme, parole, vie. Il n'y a plus de démonstration. On communie.' (An uproar of images. Tragic unity is displaced. We learn. We drink. Intoxication. Reality no longer makes any sense. It has no significance. Everything is rhythm, word, life. No longer any need to demonstrate. We are in communion.)[21]

La Perle fiévreuse

Cendrars's most wholehearted immersion in cinema was as director of the film *La Venere nera* (Black Venus) in Italy in 1921, released in 1923. The script was published as *La Perle fiévreuse* (The Feverish Pearl), appearing in serial form between November 1921 and March 1922.[22] This book is one of many instances where Cendrars blurs the boundaries of established literary genres; the title page describes the book rather misleadingly as a novel, whereas in fact it can be more accurately defined as a film découpage. The text is divided into some 850 shots, with technical instructions that provide information as to the different sizes of lens to be used, various camera angles and effects (travelling shots, close-up, *plongée*, *contre-plongée* and so on); it also employs an array of cinematographic devices including intertitles, flashbacks, fade and superimposition. The plot is a satirical send-up of the popular genre of crime serials, and indeed, the list of secondary characters includes fictional heroes of such serials: we find the Surrealists' favourite, Fantômas, cropping up alongside authors of the genre such as Arthur Conan Doyle and Gustave Le Rouge. But it is also a metatextual *mise en abyme* of cinematic production that appears to have been written consciously for the benefit of a reading public unfamiliar with the discourse of film: the first part of the text is entitled 'Ça c'est du cinéma' (That's Cinema) and professes to demonstrate how to produce a scenario découpage.[23] In spite of this confident assertion, this script, like the previous effort, must have posed some significant logistical

emploie toutes les données du monde pour

Cendrars and Cassandre, *Le Spectacle est dans la rue* (1935).

issues for Cendrars as he directed the film: the list of extras includes two Great Danes and a small bear.

The fact that Cendrars published this work as a literary text suggests that he saw cinematographic forms of writing as promising new areas to explore alongside film-making itself. He never again tried to direct a film, but in the late 1920s, cinema returned in the plot of *Les Confessions de Dan Yack*, and Cendrars also explored opportunities to adapt his novel *L'Or* for the cinema. The advent of the talkie, and developments in sound technology more broadly, would also have an impact on some of his later work. The lost film *La Venere nera* and its script *La Perle fiévreuse* certainly represent a bold step and a distinct phase of his career; the forays into cinema also offer further proof of his willingness to reinvent himself and continually reshape his identity as a writer.

The trope of original creation, already seen in *La Fin du monde filmée par l'Ange N.-D.*, anticipates Cendrars's ballet scenario, *La Création du monde*, commissioned by Rolf de Maré for the Ballets suédois and premièred at the Théâtre des Champs-Elysées on 25 October 1923. Darius Milhaud composed the score, Jan Börlin choreographed the dance and Fernand Léger produced the decor and costume; the inspiration for the latter came in part from African carvings reproduced in Carl Einstein's 1915 book *Negerplastik* (Negro Sculpture).[24] Throughout Cendrars's literary oeuvre, the theme of the creation of the world runs in parallel to that of the end of the world; the latter trope reappears in the novel *Moravagine*.

In an essay called 'Publicité = poésie' (Advertising = Poetry), written in 1927, Cendrars produced a list itemizing what he considered to constitute the seven wonders of the modern world. These are the combustion engine; SKF ball bearings; the cut of a great tailor; the music of Erik Satie; money; the naked neck of a woman who has just had her hair cut; and advertising.[25] All of these are unashamedly ephemeral: he then adds that seven or eight hundred new wonders are created every day. The entire essay is dedicated to Cassandre, whose iconic poster designs for the apéritif Dubonnet and the wine store Nicolas adorned the streets of France's cities throughout the 1930s.[26] In 1935, Cendrars wrote the text for *Le Spectacle est dans la rue* (The Spectacle Is in the Street), a volume of Cassandre's advertising images.[27]

In light of his adoption of photography and cinema as poetic stimuli, Cendrars's enthusiasm for advertising slogans and posters is easy to understand. As we have observed, he believed that literature should be accessible and in touch with the reality of modern life; his conception of poetry made no distinction between 'high' and 'low' forms, and his practice anticipated the bricolage and assemblage techniques more commonly associated with the experimentation of the late twentieth century. He understood poetry not as an esoteric and refined art form but as a multiple discourse that could embrace in an egalitarian way the language of the everyday and popular forms of speech. In other words, he understood poetry not as a self-contained, exclusive form belonging to a cultural elite, but as a diverse and multifaceted entity whose windows should be 'open onto the boulevards'. As Garrett White puts it, 'For Cendrars, literature, like film, wasn't something abstract, theoretical – hence his hatred of artistic pretense – it was something *lived*. [...] His was always a street-level point of view.'[28] This is already clear in *Le Panama* and *Dix-neuf poèmes élastiques*, where he combines elements of free verse with myriad allusions to consumer products and even brand names.[29]

An unpublished poem shows Cendrars harnessing the instantaneity of advertising, its capacity to usher forth a form of poetry born of everyday life and consumer society. The title, 'Dictated by Telephone', reinforces a notion that he found seductive, that the modern writer could dispense with putting pen to paper or even typing and rely on the modern technology of the telephone. It reads: 'Le temps c'est de l'argent,/ Oui, mais Bugatti le double en vitesse' (Time is money/ Yes, but Bugatti is twice as fast).[30]

In his essay 'Poètes' in the collection *Aujourd'hui*, Cendrars alludes to the great American poet Walt Whitman. Cendrars claims: 'En cherchant leur langue les poètes d'aujourd'hui ont pavé le trottoir.' (In searching for their language the poets of today have paved the sidewalk.)[31] In 'Publicité = poésie', he evokes an audacious advertising stunt in which an aeroplane performed a series of loops, its trail of smoke tracing the name 'Citroën' in the sky in letters measuring 100 metres.[32] Without hesitation, Cendrars acclaims this feat of bravura as a form of modern poetry, seeing the act as embodying 'l'héroïsme, la science, l'audace, la précision, la virtuosité, la candeur, l'universalité de la poésie et du poète modernes' (the heroism, science, bravery, precision, virtuosity, candour, universality of modern poetry and poets).[33]

This preoccupation with poetic language as something that should be popular, that we can read on the street or in the sky in an instant, on the move, makes Cendrars a most prescient observer of the modern

NORMANDIE
Cie Gle TRANSATLANTIQUE
French Line
ALLIANCE GRAPHIQUE

...à

LA CONQUÊTE

Cendrars and Cassandre, *Le Spectacle est dans la rue* (1935).

experience. Indeed, he could not have imagined how relevant his words would be to social trends in the twenty-first century, when technology makes it possible to read or listen to words and music wherever we go and when poetry has established an important space on social media platforms. It is no surprise that one of the essays in the collection *Aujourd'hui* should be about advertising, a phenomenon that would reach its apogee several decades after he wrote his essay on the subject. Cendrars describes advertising as 'la plus belle expression de notre époque, la plus grande nouveauté du jour, un Art' (the most beautiful expression of our era, the greatest novelty of the day, an Art).[34] In particular, he admires its international, even multilingual character, and its daring use of techniques available to rejuvenate communication and bring it into keeping with the modern era. Cendrars implies that, of all forms of language, the discourse of advertising is especially deeply rooted in the popular consciousness since it enriches everyday life, while at the same time deriving nourishment from it: 'Le langage est né de la vie, et la vie, après l'avoir créé, l'alimente.' (Language is born of life, and life, having created it, feeds it.)[35] As he did in August 1914, Cendrars here is making an impassioned call to his fellow poets, but this time in the name of advertising rather than that other product of the modern age, war.

A Poetics of Prosthetics: *Kodak*

The eighth chapter of Cendrars's 1931 volume of essays *Aujourd'hui* begins with an epigraph taken from C. F. Ramuz. It reads: 'L' "art" on sait ce que c'est: c'est une greffe sur du déjà greffé.' (We know what 'art' is: it's a graft on something already grafted.)[36] In a now famous definition, Walter Benjamin writes similarly of photography as an 'orthopaedic' practice. These words have a bearing on the collection of poems, published in 1924, that Cendrars originally entitled *Kodak*. Re-writing and plagiarism will be considered as the guiding principles of a poetic practice that can be defined as a form of grafting. We shall also explore the implications of the intertextual excision that the poet conducts on his source text, a popular novel by Gustave Le Rouge – a novel that, curiously enough, grants a privileged status to surgery.

In 1924, Cendrars published a collection of poems under the title *Kodak (Documentaire)*. When the Eastman Kodak company threatened to take legal action against him for unauthorized use of its name, Cendrars changed the title of the volume to *Documentaires*

(Documentaries). In 1945, in his autobiographical book *L'Homme foudroyé*, Cendrars admitted to having carried out a 'supercherie poétique' (poetic hoax) by 'borrowing' from the writer Gustave Le Rouge 'twenty or so original poems' that Cendrars had cut with scissors out of one of his prose works.[37] Thanks to the efforts of Francis Lacassin some decades ago, the full extent of Cendrars's poetic pilfering is known: of 44 poems in the collection, some 41 were taken more or less wholesale from Le Rouge's popular serial novel *Le Mystérieux Docteur Cornélius*.[38] Yvette Bozon-Scalzitti subsequently revealed that Cendrars took two of the three remaining poems from Maurice Calmeyn's book *Au Congo belge* (In the Belgian Congo, 1912).[39] In short, then, virtually the entire contents of *Documentaires* had a previous life, having been written by other authors. Setting aside the legality of using pre-existing published material without the authors' permission, Cendrars's appropriation of ready-made texts as the basis of poetry has far-reaching consequences and compels us to think afresh about what is and can be considered poetic practice.

As the original title *Kodak* suggests, Cendrars conceived this collection as a series of poetic snapshots; indeed, photography provides not only one of the themes of the collection, but the basis of its writing style, which emphasizes brevity, immediacy and the act of seeing. The photographic paradigm is, so to speak, the poet's modus operandi. By adopting the brand name *Kodak* as the title of his volume, Cendrars is making an important statement both about writing and about seeing; as a title, this name carries some compelling implications about the role of the modern-day poet, his relationship to everyday reality, and also to consumer society. Moreover, the title tells us much about Cendrars's understanding of the limits to which the poet may go in order to unearth the poetic.

The particular definition of visual perception that emerges from the poems anticipates by some seven years Walter Benjamin's observation that the camera's lens exceeds ocular vision and makes perceptible 'a tiny spark of chance', an ephemeral and elusive characteristic that remains imperceptible to the naked eye; we are in the realm of 'unconscious optics'.[40] For Benjamin, what distinguishes photography and film from painting is the distance between the artist and the subject; the camera – and especially the movie camera – endows the user with the capacity to penetrate as would a surgeon 'the tissues of the given reality'.[41] Benjamin was quick to foresee the potential of photography and cinematography to transform our interaction with the space that surrounds us: 'Evidently a different nature opens itself to the camera than opens to the naked eye – if only because an unconsciously penetrated space is substituted for a space consciously explored by man.'[42] In drawing this connection between the film camera and surgery, Benjamin at once recalls Freud, who identified a 'prosthetic god' created by technology, and anticipates Lacan's conception of the mirror stage:

> Le stade du miroir est un drame dont la poussée interne se précipite de l'insuffisance à l'anticipation – et qui pour le sujet, pris au leurre de l'identification spatiale, machine les fantasmes qui se succèdent d'une image morcelée du corps à une forme que nous appelerons orthopédique de sa totalité [...]
>
> (The mirror stage is a drama whose internal thrust is precipitated from insufficiency to anticipation and which manufactures for the subject, caught up in the lure of spatial identification, the succession of phantasies that extends from a fragmented body-image to a form of its totality that I shall call orthopaedic [...])[43]

In *Modernism, Technology and the Body*, Tim Armstrong examines advertising images and plastic surgery of the interwar years; he notes that in both of these practices, the body tends to be exposed in fragmented form, with the effect that only one part of it is exposed. The body can thus be seen as a whole that is continually deferred; only with the aid of technology does it become complete.[44] We shall return to these interpretations later; first, it's worth examining *Kodak* as an instance of what might be termed a poetics of grafting.

Already in its conception, *Kodak* is clearly intent on adopting the photographic paradigm as the basis of an experimental form of poetry. The approach is not entirely new but builds on some of the practices already undertaken in *Prose du Transsibérien* and *Dix-neuf poèmes élastiques*. As preceding chapters have suggested, Cendrars was intrigued by visual forms of expression, and his fascination with cinema has been the subject of considerable scholarly interest.[45] Gilles Deleuze suggests that it was thanks to Cendrars that film-makers such as Abel Gance were able to understand the 'simultanéist' aesthetic of Robert Delaunay.[46] Studies of a 'cinematographic' tendency in Cendrars's writing have tended to focus on the presence of a fragmented body: following an observation by Claude Leroy, Philippe Pilard notes, 'the Cendrarsian movie camera "operates on" what it is filming. And we must give this verb its surgical as well as its cinematographic meaning.'[47] Peter Nicholls, on the other hand, writes of Cendrars's poetry in terms of a dismembering of the body that is set in motion by the multifarious sensory experiences encountered in the modern urban setting.[48] Other critics have attempted to locate *Kodak* within the aesthetics of cinematographic writing: Henri Béhar, insisting on the subtitle of the original edition, *Kodak (Documentaire)*, interprets it as a film in ten sequences.[49] For others, *Kodak* is more akin to the photographic than to the cinematographic image: following Daniel Grojnowski, Clive Scott claims that the poem 'Elephant Hunt', for all its references to photography, does not refer even once to the movie camera.[50] But such an assertion sits uneasily alongside a line such as 'I have my three men stay put each one aiming his Bell & Howell'.[51]

Here, Cendrars is referring to one of the best-known manufacturers of film cameras of his era, a company that had been producing the Standard Cinematograph Camera since 1912. Film director Jean Epstein extolled the virtues of the Bell-Howell camera: 'Le Bell-Howell est un artiste et ce n'est que derrière lui qu'il y a d'autres artistes: metteur en scène et opérateur. Une sensibilité enfin est achetable et se trouve dans le commerce et paye des droits de douane comme le café ou les tapis d'Orient.' (The Bell-Howell is an artist and it is only behind it that there are other artists: the director and the camera operator. At last a sensibility can be bought, is commercially available and pays customs duties like coffee and oriental rugs.)[52]

Admittedly, the references to the captured image in *Documentaires* include both the still image of photography and the cinematic moving image. The line following the one cited above does suggest a still camera rather than a movie camera: 'Et je m'avance seul avec mon petit kodak sur un terrain où je puis marcher sans bruit' (And I move in alone with my little Kodak on ground where I can walk silently).[53] But other references to the Kodak brand are in all probability aimed not at the Kodak Brownie, but at the Cine-Kodak, produced in 1924: 'Je garde un homme avec moi pour porter le grand Kodak' (I keep one man with me to carry the big Kodak).[54]

It should be remembered that, before writing *Kodak*, Cendrars had already worked alongside Abel Gance on his films *J'Accuse* and *La Roue*, and that he admitted to having narrowly missed out on buying from Gustave Le Rouge the film rights for an adaptation of the latter's story *Le Mystérieux Docteur Cornélius*, about which Cendrars writes, 'l'œuvre mouvementée de Lerouge [*sic*] s'y prêtait admirablement' (the action-packed work of Lerouge lent itself very well to this).[55]

In his preface to the later edition of *Documentaires* published in 1947, Cendrars plays down the parallels with cinema and instead accentuates the analogy with photography, referring to the poems as being conceived as 'verbal photographs'.[56] Yet it is clear that both photography and cinema offered Cendrars, like Apollinaire, the exhilarating possibility of reaching a wider audience. On numerous occasions he states his preference for forms of expression that are accessible to all, and he criticizes the 'confusion fâcheuse entre la langue littéraire et la langue tout court, celle qui est parlée par tout le monde dans le pays tout entier et qui change avec le temps' (sad confusion of literary language and language *tout court*, the kind spoken by everyone in the whole country and which changes over time).[57] Cendrars's references to both photography and cinematography may best be understood in the context of his search for an absolutely modern form of 'writing'.

Cendrars's literary trajectory throughout the 1910s reveals his growing preoccupation with technical procedures whose complexity grows steadily, and in which the idea of the readymade starts to play a role. This is already perceptible in the *Dix-neuf poèmes élastiques*, discussed earlier. Jean-Pierre Goldenstein has revealed to what an extent the poet takes his inspiration not only from everyday language and advertising, but especially from the concept of the linguistic readymade. As Goldenstein has observed, the seventeenth elastic poem, 'Mee too buggi', derives entirely from an 1817 translation of a book written in English by John Martin on the indigenous people of Tonga. The sixteenth poem, 'Titres' (Titles), may be read as a meta-textual commentary on the poet's own evolution towards a new anti-poetics: 'Premier poème sans métaphores/ Sans images/ Nouvelles' (First Poem with No Metaphors/ No images/ News).[58] As this quotation and the poem's title suggest, Cendrars seems to be proposing a poetics in which naming, not writing, is the defining act. Again, here, a parallel emerges with the work of Marcel Duchamp, and with what Thierry de Duve has termed 'the syllogism "art = doing = choosing"'.[59] Duchamp underlines the importance of inscribing the readymade within time, a practice that he defines as 'cet horlogisme, cet instantané [. . .] une sorte de rendez-vous' (this matter of timing, this snapshot [. . .] a sort of encounter).[60]

On first sight, it seems legitimate to describe *Kodak* as the poetic equivalent of a readymade: in 1924, the year in which the collection was published, Cendrars declared, 'Nous ne faisons plus de la littérature' (We are no longer writing literature).[61] In the same period, Duchamp was rumoured to have abandoned painting, and the following year he devoted his energies to the creation of optical machines such as the *Rotative demi-sphère* and worked on the film *Anémic cinéma* with Man Ray and Marc Allégret. It would be a mistake, however, to overstate the parallel between Cendrars's poetry and the Duchampian anti-aesthetic of the readymade, according to which the choice of object is governed exclusively by 'une réaction d'indifférence *visuelle*, assortie au même moment à une absence totale de bon ou mauvais goût . . . en fait une anesthésie complète' (a reaction of *visual* indifference, matched at the same time to a total absence of good or bad taste . . . in fact a complete anesthaesia).[62] To define *Kodak* as the textual equivalent of the readymade would be to play down the value of Cendrars's interventions, and their relationship with their popular source that gave rise to the poems. This rewriting set in motion a series of transformations that prevent us from considering *Kodak* as a work entirely based on the copying of a textual found object. What sets Cendrars apart from Duchamp is not this transformation per se, since it already plays an important role in the readymade: Duchamp acknowledged that the short sentence that he added to his readymades 'était destinée à emporter l'esprit du spectateur vers d'autres régions plus verbales' (was intended to transport the viewer's mind to other, more verbal, regions).[63] On the contrary, it is the aesthetic character of Cendrars's intervention that distinguishes it from Duchamp. By comparing *Kodak* with *Le Mystérieux Docteur Cornélius*, we can immediately identify an aesthetic shift resulting from the simple act of converting a prose text into lines of verse. The mere adoption of the outer appearance of poetry already inscribes the poetic into a text that had originally had a more prosaic existence.

By abandoning the laws of grammar and syntax in favour of a minimal, stripped-back, elliptical, expressive form, Cendrars at times seems to approach a definition of the 'degree zero' of discourse, a phenomenon that Thierry de Duve, still referring to Duchamp, calls the 'n'importe quoi' (anything whatsoever).[64] It is nevertheless true that the process that Cendrars puts into practice goes much further than a mere rewriting in verse: rather than a readymade, *Kodak* deserves to be seen as the approximate equivalent of an assisted readymade, as the result of a collaboration between poet and linguistic matter. As in the readymade, this material is prefabricated, ready-made; but, as distinct from the straightforward readymade, that artist's task entails an act of manipulation. However minimal this intervention is, the effect of displacement that it enacts is considerable.

In 1925, when Duchamp was working on his *Rotative demisphère*, José Ortega y Gasset identified a tendency that he called the 'dehumanization of art'.[65] A decade or so before Benjamin, Ortega illustrated this new aesthetic approach, comparing the painter to a doctor sitting at the bedside of a patient. Even more than the doctor, the artist must remain at a distance from the subject: 'With the painter, we have arrived at the maximum distance and the minimum of sentimental engagement.'[66] Benjamin takes the analogy further in the sense that he brings out the contrast between the magician (whom he compares to the painter) and the surgeon (whom he likens to the camera operator):

> The surgeon [. . .] greatly diminishes the distance between himself and the patient by penetrating into the patient's body and increases it but little by the caution with which his hand moves among the organs. In short, in contrast to the magician – who is still hidden in the medical practitioner – the surgeon at the decisive moment abstains from facing the patient man to man; rather, it is through the operation that he penetrates into him.[67]

The paradoxical status of its intervention makes the camera so fascinating for Benjamin: with its capability of penetrating inside the body, it reveals an aspect of it that is 'free of all equipment'. It is precisely thanks to the discreet nature of its manipulation that the camera avoids obscuring our vision:

> for contemporary man the representation of reality by the film is incomparably more significant than that of the painter, since it offers, precisely because of the thoroughgoing permeation of reality with mechanical equipment, an aspect of reality which is free of all equipment.[68]

This insistence on an intervention that is both profoundly intimate, capable of penetrating to the heart of the subject, yet also discreet on account of its technical nature, characterizes very accurately the narrative point of view of *Kodak (Documentaire)*. Proof of this is in the virtually total absence of the first-person singular voice, which appears only in the seventh and ninth of its ten sections. It appears most frequently in the penultimate poem of the collection, 'Chasse à l'éléphant' (Elephant Hunt). Curiously, as we have already observed, it is also in this poem that the photographic and movie camera are most clearly in evidence; in a number of instances, the poet invokes these and other optical devices such as binoculars to make up for the insufficiency of human senses:

> Je garde un homme avec moi pour porter le grand kodak
> A douze mètres je distingue mal une grande bête
> [. . .]
> Quelle photo intéressante a pu prendre l'homme de sang-froid
> qui se tenait à côté de moi

> (I keep one man with me to carry the big Kodak
> At twelve yards I can barely make out a large animal
> [. . .]
> What an interesting photo the cool-headed man beside me was
> able to take)[69]

> La hauteur des herbes m'empêche de les photographier
> Du haut d'une termitière je les observe longtemps avec ma
> jumelle Zeiss

> (The height of the grass keeps me from photographing them
> From the top of a termite hill I watch them a long time through
> my Zeiss field glasses)[70]

In the majority of the poems, by contrast, the narrative point of view has the mobility and detachment that we would associate with the movie camera. The same principle of mobility applies to the geographic extent of the poems, which come and go between the United States and Africa, the Aleutian Islands and Polynesia. The first poem of the collection, 'Roof-Garden', uses alternating long and short lines, an elliptical, clipped syntax with verbs in the present tense and no punctuation; the effect is of a combination of panoramic views and close-up shots that recreate the rhythm of a cinematographic montage:

> Le vieux savant et les deux milliardaires sont seuls sur la terrasse
> Magnifique jardin

Massifs de fleurs
Ciel étoilé
Les trois vieillards demeurent silencieux prêtent l'oreille au bruit des rires et des voix joyeuses qui montent des fenêtres illuminées
Et à la chanson murmurée de la mer qui s'enchaîne au gramophone

(The old scientist and the two multimillionaires are alone on the terrace
Magnificent garden
Masses of flowers
Starry sky
The three elderly gentlemen stand in silence listening to the laughter and happy voices rising from bright windows
And to the murmured song of the sea at the end of the record)[71]

It is worth dwelling a little longer on this last word, which closes the poem and opens up a whole series of questions: it seems to confirm the impression, evident from the first line onwards, that these poems follow a dynamic that is not human but pertains to machines. Earlier in the same poem, the emphasis of certain images or sounds seems to take place autonomously, by means of repetitions that evoke the jolts and scratches of a gramophone needle:

Pendant des semaines les ascenseurs ont hissé hissé des caisses des caisses de terre végétale
[...]
Au sommet de l'édifice l'édifice de briques et d'acier

(For weeks the elevators have hoisted hoisted crates crates of loam
[...]
On top of the building the building of bricks and steel)[72]

In this way, the networks of communication that we encounter in this collection accumulate: we have not only the Kodak camera, but the movie camera, the gramophone and, as we will soon see, wireless telegraphy. In fact, all these means of communication are viable poetic devices for Cendrars, this 'very bad poet' who as early as 1913 claimed, like his friend Apollinaire, a lack of familiarity with 'the old game of verse'.[73] Elsewhere, too, Cendrars expresses his fascination for optical and audio devices and their capacity to enhance human perception. In a brilliant analysis of Cendrars's two Dan Yack novels, Philippe Bonnefis observes what he terms 'the gramophone effect'; his discussion of the role of the monocle in the first tome, *Le Plan de l'aiguille*, would merit consideration in light of the ocular theories outlined above.[74]

Cendrars's eclectic methods create movement that operates on different levels: it alerts the reader to the relationship between seeing and telling; it compels us to consider to what extent words can ever be comparable to a visual snapshot; and it creates a constant to-ing and fro-ing between poetry and the other forms of discourse and means of recording that it variously alludes to or actually uses. On a textual level, his use of bricolage, collage, montage, citation and even plagiarism propels the poems into a discursive chain in which poetic form circulates with the traces of novelistic flourishes, reportage-style observations and other fragments that it has appropriated.

In his analysis of the 'photogenic' paintings of French artist Gérard Fromanger, Michel Foucault insists not on any fixity, but rather on the state of 'transit' that they suggest. Foucault discusses a series of paintings that Fromanger made in the 1970s under the collective heading 'The Painter and His Model'; these were done in conjunction with a photographer who was enlisted to take random photographs around Paris. The paintings derive from the photographic negatives converted into slides which are projected on to the canvas and then modified with the addition of bright colours straight from the tube. This reinforces the idea of movement by allowing the different stages of the creative process to show through and, with them, the various expressive forms that contributed to the final work. As Foucault notes, 'Chaque tableau est un passage; un instantané qui, au lieu d'être prélevé par la photographie sur le mouvement de la chose, anime, concentre et intensifie le mouvement de l'image à travers ses supports successifs.' (Each painting is a thoroughfare; a 'snap' which rather than fixing the movement of things in a photograph, animates, concentrates and magnifies the movement of the image through its successive supporting media.)[75] Similarly, Cendrars's tactics have something of the palimpsest about them, in that he adds a new layer to a pre-existing text, and in the process transforms it, but without hiding the original writing.

We now know the full extent and the exact origin of Cendrars's borrowings from Gustave Le Rouge.[76] Almost every word of Cendrars's poem 'Office' derives from two lengthy sentences from *Le Mystérieux Docteur Cornélius* that describe a wealthy international businessman in his comfortable, well-equipped study. Cendrars removes the punctuation, simplifies the syntax and distils the structure into seven lines, each comprising a single idea or a mere list of nouns. This reductive transformation recalls a practice that Jean-Pierre Goldenstein, referring to *Dix-neuf poèmes élastiques*, defines as an 'inverse graft'.[77]

This process involves a number of changes: the transition from the past to the present confers on the passage an immediacy that is more characteristic of photography than textual narration; the radical reduction of syntax – and especially the removal of verbs – distances the text from its narrative context by removing any explicit relationship of cause and consequence. The various elements quoted in Le Rouge's text are connected to each other by the narrative voice that explains their function. In Cendrars's version, the objects are released from this explanatory framework and placed into a spatial relationship, as if the eye of the reader, who has become a spectator, were listing the contents of the office one by one. The telegraphic character of the poem's utterances, which enumerate without explaining, confers on the reader the task of connecting the items listed and deducing the links between them.

At the same time, Cendrars's verse gives the words a strongly rhythmic character, emphasizing groupings of four syllables: 'Radiateurs/ Ventilateurs/ à air liquide/ Douze téléphones'. According to Clive Scott, rhythm is the poetic equivalent of the backcloth of reality, that is to say, of vision.[78] Or, we might add, of what Benjamin calls 'the tiny spark of chance, the *hic et nunc* of objects'.[79]

Unlike Le Rouge's text, the poem does not refer to a character we already know, and thus gives the fourth line a completely different meaning: 'Le milliardaire ne se sent vraiment chez lui que dans ce cabinet de travail' (The only place the multimillionaire feels at home is in this office). Suddenly, the line starts to resemble an advertising text evoking a space worthy of a billionaire, rather than the description of a concrete place. In other words, it marks the passage from the specific to the generic, and the title 'Office' accentuates this same generic aspect. It is also worth noting the effect of suppressing the article in the line '[Des] Radiateurs et [des] ventilateurs à air liquide' as well as the replacement of the indefinite or partitive article with the definite article. This all goes to suggest that Cendrars's creative borrowing is indeed, as he himself claims, a 'supercherie *poétique*' (a *poetic* hoax).

By way of conclusion, a third and final aspect of *Kodak (Documentaire)* deserves to be considered, an aspect that refers both to Gustave Le Rouge's 'donor text' and to the question of the orthopaedic body. The eponymous criminal of the series *Le Mystérieux Docteur Cornélius*, a certain Dr Cornelius Kramm, nicknamed 'the sculptor of human flesh', boasts of having invented 'carnoplasty'. The list of characters at the beginning of the book qualifies him as the 'author of universally appreciated books on the rational aesthetics of the human being and scientific means to prolong youth in men and women'. But Kramm is also the leader of a group of criminals and murderers called the Red Hand. References to the orthopaedic body, enhanced by technology, abound in this book, as evidenced by this scene that takes place in Dr Cornelius's laboratory:

> trois personnages enfoncés dans de luxueuses pelisses de renard noir, leurs bonnets de fourrure [. . .] entourés d'un cercle d'or d'où s'élevaient une multitude de petites mains de rubis, de façon à former une véritable couronne. Leur visage rasé était recouvert d'un masque de caoutchouc mince qui, tout en le dissimulant complètement, laissait deviner les jeux de la physionomie.
>
> (three characters ensconced in luxurious pelisses of black fox fur, their fur hats [. . .] surrounded by a circle of gold from which rose a multitude of small hands made of rubies, so as to form an actual crown. Their shaved faces were covered with thin rubber masks which, while concealing them completely, made it possible to infer their physiognomy.)[80]

By appropriating *Le Mystérieux Docteur Cornélius*, Cendrars inscribes his poetics once again in the field of the prosthetic body, this time through the trope of the donor text on which he carries out the graft. But the most astonishing thing is that Cendrars, while constructing his collection almost entirely from fragments of Le Rouge's text, has preserved neither the main characters, nor the action, nor the style of narration, which are all displaced, stripped of their identity and placed in another context. By creating his poetic collection out of ready-made elements, Cendrars, this 'writer of the left hand', amputates the very essence of his donor text. In this respect, the relationship between Cendrars and Le Rouge illustrates the impasse in which the body in the modernist age is often held: the writer of popular fiction becomes a poet, and in the process, the literary equivalent of tin is turned into gold – but any such putative transformation is ultimately nothing other than a mirage. The alchemy of the word can only be realized at the price of its fragmentation, and the ideal, total prosthetic body is deferred forever.

As we have seen, Cendrars's appropriation of the discourses of photography and cinema came to the fore in his works that span the period from his amputation to the publication of *Kodak* and in the midst of which he became involved in the film-making process. Alongside these, his poetic practice also immersed itself in the language and concerns of everyday life and explored the creative potential of the found object, textual collage and literary graft. A preoccupation with cinema and other technologically enhanced art forms inhabits much of his later writing, too. Subsequent chapters will discuss this ongoing fascination with film and the ways in which writing can intersect with it and other expressive fields. First, however, we will consider Cendrars's work as a novelist, a transition that occurs in tandem with the crossing of another line, the equator.

four

Crossing the Line: Cendrars's American Odysseys

In January 1924, Cendrars set off on SS *Formose* bound for Brazil. Over the next four years, he stayed in that country three times, spending almost a year and a half there in total. The experience of the New World, the acquaintance with the Brazilian Modernistas and the exposure to a hitherto unfamiliar culture and literary scene all fuelled his creativity. It was a different Cendrars who returned to Paris from that first visit to Brazil, and his writing too bore the hallmarks of a life-changing experience. At the end of 1925, he published his first novel, *L'Or*, the first significant product of an experience that he himself described as a period of apprenticeship in the province of São Paolo.

For a decade, his reputation had been built on his poems characterized by their uncompromising quality and their readiness to break with convention; the transition into novel writing thus marks a significant turning point. Appropriately enough, he began writing his last volume of poetry on the ship that took him to Brazil, as if his discovery of the New World necessitated new forms of expression. Yet the adoption of prose fiction marks a shift rather than a complete rupture, since in some respects Cendrars remained a poet even when he ceased to write poems. For Claude Leroy, Cendrars is a 'poet of all discursive terrains': all of his work deserves to be considered poetry, whatever genre it notionally adopts.[1] His fascination with the allure of language, and the scope it offers for creating entire imaginary worlds, unites all of his writings in what Armand Lanoux terms a 'verbal hallucination'.[2] Indeed, one of the ways in which Cendrars continued to assert his modernity was in what may be termed an aesthetics of accumulation. We have already observed in his poems a tendency to let language run loose and threaten to destabilize its structural confines; this becomes more marked and reaches new levels in the prose writings of the interwar and post-war years. Yet the greatest commercial success of his entire career was to come from *L'Or*, his first and shortest novel, written quickly and in a concise syntax that captures the reader's attention with all the directness and urgency of his best poems.

Some of Cendrars's most prominent writings of this decade focus attention on the Americas. The three invited trips to Brazil between early 1924 and late 1927 led to his acclaim among that country's modernist writers. In Paris in 1923, he made the acquaintance of the poet Oswald de Andrade and his partner, the artist Tarsila do Amaral, who subsequently introduced him to their compatriot Paolo Prado, a wealthy businessman and patron of the arts. It was on Prado's invitation that Cendrars made his first visit to Brazil in 1924; in January of that year he left by boat and returned to France nine months later. In Brazil, Cendrars enjoyed the status of a literary hero and was celebrated as a pioneering figure of Modernism. As Le Quellec Cottier observes, such adulation was somewhat at odds with the message he communicated to his fellow writers in Brazil, whom he urged to develop their own distinct forms of writing. His contacts with Brazilian writers and benefactors not only offered him an exciting opportunity to travel and engage with a different literary culture, but bought him some more time to finish writing his novel *Moravagine*, commissioned and eagerly awaited by his publisher Bernard Grasset in Paris.[3]

The importance of Brazil in shaping Cendrars's subsequent literary career cannot be overstated. His exposure to the Americas came at a significant moment for him; his attitude towards the Parisian literary scene was uneasy, and he had a particular reticence towards the Surrealists, who would come to prominence in 1924 with the publication of André Breton's *Manifesto of Surrealism*. On his return from Brazil in the autumn of 1924, Cendrars made his base in Le Tremblay-sur-Mauldre, a rural community in the Yvelines department located some 65 kilometres to the southwest of Paris. Raymone had bought a small house there and made it available to him. He went on to write many of his books there, although it is unlikely that the two of them spent much time there together, since she was touring extensively with Louis Jouvet's theatre company and he continued to make many and frequent journeys. At any rate, having a base away from Paris seems to have suited Cendrars very well and benefited his writing. Moreover, his relations with the Surrealists were strained, to say the least. In conversation with Michel Manoll years later, he recalled that members of the group had visited him in his attic room in the rue de Savoie. His acerbic comments leave no doubt as to his feelings towards them: Philippe Soupault was 'un très gentil garçon, qui était un timide et qui est devenu velléitaire pour ne pas dire plus: flanchard' (a very nice lad, who was timid and became weak-willed, not to say a coward). His description of the 'feudal lord' André Breton is less polite: '[il] portait déjà cet air ubuesque de grand homme de province à qui, un jour la patrie SERAIT reconnaissante et qui n'a jamais pu se libérer de cette grossesse nerveuse de gloire anthume' ([he] already had this ubu-esque air of a great provincial man to whom the fatherland WOULD one day be grateful and who could never shake off this nervous pregnancy with anticipated glory). For Cendrars, Aragon was by far the most intelligent of the three, but also the most fragile, 'un révolté qui a versé dans l'hystérie' (a rebel who spilled over into hysteria). Cendrars remembers recommending Apollinaire to Soupault, who had never heard of the author of *Alcohols*, and he scoffs at Breton's mendacious boast of having been on close terms with Apollinaire in 1917 and 1918.[4]

Cendrars's neighbours in Le Tremblay at different times included the art dealer Ambroise Vollard, the publisher René Hilsum and the artists Pablo Picasso and Francis Picabia; the latter's ink portrait of Cendrars was reproduced in *Kodak (Documentaire)* when it appeared in 1924. Travel remained vitally important to Cendrars, and indeed, one of the attractions of Le Tremblay was its proximity to the Nationale 10, the route that leads from Paris to the Spanish border via Bordeaux. Cendrars bought a six-cylinder 1500cc Alfa Romeo from Georges Braque, complete with the artist's custom paintwork, and had it adapted to allow him to change gear without losing his grip on the steering wheel. In 1929, John Dos Passos had the experience of sitting beside him in the danger seat (known in French as 'la place du mort', the dead person's space) and attested to his fondness for driving at breakneck speed, taking corners on two wheels and changing gear with a hook attached to his stump.[5]

It seems telling that he preferred to live away from Paris for reasons other than having the opportunity to do more driving. It is no surprise that his relationship with the Surrealists was troubled, since he had always preferred to chart his own itinerary rather than be led by others. Even in the early years after his arrival in Paris, when he was published by avant-garde presses and surrounded by various groups, he remained very

Francis Picabia, *Blaise Cendrars*, reproduced in *Kodak (Documentaire)*, 1924.

firmly an individualist. As Jay Bochner puts it succinctly, 'Although we may consider *Profond aujourd'hui* or *L'Eubage* surrealistic in tendency and implication, we never find that Cendrars was a surrealist, or an any "thing-ist."' For Bochner, Cendrars is 'avant-garde in the most quintessential sense', a claim that may seem at odds with a writer who obstinately refused to be affiliated with any group, movement or other collective. But Bochner's distinction is well observed, since Cendrars's most genuinely avant-garde credentials lie precisely in his refusal to settle into any semblance of fixity and in his constant urge to seek out new expressive forms, eschewing all positioning that might risk holding him in any one place in order to embrace what Bochner terms the 'passing-through'.[6]

We have seen how some of Cendrars's most prominent pre-war poems already draw on his experience of travel, both within Europe and in North America. The epic poems *Le Panama* and *Prose du Transsibérien* reflect his fascination with travel and the lure of far-off places; the appeal of the distant and the other is a recurrent feature of his writing, whether or not he had actually visited the places narrated. From New York to St Petersburg, from the streets of pre-war Paris to the battlefields of the First World War, the world is poeticized in Cendrars's hands; his writings evoke a powerful sense of place, but they do more than this. They transcend the specificity of any singular locality and capture the essence of what it is to travel, to be at home nowhere and to feel at home everywhere. Whether embarking on a train journey to the furthest reaches of the Trans-Siberian express route, hunting elephants in Africa or sailing to the Antarctic, the imaginary voyage – undertaken in the imagination or through the pages of other writers' books – can prove to be as rich a stimulus for writing as any real journey.[7]

Crossing the Line: *Feuilles de route*

The voyage to Brazil was significant not only for Cendrars's life, but for his work. When he boarded SS *Formose* in Le Havre in January 1924, he took his leave of poetry once and for all. On board, he wrote his last poetry volume, *Feuilles de route* (Travel Notes), a collection of peripatetic short poems in free verse focusing on the sights, sounds, encounters and thoughts generated by the long journey by ship.[8] A first publication under the title *Le Formose* appeared in 1924 under the imprint of Editions du Sans Pareil, with eight drawings by Tarsila do Amaral. Cendrars's correspondence with René Hilsum, general editor of the publishing house, confirms that *Le Formose* was originally intended to be the first of a series of seven or even eight related pamphlets, all to be published under the collective title *Feuilles de route*.[9] The final publication contained just three sections, a change of plan probably occasioned by Cendrars's decision to move away from poetry and focus instead on writing novels; at any rate, the tripartite structure of *Feuilles de route* corresponds perfectly with the journey around which it is based. Thus the first part recounts the

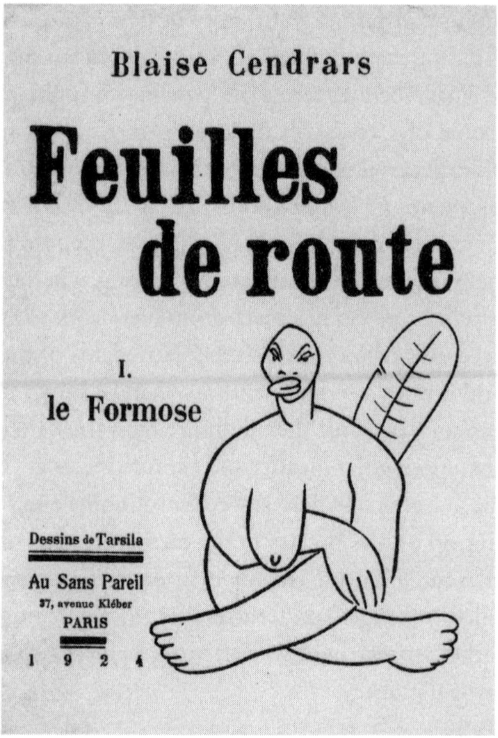

Feuilles de route, with illustration by Brazilian Modernist artist Tarsila do Amaral, 1924.

outbound journey to São Paolo; the second deals with the time spent there; and the third charts the return journey. As Claude Leroy notes, the collection in its published form thus marks symbolically Cendrars's crossing of the equator.[10]

Feuilles de route contains what can best be described as occasional poems, 'poèmes de circonstance' that share their brevity and contemporaneity with those constituting his 1919 publication *Dix-neuf poèmes élastiques*. Like the latter, the poems in this collection express the specific sensations of living in the present moment; written predominantly in the present tense, they jettison elaborate constructions, theorizations and imagery, and focus instead on short lines consisting of simple observations:

> 'réveil'
> Je suis nu
> J'ai déjà pris mon bain
> Je me frictionne à l'eau de Cologne
> Un voilier lourdement secoué passe dans mon hublot

Il fait froid ce matin
Il y a de la brume
Je range mes papers
J'établis un horaire
Mes journées seront bien remplies
Je n'ai pas une minute à perdre
J'écris

('Waking up'
I'm naked
I've already taken my bath
I rub on some cologne
A sailboat is buffeted across my porthole
It's cold this morning
There's some fog
I straighten my papers
I set up a schedule
My days will be busy
I don't have a minute to lose
I write)[11]

Crucially, the collection presents the poems as a kind of route map tracing a journey. This brings them into contact with a theme that Cendrars had already defined in *Les Pâques à New York*, *Prose du Transsibérien* and *Le Panama*. Like the poetry collection *Kodak*, which contains elements borrowed from other textual sources, the poems in *Feuilles de route* also rely on the appropriation of previously existing works by other writers; both collections can thus be regarded as textual collages that are based in part on the copying and pasting of ready-made texts, with the difference that the latter does acknowledge its sources whereas Cendrars waited until 1945 before confessing to the 'poetic hoax' that he had played on Gustave Le Rouge by copying passages from *Le Mystérieux Docteur Cornélius* and incorporating them into *Kodak*. The sources he himself cites in *Feuilles de route* are Auguste de Saint-Hilaire's *Voyage dans les provinces de Saint-Paul et de Sainte-Catherine* and *Sous la Croix du Sud* by Prince Luiz of Orléans-Braganza, the grandson of Pedro II, Emperor of Brazil.[12]

The first of its three sections, entitled 'Le Formose', dedicated to Cendrars's 'good friends in São Paolo', his 'friends in Rio de Janeiro' and finally to Léopold de Freitas, was first published in 1924 in its own right; it was not until 1944 that the three sections were published together by the Parisian publishing house Denoël.[13] The title is taken from the name of the ship that Cendrars boarded on 12 January 1924 and disembarked nearly a month later in Rio de Janeiro.

Fittingly, the opening poem charts a journey, although not by boat but by train. Its title, 'Dans le rapide de 19h 40' (On the 7.40 p.m. Express), has all the specificity we would expect of a circumstantial poem. Like 'Journal', the first of the *Dix-neuf poèmes élastiques*, this poem opens with a first-person voice reflecting on the recent past. Similarly, 'Newspaper' began with the words 'Christ/ Voici plus d'un an que je n'ai plus pensé à Vous/ Depuis que j'ai écrit mon avant-dernier poème Pâques' (Christ/ It's been more than a year now since I stopped thinking about You/ Since I wrote my next-to-last poem 'Easter'). 'On the 7.40 Express' strikes a remarkably similar tone in its opening quatrain, which lists four different modes of travelling:

> Voici des années que je n'ai plus pris le train
> J'ai fait des randonnées en auto
> En avion
> Un voyage en mer et j'en refais un autre un peu plus long
>
> (It's been years since I stopped taking the train
> I've gone by car
> Took the plane
> A boat trip and I'm taking an even longer one again)[14]

This poem sets up the same ambiguous relationship between the poet Blaise Cendrars and the narrating presence who uses the first-person personal pronoun 'je'. Like the start of 'Journal', which openly cites Cendrars's 'avant-dernier poème Pâques', the opening lines inscribe the poem within a context of travelling; they remind us implicitly that we are reading the words of the author of *Les Pâques à New York*, *Prose du Transsibérien* and *Panama*.

The poem goes on to plunge the reader into an intense profusion of sensory experiences through a sequence of lines narrated in the present tense. Thus we learn that the train is travelling at 110 kilometres per hour, has a restaurant car, makes a deafening noise as it crosses metal bridges and has a plumbing system that can be heard when the train is forced to slow down. As the train of Cendrars's poem arrives at its destination, the syntax is reduced to lists of substantives which act as a sequence of lexical snapshots: 'Le Havre autobus ascenseur/ J'ouvre les persiennes de la chambre d'hôtel' (Le Havre bus elevator/ I open the hotel room shutters).[15] Like an urban counterpoint to Rimbaud's bucolic poem 'Sensation', the closing lines celebrate the noise of the city: 'Je m'endors la fenêtre ouverte sur ce bruit de basse-cour/ Comme à la campagne' (I fall asleep with the window open on this barnyard noise/ As if in the country).[16] These lines also echo the conclusion of Apollinaire's 'Les Fenêtres' (Windows), which presents the image of a window being opened: 'La fenêtre s'ouvre comme une orange/ Le beau fruit de la lumière' (The window opens like an orange/ The beautiful fruit of the light). That poem is also a celebration of the present moment, of the wonders of modern-day technology that can enable a poem to be sent as a telephone message, and of a sense of ubiquity and spatio-temporal compression facilitated by fast travel: 'Paris Vancouver Hyères Maintenon New-York et les Antilles'.[17]

The second poem, 'Réveil' (Waking Up), acts in many respects like a continuation of the first one. The opening line reiterates the image of sleeping with the windows open: 'Je dors toujours les fenêtres ouvertes'.[18] It is now the following morning and the speaker, who continues to use the first-person voice, leans out of the window to observe the view. The reader is reminded of the symbiotic relationship between life and work in Cendrars's poetry: it alludes to a harbour station from which the poetic persona arrived in New York in 1911, which is factually accurate, since Cendrars did indeed board the *Birma* on its way to that city on 21 November of that year. The poem ends with a concise couplet that sums up the anticipation of exploring new lands and leaving the familiar world behind: 'Adieu Paris/ Bonjour soleil' (Goodbye Paris/ Hello sun).[19]

Technologies of modern travel are celebrated in the poems, but so too are other types of machine, such as the typewriter. The fourth poem, 'Lettre' (Letter), concludes with the speaker responding humorously to his addressee's wish for him to write by hand; he types his reply and then adds in ink 'Deux trois mots/ Et une grosse tache d'encre/ Pour que tu ne puisses pas les lire' (Two three words/ And a big ink stain/ So that you can't read them).[20] The musical allusion in the title of the fifth poem, 'Clair de lune' (Moonlight), extends to the typewriter, which finds the poet extolling its sonorous qualities: 'Ma belle machine à écrire qui sonne au bout de chaque ligne et qui est aussi rapide qu'un jazz' (My beautiful typewriter that rings at the end of each line and is as fast as jazz).[21] Less endearingly, the percussion of the keys interrupts the reverie of his neighbour, a young Argentinian woman. Subsequent poem titles offer snapshots of the ship's itinerary as it makes its way past the coast of Spain and Portugal to west Africa ('En route pour Dakar'), which was Cendrars's sole experience of that continent, despite the frequent allusions to it in his poems and other writings.[22]

Some poems in *Le Formose* describe the areas of land viewed from the ship's deck at different points on the journey or note the algae on the surface of the sea as well as different larger forms of marine and birdlife. Others attend to such themes as writing, and not writing: 'Je nage' tells us the ship's captain has installed a swimming pool on the upper deck: 'Je n'écris plus/ Il fait bon vivre' (No more writing/ It's good to be alive); sending letters by sea; the rising air temperature; the condition of the sea; sunsets, sunrises and starry skies witnessed on board; the goods acquired in the various locations at which the ship has berthed; occasional reminiscences of Paris and friends and loved ones there; the accidental discovery of Brazil when sea winds carried Pedro Alvares Cabral west instead of bringing him to the East Indies as he had expected; and the different toilet facilities in railway stations around the world.

Two poems are especially revealing in terms of the light they shed on Cendrars. 'Orion' is devoted to the eponymous constellation, but it is also the site of an astonishing, surreal sublimation: 'C'est mon étoile/ Elle a la forme d'une main/ C'est ma main montée au ciel' (It's my star/ It's in the form of a hand/ It's my hand gone up into the sky).[23] This allusion makes it impossible for the poem to be interpreted in any way other than autobiographically. It infuses the present moment of narration with Cendrars's memories of the First World War: the poem evokes, first, his recollections of seeing Orion from the trenches, and then the fact that the bombings conducted by the German army in zeppelins always originated from Orion. Finally, implicitly, inevitably, the poem broaches the subject of Cendrars's mutilation: 'Le grand mât perce la paume de cette main qui doit souffrir/ Comme ma main coupée me fait souffrir percée qu'elle est par un dard continuel' (The large mast pierces the palm of this hand that must suffer/ As my amputated hand hurts me pierced as it is by a continual stabbing pain).[24]

Defining this as an instance of 'mythobiographic writing', Claude Leroy notes the way the poem establishes two triads, the first of which associates Orion with the right arm and the German zeppelins, while the second brings together the trope of the cut, the image of the needle and a discreet link to the poet's mother's maiden name (her surname, Dorner, contains the word *Dorn*, the German word for thorn).[25] As we have noted, the traumatic scene of his mutilation haunts Cendrars's writing without the specific circumstances ever being openly discussed in it, yet it reappears in different mythologized guises throughout his work. *La Main coupée* contains a chapter entitled 'Le Lys rouge' (The Red Lily) in which a severed arm appears suddenly, and *Le Lotissement du ciel* returns to the constellation of Orion and its associations with the author's wound. The story of Oswaldo Padroso with his vision of the Sidereal Eiffel Tower offers another instance of a celestial sublimation.[26]

Another poem lists the contents of the poet's trunk. These include no fewer than six sets of manuscripts which he had to finish and send to their respective publishers. The backlog of unpublished writings can be explained by Cendrars's heavy involvement in the early 1920s in the world of cinema, both as Abel Gance's assistant and as a director in his own right. On the list of unfinished books are his novel *Moravagine*, to be completed and sent to the publisher Bernard Grasset, and *Le Plan de l'Aiguille*, the first of the two novels based on the character Dan Yack, commissioned for René Hilsum's publishing company, Au Sans Pareil. While on board the ship, on the way from Le Havre to La Pallice, the deep-water port in the town of La Rochelle on France's Atlantic coast, he also wrote and sent to Erik Satie a ballet script for the Ballets suédois; this was *La Création du monde*. Cendrars had also agreed to write a second ballet script with the title *Après-dîner, ballet*, again commissioned by Satie for the Ballets suédois, but in Cendrars's absence, Francis Picabia stepped in and wrote *Relâche*.[27]

Other publications that he lists here would never see the light of day; these include the poetry collection *[Au] Coeur du monde* and the manuscript of *Equatoria*, which was to be the story of an Austrian zoologist who was the governor of Equatoria at the time of the revolution of 'derviches tourneurs' and would be saved by the explorer Stanley. Cendrars also cites 'un gros paquet de contes nègres' (a big bundle of Black tales) that was to constitute the second volume of an anthology of stories based on Sub-Saharan Africa. This second volume of his *Anthologie nègre* would never materialize, even if parts of it did appear as *Petits contes nègres pour les enfants des Blancs* (1928), which was published a year later in Margery Williams Bianco's translation as *Little Black Stories for Little White Children*, and *Comment les Blancs sont d'anciens Noirs*

(1930) (How White People Used to Be Black).[28] Cendrars's appropriation of Sub-Saharan African source material, much of which had already been mediated by colonial missionaries and administrators, was characteristic of a broader avant-garde fascination with so-called 'primitive' non-European art and culture. In a compelling study, Carole Maccotta has examined in depth the problematic nature of these writings from a postcolonial perspective.[29]

The brevity of part two of *Feuilles de route*, 'São Paolo', reveals much about the respective amounts of time devoted to living and to writing during Cendrars's nine-month stay there. The six short poems in this section proclaim his fondness for this city that offers a refreshing contrast to someone whose view of the world is weighed down by European tradition: 'Ici nulle tradition/ Aucun préjugé/ Ni ancien ni moderne' (No tradition here/ No prejudice/ Ancient or modern).[30]

The third section, while longer than the second, is far shorter than the first, and this can partly be explained by the fact that Cendrars still had much to write. In 'Cabine 2' (Cabin 2) he relishes the opportunity to have a space in which he can write and make up for the previous nine months of literary inactivity in Brazil.[31] The third section, then, accompanies the poet on the return leg of the journey to Europe on SS *Gelria*.[32] Alongside him are travellers of various nationalities as well as a veritable menagerie of birds and animals that he acquired in Brazil; these include three marmosets and twelve colibris. To these he adds two more small marmosets which he names Adrienne and Jean after the eighteenth-century actress Adrienne Lecouvreur and his contemporary and fellow writer Jean Cocteau.

The style of writing throughout *Feuilles de route* is sparse and economical, as befits texts written under constraints of time. Written as free verse, their form is brief, and most lines are concise, consisting of a single main noun, a verb and an object. The tense of writing used throughout is the present, with very few exceptions. Occasionally, lines erupt and spill out. Some of the poems are self-reflexive, focusing on the act of writing or on the nature of poetry. 'Lettre-océan' (Ocean Letter), which cites a title that Apollinaire had used in *Calligrammes*, defines poetry tellingly as an extension of living:

> La lettre-océan n'a pas été inventée pour faire de la poésie

Mais quand on voyage quand on commerce quand on est à bord
quand on envoie des lettres-océan
On fait de la poésie

(The ocean letter was not invented for writing poetry

But when you travel when you do business when you're on board
when you send ocean letters
It's poetry)[33]

For Claude Leroy, *Feuilles de route* deserves to be seen symbolically as an equator crossing: as we have noted, the collection charts Cendrars's passage from Europe to the New World and back again, and it marks his transition from poet to novelist. Significantly, his first published novel, *L'Or*, would also be about a crossing of sorts, inasmuch as it would recount the story of a European – a Swiss citizen, no less – who made his life, and made and lost his fortune, in North America. *Feuilles de route*, then, is Cendrars's goodbye to poetry and marks the beginning of nearly four decades of novel writing; yet his prose would retain many of the characteristics of his best poems, as we will see in the subsequent sections and chapters.

L'Or: The Rush for *Sutter's Gold*

L'Or has an anomalous status in Cendrars's oeuvre. It is his best-known book and his greatest commercial success. It marks a watershed in his career, since it elevated Cendrars from a writer who was read mostly by a relatively small, highbrow readership of avant-garde enthusiasts to a name known throughout France. *L'Or* has also been taught on French school curricula, so for many young readers, it is the aspect of Cendrars's oeuvre with which they are most familiar. Yet a reader for whom this book is the entry point into Cendrars's fiction would find it hard to believe that its author was also responsible for the sprawling, byzantine novels of the 1920s such as *Moravagine* or the two *Dan Yack* volumes with their flights of fancy, extravagant storylines and expansive passages of prose.

The extraordinary success of *L'Or* is matched by the rapidity of its production. It does not even appear on the list of works in progress that Cendrars documented in his poem 'Bagage' (Baggage) during his journey to Brazil in 1924. He wrote the book in a mere six weeks on returning from Brazil, mostly as a stalling measure to keep the publishers at bay and give him more time to write the novel *Moravagine*; as he later admitted in a radio interview, his urge to spend Christmas 1924 in Paris fuelled his productivity to such an extent that he was able to deliver *L'Or* to Grasset in January 1925. When it appeared in print that year, the novel triggered a huge commercial success that seems to have taken even its author by surprise.

For all that it was hastily written, it was long in the making: in his poem *Le Panama*, written in 1914 and published after the war, Cendrars had already alluded to the original story matter of General Suter, his conquest of California and his financial ruin after gold mines were discovered on his land.[34] As Claude Leroy informs us, in 1912, Cendrars's old childhood friend Auguste Suter had lent him a book about his near-homologue Johann August Suter, which in all probability was Martin Birmann's biography of General Sutter (the extra t added to make the name more familiar to North Americans), some passages of which found their way into Cendrars's novel. According to Le Quellec Cottier, the former schoolfriends met again quite by chance at the Louvre in Paris in January 1911. They kept in touch, and the following year Suter passed the book to his friend. Cendrars was captivated by it and convinced that its subject, General Suter, was his friend's grandfather or great-uncle. During his period of active service in the First World War, Cendrars continued to be haunted by the story.[35]

The plot can be summarized as follows: in 1834, Johann August Suter leaves his wife and four children behind in their Swiss village and sets off on a ship bound for New York. This is where the 'marvellous story' of General John Augustus Sutter begins.[36] Penniless, he does all kinds of small jobs for two years until he can no longer resist the lure of the West. He heads first to Saint-Louis, where rumours continue to circulate about California and 'des terres, des prairies, des troupeaux innombrables qui sont à la merci d'un coup de main' (vast prairie-lands and countless herds of cattle there, to be had for the taking).[37] In 1838, he continues west, stopping first in Honolulu, where, under the guise of his newly created Sutter's Pacific Trading Company, he buys slaves and arranges for them to be shipped to a part of California that he has already named New Helvetia. In 1839, when he sets foot in San Francisco for the first time, California still belongs to Mexico, but his negotiating skills enable him to obtain permission to exploit its land and resources. He acquires huge swathes of land and becomes extremely wealthy and powerful through the vast agricultural empire that he has created. He successfully quashes attempted revolts, and even the war with Mexico and the ceding of Texas and California to the United States only bring him more power.

This all changes suddenly in January 1848, when a worker accidentally discovers gold on his land. Before long, New Helvetia is invaded by prospectors, Sutter's fields are laid to waste or abandoned, and he is ruined. His last hope lies in the title deeds he had obtained from the Mexican government which, if recognized, will make him the owner of the wealthiest gold deposits and land in this booming state. Tragically for him, his lands are invaded by numerous incomers brandishing title deeds issued by the United States. Sutter's attempts to sue the U.S. government spark riots and the destruction of his remaining land. The ensuing thirty years of legal wrangling make the lawyers and profiteers rich and leave him destitute and broken. His wife having died of exhaustion shortly after her long journey to be with him, he is alone when he dies in poverty aged 77, just moments after a young boy has relayed the false news that he has won his court case.

Cendrars's handling of this well-known subject tells us much about his own literary ambition at this point in his career: as much as it is a biography of a historically significant figure, it can also be interpreted through the lens of exofiction, a form of life writing in which an author explores his or her own story through that of another person. It does not require a huge leap of the imagination to understand why Cendrars should be fascinated by the tale of a Swiss man who left home for America, assumed a new name and identity and sought out adventure and the unknown. While it would be misplaced to interpret *L'Or* solely from this angle, it remains that the novel prompts us to reflect upon the myriad ways in which this retelling of an individual life relates both to the wider construct of literary fiction and to Cendrars's own experience. The descriptions of people thronging in the port of Le Havre, or some of the jobs undertaken by Suter on his arrival in New York, relate closely to Cendrars's accounts of his own experience of travelling to and living in that city.[38] The story of Suter's astronomic rise and catastrophic fall must also have had a personal meaning for him as the son of a failed entrepreneur, even if the scale of Suter's success and that of his subsequent ruin at the hands of lawless looters was much greater than anything Cendrars had personally experienced. Yvette Bozon-Scalzitti was one of the first scholars to acknowledge the resonances with his own life that must have drawn Cendrars to identify strongly with Suter's story. As Bozon-Scalzitti puts it, 'Suter is the first figure of the detonated man,' suggesting that Suter's life may have provided Cendrars with the inspiration for his autobiographically driven novels of the post-war years.[39] In the months following the publication of *L'Or*, numerous American readers began to complain about the way in which it portrayed Californians, and Cendrars felt compelled to defend his work in an open letter to North American booksellers in which he stressed it was a work of fiction: 'J'ai fait oeuvre d'artiste et non d'historien, un livre synthétique et non pas analytique [...] Une oeuvre de fiction. Un roman. C'était mon droit le plus absolu. Ma seule raison d'être un écrivain.' (I have done the work of an artist and not a historian, a book of synthesis, not analysis. [...] A work of fiction. A novel. That was my most absolute right. My sole reason for being a writer.)[40]

It is precisely Cendrars's skill in negotiating the tightrope between historically accurate story matter and novelistic extemporization that makes *L'Or* such an exhilarating and compelling read. Recalling his earlier poems and anticipating some of his later works in prose, his first foray into novel writing showcases his consummate dexterity in mixing literary genres, blending factual and invented elements, and even pasting ready-made passages from other literary sources into his own text. In stylistic terms, it is remarkably similar both to the observational narrative tone of the poems in *Feuilles de route* and the curt, perfunctory economy of his cinematographic stories such as *La Perle fiévreuse* or *La Fin du monde filmée par l'ange N.-D.* Like the latter, it is written largely in the present tense, employing unadorned prose. Its register is relatively informal, and the writing avoids embellishment and complex syntactical features such as embedded or relative clauses. The text is divided into chapters, which are subdivided into numbered sections ranging in length from a mere ten lines or so to a few pages; this technique resembles the style of notation that Cendrars adopted during his experience as a writer of film scripts.

The narrative approach explores the extreme ends of the syntactic spectrum: it frequently employs short sentences consisting of a single main subject and verb construction; these alternate periodically with extremely long sentences which are not grammatically complex but merely construct lengthy lists linked by commas. In the sixth section of Chapter II, in which the narrator charts Suter's progress upon his arrival in North America, the text explores both of these syntactic extremes in close succession:

> Il s'enfonce de plus en plus en ville. Il travaille chez un drapier, chez un droguiste, dans une charcuterie. Il s'associe avec un Roumain et fait du colportage. Il est palefrenier dans un cirque. Puis maréchal-ferrand, dentiste, empailleur, vend la rose de Jéricho dans une voiture dorée, s'établit tailleur pour dames, travaille dans une scierie, boxe un Nègre géant et gagne un esclave et une bourse de cent guinées, remange de la vache enragée, enseigne les mathématiques chez les Pères de la Mission, apprend l'anglais, le français, le hongrois, le portugais, le petit nègre de la Louisiane, le sioux, le comanche, le slang, l'espagnol, s'avance encore plus dans l'ouest, traverse la ville, franchit l'eau, sort en banlieue, ouvre un mastroquet dans un faubourg.
>
> (He is plunging more and more deeply into the life of the city. He works in a draper's shop, at a drugstore, a delicatessen. He goes into partnership with a Romanian and becomes a door-to-door salesman. He works as a groom in a circus. Then, as a shoeing-smith, a dentist, a taxidermist; he sells Jericho roses from a gilded wagon, sets up as a ladies' tailor, works in a sawmill, boxes a Black giant and wins a slave and a purse of one hundred guineas; for a time, he is down-and-out; he teaches mathematics with the Mission fathers, learns English, French, Hungarian, Portuguese, the pidgin dialect of Louisiana, Sioux, Comanche, American slang, Spanish. Advancing still further towards the West, he moves to the other side of the city, crosses the river, reaches the outskirts and opens a saloon in an outlying suburb.)[41]

The elasticity of his syntax, already demonstrated in his pre-war poems as well as *Kodak (Documentaire)* and *Feuilles de route*, is again in evidence in *L'Or*. In a perceptive study, Andrew Rothwell examines the relationship between accumulation and enumeration in these long lists, noting how they contribute to a 'collage' of different types of discourse that work together to undermine the normally stable signifying structures of literature.[42] Cendrars's narrative takes extreme spatial and temporal leaps which arguably also derive from his experience of the cinematic jump cut and his understanding of the visual power of montage editing. Towards the end of the fourth part of the second chapter, in which the narrative recounts Suter's journey by boat from Le Havre to New York, we encounter a sentence that jumps a full fourteen years without comment; it is followed only four short sentences later by an observation, as specific as it is laconic, which informs us that the day of the week is a Sunday.[43] By contrast, when Sutter reaches the Pacific shore, its unspoilt natural beauty, and the threat humans pose to it, are conveyed concisely in an extreme close-up: 'Quand Suter se met à marcher, il écrase un grand nombre de mollusques vésiculeux couleur de rose et qui éclatent avec bruit.' (When Sutter starts walking, he crushes a great many rose-coloured vesicular molluscs, which burst with a loud plop.)[44]

The narrative occasionally abandons grammatically correct sentence structures altogether, replacing them with anaphoric fragments that provide the minimum of information but read like a form of free verse poetry (the first three lines, read aloud, become a perfect alexandrine):

> Le port.
> Le port de New York.
> 1834.
> C'est là que débarquent tous les naufragés du Vieux Monde.
>
> (The port.
> The port of New York.
> 1834.
> It is here that all the shipwrecked souls from the Old World disembark.)[45]

Moments such as this confirm the impression that Cendrars sees the format of the novel as an opportunity to consolidate and extend the experimentation that he had already developed as a poet. The fact that the lines cited above engage with the discovery of the New World makes Cendrars's unconventional approach all the more appropriate: the discovery of the foreign land is the perfect basis for the writer's own reinvention of himself. The impression that this short sequence creates is, first, that of a cinematic close-up of a port whose location is not yet recognizable. As the camera withdraws, its environment begins to become identifiable as belonging to New York. The year 1834 reads like a subtitle of a kind that is still encountered on the cinema screen as an economical means of indicating the passage of time or simply locating a given scene at a particular historical moment. The camera then pans back to reveal the diverse travellers disembarking from the ship. Such a reading is, of course, selective and unrepresentative of the novel as a whole; yet it does offer a glimpse of the extent to which Cendrars's cinematographic experience continued to exert an influence on his writing style as a novelist.

One senses that Cendrars may have written *L'Or* with the book market and the film industry in mind. The adoption of a concise narrative style, a clear linear plot and short numbered sections containing visually charged observations does indeed point towards this. The whole of the seventh chapter runs to a mere nine lines that resemble intertitles for a silent film:

> Rêverie. Calme. Repos.
> C'est la paix.
> Non. Non. Non. Non. Non. Non. Non. Non. Non: c'est l'OR!
> C'est l'or.
> Le rush.
> La fièvre de l'or qui s'abat sur le monde.
> La grande ruée de 1848, 49, 50, 51 et qui durera quinze ans.
> SAN FRANCISCO!
>
> (Reverie. Calm. Repose.
> It is peace.
> No. No. No. No. No. No. No. No. No: it is GOLD!
> It is gold.
> The gold rush.
> The world is infected with gold fever.
> The great gold rush of 1848, 1849, 1850 and 1851. It will last for 15 years.
> SAN FRANCISCO!)[46]

The exceptionally detailed critical apparatus in the Pléiade edition of Cendrars's collected works includes three fascinating texts which confirm that he considered potential opportunities for the book to become a movie. These writings reflect the high profile that Cendrars attained in the wake of the novel's unprecedented success, both in literary circles and in the broader creative sphere.[47]

The first of these is the text of an interview from 1925, when Cendrars was interviewed by François and André Berge on the subject of cinema for the publication *Les Cahiers du mois*.[48] Having been invited to contribute an article to it, the author was unable to do so because of other commitments and instead suggested that the editors conduct the interview. He shares his thoughts on the new language of film, on the close-up technique pioneered by Griffith, on his preference for American comedies over avant-garde experimentation. He reveals his plan to make a film about the history of Brazil in which its rivers and forests would be the main characters. The interview concludes with a question about the influence of cinema on *La Fin du monde* and *L'Or*. Cendrars acknowledges that the former is 'virtually a script' but plays down the particular influence of cinema on *L'Or*. He attributes its main influence to 'the whole of modern life', which he describes as everything from motor cars to modern plumbing to navigation companies.

The second and third documents relating to *L'Or* were written by Cendrars. The earlier of these is an intriguing 'dactylogramme' (typescript) dated 1926 and containing various words typed with upper-case initials or entirely in upper case letters. In it, he sets out the details of a possible subplot to be inserted into a cinematographic adaptation of the novel. This addition was to be based around a female character, a choice that may explain his description of this imagined film as historic, sentimental and artistic.[49] This lavish production, which he dubs a 'SUPERPRODUCTION', would be 'UNFORGETTABLE' since it would have something to offer all levels of society in countries throughout the world.

The second of Cendrars's additional documents, written in 1938, is a project for a radio adaptation of the novel. It includes the detailed enumeration of various sound effects such as ships' sirens, the peal of bells, crowd noises, indigenous American music, gunshots and various other auditory embellishments, including the croaking of frogs and the howling of coyotes.

The paratextual additions that serve as bookends for *L'Or* deserve mention. The text is prefaced by two epigraphs, both of which are taken from Cendrars's writings. The first is a passage from *Le Panama* in which he alludes to the story of General Suter; the second is an excerpt from his 'Pro Domo', written in 1918, which offers proof of Cendrars's insistent preoccupation with this subject.

In the 1930s and thereafter, Cendrars embarked on a series of commissions to write reportage. In these we find him once again challenging any straightforward distinction between the novel and the journalistic essay. In some instances, the same text serves both functions; such an approach characterizes *La Vie secrète de Jean Galmot (Rhum)* (The Secret Life of Jean Galmot (Rum)), whose eponymous protagonist was a real-life businessman, traveller and writer. Cendrars's account of his life appeared as a newspaper reportage and shortly afterwards in book form. Myriam Boucharenc has spoken about these tactics that allowed Cendrars to double the return for his efforts, a practice that helped him to make a living at a time when it was far from easy to do so.[50] Later chapters will discuss Cendrars's books based on remarkable lives that bring features of reportage into the framework of prose fiction. The next two chapters, however, will examine Cendrars's next forays into novel writing; as they attempt to demonstrate, his publications in this genre are strikingly varied and encompass an extraordinary stylistic breadth. *Moravagine* and the two tomes based on the character Dan Yack move away from the portrayal of historical figures in order to create fictional personae; for all that these novels are stylistically poles apart from *L'Or*, they share with it their obsession with characters who reflect and project aspects of their author's personality. All of them, in their dramatically different ways, prove Cendrars to be a writer of exceptional talent.

five

A Dangerous Mind: *Moravagine*

At the start of 1926, Cendrars set off to Brazil for the second time, arriving in Rio on 25 January to join Paolo Prado. He was thus far from the Parisian literary scene, and at a safe distance from the French press, when his brilliant and deeply troubling novel *Moravagine* was published by Grasset the following month. He had spent time working on it during his previous stay in Brazil in 1924, when he was living at Santa Veridiana, Prado's fazenda in the state of São Paulo; but the book was not completed until the following year, when he was back in France and living at the home of Eugenia Errázuriz in Biarritz. This novel, diametrically different in almost every way from *L'Or*, is one of the most intense and hallucinatory books of that era and has attracted comparisons with Beckett and Céline.

The fact that the book made it into published form at all is surprising, given that in 1917, in a letter to his friend Jean Cocteau, Cendrars described his literary project as 'a monster'.[1] The personification applies equally well to the task of writing the book and to its eponymous principal character, a mentally unstable and violent mass murderer and child molester. As Christine Le Quellec Cottier has observed, the parallels between the eponymous character Moravagine and Cendrars's book project are many and far-reaching.[2] The combined presence of Moravagine/*Moravagine* in Cendrars's consciousness over such a long period tells us much about the book's particular identity as a textual construct.

Moravagine is a highly complex novel, so much so that it is difficult to reconcile with any straightforward definition of this literary genre. It is a multilayered textual artefact that employs an array of narrative strategies that intrigue and often disconcert the reader. But the book's single most troubling aspect is the titular character himself. In the novel we encounter a trope that runs through much of Cendrars's oeuvre, namely the idea of an alter ego. Curiously, a character called Blaise Cendrars appears in *Moravagine* – just one of many instances in which the author explores the ambiguities of the first-person narrative voice – but there are strong grounds for suggesting that Cendrars created the novel's eponymous anti-hero as a negative double of himself. As he writes elsewhere, and repeatedly, citing the words of Gérard de Nerval, 'Je suis l'Autre' (I am the Other).[3]

After the death of his friend Hélène Kleinmann in 1907, Cendrars was treated for depression in the Waldau clinic, and it is thought to be there that he first made the acquaintance of Adolf Wölfli, who is best known as an outsider artist; this experience may have given rise to the characterization of Moravagine. In addition to this real-life source, an array of literary and cinematic intertexts suggest that as much of Cendrars's inspiration came from the pages of books as it did from lived experience: besides Remy de Gourmont's *Sixtine*, openly acknowledged in the epigraph, Flückiger has identified a range of possible literary influences that range from Maupassant, Huysmans and *La Messe des morts* by the Polish novelist Stanislas Przybyzewski to the popular serial *Fantômas* and Camille Flammarion's *Astronomie populaire*.

The Pléiade edition of Cendrars's collected works also contains two highly revealing source texts, parts of which found their way into Cendrars's novel. The first of these is an extract from the memoirs of a Swiss man, Joseph Fessler, significant aspects of whose life (a childhood leg injury; fanatical views; the perpetration of child abuse; incarceration) reappear in the character of Moravagine.[4] Fessler is thought to be the 'sad individual' and child molester whom Cendrars met in 1907 and who he claims inspired the character Moravagine.[5] More compelling still is the segment from a book called *La Philosophie de Golgotha* written in 1906 by the German author Franz Blazek, which Cendrars translated into French in 1912.[6] The book's main protagonist and first-person narrator becomes involved in an anarchist revolutionary party in Central and Eastern Europe with a clandestine press in Warsaw. He has a violent and abusive relationship with a woman called Mascha, who falls pregnant and commits suicide by swallowing poison. He witnesses the Russo-Japanese War. He acclaims Nietzsche's *Übermensch* and aspires to emulate this figure of superhuman strength. He takes part in brutal raids of the Jewish quarter and commits numerous acts of torture. Moravagine does indeed seem to walk in his shadow.

Moravagine also contains numerous borrowings from, and references to, other works by Cendrars: these include expressions, descriptive passages or lines of his poems, which are inserted into chapters of the book; Chapter w is entirely devoted to a literary work called *La Fin du monde*, which, as we have seen, occupied an especially important place in Cendrars's body of work; here, however, the title appears in fictionalized form and is attributed to Moravagine, who is said to have used it for a portion of his manuscripts. The narrator, Raymond la Science, informs us that he has enlisted a certain Blaise Cendrars with the task of publishing Moravagine's notes and possibly even making a film based on them.

Perhaps the most high-profile intertextual connection involving *Moravagine* is with Céline's first novel *Voyage au bout de la nuit*, published in 1932. When it appeared in print to great acclaim that year, Cendrars expressed his astonishment that none of its commentators had spotted the close similarities between Céline's book and his own novel, which had appeared in the previous decade.[7] Jay Bochner concurs, writing: 'the similarities between *Moravagine* and *Voyage au bout de la nuit* are flagrant, and I do not know why no one has chosen to explore them.'[8] He points to the extensive and troubling catalogue of parallels between the novels:

> Both novels have doctor-narrators, Céline's Bardamu and Cendrars's Raymond, and both doctors have complex, obsessional relationships with mad doubles – Bardamu with Robinson, who lives like an outlaw and precedes Bardamu in all his escapades, whether to the front, Africa, or America, and whose death from morphine injections ends the novel; and Raymond with Moravagine, whom he frees to lead an outlaw life, who drags Raymond across Germany, Russia, North and South America, and who haunts Raymond's imagination at the front. Like Robinson, Moravagine dies from morphine at the end. Even the name Moravagine finds its counterpart in Céline's Doctor Parapine (playing, I suppose, hoist-the-male-member to Cendrars's death-to-the-vagina). Parapine lies in wait for little girls outside schools and ends up in an asylum; Cendrars begins with Moravagine in an asylum, and after Raymond helps him to escape he immediately begins killing little girls.[9]

As archival research has revealed, the tortuous process from conception to completion led Cendrars up several blind alleys before arriving at the definitive version of *Moravagine*. Flückiger notes that in 1916,

Cendrars still intended to write various novellas, one of which would bear the title 'L'Indifférent' (The Indifferent Man). The connection with *Moravagine* is confirmed by a letter that Cendrars wrote that year to Robert Delaunay:

> [. . .] puis j'ai repris mon roman Moravagine l'idiot, quelque chose que je ne sais comment appeler sur l'Indifférent qui se fiche de tout, qui est fatigué de tout et qui aime passionnément tout, qui perd dans la vie, multiple. Je ne sais ce que cela deviendra.
>
> ([. . .] and I have returned to my novel Moravagine the idiot, something I am struggling to put into words about the Indifferent Man who couldn't care less about anything, who is tired of everything and loves everything with a passion, who loses in life, who is multiple. I don't know what will become of it.)[10]

Flückiger and other researchers have trawled the Cendrars archives in Bern in order to construct a detailed genealogy of the intra- and intertextual connections that radiate from *Moravagine* at various stages of its composition and bring it into contact with Cendrars's other writings. As discussed above, the novel was intended to be a part of the vast project with the overarching title *La Fin du monde*. This never reached completion, but it did spawn *Profond aujourd'hui*, 'Les Armoires chinoises', *L'Eubage* and *La Fin du monde filmée par l'Ange N.-D.*, all of which originated in 1917, an extraordinarily productive period in Cendrars's career as he recovered from his mutilation on the battlefields of Champagne.

Structure

Narrative structure is just one of the many respects in which *Moravagine* is an extraordinary novel; indeed, it is characteristic of Cendrars's relentless desire for experimentation that he should have produced this complex, intriguing composition so early in his career as a novelist. The title, which is the name of the eponymous anti-hero, is itself symbolic: it is no coincidence that the name of a pathological mysogynist and mass murderer of women should be so phonetically and orthographically close to 'mort-à-vagins' (death-to-vaginas). But the name Moravagine also refers us back discreetly to Cendrars's own experience, and in this respect, it is just one of many respects in which this book blurs any straightforward distinction between fact and fiction. In the opening lines of 'Vol à voile', the first part of the autobiographical prose text *Sous le signe de François Villon*, Cendrars claims that at the age of fifteen he worked for a man called Rovogine.[11] Scholars initially dismissed this as an invention, but Oxana Khlopina's doctoral thesis asserts that a Grigori Alexandrovich Rogovin did indeed work for the jeweller Leuba, who was Cendrars's employer at that time.[12]

A feature of this novel that deserves mention is its extensive apparatus of paratextual additions. The first we encounter are the epigraph, taken from a novel by Remy de Gourmont, and the preface, which bears the signature of Blaise Cendrars but contains a letter from Raymond la Science. After these, we encounter the main body of the novel itself, which falls into 26 chapters, listed from a to z. The language used in these varies considerably in tone, register and content, and the length of the chapters is extremely divergent too, ranging from a mere two lines to sixty pages of the Denoël edition.[13] Here as elsewhere, Cendrars's approach to narrative structure is characterized by its extraordinary elasticity. At the end of the novel, we encounter a further autobiographical text, largely written in 1917 but added by Cendrars over three decades later, in 1951. Entitled 'Pro domo: comment j'ai écrit *Moravagine* (papiers retrouvés)' (Pro Domo: How I Wrote *Moravagine* (Rediscovered Papers)), this supplementary text helps to shed considerable light on the lengthy and complex creative process of which the novel is the product. This additional text far exceeds the function and scope normally allocated to appendices or other paratextual additions, thereby adding a further layer of complexity to the multilayered textual construct initially published in 1926.

Such an accumulation of literary apparatus on the margins of *Moravagine* stands in sharp contrast to the core of the novel itself, which in certain significant respects is lacunary. The gap or hole at the centre of the novel has been analysed in detail, but it is worth returning to this topic, especially in light of the excesses that characterize the novel's plot and coexist with it in a contrapuntal relationship. In one of the earliest detailed analyses of this theme, Stephen K. Bellstrom focuses on the book's longest chapter, k, 'Mascha', and the eponymous character around whose life and death it revolves.[14] Mascha is a Lithuanian Jew whom Moravagine and Raymond first encounter in Warsaw, where she is running their anarchist terrorist group's clandestine press.[15] She quickly becomes heavily involved in plotting their activities, demonstrating a capacity to be cold-hearted and calculating; she also becomes

Moravagine's lover, and it is when she is with him that an unexpected aspect of her character comes to light. She expresses a sentimentality and vulnerability, both exploited by Moravagine, that seem quite out of keeping with her cold-hearted nature and her brilliantly calculating ability to engage the support of the group's followers.[16] As Bellstrom observes, this vulnerability is expressed in terms of an emptying out that connects with other lacunae throughout the novel and constructs a unity from accumulated absences: the book's narrative structure and its network of symbolic references are thus inhabited by 'a narrative gap, a philosophical void, an anatomical hole, and a *lapsus memoriae*'.[17] Moravagine's chosen method of killing involves disembowelling his victims. To these we can add the numerous architectural and topographic references to empty interiors and hidden spaces, including the clandestine group's base, which is hidden away inside a hollowed-out structure in the polytechnical institute. At the end of the chapter, Raymond and Moravagine attempt to evade capture and certain death by looking for a hiding place in the dark carriage of a goods train; in the 'holes' of Raymond's torchlight they discover Mascha's hanged, disembowelled body and the dead foetus suspended between her legs. The two fugitives promptly hide inside large barrels, leaving Mascha's corpse suspended in the knowledge that this grisly sight will provide sufficient distraction to enable them to go unnoticed when the carriage door is opened at Riga.

Themes

The storyline centres on Raymond, a young medic specializing in psychiatric care, who takes a close interest in a patient named Moravagine, whose symptoms are deemed to be beyond help. Raymond develops a friendship with him and eventually helps him to escape from the institution where he has been incarcerated. Upon his liberation, Moravagine embarks on a spree of violence that takes him around the world, leaving a trail of destruction and death in his wake. The book charts his entire life from his birth to his death. Along the way, he and his companion travel to numerous cities, including Berlin, Moscow, Tokyo, Beijing, London, New Orleans, San Antonio, Montreal and Quebec. But Earth alone could never suffice in a novel like this; so, in Chapter w, we learn that Moravagine had even stayed on Mars and had created a dictionary of the 200,000 principal meanings of the sole word of the Martian language.[18]

The book opens with a quotation from *Sixtine*, the novel by Remy de Gourmont. The choice is significant for this book specifically, but also for Cendrars's literary oeuvre as a whole, since it sums up the ideal to which he aspires:

> Je montrerai comment ce peu de bruit intérieur, qui n'est rien, contient tout, comment, avec l'appui bacillaire d'une seule sensation, toujours la même et déformée dès son origine, un cerveau isolé du monde peut se créer un monde.
>
> (I shall show how this little inward bluster, which is nothing, contains everything, how, with the support of a single sensation always the same and distorted from its very inception, a brain isolated from the world can create a world for itself.)[19]

In these lines we find an echo of Schopenhauer's words as expressed in *The World as Will and Representation* that served as a mantra for Cendrars: 'Le monde est ma représentation.'[20]

The epigraph can be interpreted as serving advance warning of what is to come. It leads on to the preface, written in the first person and identifying its author as Blaise Cendrars. The addition of the place and date of writing, La Mimoseraie, April–November 1925, immediately confers on this paratext a factual status that throws readers into confusion as to what kind of work they are reading. (Located in Biarritz, La Mimoseraie was the home of Cendrars's patron and friend Eugenia Errázuriz.) Our puzzlement merely grows as the preface refers to manuscripts hidden away along with a syringe in the secret compartment of a locked trunk in the author's attic, which is also locked shut. The manuscripts, syringe and trunk, we learn, belong to a Spanish prisoner, who is then revealed to be Moravagine. The narrator, identifying himself as Blaise Cendrars, reveals that the story we are about to read consists of Moravagine's notes, transcribed from the manuscripts in the trunk; as he points out, these notes are themselves a mere preface to Moravagine's complete works, which the narrator will one day edit. The narrator 'Blaise Cendrars' then reproduces in full a letter that he had received from a condemned man called Raymond la Science. This letter, 'Cendrars' tells us, had come into his possession during his stay in Brazil, and so alarming were its contents that he was forced to return to Europe. The letter had been written in a prison cell in Barcelona, where Raymond was waiting to be executed on a charge of regicide.

As this makes clear, the preface already conflates fact and fiction, observable reality and invention. Numerous specific details evoke an entirely plausible facticity, starting with the address in Paris where Cendrars actually lived. This is just one of a whole string of elements that conspire to suggest that we are reading a factual report: other compelling details include the place and time, the brand of syringe, the use of real names and the fact that 'Blaise Cendrars' reports that he was staying at a fazenda in Santa Veridiana, which is not only a real location, but moreover is exactly where he lived during his first visit to Brazil in 1924 as a guest of Oswald de Andrade. Another element of the preface that inevitably brings fiction and real life into close proximity is Raymond's mention that he lost a leg in the war. The reader's suspicion that this is an allusion to Cendrars's own war trauma is borne out in Chapter 1, 'L'Ile Sainte-Marguerite' (Saint-Marguerite Island), where Raymond narrates his encounter with Blaise Cendrars in a hospital in Cannes shortly after the latter had had his right arm amputated. Even the name of Raymond la Science, while not the name of an actual person, was the nickname of Raymond Callemin, a member of the Bande à Bonnot, a notorious anarchist criminal gang led by Jules Bonnot which was active in and around Paris in the pre-war years, and whose nefarious activities are mentioned in Chapter 0. Running counter to these invocations of the real, and threatening to undo their claims to veracity, are various references to more inherently inventive – not to say fictitious – ways of relating events. The narrator 'Blaise Cendrars' hints that Raymond la Science is not the prisoner's real name but merely a convenient pseudonym; he also explicitly invokes the act of artistic representation by means of different creative practices, describing Raymond la Science's miserable appearance in the prison cell as being 'comme sur une estampe de Goya' (like on a Goya print).[21] Raymond la Science describes himself in his letter as being neither an anarchist nor a thug 'comme on nous représente habituellement au cinéma' (as we are usually depicted in films).[22] These overt allusions to different forms of artistic practice may be intended to serve as a warning to the reader not to interpret what follows as the truth, even though the context in which they are presented seems to assert the reality and credibility of what we are reading. These conflicting impressions create a tension that runs throughout the entire novel and anticipate the questions we will ask ourselves as we read it: is this real or fictitious? As is so often the case with Cendrars, the answer lies somewhere in between these two poles.

The 26 chapters are as widely divergent in subject-matter and location as they are in length. The book is divided into three sections entitled, respectively, 'L'Esprit d'une époque' (The Spirit of an Era), 'La Vie de Moravagine, idiot' (The Life of Moravagine, Idiot), and 'Les Manuscrits de Moravagine' (Moravagine's Manuscripts). In the first of these, Cendrars has his narrator Raymond launch into a diatribe against what he sees as the unacceptable behaviour of the medical profession regarding its punitive treatment of the insane. As Raymond puts it: 'je voulais dresser un réquisitoire terrible contre les psychiatres, déterminer leur psychologie, circonscrire, définir leur conscience professionnellement déformée, détruire leur pouvoir, les livrer à la vindicte publique.' (I wanted to draw up a terrible accusation against these psychiatrists, expose their psychology, circumscribe and define their misshapen professional conscience, destroy their power and deliver them up to public obloquy.)[23] Criticism of the psychiatric profession is a recurrent theme in Surrealist writings and appears prominently in André Breton's *Nadja* (1928). The psychiatric institutions that open and close *Moravagine* represent the forces of authority and convention; they are the manifestation of state-sanctioned powers that are staunchly opposed to free spirits or those who transgress their laws. Moravagine is the archetypal individualist, never complying with rules laid down by society, wholly and uncompromisingly committed to his chosen path of destruction and violence. He is above all an allegorical figure, and his fate is unmistakably, ineluctably, tragically, that of the nascent century in which the action takes place.

Early in the second part of the book, Raymond transcribes Moravagine's verbal account of his upbringing. It is a tale of perpetual motion, a journey to the very darkest recesses of human depravity. Moravagine is the last descendant of the Hungarian royal family, denied accession by the establishment of the Austro-Hungarian Empire. His life story is remarkable, and from an early stage it becomes clear that he is precociously brutal: he is raised alone in a huge castle and married at the age of six to little princess Rita. The two are separated almost straight away, but each year she pays him a visit on the anniversary of their marriage. Moravagine becomes worryingly, dangerously possessed by his absent love, whom he raises to the status of an ideal. Aged ten, he attempts to escape by burning down the stables and strapping himself to his horse, but the horse is shot, and he sustains permanent injury to his legs. A sickening glimpse of the evil of which he is capable occurs when, aged fifteen, he tires of his pet sheepdog and, after gouging its eyes out slowly and expertly, he kills it by breaking a chair on its back.[24] When he turns eighteen, Rita visits him again, but on this occasion she tells him that this is the last time they will see one another. Moravagine's displeasure at this news can be measured by the fact that he strangles, then stabs and disembowels her. He is imprisoned for ten years, then interned for a further six at the Waldensee asylum, where he makes the acquaintance of Raymond. With the latter's help, he escapes, stopping only to kill a little girl as she collects wood in the hospital grounds. The two men spend three years in Germany, where Moravagine continues to kill women and children, sowing terror throughout Berlin and acquiring the nickname 'Jack the Ripper'. The two protagonists then flee to Russia, where they become active members of a nihilist terrorist organization. Moravagine develops a relationship with a young woman, Mascha, who becomes pregnant by him. She betrays the entire group to the authorities, as a result of which all the conspirators are killed, except for Moravagine and Raymond, who manage to reach Great Britain, from where they travel to the United States. There they meet a Frenchman, Lathuille, with whom they travel by boat up to the source of the Orinoco River. Having inflicted substantial damage on the Jivaro people who hosted their stay there, they return to France, and both end up fighting in the First World War. It fails to kill them but does leave Raymond with an amputated leg and Moravagine again incarcerated, this time in a state of irretrievable insanity in an asylum on the Ile Sainte-Marguerite, a tiny island near Cannes, where he writes sheaves of notes about his travels to Mars. He dies in the asylum on 17 February 1917, aged 51, in the same room once occupied by the individual known as the Man in the Iron Mask, most famously immortalized in the novel of that name by Alexandre Dumas *père*. Raymond was not present at the time of death or at the funeral, but he reproduces all five pages of the medical report setting out in considerable detail Moravagine's year-long decline. True to form, Cendrars based this report on a textual readymade, a scholarly article that had appeared in *La Presse médicale* in July 1917, which he incorporated virtually unchanged, preserving the subject-specific complexity of its terminology and importing it into the novel.[25]

The frenetic action that carries the reader from chapter to chapter, baroque in its excess and disturbing in its perversity, suggests a profoundly troubling world view. Yet, like the preface, the book's chapters contain passages that clearly derive from Cendrars's own experiences. An example of this is Chapter j, 'Arrivé en Russie' (Arrived in Russia), which unfolds in late September 1904. As Flückiger confirms, the young Freddy Sauser went to Russia at the end of that same month, having fared badly in his studies at the business school in Neuchâtel. He spent three months in Moscow before embarking on an apprenticeship in St Petersburg with the jeweller Henri Albert Leuba, for whom he would work for a little over two years.[26]

The chapter recounts the end of the Russo-Japanese War and the first stirrings of the 1905 Revolution; still to follow are 'des actes inouïs d'héroïsme et de sadisme' (unheard-of acts of heroism and sadism) that will reach ever more extreme depths of depravity.[27] Yet the chapter opens with an elegant evocation of Moscow as the young Freddy Sauser must have seen it in 1904:

> Moscou est belle comme une sainte napolitaine. Un ciel céruléen reflète, mire, biseaute les mille et mille tours, clochers, campaniles qui se dressent, s'étirent, se cabrent ou, retombant lourdement, s'évasent, se bulbent comme des stalactites polychromes dans un bouillonnement, un vermicellement de lumière.
>
> (Moscow is as beautiful as a Neapolitan saint. An azure sky reflects, examines, marks the bevel of the thousand-thousand towers, steeples, and campaniles that rise and stretch up, rearing, or fall back heavily in fat, bulbous forms like many-coloured stalactites, bubbling and crawling with light.)[28]

This passage reminds us of Cendrars's earlier description of that city in *Prose du Transsibérien*; but it also calls to mind the vision of the modern city, unspecified but presumably Paris, that resembles a primal forest in the opening lines of *Profond aujourd'hui*, with its profusion of trams squealing like monkeys holding each other by the tail.[29]

The close coexistence of narrative beauty and passages conveying acts of extreme violence alerts us to the fundamentally dualistic nature of *Moravagine* – or rather, to the absence of any differentiation at the level of narrative between such contrasting experiences. This is just one of the respects in which the book inhabits and conflates realms normally regarded as incompatible. Against this background, Cendrars's choice of a passage from *Sixtine* as the epigraph seems judicious: the fact that Gourmont's novel is subtitled 'novel of cerebral life' is significant in light of what Cendrars does with his book and the relationship he creates between the eponymous main character and his travelling companion-cum-narrator, Raymond la Science. The latter insists on his role as a detached observer and a scientist; he adopts a degree of distance from the unhinged actions of Moravagine and repeatedly retreats into the world of books, in which he clearly and understandably feels safer than in the violent world that Moravagine inhabits. Yet Raymond finds himself increasingly contaminated by his sustained exposure to Moravagine's immoral behaviour: by Chapter p, Raymond tries to return to his studies but finds himself hamstrung by inactivity and unable to write a word. Even reading becomes a struggle, and a decade spent with Moravagine has muddled his thoughts. Fittingly, as he puts his book down, he leans against a gargoyle in the form of a braying donkey clad in a hat, while Moravagine performs aerial stunts in his aeroplane.[30]

Still in Chapter p, an exchange between Moravagine and Raymond reflects their respective attitudes towards the realms of action on the one hand and reading on the other. As Moravagine addresses his companion, he expresses his undisguised scorn for him and those of his ilk who read books, intellectualize and attempt to categorize the world:

> Laisse donc ça aux archivistes-policiers. Tu n'as donc pas encore compris que le monde de la pensée est fichu et que la philosophie c'est pis que le bertillonnage. Vous me faites rire avec votre angoisse métaphysique, e'est la frousse qui vous étreint, la peur de la vie, la peur des hommes d'action, de l'action, du désordre. Mais tout n'est que désordre, mon bon.
>
> (Why don't you leave that to the police archives? Haven't you got it through your head that human thought is a thing of the past and that philosophy is worse than Bertillon's guide to harassed cops? You make me laugh with your metaphysical anguish, it's just that you're scared silly, frightened of life, of men of action, of action in itself, of lack of order. But everything is disorder, dear boy.)[31]

At the start of the novel, it seemed that in certain senses Moravagine and Raymond represented opposite approaches to life: on the one hand, the world of deeds and instinct, and on the other, that of reflection and conceptualization. This dualistic pattern is steadily effaced and replaced by a more nuanced one whereby Raymond tacitly approves of

Moravagine's atavistic urges and his violent impulses. His veil of scientific detachment is nothing but that; he fails to stop Moravagine from wreaking havoc wherever he goes. As Bochner puts it:

> the two men are an indissoluble pair, the seemingly coincidental, but actually destined, or synchronistically determined meeting of an ambitious but weak, overcivilized doctor with a fauve humain who has no ambition but is extraordinarily powerful and entirely uncivilized. In this meeting of pure force and its repressed aspirant Cendrars split the schizoid personality of the times into its two natural parts, each hidden from the other. Thus separated, the beast became mythical, and the socialized recognized his own cruel depths.[32]

Bochner's persuasive socio-political reading reminds us that even through his most seemingly fictional characters, Cendrars is making pertinent and probing comments on the times he was living in. Moravagine continues:

> Ça a toujours été comme ça. Pourquoi voulez-vous y mettre de l'ordre ? Quel ordre ? Que cherchez-vous ? Il n'y a pas de vérité. Il n'y a que l'action, l'action qui obéit à un million de mobiles différents, l'action éphémère, l'action qui subit toutes les contingences possibles et imaginables, l'action antagoniste. La vie. La vie c'est le crime, le vol, la jalousie, la faim, le mensonge, le foutre, la bêtise, les maladies, les éruptions volcaniques, les tremblements de terre, des monceaux de cadavres. Tu n'y peux rien, mon pauvre vieux, tu ne vas pas te mettre à pondre des livres, hein?
>
> (It's always been that way. Why are you trying to make something out of it? And what would you make? What are you looking for? There is no truth. There's only action, action obeying a million different impulses, ephemeral action, action subjected to every possible and imaginable contingency and contradiction. Life. Life is crime, theft, jealousy, hunger, lies, spunk, stupidity, sickness, volcanic eruptions, earthquakes, piles of corpses. What can you do about it, my poor friend? You're not about to start writing books, are you?)[33]

Three days later, history seems to prove Moravagine's point as the Great War breaks out, confirming the futility of any attempt to impose order or rationalism on life. The story of Moravagine had begun in 1900, the year of his and Raymond's encounter, and in a sense the chaos and turmoil that characterize the action throughout the entire novel up to this point pave the way for the mass insanity that would be unleashed throughout Europe from 1914 to 1918.

The overriding tenor of the book is unremittingly despondent, but some critics argue that it offers glimpses of more positive interpretations. For Bochner, Moravagine encapsulates 'a return to instinct, thus to nature, which is the reflex of an oppressed, over-socialized civilization heading straight for the catastrophe of world war'. Observing that Moravagine had initially embarked on the study of music when he and Raymond went to Berlin, Bochner draws a useful distinction between this and the course of action he chose to take shortly afterwards: experiencing the world, immersing oneself in the rhythms of life, is a far cry from merely analysing it from the position of detachment that comes with academic study. If there is a positive message to glean from the book, then perhaps it is that life is to be lived and relished, and not merely viewed from afar. As Bochner puts it, '[Moravagine's] life is a curse, but he abandons himself to it because it *is* life, which the study of life manifestly was not.'[34] Bochner argues that Moravagine deserves to be regarded as someone who remains admirably in control of situations, even when they result in his defeat and necessitate his hurried departure. His life can be considered a success 'because he is a man of action who has no prejudices, carries no imperative and compelling past, and thus instinctively discovers and submits himself to the revealing rhythm of all he encounters'.[35] Persuasive as this rationale is, it is still not quite enough to deter readers from objecting to the shockingly misogynist violence that runs throughout the book.

One of the other few signs of hope in the novel lies in the principle of utility, a subject about which Cendrars wrote an eponymous essay, which he imported into the novel, becoming its Chapter III, 'Nos randonnées en Amérique' (Our Travels in America). It makes for an unusual chapter in the book, since it dispenses with Raymond's narrative voice and interrupts the narrative flow. Instead of Moravagine's debauched actions, we read an appraisal of contemporary life in the USA; the narrative celebrates modern industry and civil engineering and hails some of the developments in science and technology that have changed people's lives. Not only is this chapter an odd insertion, wholly out of place amid the tumultuous actions that precede and follow it, but it is a bold one, since it contains elements copied and pasted from other sources. These include a passage lifted virtually wholesale, and without quotation marks or any bibliographical acknowledgement, from a book by the author Charles-Albert Cingria – whose name is cited before the passage in question starts, as if to throw a clue to the inquisitive reader. The second borrowed passage is taken from a volume of the *Nouvelle Géographie universelle*. In appropriating and relocating these excerpts, perhaps Cendrars wished to undertake a 'supercherie poétique' of the sort that turned Gustave Le Rouge's popular novel into the poetry collection *Kodak*? Or perhaps his intention was to initiate what we could think of as a form of 'uncreative writing', to use a concept coined in reference to the experimental literature of the late twentieth and early twenty-first century?[36] The place that such borrowed passages as these occupy alongside the rest of the novel points towards the very tension that runs throughout the book and underpins its implicit message: it blurs the identity of the narrating self, negates any straightforward dialectical relationship between self and other, problematizes both, and suggests that neither is wholly intact or free of the other, like the couple of misfits who form a dysfunctional yet brotherly bond throughout the pages of *Moravagine*.

In 'Pro Domo', Cendrars explains that he was haunted by Moravagine for many years. The idea of writing this character first occurred to him before the Great War, springing up quite unexpectedly during a conversation in a bar in Paris. The figure of Moravagine continued to inhabit his consciousness throughout his time at the front and during his recuperation from his amputation. He acknowledges that the character was based on real people: one was Sadory, a descendant of the Hungarian royal family whom he had met in Paris before the war. Another was a former prisoner whom he had encountered in 1907 in Bern.[37] But over time, this Other named Moravagine had begun to inhabit the writer's psyche so profoundly that Cendrars could no longer separate himself from his creation: 'J'ai nourri, élevé un parasite à mes dépens. A la fin je ne savais plus qui de nous deux plagiait l'autre.' (I had raised and nourished a parasite at my own expense. By the end I no longer knew which one of us was plagiarizing the other.)[38] Probing further what exactly the figure of the Other means to him, he concludes that all great books are autobiographical in that their protagonists are extensions of their authors. 'C'est pourquoi il n'y a qu'un seul sujet littéraire: l'homme. C'est pourquoi il n'y a qu'une littérature: celle de cet homme, de cet Autre, l'homme qui

Poster from the 1900 Universal Exposition advertising a visitor attraction based on the Trans-Siberian railway. This featured four railway carriages, in which visitors could 'travel' against a moving backdrop, and Moscow and Beijing 'station restaurants'.

BLAISE CENDRARS
La Prose du Transsibérien
et de la Petite Jehanne de France
TIRAGE DE LUXE
EDITIONS
HOMMES NOUVEAUX
PARIS
1913
PROSE DU TRANSSIBÉRIEN
ET DE LA PETITE JEHANNE DE FRANCE
« Blaise, dis, sommes-nous bien loin de Montmartre? »
« Dis, Blaise, sommes-nous bien loin de Montmartre ? »

Blaise Cendrars, *La prose du Transsibérien et de la Petite Jehanne de France*, illustrated with watercolour applied through pochoir and relief print by Sonia Delaunay-Terk (1913).

PANAMA

OR THE ADVENTURES OF MY SEVEN UNCLES

By **Blaise Cendrars** *translated from the French and illustrated by* **John Dos Passos**

HARPER & BROTHERS · NEW YORK AND LONDON

Blaise Cendrars, *Panama; or, The Adventures of My Seven Uncles*, translated and illustrated by John Dos Passos (1931).

Double page of Blaise Cendrars, *La Fin du monde filmée par l'Ange N.-D.*, with illustration by Fernand Léger (1919).

Double page of Blaise Cendrars, *La Fin du monde filmée par l'Ange N.-D.*, with illustration by Fernand Léger (1919).

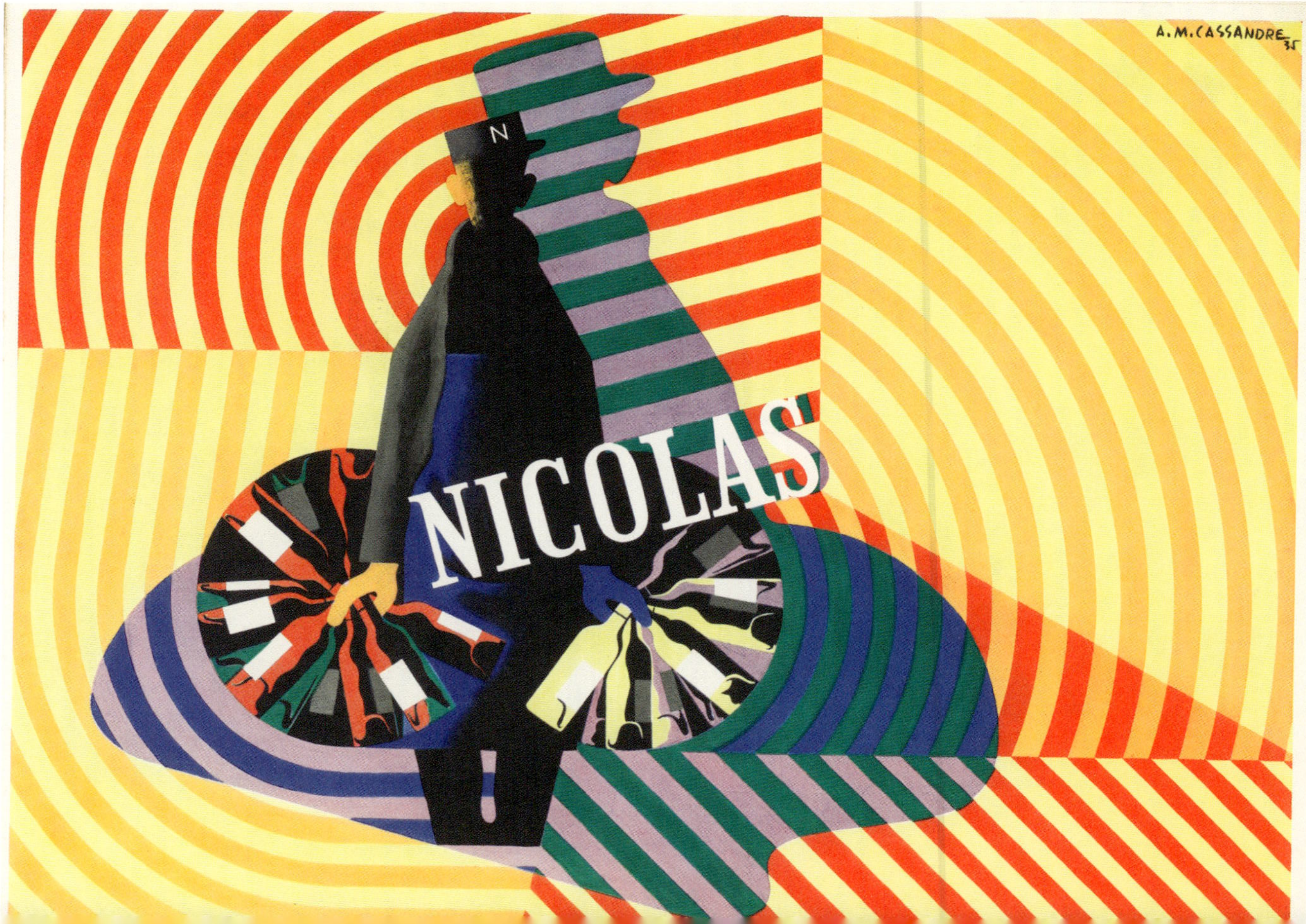
A.M.CASSANDRE 35
N
NICOLAS

...sur les portées de la lumière,

Cendrars and Cassandre, *Le Spectacle est dans la rue* (1935).

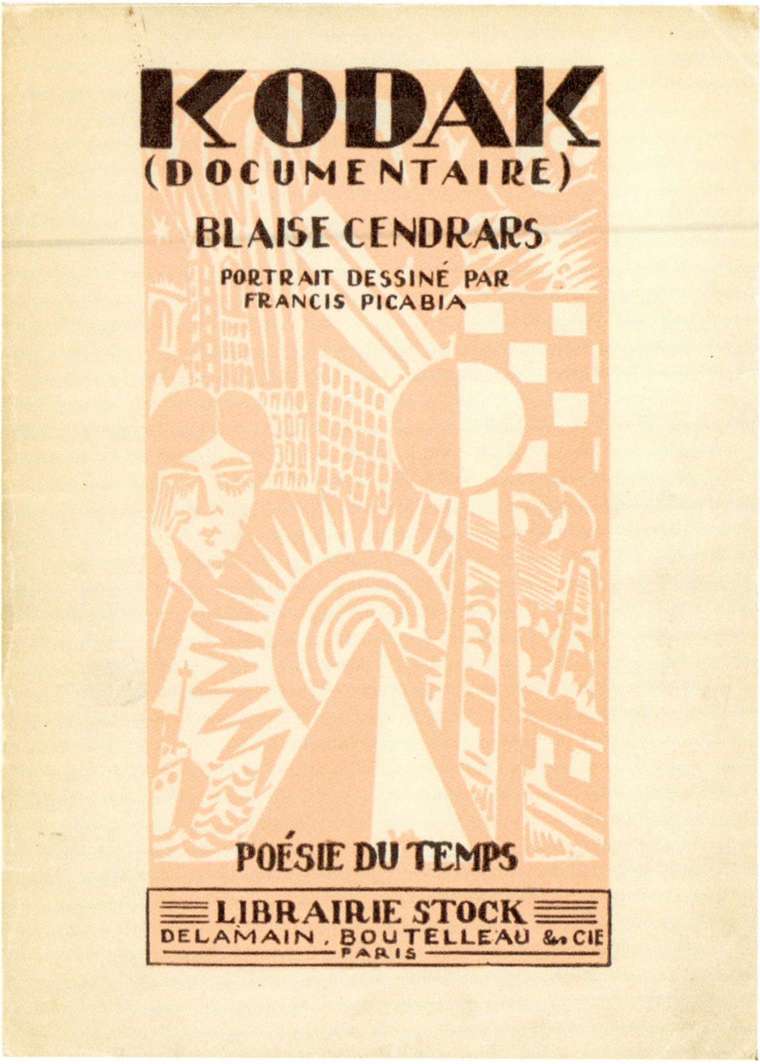

Kodak (Documentaire), with cover illustration by Frans Masereel, 1924. The book's title was changed to *Documentaires* after the Eastman Kodak Company threatened legal action against the unauthorized use of its name.

écrit.' (It is why there is only one literary subject: Man. It is why there is only one kind of literature: that of this man, this Other, the one who writes.)[39]

The relationship between the writing self and the written other haunts Cendrars from the early years onwards: he cites the words 'Je suis l'Autre' (I am the Other) in 'Journal' (Newspaper), the first and most openly autobiographical of his *Dix-neuf poèmes élastiques*, and the imbrication of the other in the self continues to inhabit his writings in the post-war years. It seems telling that the character Moravagine, and the book that bears his name, both occupied Cendrars's thoughts for so many years, particularly since they straddled the two crucial periods of his life, the time before and after his amputation. As scholars have suggested, the loss of the right arm was the traumatic moment at which Cendrars was forced to adopt, acquaint himself with and adapt to his 'left side'.[40] The exceptionally long trajectory of this novel from conception to completion straddles that fundamental breach in Cendrars's life and work. If Moravagine represents an uncompromisingly destructive impulse within him, then Raymond too stands for a part of his character, more prone to reading, writing and reflecting and less conspicuously stimulated by violent action, but he does nevertheless share Moravagine's hostility towards women and towards sexuality more generally.

Perhaps the single most striking figure of the entire novel is that of literature itself. *Moravagine* is an act of literary bravura, and it is through language and the power of the imagination that it succeeds in summoning forth a whole world. In turns gently poetic and uncompromisingly experimental, violent and violently funny, action-packed and quietly contemplative, this novel is infuriating, perplexing, yet still breathtakingly original. It conveys an unremittingly bleak vision of humanity through the protagonists' journey of violence and relentless destruction; yet it does so thanks to its author's orchestration of an extraordinary patchwork of textual matter. This saga of devastation thus ultimately attests to the creativity of writing as a force that enables the pen to prevail over the sword.

six

Polar Extremes: *Le Plan de l'Aiguille* and *Les Confessions de Dan Yack*

As early as 1922, Cendrars had signed a publishing contract to write a book entitled *Le Plan des Aiguilles*. In the years that followed, this project evolved in fits and starts. In the spring of 1927, he travelled to the village of La Redonne near Marseille with the aim of completing the book, but failed to write more than a handful of lines. The poet André Gaillard was a frequent visitor to the house that Cendrars was renting and often used it as a base for trysts with women when his friend was away. On several of those occasions, Gaillard left traces of his presence: besides the unmade bed and a trail of cigarette butts, he habitually added a few lines to Cendrars's unfinished typescript. Gaillard's words remained unchanged in the published book.[1]

It was during his stay at La Redonne that Cendrars decided to split the book into two volumes united by their main character, Dan Yack. Both books were published in a single year, 1929: the first appeared in February, the second in September, both under Parisian imprint Au Sans Pareil, directed by René Hilsum, who published work by the Surrealists as well as Marguerite Yourcenar's first novel. Like *Morvagine*, the *Dan Yack* volumes owed something to the generosity of Paolo Prado, Cendrars's patron in Brazil: he made his third and final sojourn in that country from August 1927 until January 1928 and worked on the book while staying at the Art Deco Copacabana Palace Hotel in Rio de Janeiro, which had first opened its doors to the public four years earlier.[2]

The original title with its plural form 'Aiguille*s*' is intriguing by virtue of its departure from the singular form, Le Plan de l'Aiguille, which is the name of a summit in Mont-Blanc and became the title of the first volume. The 1922 title is unlikely to have been devised in error, given that Cendrars was familiar with the cartography of Mont-Blanc, having spent several months in 1920 not far from there working alongside Abel Gance on *La Roue* and seeking out locations for mountain scenes.[3] A probable explanation for the play on the place name is that Cendrars wished to draw attention to the role of mechanical recordings in the novels: 'aiguille', meaning needle, refers to the stylus of a gramophone, a device so important to Dan Yack that he even takes a portable one with him to the Antarctic. 'Aiguille' could also refer to the needles on the phonogram's wax cylinders used to record Mireille's and Dan's voices in *Les Confessions de Dan Yack*. Both of the Dan Yack volumes feature gramophones extensively; and the medical connotations of the word 'needle' relate all too vividly to Cendrars's amputation and the terms in which he described the searing pain he experienced after it.[4]

This is just one of the peculiarities of the title of the first volume. Perhaps the most surprising aspect of it is that, of all the many locations that appear in *Le Plan de l'Aiguille*, perversely, the geographic place in Mont-Blanc that carries this name does not feature at all in the book; by contrast, the place known as Le Plan de l'Aiguille not only appears in the second volume but is its sole location, since it is there that Dan Yack listens to the recordings that constitute its narrative.

Of course, this anomaly is less serious when we consider that the two books were originally intended to be published as a single tome. As Cendrars later explained, the reason for having them appear separately had much to do with the particular binary relationship that they embody:

> Le monde est ma représentation. J'ai voulu dans *Dan Yack* intérioriser cette vue de l'esprit, ce qui est une conception pessimiste ; puis l'extérioriser, ce qui est une action optimiste.
>
> D'où la division en deux parties de mon roman: la première, du dehors au dedans, sujet du *Plan de l'Aiguille* ; du dedans au dehors, objet des *Confessions de Dan Yack*, la deuxième. Systole, diastole: les deux pôles de l'existence. Outside-in, inside-out: les deux temps du mouvement mécanique. Contraction, dilatation: la respiration de l'univers, le principe de la vie, l'Homme, Dan Yack, avec ses figures.
>
> (The world is my representation. I wanted in *Dan Yack* to internalize this view of the mind, which is a pessimistic conception; then externalize it, which is an optimistic action.

> Whence the division of my novel into two parts: the first, from outside to inside, the subject of *Dan Yack* [*Le Plan de l'Aiguille*]; the second, from inside to outside, the object of *Confessions of Dan Yack*. Systole, diastole: the two poles of existence. Outside-in, inside-out: the two stages of mechanical movement. Contraction, dilation: the breath of the universe, the principle of life, Man, Dan Yack, with his figures.)[5]

These words shed much light on how Cendrars wished the two books to relate to one another and reinforce the fact that the binary structure is essential to their meaning. As Bochner puts it succintly: '*Le Plan* breathes in, *Les Confessions* out, but only together do they breathe and become Dan Yack.'[6] In the first novel, Cendrars turns his gaze inwards, drawing the experience of the outside world into the mind, a space of contemplation and immersion where it is vulnerable to sombre impulses. In the second novel, the thinking and feeling self is directed outwards, into the world and into society. As a result, this book strives towards a relationality that is absent from the first one. This does not mean, however, that the tone of the book is upbeat, as we might expect, since the brief period of happiness and balance in Dan Yack's life is already over by the point at which it begins.

Storyline

The first tome, entitled *Le Plan de l'Aiguille*, introduces the main protagonist, Dan Yack William. The wealthy English inheritor of a shipping firm, he is far more interested in frequenting the social scene of St Petersburg than in running the family business. We first encounter him in that city; he has been jilted by his love, Hedwiga, and is determined to deal with this situation by drinking himself into a stupor in a bar. Meanwhile, close by, a poet, a musician and a sculptor are deep in conversation, sharing their disillusionment about art and life. Yack awakens in time to overhear some of their words and hatches an ambitious, not to say crazy, plot to take the three men with him on an expedition to the South Pole, on one of the whalers belonging to his family firm. The intention behind his decision to bring the artists with him is to encourage them all to engage with their respective creative practices and, in this most extreme of environments, to explore the outermost boundaries of artistic expression in the hope that it might allow them to take that art to its logical conclusion.

The ship becomes trapped in pack ice and Dan orders his crew to allow him and the three artists to disembark and attempt to endure the long dark winter on the Balleny Islands.

The men survive the winter, albeit not without psychological and physical deterioration, but the real damage is done when finally, after several months, the sun makes an appearance. At this point the perilous expedition ends in tragedy as one by one the artists lose their sanity and then their lives. Arkadie Goischman, the poet, descends into madness and uses Dan Yack's knife to cut off his own nose and offer it to him as a gift. Ivan Sabakov, the sculptor, creates a giant effigy of Dan Yack in ice; he then becomes ever more obsessed with the idea of reducing the artistic idea to its most elemental form, and then to whittle even that down to absolute immateriality, a kind of Mallarméan attenuation to the pure essence. He realizes this in a huge sculpture based on a monocle, a metonym for Dan Yack. Ivan dies when one of his huge ice sculptures falls and crushes him. André Lamont, suffering from the final stages of syphilis, walks off into the distance, a bottle in his hand but wearing clothes that are far too insubstantial to protect him from the cold.

Ultimately only Dan Yack survives unscathed. He leaves Struge and, after a brief return to the excesses of old, he decides to embark on another radical adventure. One night, after a long evening of heavy drinking, he hatches an idea that will reverse his fortunes: he decides to set up a company to process and sell an array of whale by-products, and in so doing he founds Community-City, a settlement of 711 inhabitants, and not one woman among them. By the point at which this has grown into a large and successful business, he has already tired of profiting from his capitalist schemes and decides to share out his wealth. He also relinquishes his long-held principle of celibacy. He falls in love again; but this potentially positive turn of events does not bring much hope, since the woman who captures his heart is the wife of his colleague and second-in-command Gonzalo Hortalez.

The storyline of *Le Plan de l'Aiguille* is entertaining but implausible in its sheer excess; this, along with its diverse locations, gives the book some of the restlessness and picaresque character of *Moravagine*. Some of the plot developments are abrupt, and character development does not always keep up with the pace. In the wake of the epic failure of the Antarctic voyage, it is hard to believe in Dan Yack's rapid transformation into a hugely successful businessman thanks to his large-scale whalemeat processing operation in Port-Deception.[7] This matters little, since the narrative sweeps the reader along in its fast-flowing sequence of adventures, business ventures and misadventures.

Yet as in *Moravagine*, significant elements of the basic story matter derived from fact. The itinerary of Dan Yack's expedition, reaching the Antarctic via the coast of Argentina, was borrowed from that of the famous French explorer Jean-Baptiste Charcot, who led two celebrated expeditions to the Antarctic in 1903–5 and 1908–10; Cendrars's text reveals that he had read Charcot's two volumes of writings on these voyages, published as *Autour du Pôle Sud*.[8] The ship in which Charcot and his crew sailed on the second expedition was named *Le Pourquoi pas?*, an echo of which appears in the name of Dan Yack's favourite bar, the Pourquoi Pépita?, which features in *Le Plan de l'Aiguille* and is mentioned again in the opening pages of *The Confessions of Dan Yack*. Besides the obvious appeal of the subject-matter, Claude Leroy has written suggestively about the personal reasons that may have compelled Cendrars to base much of his story on Charcot. The latter was the son of Jean-Martin Charcot, the famous psychiatrist and founder of Pitié-Salpêtrière Hospital in Paris. For Charcot junior to step out of his father's shadow, earn a name for himself and establish a reputation in his own right, he had to make his journeys to the end of the Earth. Dan Yack too manifests a reluctance to be burdened by the family name whose reputation goes before him and has made him wealthy. He repeatedly insists that he is not a William and orders others to address him simply as Dan Yack.[9] Cendrars, the son of an unsuccessful entrepreneur, reinvented himself, partly by shedding his own family name. It is hard not to see in Dan Yack a projection of certain aspects of Freddy Sauser's own family history.

As in *Moravagine*, *Le Plan de l'Aiguille* brings together widely divergent moods, and amid the turbulent events narrated, we encounter some descriptive passages of intense beauty. Typically for Cendrars, many of these focus on the natural world:

> L'aube tarde à venir. Dans le nord-est deux petits nuages arrondis présentent chacun à leur extrémité une ébauche d'arc-en-ciel formant une double arche de pont en amorce sur une cataracte fumante de brouillards verts, violets, orangés. La calotte du ciel est absolument noire et une splendide bande azurée rejoint l'est à l'ouest. Dans le sud se dresse un éventail gigantesque, un pied de vent rouge et rose s'éparpillant en cirro-stratus ocre rouge et

Photograph of the ship *Pourquoi-pas?* in Jean Charcot, *Le 'Pourquoi-pas?' dans l'Antarctique: journal de la deuxième expédition au Pôle sud, 1908–1910* (1910), upon which Cendrars based his novel *Dan Yack* (1929).

bleu sombre. Le large est un immense cercle d'eau libre où flottent les icebergs comme des tampons d'ouate colorée.

(The dawn is late in coming. To the northeast, two little round clouds are fringed with just a hint of a rainbow, a half-built bridge whose double arch spans a smoking cataract of green, violet and orange haze. The vault of the sky is utterly black and a resplendent azure band joins east to west. To the south, a gigantic fan opens up, a red and rose-coloured pillar of wind that disperses in the form of red ochre and dark blue cirro-stratus. The ocean is an immense circle of open water on whose surface icebergs float like wads of coloured cotton wool.)[10]

The parts of the narrative that describe the extreme weather conditions of the Balleny Islands paint an evocative picture of the quasi-biblical force of the natural elements:

Tout se concassait, se rompait, s'émiettait, se disloquait et, pris de frénésie, se mettait hystériquement en branle. Tout se lâchait, se vidait, par en haut ou par en bas, tout partait à la dérive tumultueusement éperdu, désordonné, défaillant, aspiré, refoulé, tohu-bohu, fuite, cohue, panique des éléments en pagaïe, panique de la nature mise en déroute par la lanière claquante et cinglante du blizzard.

(Everything was in collision, breaking up, shattering into smithereens, dislocated and, seized with frenzy, flung itself hysterically into the fray. Everything was breaking loose, emptying itself out from above or below, everything was coming adrift, tumultuous, bewildered, in total disarray, faltering, sucked in, spat out in the hurly-burly of flight, the thronging, the panic of the elements in chaos, of nature put to rout by the stinging, cracking lash of the blizzard.)[11]

For all the bleakness of its subject-matter and mood during the Antarctic expedition, the book has unexpected moments of levity. One is provided when Dan Yack is spending six months in the town of San Carlos in Chile and discovers the pleasures of the *guesquel*. As the author's lengthy footnote explains, this is the native American name for a contraption made of mule hair attached to a thin tricolour cord to be worn around the penis. During sex, it provides the woman with intense pleasure. The footnote continues:

Ces crins sont raides et longs d'un bon doigt; leur effet est si violent que la femme hurle, pleure, grince des dents, mord, éclate de rire, sanglote, s'agite, écume, bave, fait des soubresauts, se tortille [. . .]; l'orgasme est si puissant, qu'après la détumescence la femme reste épuisée, râlante, rassasiée, satisfaite, comblée, étourdie de bonheur, bête à pleurer, n'en pouvant plus.

(These tufts are stiff and at least as long as a finger; their effect is so violent that the woman cries out, weeps, grinds her teeth, bites, bursts out laughing, sobs, tosses, foams at the mouth, slobbers, twitches and writhes her hips [. . .]; the orgasm is so powerful that, after detumescence, the woman remains exhausted, at her last gasp, sated, replete, overcome, dizzy with happiness, stupefied to the point of tears and utterly helpless.)[12]

The note goes on to explain that the *guesquel* is so prized in some communities, 'even in marriage', that a good one can be worth between three and six horses depending on the quality of its manufacture and materials.

Dan Yack is so delighted with his *guesquel* and its effect on the recipient of its action that he never removes the device, so its bells tinkle whenever he walks.[13]

Dan Yack's obsession with such toys, and gadgets more generally, prompts us to speculate on their wider implications in relation to his behaviour. In numerous instances, he displays a lack of emotional maturity; on his own admission, he is a 'brute' who lacks subtlety of judgement. Very much a product of his era, he displays misogynistic as well as racist tendencies, not to mention his cheerful acceptance and perpetration of animal slaughter on an industrial scale. When he ends his period of celibacy, he does so with an 'anonymous Indian woman', and this adjective is used twice to describe the indigenous women he encounters in Chile. We are never told this woman's name, and we are left with the impression that Dan Yack neither knows it nor wishes to do so.

Throughout the novel, we are often made aware of Dan Yack's intense pleasure in listening to recordings. As noted above, he brings several gramophones and phonographs to the Balleny Islands, at one point almost prompting André Lamont to attack him when he plays them all at once. In the Pourquoi Pepita? bar, he becomes obsessed with the cat orchestra, a music-playing machine adorned with mechanically animated stuffed cats. When his crew are out on the town celebrating their return, he indulges his pleasure, repeatedly and compulsively inserting coins into the slots of machines that were the early twentieth-century equivalent of juke boxes. In the sheer pleasure it brings him, this action can be likened to a form of auditory masturbation. Similarly, Dan's fondness for listening to his many recordings of seals leads us to suspect that technology, and especially audio technology, is to some extent a surrogate for a loving relationship. Dan Yack has been described as one of the most autobiographical of all of Cendrars's fictional characters. The author's estrangement from Féla and his long-term but allegedly unconsummated relationship with his second wife, Raymone, suggest that Dan Yack's unhappiness in love and his largely solitary existence may indeed be modelled on his author's own experience.

His Master's Voice: *The Confessions of Dan Yack*

As early as 1878, the prolific North American inventor Thomas Edison predicted with astonishing foresight that his phonograph would bring an array of benefits to future generations:

1. Letter writing and all kinds of dictation without the aid of a stenographer.
2. Phonographic books, which will speak to blind people without effort on their part.
3. The teaching of elocution.
4. Reproduction of music.
5. The 'Family Record' – a registry of sayings, reminiscences, etc., by members of a family in their own voices, and of the last words of dying persons.
6. Music-boxes and toys.
7. Clocks that should announce in articulate speech the time for going home, going to meals, etc.
8. The preservation of languages by exact reproduction of the manner of pronouncing.
9. Educational purposes; such as preserving the explanations made by a teacher, so that the pupil can refer to them at any moment, and spelling or other lessons placed upon the phonograph for convenience in committing to memory.
10. Connection with the telephone, so as to make that instrument an auxiliary in the transmission of permanent and invaluable records, instead of being the recipient of momentary and fleeting communication.[14]

Edison would doubtless have approved of *The Confessions of Dan Yack*. This, the second volume, or the second part of Dan Yack's adventures, was written at Cendrars's home in Le Tremblay-sur-Mauldre and published in 1929, hot on the heels of *Le Plan de l'Aiguille*. In literary terms, there is much to say about this book; as is so often the case in Cendrars's oeuvre, we encounter a prefatory note that far exceeds the role normally expected of such a marginal addition. This note explains that the book was not written, but entirely dictated on a dictaphone. As the preface suggests, this new procedure was much more than a mere technical novelty: for Cendrars, who never ceased to experiment, it offered an opportunity to explore new creative methods. He laments that books are not yet able to reproduce sounds such as Dan Yack's voice, but he predicts quite presciently that this would eventually be possible. Indeed, Cendrars and Colette Godard adapted the novel for radio in 1956.[15]

The realization that technology could transport moments from the past into the future was hugely significant. Similar claims were made of Edison's Kinetograph and, after it, the Lumière brothers' Cinématographe when it was launched in 1895. The opportunities to 'freeze' time that these recording devices opened up were exhilarating, but they would also intensify the sense of loss experienced by the bereaved. This paradoxical situation is at the core of *Les Confessions de Dan Yack*.

In numerous respects, the second tome of the Dan Yack saga is the inverse of the first one. The fast pace of the first book conveys an energy that befits the eponymous protagonist's ebullient personality; this dynamism prevails even when the action turns to tragedy. In contrast, by the time the second book begins, Dan Yack has met, married and lost to a mysterious illness his young wife, Mireille, whose death he is mourning. The tone of much of the narrative is more tender and contemplative, and an atmosphere of despondency pervades the entire book.

Narrative voice plays an important and varied role in the two novels. The first tome is narrated predominantly in the third person and in the past tense, with conversations in direct speech. At moments, however, the use of the dramatic present conveys a sense of immediacy and intensity. Towards the end of Chapter Four, as the longest day of the year arrives, the four men on Struge face appalling weather conditions. At this point, the narrative adopts a lineation and a syntactic elasticity that give it a visual appearance similar to Cendrars's pre-war poems written in free verse:

> Le vent vient de sauter. Il souffle un mélange de neige et de verglas.
> Il y a un petit lac, formé par la fusion de la glace pendant les premiers jours d'été, qui vient de se vider comme une tasse renversée.
> Lumière crépusculaire, bouffie.
> Il pleut.
> Tout danse dans une ornière d'eau.
> Tout se secoue et remonte.
> Il neige.
>
> (The wind has just shifted. It is blowing a mixture of snow and verglas.
> A small lake, formed by the melting of the ice during the first few days of summer, has just emptied itself like an overturned cup.
> A swollen, crepuscular light.
> It is raining.
> Everything is dancing in a runnel of water.

Everything is shaking itself out, winding itself up again.
It is snowing.)[16]

The syntactic contrasts here are strongly reminiscent of the *Dix-neuf poèmes élastiques*: monolexical lines are interspersed with short sentences and long lines, creating a pattern of rhythmic contrasts; the paratactic structure and the typographic separation of individual sentences into paragraphs contribute towards an effect of urgency and immediacy, as if we are witnessing the natural phenomena taking place even as we read.

In the following chapter, by which time Dan Yack is in San Carlos in Chiloé enjoying the libidinous advantages of the *guesquel* with an unnamed woman, the narrative again hints at the author's abiding fascination with language and the poetry that can emerge from a wide range of situations. The text transcribes the woman's words in her unspecified indigenous language. Her utterances are profoundly physical and embodied as well as musical: '*MAI – MAI – – – CARA – CARA – – – CACA – – – CACA – – – MOU – TCHI*'.[17] The reader is reminded here of the words and sounds uttered by the narrator/protagonist of *Prose du Transsibérien* to help lull the feverish Jeanne to sleep. The woman's words of affection are interspersed with curt instructions that Dan Yack sends by telegraph to his staff. These are presented in exactly the same way, in italicized upper-case letters, followed by the French translation:

IBOA CHARCOT FOUZKAOOS JYLONEXWEY
Circonvenez membres expédition Charcot stop obtenez nouveaux renseignements, écrivait Dan Yack en consultant son code télégraphique.

(*IBOA CHARCOT FOUZKAOOS JYLONEXWEY*
Circumvent members of Charcot expedition stop obtain further expedition wrote Dan Yack, consulting his telegraphic code.)[18]

The typography here elides the gap between two fundamentally unrelated kinds of discourse – terms of endearment and instructions tapped into a telegraph machine – as if to emphasize an underlying similarity; perhaps Cendrars is suggesting that their common identity as language overrides the differences between them. At first glance, this page too resembles lines of avant-garde poetry and calls to mind the abstract Dada sound poems of the 1910s and '20s and Lettrist experiments of the 1940s, which experimented with typography as well as departing from the notion that the word is a meaningful unit.[19]

In other respects, too, the two tomes contrast significantly with one another. The first was more or less entirely devoid of women: Dan Yack's plot to establish Community-City and populate it solely with men was a typically extreme reaction to his own unhappiness in love, since Hedwiga had decided to marry another suitor. The second *Dan Yack* volume reverses this tendency, placing female characters to the fore; alongside Mireille, these include her mother, who is a prostitute called Théréson, and various other women with whom Dan Yack becomes acquainted.

By the time the second book begins, he has met, married and witnessed the suffering and eventual death of his young wife, Mireille, who succumbs to cardiac illness. This tragic circumstance makes the role of the recordings especially poignant, since the act of reading brings her closer to Dan Yack. Even though we do not hear her – her silent films preserve her image, but not her voice – the fact that Dan Yack is able to read her words, written in the present tense and expressing her thoughts and feelings at a specific time, reduces the temporal gap between her at the moment of writing down her words and him at the moment of reading them and recording them on to phonograph cylinders.

Mireille's story was inspired in part by Ida Danis. She met Abel Gance during the First World War when she was working as a secretary for the Film d'Art production company. Gance, who had been married since 1912, fell in love with Danis and decided to live with her in 1918. She was still with him throughout the filming of *La Roue*, which began in Nice in 1919. Both Gance and Danis had fallen victim to the Spanish influenza pandemic in 1918, and whereas Gance recovered, Danis fell seriously ill with tuberculosis in the winter of 1919. Her condition deteriorated so dramatically that Gance rewrote the script of *La Roue* and moved the filming into the Alps, where he hoped Ida could convalesce. She died in April 1921 as Gance was making the final edits of the film.[20] Gance married her sister Marguerite in November 1922, while their brother Pierre eventually became Gance's director of production.[21]

The Confessions of Dan Yack proffers the intriguing literary conceit that it is composed from transcriptions of audio recordings stored on cylinders which Dan has sent to a typist for tidying up and transcribing. Early in the book, he uses one of the cylinders to record instructions for the typist, pointing out that all of the cylinders are damaged, and urging her to cross-refer to Mireille's written entries in her exercise book. The book is proof that the typist has not followed Dan Yack's instruction to edit out his random musings and comments; alongside the transcriptions of Mireille's diaries, we read Dan Yack's words. The result is a fascinating composite of both voices. The book thus offers scope for reflection on how and to what extent this novel, not written but dictated, relates to Cendrars's practice as a writer. First, the dictaphone is the ideal device for an author who repeatedly expressed frustration at having to write. The availability of technology that has the potential not only to preserve the past, but to record one's thoughts, must have been an extraordinarily liberating discovery. Cendrars's epigraph at the start of *The Confessions of Dan Yack* also prompts us to consider the recording device as a form of prosthesis replacing the author's missing right, and writing, hand.[22]

In Cylinder 5c, which contains transcriptions of Mireille's entries, we learn that Dan Yack was displeased when she was given a role in Villiers de l'Isle-Adam's play *Eve future* and was expected to play the part of a robot.[23] As she recalls in her notes, 'Ce rôle de femme artificielle qu'un inventeur met au point et anime petit à petit jusqu'à lui insuffler la vie, déplut beaucoup à mon grand.' (My big man was very displeased to see me in this role of an artificial woman constructed by an inventor who animates her, little by little, to the point where he can actually breathe life into her.)[24] This suggests that he is unable to accept her automation, her mechanization, her being absorbed into the world of machines rather than that of humans. And yet, after her death, he regrets that he does not have more films of her, since this technical reproduction could offer a semblance of her presence and bring her back from the dead.

While Mireille's recollection ostensibly suggests that Dan Yack was determined for her to retain her agency and her autonomy, the same paragraph ends with her reflecting on the impact that Dan Yack has had in her life; while she expresses gratitude to him, confirming the view that he has supported her, her words make it clear that their relationship is emphatically not one of equals, which allows us to infer that Dan Yack had a controlling influence on her. This can be measured in Mireille's portrayal of her own subservient behaviour in her depiction of their life together. She acknowledges that Dan taught her everything she knows about screen acting and attributes her acting success in *L'Eve future* to his advice and support.[25] In light of her early death, the eagerness with which she subordinates herself to the men closest to her – not only Dan

Yack, but the director Lefauché too – prompts the reader to question their failure to prevent her from working to exhaustion on the film set.

Katherine Shingler has written persuasively on the two Dan Yack tomes and situates them within the genre of the art novel. She argues that the book's binary structure is intimately tied to its discussion of the ways in which art can best respond to changing times and propose new ways of seeing the world. The art forms that we encounter in the first tome are steeped in tradition and heritage, however hard the three artists may try to free themselves from the past; even Ivan Sabakov's quest, first to produce an abstract sculpture, and then an entirely immaterial one, potentially a radically original way of understanding sculptural practice, cannot dispense with the weight of the past. Paradoxically, his drive to create a sculpture made of pure geometric forms, potentially a radical act of breaking with tradition, is nothing other than a way of reflecting the divine force that, he believes, governs all artistic creation:

> 'Il me faut serrer la réalité de plus pres encore et la réalité c'est Dieu.'
> 'Un cercle, un carré, un cube, une sphère, un disque, une ellipse sont les manifestations de sa perfection.'
>
> ('I must cling even more closely to reality, to the reality that is God.'
> 'A circle, a square, a cube, a sphere, a disc, an ellipse, are manifestations of His perfection.')[26]

Paradoxically, shortly before his death, Sabakov makes a proclamation that suggests he is retreating from artistic experimentation into convention: 'J'ai retrouvé la voie de mon père: la Vérité.' (I have rediscovered the way of my father: the Truth.)[27] Fittingly, the huge ice sculpture that falls over and fatally injures him is not one of his new minimal, geometric forms, but a large figurative portrait depicting Dan Yack's likeness, a literal manifestation of the crushing weight of the past. To reinforce the message, we learn that the sculpture was made from fossil ice. In an echo of Moravagine's disembowellings, it is the belly of the giant sculpted form that crushes Sabakov to death.[28]

This account of events is only partly convincing, however. A more compelling interpretation is that the artists fail because they are in the thrall of the modern consumer society and it is this, rather than any excessive adherence to tradition, that brings about their downfall. André Lamont fails because he is unable to write a musical composition in the absence of his fawning admirers; he is, in other words, a victim of the cult of personality and the values of a society more interested in celebrity than in genuine talent or significant achievement; as a result, his self-awareness and vanity have impeded artistic creativity. Arkadie Goischman's most significant incentive for writing poetry is the lure of money rather than the love of poetry itself. He longs for the trappings of success rather than the readers' appreciation of his literary efforts. He too, then, has fallen victim to the values of capitalism, in which respect Dan Yack can only have served as a dangerous example as someone who had profited enormously from that system. Even Goischman's self-mutilation, the single most significant gesture he will ever make, is devoid of originality and ultimately nothing more than a mere pastiche, since it mimics Van Gogh's self-inflicted injury but lacks the latter's sincerity of intent. In other words, it is a simulacrum, a mere semblance of the act itself.

The relationship between the real and the simulacrum is a crucial trope of the second tome, since technologies of reproducing the real proliferate throughout this book. Their most obvious and consistent presence occurs in the phonograph recordings that constitute the book's chapters; cinema too haunts the book's pages, primarily through the accounts of Mireille's big screen roles, but also in the many other references to cinema. Already in the first tome, Ivan Sabakov's yearning to produce an immaterial form of sculpture takes on a distinctly cinematic quality: he begins to dream of creating an art form which would consume itself by radiating shapes as the sun emits rays. He dwells on what this might entail: 'Ne plus sculpter la main, mais l'espace infini qui circule entre les doigts écartés.' (No longer to sculpt the hand but the infinite space that circulates between splayed fingers.)[29] Both of these descriptions convey the image of an art form consisting essentially of light; indeed, he concludes that the only possible sculpture is one made of pure light.[30] The image of a light source consumed by flames not only evokes primal and cosmic forces but, more pertinently, it also brings to mind the all too familiar trope of destruction and rebirth that leads us back to Freddy Sauser's pseudonym and the richly symbolic image of the phoenix rising from the ashes (*braise*, *cendres*). Energized by his epiphany and intent on creating an art form dematerialized to its merest essence, Sabakov proceeds to make a series of identical sculptures by hewing and polishing giant circular forms of ice from the walls of icebergs. Even in his incipient madness, the sculptor seems to have intuited that the circular form is the perfect symbol with which to express a supernatural, all-encompassing force: not only does the disc suggest the form of the sun whose rays it refracts, but it imitates the shape of the eye, that organ of vision with which we perceive light, as well as the round optical lens that summed up Dan Yack, the monocle:

> Le monocle c'est tout.
> L'homme.
> Une cristallisation.
> Un gel.
> Un micelle.
> Dieu.
>
> (The monocle is everything.
> Man.
> A crystallization.
> A gel.
> A micella.
> God.)[31]

The monocle and the series of transparent discs that Sabakov carves out of ice also foreshadow another eye, and another way of seeing, that will take centre stage in the second tome, namely the lens that serves as the eye of the movie camera, recording and documenting reality with precision. Sabakov's discovery of the giant lens as the ultimate sculptural form, capable of transmitting and refracting the sun's powerful light, hints at his nascent fear that his own practice as a sculptor will be overshadowed by more technological forms of art. Cinema will indeed figure prominently in the second tome, although it too will prove to be a complicated and problematic heir to the more traditional forms of art.

As someone who on his own admission has never read a book, does not understand art and is innately distrustful of all that cannot be empirically proven, Dan Yack unsurprisingly has more of an affinity with cinema: its technological means of recording and reproducing fragments of reality are better suited to his character than the speculative and imaginative forms of artistic practice that the three artists of the first tome represent. The fact that their projects in the Antarctic fail might seem to confirm Dan Yack's faith in technology over art, as Shingler argues.

Yet the events that unfold in the book's two tomes repeatedly demonstrate that Dan Yack's perception does not match reality. As we have argued, the deaths of the three artists were not occasioned by any inherent weakness in their own work, but rather occurred because they made the mistake of placing their faith in Dan Yack's fantastical and irresponsibly hazardous project. Their first and most damaging mistake was to allow themselves to be persuaded to join him on his mission, a decision no doubt inspired as much by the lure of financial security as by any real desire to visit Antarctica. This again reiterates the book's implicit message that art cannot survive commercialization unscathed.

Yet throughout the first tome, Dan Yack shows no sign of accepting the very significant part he had played in the deaths of the three artists. After a short hiatus, he continues to pursue his career ambitions, and when he eventually tires of making huge financial gains from his business, this is not the result of any crisis of conscience occasioned by the artists' deaths. The narrative does not at any stage suggest that he has taken responsibility for his actions.

We have to wait until close to the end of the second tome before Dan Yack reflects on that disastrous experience; even now, he is completely unrepentant. He begins to reminisce about the First World War; he reflects on the fact that his most terrible memories of that period take him back, surprisingly, not to the combat itself but to the nights he spent on lookout duty, when he had to endure the sights and sounds of his fellow troops sleeping noisily, wriggling, groaning, having nightmares in their sleep. These various sounds, which emanated from deep in the very being of his fellow troops, rivalled the noises of battle; if these sounds horrified him so much, then perhaps it was because they reminded him briefly of the real human cost of this massively dehumanized war. In the 'terrifying silence' of the night that would be punctuated by exploding shells, his thoughts wander back to the Antarctic expedition and the 'symphonie singulière' of the storms he had witnessed there. His recollection of those occasions is revealing, as it becomes clear that what he really feared was not the storm itself, but the presence of his three companions. As he now recalls, his way of coping with such situations was to play all of his phonographs and gramophones simultaneously so as not to hear their groaning above the noise of the storm.[32] This admission makes it clear just to what an extent Dan Yack sought solace in machines, and even the machines of destruction, in preference over the company of his fellow humans. At this moment his thoughts take a Nietzschean turn as he insists that he alone survived the expedition because he wanted to live, unlike the three artists who accompanied him there:

> Arkadie Goischman, André Lamont et toi, petit Ivan, que me voulez-vous ? Je ne partage pas plus aujourd'hui vos souffrances que je n'ai jamais compris vos angoisses, vos rêves et pourquoi vous êtes morts d'impuissance en voulant vivre votre vie.
>
> (Arkadie Goischman, André Lamont, and you, little Ivan, what did you want from me? Today, I still do not share your sufferings, any more than, at the time, I understood your agonies and your dreams, nor why you died impotently, even though you wanted to live your lives.)[33]

Dan Yack's insistence that the three men were entirely responsible for their own deaths seems disingenuous to say the least, given the extreme location and circumstances of sensory privation into which he had knowingly led them, and in which all three had lost their minds. This moment offers further confirmation of the book's underlying symbolic message that art is doomed to fail in its encounter with the relentless force of commercialization and profiteering. This is a theme with which Cendrars must have had considerable empathy. Having befriended many artists on the pre-war Parisian avant-garde scene, he had witnessed the astonishing rise in profile and associated wealth of some of these individuals as they became internationally renowned in the interwar years.

Film

For a time, Cendrars envisaged cinema as the context in which his career would develop. By the time of writing *Dan Yack*, that dream had failed, and his view of that art form must have been tainted by his negative experience. Cinema, the art form that becomes central in the second Dan Yack tome, fails to provide a promising future for artists. It falls short of providing a viable alternative to the other art forms embodied by the three artists, and moreover, it contributes to Mireille's premature death. Once more, Dan Yack can be held partly responsible for this, since it was his decision to propel her into a film acting career; and once again, he shrugs off any accusation of guilt, directing his anger at others instead.

Yet throughout the second tome we are presented with evidence of the close and keen interest that Dan Yack took in Mireille's acting exploits. In her red notebook, Mireille wrote about the close attention Dan Yack had paid to her acting style and his efforts to help her perfect certain techniques. It transpired that he had an uncanny sense of how she could best surrender herself to the gaze of the movie camera. As Mireille recalls,

> 'Maintenant, il faut te mettre à la hauteur de cette machine,' me disait mon grand en me parlant de l'appareil de prise de vues. Et il me réapprenait à marcher, géométriquement, pour le cristallin gradué des objectifs et non plus pour la sensibilité des yeux.
>
> ('Now, you must be equal to the demands of this machine,' my dear man said to me when we talked about the film camera. And he taught me, all over again, how to walk, geometrically, for the crystalline eye of the lens and not for the sensibilities of the human eye.)[34]

Here we have a distorted echo of the scene that introduced the second tome, namely, the iconic image of the dog listening through a trumpet to His Master's Voice. Dan Yack has become Mireille's master and she his faithful servant, waiting on his every instruction. When Dan Yack visits his old acquaintance to ask his advice on what might be done to help Mireille, he refers to the latter as his 'petite fille' (little girl) rather than his wife.[35]

But Mireille has also been shaped by the movie camera, and in the process she has become a victim of the machinery of cinema, its relentless rhythm and its frenetic work rate that will precipitate her illness and eventual death. Not only that, but the camera's capacity to zoom in close and expose every imperfection, every flaw in an individual's body or soul, ultimately takes its toll on her. Lefauché, the director who films Mireille, does so with such intrusiveness that she feels violated. Her account of the filming process resembles that of a violation: he points his 'monstrous lens' at her and films her at the very brink of collapse from exhaustion.[36] The director's name connotes phonetically the Grim Reaper, and the novel suggests that he – or rather the filming – actively contributes to her premature death.

Dan Yack, who places his faith in technology, cannot cope with Mireille's illness and when she dies, he repeatedly describes himself as 'finished'. Their relationship, which was never consummated, is characterized by an avuncular love and affection. This is especially revelatory for the perennial playboy Dan Yack, who used his immense wealth as a substitute for emotions and was always more at ease in dealing with the reliable world of machines than in interacting with other humans who are all too prone to behave in unpredictable ways. His tendency to surround himself with machinery and technology offers him a means of escaping from emotionally trying situations. Despite this, Mireille awakened an affective side of him that we, and probably he, had not seen before.

The characters of Moravagine and Dan Yack can both be understood as bearing out aspects of Cendrars's own personality. If the former represents his negative double, then the latter is an exaggerated reflection of his solitary nature, his ambition and his love of the world. The next chapter will explore some of the books that he wrote about real-life individuals whose lives had in some ways been remarkable. The figures in question spanned various historical eras, cultures and geographic realms; what unites them is that they all, in myriad ways, had a strong appeal for Cendrars, no doubt in part because he recognized aspects of himself in them. In narrating their extraordinary lives, he was also, once again, retelling his own.

seven

Extraordinary Lives: From Homer to Hollywood

The remarkable creative output of the 1920s, and the popular and commercial reception that greeted the publication of *L'Or*, spurred Cendrars into plotting out numerous projects that offered scope for building on the success that his account of Suter's rise and fall had garnered. Correspondence from the period points to the end of the 1920s and the start of the '30s as a fertile period of creativity in which he variously discussed the film adaptation of *L'Or*, completed the two Dan Yack novels, began working on *Une Nuit dans la forêt* and *Eloge de La Vie dangereuse*, and wrote *L'ABC du cinéma*, *Petits contes nègres* and *Rhum*, among other books. The great film-maker Sergei Eistenstein met him in 1929 to discuss a film adaptation of *L'Or*. This project failed to attract funding, but Cendrars's reputation grew in the USA through John Dos Passos's 1931 translation of *Panama; or, The Adventures of my Seven Uncles*. Cendrars also found an ardent supporter in Henry Miller, with whom he visited the bars of Paris and corresponded at length. Miller wrote of him: 'I always see him there in the hub of the universe, slowly revolving with the vortex.' Yet the 1930s would eventually prove to be a low point in Cendrars's creative career: his novel writing slowed down to a virtual standstill, and many of his ambitious literary projects stalled, never to find their way into print. Instead, he found himself anthologizing some of his earlier essays and embarking on more journalistic forms of writing. Many of these, however, are remarkable, and even the unfinished projects provide further proof of his boundless eagerness to broaden the scope of his writing, embrace new literary genres and erode hierarchical distinctions between 'high' and 'low' literary forms. When the daily newspaper *Paris-Soir* invited him to write a reportage about the maiden voyage of the Transatlantic liner SS *Normandie* from Le Havre to New York in 1935, he chose to stay in the engine room rather than go above deck, preferring the company of the engineers to that of the guests. This decision was especially significant since the vessel's interior was finished to an especially high level of luxury and its accommodation catered primarily for passengers travelling in first class.[1]

Shortly after *L'Or* was published, Cendrars corresponded with his publishers in France and the USA with a view to writing an entire series of books based on the lives of extraordinary individuals; as early as 1925, he proposed this to the New York publishers Harper & Brothers and received a positive response.[2] Under the heading 'Les Têtes brûlées' (The Daredevils), this series was to continue in the vein of *L'Or* by focusing on the lives of four founding figures in the history of the USA, Alexander Hamilton, John Paul Jones, Abraham Lincoln and George Washington. In the event, only two volumes in the series appeared in print: these were *Feu le lieutenant Bringolf* (1930) and *Al Capone le Balafré* (1931). The former is presented as a translation from the German autobiography of Bringolf, a Swiss former soldier who had fought in the same regiment as Cendrars and whose malpractice while in the Swiss diplomatic service had him expelled from it, but did not prevent him from committing further acts of deceit in Latin America. Like the Bringolf volume, Capone's story is presented as Cendrars's translation of a pre-existing text, in this case Fred D. Pasley's biography of the Chicago gangster;[3] but there is much to suggest that Cendrars's input exceeded this role and spilled into some more creative rewriting.

Another closely related project, which gave rise to a plan and a draft text but never reached completion, is *John Paul Jones ou l'ambition* (*John Paul Jones; or, Ambition*). Cendrars worked on this initially from 1926 until 28 and returned to it in 1932–3, but by 1945, he had finally given up on the project altogether, citing the fact that his house had been pillaged by the Nazis during the Occupation.[4] Before this, it seems his other writing duties, the complexity of the undertaking and the discovery that Jones himself had written his own story all conspired to prevent the book from reaching completion. In *The Books in My Life*, Henry Miller writes about this and suspects that Cendrars simply felt overwhelmed by the scale that the project had acquired:

> The spectacular story of this man's life is one of those projected books which Cendrars has not yet written and probably never

> will. The reason is simple. Following the trail of this adventurous American, Cendrars amassed such a wealth of material that he was swamped by it. In the course of his travels, searching for rare documents and buying up rare books relating to John Paul Jones' myriad adventures, Cendrars confessed that he had spent more than tenfold the amount given to him by the publishers in advance royalties. Following John Paul Jones' traces, Cendrars had made a veritable Odyssean voyage. He confessed finally that he would one day either write a huge tome on the subject or a very thin book, something which I understand perfectly.[5]

The book was based on the life of the Scottish-born seafarer who rose to prominence as a lieutenant in the Continental Navy. By the time he died in Paris in 1792 aged 45, Jones had fought against Britain in

Roger Schall, photograph of Cendrars on the maiden voyage of the *Normandie*, 1935.

the American Revolutionary War, become an admiral for the Russian Imperial Navy, and been appointed to the position of commander of secret missions by Louis XVI and honoured by him for his service to the French nation.[6] In December 1925, Cendrars signed a contract for his book with Grasset, and one month later he obtained a contract for its English translation from Harper & Brothers.[7] In early January 1926, Cendrars had embarked on his second journey to Brazil. It was there, in March and April of that year, that he wrote most of the extant parts of this book, which end partway through the first of its four sections.

The fragments that do exist are fascinating, as much for the light they shed on Cendrars as for what they tell us about the book's subject. The first part of the book, written in the first person, asserts the narrator's identity as synonymous with Cendrars himself. It reveals that the book was written en route to Brazil and during his stay there, 'dans cet immense pays en formation que l'on défriche de plus en plus au nord et à l'ouest (caoutchouc, café) et qui peut encore recevoir plus de cent millions d'hommes' (in this immense country in the making that is being exploited more and more in the north and west (rubber, coffee) and which can still take more than a hundred million men).[8]

The book offers captivating insights into Cendrars's conception of writing about historical subjects; this is particularly significant in light of his subsequent work, and not least the four volumes of memoirs that appeared in the latter part of the 1940s. For a writer as openly averse to theorization as Cendrars, the introductory pages of *John Paul Jones ou l'ambition* bring us as close as we ever get to a statement of his methods; what he writes in this regard is especially instructive in suggesting possible reasons behind his decision to write about the lives of others. This first section makes some intriguing arguments about the relationship that writing can, and should, establish between author and reader. Suggestively entitled 'Touchez du doigt' (Touch with Your Finger), it asserts the importance of getting close to the subject so that a strong human connection can be established. This entails, first, looking closely, but also other sensory ways of engaging.

Cendrars's narrator admits that, while he has limited experience of archives, he has an appreciation of documents that can give rise to discussion, interpretation and misinterpretation.[9] He goes on to express his dislike for theories that are allowed to become dogmas and then remain unchallenged.[10] In order for theories to avoid the risk of calcification, they need to be sufficiently supple to move with the times and to accommodate the imaginative input of other parties. Above all, one senses, theories are only viable as long as they can be brought out of the abstract realm and into the world of concrete reality. Only then can they be put into practice and related to real-life individuals. Here as before, we find Cendrars negotiating the shifting, indeterminate space that connects literature and life but also distinguishes them from one another.

> Qu'est-ce que la Vérité Historique ?
> Et qu'est-ce qu'un Document ?
> Une interprétation toujours, tendancieuse ou artistique.
> Un tremplin.
> Pour bondir.
> Dans la réalité et la vie.
> Au coeur du sujet.
> [. . .] La Vérité Historique c'est le point de vue de Sirius. On ne distingue plus rien de cette hauteur. Il faut descendre, se rapprocher, fair un gros plan. Voir. Voir de près. Se pencher sur. Toucher du doigt. Découvrir l'humain.
>
> (What is Historical Truth?
> And what is a Document?
> Always an interpretation, tendentious or artistic.
> A springboard.
> For leaping.
> Into reality and into life.
> Into the heart of the subject.
> [. . .] Historical Truth is Sirius's point of view. Nothing can be distinguished from that height. You have to go down, get closer, take a close-up. See. See closely. Lean on. Touch. Discover the human.)[11]

The underlying ideas here, and the specific terms in which they are expressed, are equally intriguing. Cendrars suggests that a given entity or reality becomes fully meaningful only at the point at which it is possible for the individual to engage with it on a human level. His terminology brings us back to cinema: the 'gros plan' (close-up) is the cinematographic equivalent of close reading or of becoming closely acquainted with the subject by other means. Underpinning his words here is the notion that rigorous scrutiny can reveal an underlying truth, one that might otherwise have remained unknown and invisible to the naked eye. Implicit in this is the notion that the imperious stance of theoretical knowledge is only partially useful and requires us to bring it down to the level of humanity before it can be fully applied and exploited. The close-up, revered by early film-makers, is the key to unlocking the affective potential of cinema; as Gilles Deleuze formulated it, 'The image-affection is the close-up, and the close-up is the face.'[12]

In the cinematographic context, Cendrars's allusion to the sense of touch in this passage merits consideration. His conflation of the acts of seeing and touching chimes with some of the claims that his acquaintance Jean Epstein makes in his theoretical writings on cinema and modern poetry.[13] Cendrars's words come particularly close to a 1923 essay on photogénie, in which Epstein argues that the phenomenon of the close-up brings the act of seeing into contact with other, non-visual sensory experiences.[14] In his study of Epstein, Christophe Wall-Romana observes that 'the medium of film is tightly intertwined for Epstein with bodily affects and non-visual sensations.'[15] Rather than reducing photogénie to the sum of its technical properties, Epstein insists on it as an embodied experience; moreover, it is no static, categorical condition but involves the spectator's subjectivity in dynamic ways. In order to stress the particular character of the phenomenon, he resorts to a linguistic analogy, one that aligns itself neatly with Cendrars's order to the reader to reach out and touch the subject: '*photogénie* is conjugated in the future and the imperative.'[16]

Cendrars's words also prefigure other more recent theories that break down rigid differentiations between sensory impressions. Cendrars's words seem to anticipate the theory of 'haptic visuality' as expounded by Laura U. Marks. Following Deleuze and Guattari, Marks defines her understanding of this phenomenon in terms of a 'kind of seeing that uses the eye like an organ of touch.'[17] Cendrars had already intuited a dislocation of the senses in *Profond aujourd'hui*; yet rather than a synaesthetic overlapping in which one sense dissolves into another, the sensory experiences he described there remain discrete, although their natural functions have been reversed, with the effect that optical and haptic sensations assume each other's properties: 'Des centres de sensibilité se polarisent. Indépendance de toutes les fonctions. L'oeil tend à toucher; le dos mange; le doigt voit.' (Nerve centres are polarized. All functions are independent. Eyes reach to touch; backs eat; fingers see.)[18]

John Paul Jones ou l'ambition thus continues his long-standing interrogation of the boundaries that separate the senses; it also explores and questions other kinds of categorical borders relating to selfhood and its representation. As the introductory section of the book reaches its end, the narrative returns to the question of what it means to write about the life of another human being. Here, Cendrars insists upon humanity as an essential condition of any such literary endeavour. As he reflects, the mark of a hero does not lie in the number of monuments erected in his honour; a hero is 'avant tout un être humain, c'est-à-dire un souffle, un coeur, des poumons, cinq sens, un cerveau, des réflexes, mille impressions chatoyantes, de la timidité, et de l'ignorance, et de l'impuissance, et de la peur' (above all a human being, that is to say, a breath, a heart, lungs, five senses, a brain, reflexes, a thousand shimmering impressions, shyness, and ignorance, and helplessness, and fear).[19]

Cendrars goes on to explain the consequences of this humanist vision for his writing, whose very nature is shaped by it. Crucially, he acknowledges that the life of the other has become a means of exploring the self, and that he has decided to call this book a novel because it does not so much contain the official biography of Admiral John Paul Jones as 'ma propre autobiographie prêtée à un personnage historique' (my own autobiography lent to a historical figure).[20]

Cendrars's choice of the term 'novel' is radical, since it has serious implications for our understanding of what constitutes a novel and a biography alike, and the relationship that each of these genres can have with lived experience. He suggests that any literary account of a life is, to some extent, a fictionalization. His approach has something in common with both autofiction and exofiction, which both serve to blur conventional distinctions between factual and fictional modes of discourse. Exofiction, the more recent of these two literary categories, relates to ostensibly fictional forms of writing that incorporate factual elements.[21] Exofictional writings usually focus on an individual who is not the author; autofiction, by contrast, is broadly autobiographical in nature, and presents certain aspects of the writer's own life, but does so in fictionalized form. In documenting the extraordinary lives of others, Cendrars is exploring himself. Thus, when he describes John Paul Jones as 'un solitaire qui ne pouvait quitter les hommes, un contemplatif jeté dans la mêlée' (a loner who could not be away from people, a thinker thrown into the fray), it is impossible not to see this as a self-portrait.[22] Indeed, Henry Miller describes Cendrars in strikingly similar terms: 'The most gregarious of men and yet a solitary one.'[23] The section entitled 'Touchez du doigt' ends with Cendrars admitting that he could not think of a term other than 'novel' that was better suited to the act of writing about a person's life, with all its flaws, contradictions, false starts, trials and tribulations. As Cendrars acknowledges, 'on ne peut pas raconter d'autre vie, que la sienne propre' (you can't recount a life other than your own).[24]

Cendrars is particularly interested in the point at which our understanding of self and other can become porous and indistinct. Here we are reminded of his insistent questioning of identity in the wake of Rimbaud's declaration that 'je est un autre' (I is another) and Nerval's claim that 'je suis l'Autre' (I am the Other). Identity, Cendrars seems to suggest, is always inevitably overlaid with alterity; the notion of the stable self, identical to the voice that writes 'I', has been superseded by a multitude of possible selves who are constantly evolving and whose identity can take shape in the act of writing. This view that the self is not essentialist in nature, is not pre-determined and fixed from birth to death, but is shaped and reshaped by experience, brings us close to the notion that the world is coterminous with our representation of it. As we have noted, Cendrars repeatedly invokes Schopenhauer's dictum 'Le monde est ma représentation' (The world is my representation). Indeed, the belief that it is possible to create one's own world through the creative act seems like a natural corollary for an individual who invented his name and shaped his identity as a poet.

Another aspect of *John Paul Jones ou l'ambition* that deserves mention is its structural complexity. The plan that Cendrars produced in 1935 maps out its four sections, followed by an epilogue. Three of them are sketched out only vaguely, and he notes that their writing will depend on his obtaining access to Jones's diaries. But the first section, the only one to be fleshed out in any detail, consists of four sub-sections, each of which is subdivided into seven sequences. Cendrars's filmic imagination is again here in evidence, and the practice of breaking a text down into many short, numbered sequences has much in common with the notational technique that he had employed in writing his cinematographic novels such as *La Perle fiévreuse* and *La Fin du monde filmée par l'Ange N.-D.* The compositional complexity of *John Paul Jones ou l'ambition* also points ahead to some of Cendrars's later writings; Flückiger sees a particular parallel with the 'magistral jeu de cartes' of *L'Homme foudroyé*, which would construct the four 'Rhapsodies gitanes' from 32 evenly distributed chapters.[25]

Cendrars also planned to write biographies of artists who had led extraordinary lives. In 1929, the publishers Grasset advertised a forthcoming book of his in a series called 'La Vie de bohème' (Bohemian Life); this was to be a biography of Cendrars's erstwhile friend from La Ruche, Amedeo Modigliani, who died of tuberculosis aged 35. He also planned a book on the legendary Brazilian sculptor Aleijadinho (*c.* 1738–1814), who created numerous church statues despite a severely debilitating illness, suspected to be leprosy, that required his sculpting tools to be bound to his palms.[26]

The one unfinished book that would have been most similar to *L'Or* in theme and conception was *L'Argent*, subtitled 'Histoire mirobolante de Jim Fisk' (The Amazing Story of Jim Fisk). Based on real-life events, this story too had much appeal for Cendrars. Fisk ran away from home at an early age to join a circus and went on to make his fortune trading cotton before losing it all on the black market. He was murdered by his former business associate Edward Stokes after the latter tried to extort money from him with the help of Fisk's wife, with whom Stokes was by then living. Cendrars wrote a draft plan of this book in 1934 and a few pages of the story the following year, but it never reached completion.[27] Even in its draft form, it is clear that this book shared some features employed in *L'Or*. Besides the theme of financial intrigue leading to the principal character's downfall, the draft reveals that its writing style possessed the same attention to cadence and syntactic concision as the earlier novel. Moreover, the third section of the first chapter of *L'Argent* makes an explicit reference to the Gold Rush and suggests that the expansion of Wall Street was a corollary of the speculative frenzy that it inaugurated in 1848.[28]

The Secret Life of Jean Galmot: Rum

The one book about a remarkable individual that did make it into print was *La Vie secrète de Jean Galmot [Rhum]*, published by Grasset in 1930. The book recounts the real-life story of Jean Galmot, who settled in Guyana in 1906 and went on to establish a successful and, by the standards of its time, ethical business exporting gold and rosewood. When he began producing rum, his unusually fair treatment of his indigenous suppliers led to conflicts with his competitors. Charged and imprisoned on highly spurious grounds for fraud in the 'Rum Affair' of 1921, he ran for election as Deputy of Guyana in 1924 but lost to his rival Eugène Lautier amid widespread rigging. When Galmot died of suspected poisoning in 1928, riots broke out. What sets him apart from the historical figures who interested Cendrars at the time is the contemporaneity of his story: Galmot had died only a few months before work on the book began.

Rhum began life as a commission for the newspaper *Vu*: Cendrars signed a contract in October 1929 for ten submissions of three hundred lines apiece, to be published in serial form.[29] This publication brought Cendrars to the attention of a wider readership. Initially unconvinced by the prospect of expanding this material into a book, Cendrars changed his mind after reading a newspaper headline that declared: 'L'homme qui a perdu son coeur. Thémis a égaré le coeur de Jean Galmot. Bonne récompense à qui le rapportera.' (The man who lost his heart. Thémis has misplaced Jean Galmot's heart. Good reward to whoever returns it.)[30] The headline found its way unchanged into the book and even became the title of its first chapter. Cendrars instructed the newspaper's editors to do some initial research on Galmot and enlisted his friend and fellow writer Nino Frank to help with the drafting of the text, which he then edited and partially rewrote after visiting Galmot's birthplace, the village of Monpazier in the Dordogne, in January 1930. The book incorporates texts from various other sources, including Conrad Moricand's astrological reading of Galmot based on his birthdate; the text of an electoral speech from 1924 made by Galmot after his five-year stint as Deputy of Guyana; testimonies written by those who knew and worked with Galmot; extracts of speeches from his trial, which began at the end of 1923; a passage from a poem by Louis Roubaud; traditional songs in Creole; and the sole remaining page of a book written by Galmot. As Myriam Boucharenc aptly puts it, the book is 'un récit profondément polyphonique' (a profoundly polyphonic narrative).[31] In spite of its status as a textual assemblage culled from diverse sources, *Rhum* is unmistakably the work of Cendrars. Like *L'Or*, extensive passages are written in the present indicative and in short sentences, conferring upon it a directness and a lack of 'literariness'. Another distinctive feature is the syntactic elasticity that alternates between short utterances, at times clipped to a single word, and lengthy sentences with lists of words linked by commas. The book is dedicated 'aux jeunes gens d'aujourd'hui fatigués de la littérature pour leur prouver qu'un roman peut aussi être un acte' (to the young people of today who are tired of literature to prove to them that a novel can also be an act).[32]

The story is structured in twelve chapters, which disrupt chronology in ways that anticipate the post-war 'prochronies'. The first chapter asserts the text's status as a reportage, announcing that Galmot has died of suspected poisoning; the remaining chapters take the reader through Galmot's life, concluding with the poisoning and giving Galmot the (nearly) last word by citing a page of his authored book. The definitive version of the book features an 'Epilogue in the guise of a preface' that Cendrars added in 1934. This single page is emblematic of the textual polyphony that characterizes the rest of the book. It outlines the suspicious circumstances of Galmot's death, cites the official inquiry into it, and inserts lines from Moricand's horoscope of Galmot followed by a quotation from Galmot that intensifies its ominous quality.

Cendrars later dismissed *Rhum* as his weakest novel; while it does not achieve the complexity or imaginativeness of his best work, it marks an important point in his literary career, and its particular combination of factual events relayed through a terse narrative voice allows us to imagine what an exciting series of extraordinary lives he might have written had circumstances allowed it.

Gliding

After the flurry of publishing that ended the 1920s, the early '30s heralded an abrupt drop in productivity. By the end of 1929, Cendrars was living in Biarritz in the home of Eugenia Errázuriz. In the spring of 1930, he began working on *Vol à voiles* (which translates as *Gliding*), a collection of memories of his childhood in Neuchâtel commissioned by the Swiss publishing house Payot.[33] By the end of 1930, though, Cendrars was beset with health problems: he fell ill with depression, which seriously affected his ability to write for the next two years. He did manage to finish *Vol à voiles*, which was published in June 1932, but lost his momentum with *John Paul Jones ou l'ambition* and another planned novel, *La Vie et la Mort du Soldat inconnu* (The Life and Death of the Unknown Soldier), both of which would eventually be abandoned. Meanwhile, John Dos Passos published his English translation of *Panama* in 1931, and the same year Cendrars published under the title *Aujourd'hui* a collection of short essays that he had written in the previous decade.

Despite its insubstantial length, *Vol à voiles* is significant for the place it occupies within Cendrars's work as a whole, since it anticipates and inaugurates the many works of prose in which he recounts episodes of his life. It can be seen as a companion piece to *Prose du Transsibérien*, in the sense that it returns in more detail to some of the autobiographical events that appear only elliptically in that poem. In *Vol à voiles*, recounting the departure from the family home in order to work for a jeweller in St Petersburg, he adds that his boss was Rogovine, a Jew from Warsaw who was profitably involved in numerous businesses for which he seemed not to be commissioned.[34] He also paints a poignant picture of his father, who had died in 1927. If it thus provides some resolution to questions prompted by *Prose du Transsibérien*, it also opens other new chapters; as his earliest attempt to write an explicitly autobiographical account in prose, it foreshadows the autobiographical works that became an important element of his post-war output. And in stylistic terms it is highly innovative, since it provides the first occurrence in his or any other oeuvre of a new literary genre, the 'prochronie', which is how the front cover defined the book on its publication on the last day of 1931. This neologism of Cendrars's invention reappears in his post-war memoirs.

Vol à voiles nearly had another lease of life as one part of a trio of autobiographical essays prefaced by a lengthy letter. Having signed a contract to write a book about François Villon, Cendrars failed to produce the expected tome; instead, he tried to republish *Vol à voiles*, renamed 'Vol à voile', as one of three parts of an autobiographical book to be entitled *Sous le signe de François Villon* (Under the Sign of François Villon). The other two sections were to consist of a hitherto unpublished essay entitled 'Le "Sans-Nom"' (The 'Nameless One') and 'Une Nuit dans la forêt' (A Night in the Forest), originally published in 1929. Most significantly, he presented his three autobiographical accounts as belonging to an entirely unknown literary genre that he called the 'prochronie'. This new label underlines the role of time as an essential part of the stories' conception: each of the three texts is introduced by a year that indicates the date of the events to which it refers, namely 1901, 1911 and 1921. The three narratives would be prefaced by a dedicatory letter from the author to his first editor, Paul Laffitte, with whom he had been friends since 1916, when they had first worked together 'under the sign of François Villon'.[35] More specifically, as Cendrars recalls in his letter, Laffitte had invited him that year to join him in establishing the Editions de la Sirène. At that time, Cendrars was obsessed with the idea of publishing a new edition of Villon's poems; moreover, he was insistent that this should neither be a luxury tome targeting the wealthy, nor a heavily annotated one for the exclusive interest of academics. Instead, it was to be cheap and accessible to all. As Cendrars correctly recalls, it sold for a mere ten francs when he and Laffitte reprinted it in 1918, accompanied by illustrations from Villon's era.[36]

The long letter to Laffitte is the one part of this proposed book that engages with Villon. Significantly, though, it does so by establishing a series of comparisons between the fifteenth-century poet and the twentieth-century one: as Cendrars points out, they were both hard-drinking travellers who dropped out of their studies and found themselves banished from their homeland. He also asserts the natural alignment of his and Villon's modes of writing, citing the medieval poet's use of slang, his wide range of popular registers and his discussion of social inequality as important influences on his own development as a poet through his 'ardent, adventurous adolescence' spent in St Petersburg, China and New York.[37] Cendrars goes on to pour scorn on the way in which Villon has been subjected to exhaustive scholarly studies of a particularly Parisian sort. For all their earnest intent, such works of criticism fall into the trap of delving into too much detail and, as a result, lose sight of the life of the poetry and end up skewing what Cendrars, citing Albrecht Dürer, terms the *Idealbildnis* or ideal portrait.[38] This sheds revealing light on Cendrars's own writing and his understanding of the relationship between factual accuracy and a deeper, more poetic kind of truth.

Cendrars's dedicatory letter goes on to focus on a modern-day *poète maudit*, namely Arthur Rimbaud, who, like Villon, has fallen victim to an excessively intellectualizing form of criticism practised by those poets who inhabit the 'sombre Sorbonne'.[39] Here, he explicitly names Claudel and Aragon among those guilty of maltreating the memory of Rimbaud. His onslaught levelled against stale academicism continues as he attacks those who have attempted to explicate the words of his literary hero Gérard de Nerval with scholarly erudition but a disregard for the spirit and life of the poetry.[40] Academics are not the only culprits, however; he also criticizes the Hollywood film industry for sidestepping Villon's identity as a leading poet and instead reducing him to a truant.[41] Towards the conclusion of his letter, Cendrars admits that he will not furnish Laffitte with a 'Life of Villon', a 'romanticized life' or yet another attempt to explain his poems in depth. Instead, Cendrars's three essays, covering three decades of his own life, will present his three important 'encounters' with Villon over a period of a quarter century (the fourth encounter being his letter itself) as a way of creating a freer, less literal, more allusive response to Villon's life and work. In concluding his letter, he makes some fascinating observations that help us understand what he is aiming to achieve with his 'prochronies' and how he conceives of writing in the first person. Here, his remarks on Villon are clearly intended to reflect his own practices as a writer: 'qui te dit que ce *je* que François emploie tout le long du Testament est un *Je* biographique et non pas le *Je* idéal, lyrique, en somme impersonnel de Villon, le poète [?]' (What tells you that this *I* that François uses all the way through the *Testament* is a biographical *I* and not the ideal, lyrical, impersonal I of Villon the poet[?])[42] Finally, he acknowledges openly that his essays will be about himself, albeit only in order to reflect wider society. As he notes, the act of writing about himself, even in the first person, is above all a means to explore wider questions about the world and our place in it: 'Il ne s'agit donc pas seulement de moi dans ce "Je".' (This 'I' is thus not only about me.)[43]

The notion of creative collaboration and the benefits of learning from others is central to 'Vol à voile'. It ends with a lengthy meditation on music, prompted by Cendrars's memory of his efforts to find casual work in Munich, which culminated in a spontaneous duet with a talented employee of a piano showroom. This in turn takes him back to Neuchâtel and to Hans Hess-Rüetschi, the elderly organist at the old temple in that city, for whom Cendrars served as an assistant and drinking partner during his year there. Under Hess-Rüetschi's informal tutelage, he learned to improvise, or 'invent', as the organist put it. This taught the young Sauser an important lesson, namely that in life, as in music, it is beneficial not simply to accept received ideas but to look beyond them and strive to create new thoughts. Decades later, as he reflects on the fact that the loss of his arm brought his musical education to an end, Cendrars nevertheless acknowledges his ongoing debt to Hess-Rüetschi's wisdom and his life lessons. He concludes by citing his mentor's adage that the best way to make life bearable is to reinvent it repeatedly.[44]

The book's two further chapters, 'Le "Sans-Nom"' and 'Une Nuit dans la forêt', both contribute rich material for an understanding of Cendrars's evolution as a writer and his shaping of a form of life-writing. 'Le "Sans-Nom"' was written between 1935 and 1938 but never finished; even in its incomplete state, it tells us much about Cendrars's enlisting of invention into what is ostensibly a factual account. From the opening paragraph, it is clear that we are dealing with a kind of truth that cannot be reduced to factual accuracy: the 'Sans-Nom' (the Nameless One), his first-person narrator informs us, refers to the ship on which he travelled from Libau to New York in December 1910, and whose name he claims not to recall. Contemporaneous manuscripts reveal that Cendrars not only remembered that the ship was called the *Birma* but even intended to use its name as the title of another essay.[45] Moreover, he travelled on it in 1911, a full year later than the narrative suggests. The nameless entity of the title, then, is surely not the ship but the author himself, as he shed his birth name and prepared to assume the new persona of the poet Blaise Cendrars. It seems fitting that the self-styled *bourlingueur* in the making should commemorate this hugely significant moment within the framework of a journey: the literal, physical displacement across the Atlantic would then stand in for the slippage of identity from the patronym Sauser to the pseudonym Cendrars and the rebirth that this act symbolized.

When it was published in modified form in the journal *La Revue de Paris* in 1952, this story was called 'Partir' (Leaving), and indeed, the central theme is his restlessness.[46] The story narrates his insatiable wanderlust and his recourse to literature as a vicarious means of escape: he acknowledges that books offered the solace he needed.[47] One of his bedside favourites was Leonardo da Vinci's *A Treatise on Painting*, and in particular the passages in which the artist describes a powerful storm that leaves humans powerless to defend themselves against it. These passages from the *Treatise* inspired the young Cendrars to translate it into music to make it 'retentir dans une grande symphonie cosmique sur le Déluge' (resound in a great cosmic symphony on the Deluge).[48]

The same source inspired another creative act that features in this story; the circumstances in which it occurred make it one of the most important turning points in Cendrars's life as a writer. The event in question is the miraculous night of writing that he experienced in Méréville, a small village just over 65 kilometres south of Paris, on 1 September 1917, his thirtieth birthday. As he narrates it, the circumstances could not have been more unprepossessing: at the time, he was living in an abandoned barn; his writing desk was a door that he had removed from its hinges and propped up on two old crates. By candlelight, he sat on a bale of hay and began to write 'comme un inspiré, de la main gauche, d'une traite, et sans une rature, et sans avoir à chercher les mots' (like a man inspired, with my left hand, in one go, without scoring anything out and with no need to search for my words).[49] By the following morning, to his astonishment, he realized he had written *La Fin du monde filmée par l'Ange N.-D.* from start to finish. Writing from the standpoint of the mid-1930s, he acknowledges that the memory of this feat has become 'le témoignage d'une longue, lente, douloureuse et double cicatrisation, sinon d'une guérison parfaite' (the testimony of a long, slow, painful and double healing of scars, not to say a perfect recovery).[50] The adjective 'double' reflects the importance for Cendrars not only of returning to health but of regaining the ability to write, as if these two factors were of equal importance to him. Like the initiatory journey to New York, this uncanny, almost involuntary resurgence of his creative impulse represents a rebirth; reflecting on the text that emerged from his hand that night, he admits to realizing after the event that he had been carrying an 'embryo' inside him.[51] Paradoxically, the act of writing a tale about the end of the world engendered the beginning of a new life as a left-handed writer; the tropes of creation, destruction and rebirth that crop up repeatedly in his writings seem so tightly connected as to be inseparable. As Claude Leroy states, it was in Méréville that Cendrars became *the other*, the man and poet of the left hand.[52]

Perhaps there is a third wound in 'Le "Sans-Nom"', and this is the story itself, which is prematurely excised. As we have seen, it begins by alluding to the author's journey by ship to New York, but it tails off as he is in the train waiting for it to depart for St Petersburg. He attributes the choice of destination to pure chance: having little more than the cost of a train ticket to his name, he arrives at the Gare du Nord with the intention of travelling as far as his money will allow. The unhelpful employee working in the ticket office, whose unpleasant appearance and manner Cendrars later recognized in the writer Joseph Delteil, refuses to help him, so from a list of destinations printed on a board, he chooses the city simply because its name happens to be at his eye height. Of course, we know that this was not true; he had been invited to St Petersburg by the family of Hélène, his girlfriend who had died in a fire four years earlier. But such liberties do not detract from the fact that this story communicates a poetic truth about the power of creative inspiration and the irresistible urge to travel that characterized Cendrars from an early age onwards.

'Une Nuit dans la forêt', the book's third and final prochronie, was written between March 1925 and March 1927, thus, some years before 'Le "Sans-Nom"'. It shares with the previous two prochronies its emphasis on travel and its loose treatment of chronology and factuality: bearing the date 1921, the story begins as Cendrars arrives in Paris from his first trip to Brazil; the narrative thus situates the journey three years before its actual date; it unfolds over an extremely short space of time, a matter of hours he spent in the French capital between returning from Brazil and setting off to Spain. Cendrars claimed to have written the story in Castets-les-Landes, a village in the south of France, and in Rio, conferring further globetrotting cosmopolitanism upon the narrative. The heavily autobiographical narrator and protagonist who emerges in this text is a writer and seasoned traveller, yet somewhat world-weary, and professes to have lost the desire to live the kind of life of frivolity and risk-taking that leaves a trail of debts, furious mistresses and a distraught wife in his wake.[53] The one remnant of his earlier life that Cendrars's narrator still retains is an insatiable need for renewal. He acknowledges that his curiosity to learn foreign languages and discover unfamiliar environments stems from a need to break with old habits and 'perdre pied' (lose footing).[54]

He seems particularly jaded with contemporary society's obsession with sex: his own recent stay in the virgin forests of Brazil had led to amorous encounters that he had abandoned suddenly in order to finish a long-awaited manuscript which transpires to be *Dan Yack*. When he returns to France and hands it to his publisher, Jean, a thinly disguised René Hilsum, the latter complains that it has not one sex scene in it, and Cendrars agrees to add one, but featuring whales.[55] His disaffection with love becomes clearer in the second half of the story, which revolves around Pompon, a fragile young woman scarred by self- and love-inflicted wounds: she had shot herself in the abdomen on discovering she was pregnant by the boyfriend who had abandoned her. Pompon's character bears traces of Dourga, the star of Cendrars's film *La Venere nera*, who had died shortly after completing the shooting, and also Raymone, his real-life muse, whom he addresses, but without naming her, in the closing lines. The evocation of the actress unites the different geographic and temporal layers of the story, as the imminent prospect of watching her onstage revives memories of sleepless nights in Brazil during which he would think of her as he lay in a hammock smoking a cigarette. In a beautiful evocation that recalls the opening sentence of *Profond aujourd'hui*, the text describes how the glowing embers of the cigarette tip become as one with the countless stars in the sky.[56]

IN AUGUST 1939, when he wrote his dedicatory letter to Paul Laffitte, Cendrars was about to set off on a year-long journey around the world on one of the last remaining large windjammers, the *Moshulu*.[57] He had proposed to write a report on the voyage for *Paris-Soir*, to be accompanied by photographs by his friend Elisabeth Prévost, whose experiences of hunting in Africa would find their way into the stories on this topic in *D'Oultremer à indigo*.[58] He anticipated sending his letter/introduction to Laffitte in early 1939 and completing the writing some time thereafter, but the outbreak of war on 2 September 1939 put a stop to the book and the trip. Instead, Cendrars signed up as war correspondent for the British Expeditionary Force in France, leaving the unfinished book in a trunk, probably at La Mimoseraie, the home of his friend Eugenia Errázuriz in Biarritz, where he spent much of his time in the 1930s. During the war the trunk went missing, along with much of his book collection, presumably when La Mimoseraie was sold. By an extraordinary coincidence, Cendrars found the trunk and most of his books again in an antiquarian bookshop in the same town in 1950.[59]

In one sense, the trajectory that led from the commission to write about Villon to an essentially autobiographical trio of narratives is a reflection of Cendrars's skill, not to say deviousness, in circumventing his obligations towards his publishers and persuading them to accept a fundamentally different literary entity from him. In another sense, the choice of overarching title, with its overt reference to the most famous French poet of the Middle Ages, compels us to think differently about the accounts. The appropriation of Villon's name asserts the heavily intertextual nature of Cendrars's three essays and displaces them from the sole realm of autobiography, multiplying their literary identity and overlaying them with a palimpsest of poetic history. Cendrars was probably drawn to Villon for his non-conformism, his anti-elitist views and his peripatetic lifestyle as much as for his radically innovative approach to poetic language; by enlisting the fifteenth-century poet to his cause, he subscribes to a vision of the poet as a free spirit, a wanderer, a man of the people and an enfant terrible. In literary terms, Cendrars's adoption of Villon as the patron saint of his writing compels us to think anew about the testament as a form of writing. The finality that it implies – a testament as an account of a life intended to be read posthumously – invites us to think of the particular temporality of Cendrars after the loss of his right arm, reliving or imagining anew experiences undergone before that loss. All of his writings after the devastating events at the Navarin Farm in 1915 must have been marked by an especially acute consciousness of his own mortality. In a symbolic sense, his writing after the amputation embodies this awareness, and the act of writing brings into existence a body of literature that in some respects may represent an effort to replace or supplement another damaged, incomplete body.

In this light, an aspect of 'Une Nuit dans la forêt' that deserves comment is its depiction of cinema and the capacity of the camera to reveal hitherto invisible aspects of physiognomy. It is all the more remarkable given that it was written as early as 1925; thus, it anticipates by several years Walter Benjamin's 'The Work of Art in the Age of Mechanical Reproduction', which famously likened the incisive action of the camera to that of the surgeon's scalpel.[60] Like Benjamin after him, Cendrars in this short story expresses his fascination with the surgical invasiveness of filming. He reflects on how an early intervention with the camera could have 'cured' Pompon of her chronic depression. Yet his narrative is to say the least ambivalent, describing the filming process as akin to pointing a gun, capturing, tying up, lassoing, drugging, luring and rendering the subject unconscious as if with chloroform. The camera even has the capacity to penetrate the victim and replace her personality.[61] Immediately following these sentences, Cendrars's narrator portrays the work of the movie camera in terms that situate it somewhere between a surgical operation and death by a thousand cuts, but claims that the experience would have brought Pompon relief, like the removal of a cyst.[62]

Like many of his generation, Cendrars lamented the demise of the silent era, which he felt had a level of artistry that the talkie could not equal. Yet he was quick to exploit the creative possibilities of recording sound and to consider its implications for literature. We have seen how *Les Confessions de Dan Yack*, some thirty years before Beckett wrote *Krapp's Last Tape*, exploits the potential of the tape recorder to explore the relationship between memory and identity.[63] Cendrars's close encounter with Hollywood brought his feelings about the film industry into sharp focus.

Hollywood

The passage cited above from 'Une Nuit dans la forêt' suggests a profoundly ambivalent relationship to cinema; the movie camera with its penetrating quality has the capacity to heal but also to kill the subject caught in the gaze of the lens. A similarly paradoxical vision of the film industry emerges from Cendrars's assignment to Hollywood in 1936. He was, in many respects, the perfect candidate for the job: preceding chapters have considered his deep and wide-ranging involvement in cinema, be it as the author of screenplays, essays on cinema or cinematographic poems, a production assistant and bit-part film actor, or as a film-maker in his own right. Whether theoretical in nature or embedded into fictional or autobiographical works, his authored texts on the subject of cinema are valuable documents of this art form, which was still in its infancy.

At the end of January 1936, he was sent on an assignment to the epicentre of cinema in Los Angeles; the fruit of his stay was not a film but an essay, 'Hollywood, la Mecque du cinéma' (Hollywood, Mecca of Cinema). He was there in his capacity as a writer, but also as the author of a script that had been adapted for a Hollywood movie. Indeed, his visit coincided with the release of *Sutter's Gold*, James Cruze's film adaptation of his novel *L'Or*.

As early as 1928, Cendrars had signed a deal that gave Universal Pictures the rights to a film adaptation of his book. According to Ivor Montagu, in 1929, the internationally renowned film director Sergei Eisenstein was already considering adapting the novel for the cinema, and a letter from Cendrars to him at the end of September 1930 refers to a dinner that they had had together in Paris.[64] Eisenstein went on to produce a complete script, 'The Golden Demon', and Paramount gave the green light to the project, but the film was never made. Daniel Winkler cites as a possible reason the fact that Eisenstein, as a European Jew, was unlikely to be a popular choice of director for a film about the history of North America.[65] Christine Le Quellec Cottier notes that the next attempt to adapt the novel was under the auspices of Howard Hawks, who enlisted William Faulkner to write the screenplay. Charles Laughton was considered for the key role.[66] This project, too, fell by the wayside, leaving Cruze to pick up the reins.

In Hollywood, Cendrars met the actor Edward Arnold, who played the title role in Cruze's film. In spite of its commercial success, Cendrars was disappointed with the adaptation, which he felt was an inaccurate reflection of the novel. But worse was to come: the same year saw the release of an unauthorized German film, also based on his book, but which failed to acknowledge its source. Its Italian Austrian director Luis Trenker played the leading role in the film. The fact that this version of the story is widely judged artistically superior to the Hollywood adaptation must have been galling to Cendrars, especially in view of the fact that the unauthorized film was a product of Nazi Germany. Cendrars commenced legal proceedings against Trenker on grounds of plagiarism, but the outbreak of war halted them. By the time peace was resumed in 1945, he had run out of energy to pursue the case.

Cendrars's Hollywood essay expresses fascination with the stars of the movie industry and its high-profile figures such as Walt Disney, and

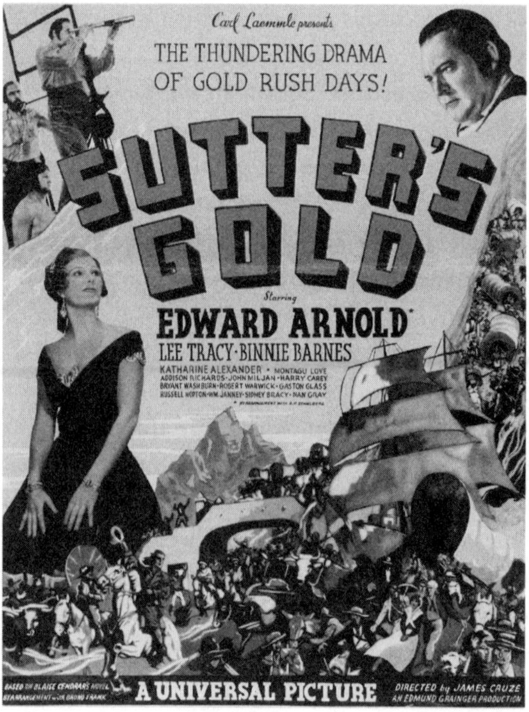

Poster for *Sutter's Gold* (1936, dir. James Cruze).

disgust with its blatantly commercial interests and factory-style production. One huge sentence enumerates the panoply of technicians, engineers, assistants, secretaries, costume and make-up artists, drivers and hangers-on who populate the set for the painstaking and time-consuming takes and retakes of a simple close-up shot of a screen kiss. All this happens under the critical eye of the cigar-puffing producer, his wife and her friends. Cendrars observes drily:

> Alors, on est beaucoup plus que cinquante et tout cela papote, ergote, cancane, compare, donne son avis, commente, s'esclaffe, rit, jalouse, censure, applaudit ce baiser – ce faux baiser – et la chose finit, toute la smala enjuponnée et caquetante s'en va boire un cocktail en ville, un 'kiss-me-quick', celui que Mae West aime, au *Vendôme* ou au *Trocadéro*, les deux boîtes à la mode.

> (So there are well over fifty people, and the whole lot are chatting, quibbling, gossiping, comparing, giving their opinion, commenting, guffawing, laughing, envying, censoring, applauding this kiss – this false kiss – and when it's over, the

> entire beskirted and prattling tribe goes off into town to drink a cocktail, a 'kiss-me-quick', the one that Mae West likes, at the *Vendôme* or the *Trocadéro*, the two fashionable nightclubs.)[67]

For all his irritation with the paraphernalia of the industry, he recognizes the power that a single shot can wield when viewed by millions across the globe. The idea of cinema as a form of communion pervades his writing on the subject.

The late 1930s saw Cendrars publishing three further related volumes of essays, the first two of which were intended to form a pair. On Christmas Eve 1937, *Histoires vraies* (True Stories) was published by Grasset. It was followed by *La Vie dangereuse* (Dangerous Life) in 1939; the third, *D'Oultremer à Indigo* (From Ultramarine to Indigo), appeared in 1940. These have something in common with his earlier books based on remarkable lives, but this time they present Cendrars explicitly as the narrator and main protagonist for the first time. In fact, he is present and mentioned in all but one of the stories, the exception being 'T.P.M.T.R.', which opens *Histoires vraies*. The tales of all three volumes are as disparate in their contents as they are in their geographic reach, with stories that reflect the author's travels in Brazil, his journeys by ship and his experience of the trenches of the First World War, as well as numerous anecdotes that are as much the product of invention as of any lived experience. In this last sense, they are exemplary of Cendrars's understanding of poetic truth, which is emphatically not identical with factual events, even if the two cross paths at many points along the way.

Histoires vraies

This is the most diverse of the three books, yet it is driven by the same guiding principle as the others, namely that its stories focus on identifiable places and individuals whose veracity is presented as being beyond question. Across the range of stories, some subtle parallels emerge: the opening and closing tales are set aboard ships, and the penultimate one, 'L'Actualité de demain' (Tomorrow's News), also features an anecdote about a ship and its crew. Brazil and, more broadly, Latin America feature repeatedly, as do North America and other parts of the world. The opening story, 'T.P.M.T.R.', locates us in familiar Cendrars territory: it takes place on a cargo ship making its way in extreme weather from Le Havre to the coast of America. When one of the crew members, a corpulent,

Photograph of Cendrars with writer and editor Henry Poulaille at the Brasserie Lipp in Paris, 1937.

heavy-drinking man from Bordeaux, dies while aboard and the ship is unable to dock or store the body safely, the crew are forced to dispose of the body and its ornate coffin at sea. Remarkably, some time later they discover that the dead man, driven by currents and probably kept buoyant by gas escaping from his decomposing corpse, had reached the shore of Miami. The ship's captain reflects on the impressive speed of 5.4 knots at which the body must have travelled to reach Miami in little over two days; a crew member retorts and, in the process, explains the enigmatic title of the story – 'Tu pars, mais tu reviendras!' (You leave, but you will return!)[68] The dead man is identified in part thanks to a tattoo on his pubis, partly obscured by hair, which the authorities assume to be his name, but fail to read in its entirety; one of the crew corrects this, revealing that the tattoo reads neither Robert Durnand, nor Robert Dournant, nor Robert Dournour, but 'robinet d'amour' (love tap).[69] On a narrative level, too, the opening story foreshadows the multiplicity of textual levels and sources: it contains a reproduction of a form detailing the post-mortem handling of the body and a long letter purporting to come from the shipping company in which is contained the report it received from the United States port authorities, forwarded by the consul in New York. Such devices assert the material's veracity and lend even its most implausible anecdotes an air of credibility.

Seemingly insignificant pieces of information emerge that become more meaningful as we read the other stories. The ship's name is the *Saint-Wandrille*, which refers to an abbey located in a community in the Seine-Maritime department of Normandy. It is the resting place of various saints, a theme that reappears in the third story, 'Le Saint inconnu' (The Unknown Saint), set in Santiago de Chile. This subject foreshadows the fourth of Cendrars's post-war memoirs, *Le Lotissement du ciel*, which devotes considerable amounts of space to the lives of saints. Other stories in the book are heavily inter- and intra-textual too: 'Le Cercle du diamant' (The Diamond Circle) cites a paragraph from the Antarctic explorer Charcot's written account of his expedition to the South Pole, a journey that formed the basis of the first Dan Yack volume.[70]

One of the most surprising examples of this book's range is its inclusion of an entire story written by Al Jennings and presented in Cendrars's translation. As Cendrars explains in his introduction to the chapter, he had met Jennings in person on the last day of his trip to Hollywood.[71] It is easy to understand the appeal of Jennings for Cendrars: the American would have made a worthy candidate for an entire book in Cendrars's series focusing on extraordinary lives. A former train robber and one-time suspected murderer, Jennings had served part of a life sentence before being released from prison and receiving a presidential pardon from Theodore Roosevelt in 1904. He went on to have a career in politics, standing for election as governor of Oklahoma in 1914 (where his campaign focused on his pledge to obey the law for a whole year), and worked as an attorney before establishing a new career in the film industry making westerns. As a writer with a life of adventure behind him, Cendrars must have found it easy to relate to Jennings, and this is indeed the impression that the chapter's introductory paragraphs give. Moreover, Jennings and Cendrars were connected through literature: in 1921, Jennings had written a book, *Through the Shadows with O. Henry*, described by its publishers as 'a colourful and tall-tale memoir'; by the time of their encounter, Cendrars had already translated Jennings's text 'from the American and slang'.[72] Noting that Jennings had not yet written a story with a main female protagonist, Cendrars invited Jennings to pen a story for him, which constitutes this chapter of *Histoires vraies*. Set in 1875 in Dog-Town, New Mexico, it centres on Dollie Madison, the owner of a seedy saloon atmospherically named Le Bidon de Sang (The Can of Blood). It is easy to see why Jennings's story had such an appeal for Cendrars, who admits that he translated it 'telle quelle' (as it is).[73] Jennings's life is, for Cendrars, 'un roman duquel il manque le vraisemblable' (a novel that lacks plausibility), so there was no need to further embellish its already remarkable facts.

From the start, *La Vie dangereuse* follows in the vein of *Histoires vraies* by presenting its author as a world traveller. Its opening story finds Cendrars aboard a cargo ship on its way from Dunkirk to Bahia Blanca in Argentina via Port-Vendres, Oran, Tangier and Dakar. On his own admission, nothing awaits him in Latin America apart from the opportunity to visit his acquaintances.[74] The journey thus presents excellent opportunities to observe life on board and to recall previous voyages and experiences. The short stories also recall the *Histoires vraies* in their praise of adventure and their fascination with those individuals who, like Al Jennings, flirt with danger: 'Febronio, Indio do Brazil' is about a notorious and highly violent criminal, sadist and religious fanatic who removes his victims' teeth. Conflating fiction and fact with characteristic insouciance, Cendrars compares him to Moravagine and to Don Pedro, another Brazilian criminal who appeared in his essay 'Eloge de la vie dangereuse', published in *Aujourd'hui* in 1931.

One of the most harrowing stories, and also one of the most significant for its proximity to Cendrars's own experience, is 'J'ai saigné' (I bled). This narrative brings us closer than almost anywhere else in his oeuvre to the primal scene of his mutilation; it begins only 48 hours after the amputation of his right arm, with Corporal Cendrars lying on a stretcher in the courtyard of the military hospital where the operation took place. The opening pages evoke the agony of this period in which his life seemed to be at risk of slipping away; but very quickly, the spotlight shifts away from him and onto Sister Philomène, the nurse who tends him and his fellow *mutilés de guerre* with extraordinary energy, empathy and strength. Philomène, a Florence Nightingale for the age of mechanized warfare, is a rare example of a female protagonist in his work who is fully developed, compassionately drawn and not merely the writer's other. The story is also an opportunity for Cendrars to vent his fury towards those figures of authority whose inflated self-confidence and conviction in their superior knowledge cause grievous harm. In this case, an Inspector General arrives to show off his surgical skills and insists on demonstrating them on a seriously weakened soldier whom Sister Philomène has been tending with patience and dexterity. Even as the great expert tries to dazzle his audience with his tricks, the soldier dies an agonizing death.[75]

D'Oultremer à Indigo derives its title from one of the stories in which Cendrars claims to have spent 97 days travelling the length of the Orinoco river by canoe. On that expedition, he found one of the rarest of all flowers, revered for its extraordinary characteristic of changing colour, not once but several times: over the course of a day it transforms from white, through pink, red, orange and violet to bright blue, which it maintains throughout the night before returning to white by the following dawn. One of the longest stories in the book, a five-part account of hunting in Africa entitled 'Mes Chasses' (My Hunts), asserts the author-cum-narrator as a seasoned expert and, somewhat troublingly, begins with an analogy between big-game hunting and firing at the enemy in wartime: 'I love hunting. I know what it is to bring down a charging being with a devastating bullet. At the front they always came to look for me. I was the best rifle in the company.'[76] Once again, care must be taken to distinguish the first-person narrative from fact: while Cendrars admitted to Michel Manoll that he had a keen interest in the life of animals, and had even made films about them, he dispels any assumption that he is a keen hunter, a fact that may come as a surprise to readers who assume that the first-person narrator of the poems in *Documentaires* describing elephant hunts is autobiographical.[77]

The narrator goes on to boast of having shot 27 Germans in a single morning at the Somme, spurred on by the lieutenant's reward of 50 litres of wine per hit. Four of the five parts take place in Brazil, the fifth in Naples; but while the locations do relate to the author's first-hand experience, the tales of hunting leopards, crocodiles and boa constrictors are borrowed and imported into their Brazilian setting. The true source of these accounts is his friend Elisabeth Prévost, an experienced solo traveller who had hunted in Africa. Cendrars had met her in Paris in February 1938 and dedicates the story to her under the nickname 'Bee and Bee'. Appropriately enough, Cendrars enjoyed board and lodging on her stud farm in the Ardennes between 1938 and 1939, and it was there that he translated Portuguese novelist Ferreira de Castro's *A Selva* as *Forêt vierge*

(Virgin Forest).[78] Cendrars saw in Prévost a kindred spirit who shared his love of travel and exploration. They remained on close terms until the war separated them.[79]

Even if the 1930s are often regarded as a relatively fallow period in his career, Cendrars's reportage and his essays are a valuable contribution to his literary legacy. They reveal an imagination that has lost none of its creative energy, and they confirm his mastery of the short story genre, whether it be fictional, autobiographical or a combination of the two, as is often the case. In their use of the first-person narrative voice, their breadth of scope and their remarkable erudition, these books set the tone for much of his post-war output. Perhaps most significantly, the books set in place a creative practice in which the author absorbs fragments of information and weaves them into intricate tales of lives invented and created, including his own. Elisabeth Prévost notes:

> Il captait tout. Enregistrait tout. Ensuite, longtemps après, remis dans ses moules à lui, réécrivait superbement des vérités qui étaient devenues mensonges ou vice-versa. C'est cela sans doute l'imagination ou l'imaginaire. Le transfert. Je l'ai constaté beaucoup d'années plus tard, presque vingt ans après, dans un chapitre de *L'Homme foudroyé*.
>
> (He captured everything. Recorded everything. Then, much later, back inside his own mould, he would rewrite truths that had become lies or vice-versa. No doubt that is imagination or the imaginary. I noticed it many years later, nearly twenty years afterwards, in a chapter of *L'Homme foudroyé*.)[80]

Prévost alludes here to a section of the book entitled 'Une drôle de vierge' (A Curious Virgin), in which certain aspects of her appear in the fictional character Madame de la Panne. The chapters that follow will explore this and the other first-person memoirs written after the war and consider how they unearth myriad ways to reinvent a life.

eight

Memoirs Without Being Memoirs: Reinventing the Self

The preceding chapters have attempted to reflect the breadth and richness of Cendrars's literary output. The picture that emerges of the man himself is no less multi-dimensional; indeed, it is worth pausing for a moment to reflect on the extraordinary ways in which not only his literary work but his personality evolved over the decades, a development mirrored by his thickening physiognomy. His own early letters and diary entries point to a sensitive, intense and serious individual, an impression reinforced by the accounts of friends and acquaintances of the young Cendrars. As we saw earlier, Sonia Delaunay recalled her first encounter with Cendrars at Apollinaire's flat in Paris before the First World War; the impression he made on her was of a physically small, reserved character who paled into insignificance alongside the more corpulent and extrovert Apollinaire.[1] A very different image of Cendrars emerged later in his life, and particularly in the post-war photographic portraits of Robert Doisneau, and this ultimately became his defining iteration for the wider French reading public: this older Cendrars was a genial globetrotter and raconteur, sharing drinks and anecdotes with those prepared to listen, cigarette permanently jutting from the corner of his mouth. It is difficult to reconcile these contrasting versions of Cendrars, but despite the very significant changes he underwent throughout his life, we can identify points of contact across the different stages of his career that help us to understand the underlying connections between them. The mature figure was shaped, both physically and in terms of character, by the wealth of experiences lived and recounted in his writings. That literary output is the tangible evidence of his compelling need to live life to the full; and this compulsion connects the earliest writings of a young man, impatient to explore the world, with the post-war tetralogy of books that speak of countless adventures. The tension between the need to write and the desire to live accompanies him through his entire literary career.

On the outbreak of hostilities in 1939, Cendrars was in Paris. Having fought in the Great War a quarter century earlier, he was now too old to enlist in the French army, having turned 52 years old just two days before Britain and France declared war on Germany on 3 September 1939. Neither his age nor his disability prevented him from trying to volunteer for the armed forces, and he managed to be taken on as a war reporter for the British Army. This experience is recounted in his book *Chez l'Armée anglaise*, which appeared in 1940.[2] This book assembles articles previously published in the press dealing with various aspects of British military policy. It expresses his admiration of the strength of the British Army, the prodigious output of munitions and aircraft manufacturing, and the quality of military training. Fittingly in view of the author's extensive experience of sea travel, it concludes by considering the important role of the Royal Navy in clearing mines and recounts his visit to the Port of London.

In terms of his literary output, the years of the French Occupation were overwhelmingly unproductive. Cendrars must have felt profoundly affected by the return of war to Europe. At the start of Nazi Occupation, he left the capital for Bordeaux and went on from there to Aix-en-Provence, where he ended up staying until January 1948.[3] The period 1940–43 was uncharacteristically barren for him: he suffered from writer's block, a state that is hardly surprising in light of the prevailing world events. Reflecting on the gravity of this situation for Cendrars, Claude Leroy alludes to this as a second 'amputation' in which his ability to write was brutally and unexpectedly curtailed.[4] Fellow writer and former seafarer Edouard Peisson, who befriended Cendrars during the war years, dedicated his novel *L'Homme couvert de dollars* to him 'en souvenir de quatre années de tristesse vécue côte à côte' (in memory of four years of sadness experienced side by side).[5] Nevertheless in July 1944 he wrote to Raymone announcing that he had finished *L'Homme foudroyé* and would send the complete manuscript to the publishers by September.[6] There is palpable relief in his words, and one senses his sheer exhilaration at having managed to see the book through to completion, a remarkable achievement in light of the difficult circumstances in which he had been working.

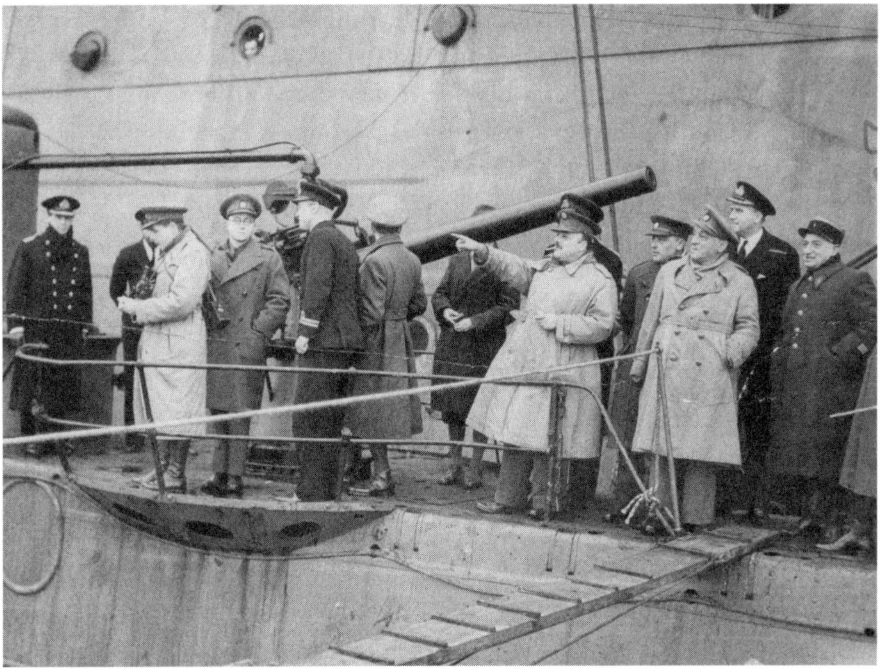

Photograph of Blaise Cendrars (third from the right) and a group of journalists aboard a submarine in England, 1940.

But far from being an isolated feat, this would become the first volume of a tetralogy of works as remarkable for their expansiveness as for the speed with which they came into being. After his three lean years, the fecundity of this period of Cendrars's career exceeded anything he had achieved before. After *L'Homme foudroyé* (1945, trans. *The Astonished Man*, 1970), he would go on to publish in close succession three other volumes that are similar in length and style: these are *La Main coupée* (1946, trans. *Lice*, 1973), *Bourlinguer* (1948, trans. *Planus*, 1972) and *Le Lotissement du ciel* (1949, trans. *Sky*, 1992). All four volumes together amount to nearly 2,000 pages.

L'Homme foudroyé sets in motion a conversational, seemingly loosely structured form of discourse, narrated in the first person, that is far removed from the stylistic economy of his poems of the 1910s and the terse notational style of his novels and cinematographic writings of the 1920s and '30s. The four books are broadly autobiographical in nature, but we find Cendrars here, as so often in his work, diverting from any single straightforward genre and creating a new form of writing entirely his own. Bochner notes that some of the preliminary research was conducted at the Bibliothèque Méjane in Aix-en-Provence, but in order to accomplish the writing, Cendrars simply 'mixed erudition with a rich past'.[7] In an interview with Michel Manoll, he described the books as 'des Mémoires sans être des Mémoires' (Memoirs without being Memoirs).[8]

The scope of the present study does not allow for a detailed discussion of theories of autobiography, but it is helpful to consider some of the most significant ones. Rousseau's *Confessions* is often considered to be the founding autobiographical text, at least for the modern era; Augustine's *Confessions* clearly provided the original model. Rousseau's stated aim, 'montrer à mes semblables un homme dans toute la vérité de la nature ; et cet homme ce sera moi' (to display to my kind a portrait in every way true to nature, and the man I shall portray will be myself), effectively paved the way for the entire genre of autobiography, but as critics have ascertained, even this definitive book is a literary entity and departs from neutrality and objectivity in many instances.[9] In the twentieth century, Gérard Genette made important distinctions between writing in the first person and autobiography per se. As Genette notes, a book written in the first person need not express the author's opinion or be seen as synonymous with the author; nor does an account require a first-person narrator in order to be autobiographical.[10]

Writing after Genette, Philippe Lejeune has had widespread influence with his concept of the autobiographical pact.[11] Highlighting the ambiguity of the word 'person', which can refer both to a grammatical figure and to a living entity, Lejeune focuses on what is happening at the level of the text. The pact to which his title refers pertains to the relationship between author, narrator and character. He makes a meaningful distinction between identity and resemblance,[12] and indeed he detaches the autobiographical text from problematic constraints such as 'truth' and resemblance; Lejeune thus argues that the essence of autobiography resides in the act of narrating rather than in a putative verisimilitude.

Building on Lejeune's thinking, Michael Sheringham contends that autobiography is essentially governed, not by fixed structures, but by processes that are fluid and characterized by otherness.[13] This alterity is by definition multiple: first, the act of writing inevitably establishes a distance between the person who writes and the 'I' about whom s/he writes; however much a text may aspire to truth, it can never be identical to lived experience. Moreover, by writing, the author engages in relationships with external parties: the unknown reader, whose perspectives and sphere of reference will differ from those of the author; but also the tradition and the infrastructure of writing and publishing, which are external to the writer's subjectivity.

Max Saunders argues that '[the] writing of the self as an "I" becomes an impossible project. No autobiographical project will be able to capture the chaos of the "I", because the very act of articulating the self as an "I" presupposes a unity in it, or imposes a unity upon it.'[14] In keeping with the notion that autobiography is necessarily a diverse and complex genre, he proposes the term 'autobiografiction'. In literary terms, Cendrars's tetralogy encapsulates much of the indeterminacy and otherness that the above theorists and others have identified in recent years as a predominant feature of autobiography.

'Prochronies' and 'Rhapsodies'

It is entirely characteristic of a writer who never ceased to experiment with literary categories and forge new ground that Cendrars devised a wholly new literary genre into which these books would fit: the name he chose for this is 'prochronie'. As Christine Le Quellec Cottier has noted, this neologism derives from the word *prochronisme*, a term used to denote a form of anachronism in which a narrative situates an event in the past at a point in time before its actual date of occurrence.[15] As we have discussed above, one of the most ambitious of the many unfinished book projects that Cendrars was planning in the 1930s was to be entitled *Sous le signe de François Villon* (Under the Sign of François Villon). It was to consist of three short essays, 'Vol à voile', 'Le "Sans-Nom"' and 'Une Nuit dans la forêt', all of which would be prefaced with the generic heading 'Prochronie' and followed by the dates 1901, 1911 and 1921 respectively.[16] Setting the pattern for the subsequent works constituting Cendrars's tetralogy, *L'Homme foudroyé* employs this technique to recast time outside its most conventional linear, sequential guise; instead, it brings together chronologically disparate recollections that are periodically interspersed with allusions to the time of writing.

But there is more to the 'prochronie' than the manipulation of sequential time; another distinguishing feature is the combination of factual events and real characters with some elements of the author's invention. In these books we encounter an array of figures who were known to Cendrars, but they appear alongside characters of his creation as well as some fictionalized versions of real people. The implications of this narrative technique will be discussed later. For the time being, let us focus on what can be ascertained with confidence: Cendrars creates a narrator and protagonist called 'Blaise' who is ostensibly synonymous with the author but should not be confused with him.

Another innovative term that Cendrars chose in the context of these experiments is the 'rhapsodie': less overtly striking than 'prochronie', the label is nevertheless meaningful, particularly in a literary context. We encounter this category in *L'Homme foudroyé*, in which a quartet of 'Rhapsodies gitanes' constitutes the third of three sections and occupies more than half of the book. The category of the rhapsody originates in ancient Greece, where it referred to a series of epic poems sung by an itinerant poet. In its evocation of epic poetry, but also in its association with travel, the rhapsody is the ideal category in which to present such a peripatetic narrative. The choice of word is also a throwback to Cendrars's early years on the pre-war Parisian literary scene and his *Prose du Transsibérien*, whose title was intended to reflect his preference for the popular associations of the term 'prose' over the more elitist 'poème'.[17]

The rhapsody as a genre entered the musical context in the eighteenth century, and in the mid-nineteenth century composers including Franz Liszt adapted it for musical compositions that incorporated Romany violin playing. Cendrars's adoption of the term seems to allude to this conception of the rhapsody, since the 'Rhapsodies gitanes' focus on various Romany characters. At a more general level, too, the trope of the rhapsody lends itself well to *L'Homme foudroyé*, and for many reasons. Not only does it relate to the nomadic nature of Cendrars's writing, which inhabits a range of geographic locations, but it is germane to the book's apparent structural looseness as well as its informal narrative style: the stories that constitute the book are not presented chronologically, and nor do they all follow the logic of cause and consequence. As a result, Cendrars partly masks the fact that his text is extremely neatly organized, with each of the four rhapsodies subdivided into eight parts. This combination of rigorous order and elements that appear more spontaneous is well suited to his chosen literary genre: in the musical context, a rhapsody denotes a composition that has an improvisatory character, consisting of a single movement, but is typically episodic in nature and often contains juxtapositions in mood and dynamics. This term is eminently well suited to the unexpected excurses and digressions that intersperse Cendrars's narrative.

While Cendrars's post-war 'prochronies' are closely related to autobiographies and memoirs, they can also be described as precursors of a literary form that became known as autofiction. This term, coined in 1977 by the French novelist Serge Doubrovsky in his novel *Fils*, alludes to a broadly autobiographical form of writing in which the author's name is shared with a protagonist in the story.[18] In Cendrars's case, not only do all the post-war books in question have a narrator called 'Blaise', but they allude to various friends and acquaintances of his; *L'Homme foudroyé* alone includes anecdotes involving Fernand Léger and André Gaillard, as well as Gustave Le Rouge. These figures appear alongside others whose identities have been partly fictionalized, such as Le Rouge's second wife, Françoise, and Paquita, who is almost certainly based on Cendrars's real-life patron, the wealthy Chilean silver mine heiress and style icon Eugenia Errázuriz, who had encouraged him to live and write in her home in Biarritz in the interwar years. Cendrars's technique of combining straightforwardly factual details with those of his own invention poses intriguing questions regarding the representation of truth; not the least significant is to what extent facts and truth can differ from one another. Does a factual account of events necessarily tell the truth? And conversely, in order to be a reliable record, does a story need to recount all of the facts? Can a fictional story convey a given truth more effectively than a factual one? Such questions compel us to reconsider the relationship between fact and fiction, which should not be seen as mutually exclusive categories but can instead be regarded as complementary aspects of the same phenomenon that is experience. As Lee Rourke noted shrewdly in an article on Cendrars in *The Guardian*, 'it is his mockery of biographical details and the very notion of literature that fascinates me the most. If, like me, you're not a fan of autobiography, then Blaise Cendrars is the memoirist for you [. . .] Cendrars dances on the ashes of outmoded literary styles to create his own pioneering art.'[19] In her introduction to *Sky*, the English translation of *Le Lotissement du ciel*, Marjorie Perloff likens his literary approach in the memoirs to the principles of heterogeneity and collage that he had first explored in *Prose du Transsibérien*.[20] These appraisals reinforce the idea that Cendrars is continually striving to unearth new ways of thinking about literature and its relationship to lived experience.

Myth

The life and literary work of Cendrars are bound up with various experiences that have achieved a quasi-mythical status. Prominent among these are the tropes of death, rebirth and reinvention that appear throughout

Daniel Wallard, photographs of Fernand Léger and Blaise Cendrars in Trouville-sur-Mer, 1954.

his entire literary oeuvre; a barometer of these recurrent themes is the author's own name, which itself undergoes a series of transformations. First, his birth name evolves from Frédéric-Louis Sauser to Freddy Sauser; then he changes his name to Blaise Cendrart before definitively becoming Blaise Cendrars. Such radical shifts of identity are entirely in keeping with an author whose entire life can be summed up as a series of reinventions. The first of these is that of the young man casting himself in the guise of poet of the pre-war Parisian avant-garde. He would soon accrue another identity, that of the *mutilé de guerre*, the wounded war hero. The image of the *manchot*, the writer with one arm missing, comes to define him in the later years of his life. Added to this is perhaps the best-known version of the mythological Cendrars: the genial raconteur who expounded at length on radio interviews in the early 1950s and whose anecdotes are often regarded as inventions. Bruno Frank is one of those who identify in Cendrars a tendency to embellish the truth, although he argues that it matters not one jot whether Cendrars actually took the Trans-Siberian express, given how vividly he conveyed it in written form.[21]

Cendrars is unquestionably responsible in large part for the creation of these myths. Indeed, it might be said that a part of his literary identity, or indeed his literary project, revolves around the imbrication of his life in his literature. In interviews he expresses the view that writing is a tedious and tiring activity, and that it is not living in any real sense, but rather an abdication, since when we write, we are not existing as physical beings. Cendrars's writing often creates the impression that he is addressing the reader as his personal interlocutor; his humanity and humour shine through, whether he is writing about everyday matters or arcane subjects. At times, his narrative style is so stripped of literary artifice that it resembles the most direct transcription of thoughts or actions.

The post-war autobiographical writings are another instance of how Cendrars is always one step ahead of his reader. These writings are remarkable for the sheer scale of their ambition and for the fact that the four books have a shared identity as a series of interrelated works while also operating autonomously at an individual level. This inevitably prompts comparisons with Proust and other figures who pursued an overarching artistic idea spanning several years and several works; Cendrars's creative process may be likened to artists such as Monet or Robert Delaunay, who produced extensive series of paintings on given themes.

According to Claude Leroy, we should see the young Cendrars and the mature one as contiguous parts of the same single entity. The connection between these two phases of the writer's life lies in the incessant desire to innovate, be it in the audaciously experimental pre-war poems or the post-war autobiographical writings, which are extraordinary in a very different way. In a sense, the later works are more discreetly provocative, since they enact their subversion beneath the guise of an ostensibly conventional literary form. It is easy to see why Cendrars's readers were not ready for the act of insurrection that his post-war books articulate. They can be read simply, straightforwardly, as mythologized reworkings of an autobiography, but they are much more than this. Seen either individually, or over their entirety, the four lengthy volumes that constitute his immediate post-war published output deserve to be regarded as a thoroughgoing re-articulation of writing through one's subjectivity. Cendrars's unique legacy is to have created not only the myth of the wounded writer, but the mythical reconfiguration of the self into a literary genre. For this reason, it seems fitting to identify the later works with precisely the spirit of invention and experimentation that scholarship has more commonly reserved for appraisals of his earlier work.

Cendrars was quick to refute any accusations that he was following a formula in those post-war years, and hindsight compels us to agree that each of the four volumes articulates a distinct form of literary innovation. Moreover, he continued to produce more conventional novels, alongside which the autobiographical writings carve out their own distinctive identity.

Cendrars's attitude to his peers on the visual arts scene is very revealing of the respective statuses of writers and poets at the time in which he was active. He comments that writers were approximately fifty years ahead of their artistic peers. Picasso, he observed, continued to produce work that fell easily onto the canvas. For Cendrars, this represents the complacent act of somebody who is no longer legitimately a member of any avant-garde, but who merely trots out facile visual exercises. He argues that none of the so-called artistic avant-garde came even close to the inventiveness of a Rimbaud. One suspects there may be a measure of envy in this account of the visual arts scene. After all, Cendrars had been acquainted with a huge array of early twentieth-century avant-garde artists in Paris at a time when they were living in poverty, with the exception of Picasso and the Delaunays, who already enjoyed a comfortable standard of living in the pre-war years. He had then seen how Picasso and others had become immensely wealthy on the strength of work that, for Cendrars, was certainly no more innovative or more original than the type of creations that some writers had produced. It must have been galling for him to see such a wide disparity emerging between their respective communities.

L'Homme foudroyé

From the outset it is clear that the writing of this book meant a great deal to Cendrars. As we have seen, its completion marked the end of three frustrating years in which none of his many writing projects had seen the light of day. Its preface, 'Dans le silence de la nuit', is a letter from Cendrars to fellow writer Edouard Peisson, who had become his friend during the Occupation when both were living in the south of France.[22] In it, Cendrars thanks Peisson for his crucial role in helping to break his pattern of inactivity. Curiously, the catalyst for this is an anecdote that Peisson tells about how a German lieutenant lodging in his home had persuaded him to go outside to view a lunar eclipse. Peisson obliged, only to discover that the German's true motivation was to distract his host and keep him outside while he spent the night indoors with a prostitute whom he had brought back from Marseille. Peisson's sense of wonder at the nocturnal spectacle is tempered only by his humiliation at being duped by the occupying enemy officer. Having told this story, Peisson promptly leaves, just at the moment when Cendrars feels the urge to respond by sharing similar anecdotes with him. Deprived thus of his interlocutor, Cendrars is prompted to fetch his typewriter and narrate his own experiences in what has become the book.[23] The reader is invited to conclude that Cendrars has simply sat down and unleashed a torrent of stories, as if he had been storing them inside his head for years, waiting for this moment to arrive.

Much about this preface calls to mind Cendrars's early years as a poet and the myths that surround his work: the notion that this book is the product of an uninterrupted stream of creativity reminds us of *Les Pâques à New York*, which he claimed to have written in a single night. A degree of proximity with the *Prose du Transsibérien* can be felt, too, in their multi-perspectival composition, their tendency to shift unexpectedly from one location and time to another, their emphasis on similar themes, and their use of a first-person narrator called 'Blaise' who, in the early poem and the post-war tetralogy alike, undermines any straightforward distinction between autobiographical fact and fiction.

Writing About (Not) Writing

Given the creative difficulties that Cendrars encountered before he managed to overcome them by writing *L'Homme foudroyé*, it is unsurprising that his narrative frequently alludes to the writing process itself, as well as to the difficulties that writers face. Indeed, the book explores a tension that Cendrars felt throughout his entire life. On the one hand he is acutely aware of the world around him and feels an irrepressible urge to live and experience it at first hand. On the other, he intends to document it in writing, but the demands that the writing process places upon his time threaten to make this impossible. As we have observed, this situation very nearly prevented the book from making it into print at all.

The paratextual additions that fill the margins of the book reinforce the impression that Cendrars intended to forestall any suggestion that it belongs within a singular, straightforward literary genre. It begins with an epigraph, a slightly modified passage taken from Descartes's *Discours de la méthode* that alludes to the 'grand livre du monde' (great book of the world); this, Descartes contends, consists 'à voyager, à voir des cours et des armées, à fréquenter des gens de diverses humeurs et conditions, à recueillir diverses expériences, à m'éprouver moi-même dans les rencontres que la fortune me proposoit' (in travelling, seeing courts and armies, mingling with men of diverse tempers and conditions, gathering a variety of experiences, proving oneself in the fortunes of life).[24] Cendrars could hardly have chosen a more apt way to describe the ambition of this book; certainly the impulse to portray a diverse array of individuals and gather a range of experiences rings true. For Cendrars, this does not mean spreading gossip or salacious facts about the many high-profile personalities he had encountered on the literary scene, some of whom he knew well. The book refuses to shed light on his uneasy relationship with the Surrealist group; Cendrars would reserve that for his radio interviews with Michel Manoll in 1950. On the contrary, the book does mention Raymond Radiguet and Charles-Albert Cingria briefly, and devotes considerably more space to the lesser-known writer Gustave Le Rouge, author of the popular serial novel *Le Mystérieux Docteur Cornélius*.[25] As already mentioned, in 'Rhapsodies gitanes', the third part of *L'Homme foudroyé*, Cendrars admits that he had copied, pasted and reformatted in verse form several lines from Le Rouge's serial novel into a book of poems that he published under his own name with no acknowledgement of the original source. Cendrars refuses to divulge the name of the offending poetry collection, but scholars have subsequently revealed it to be *Kodak (Documentaire)* (1924), which, fittingly enough, had to be renamed *Documentaires* after the Eastman Company threatened to sue him for infringement of copyright.[26] It was only several years after the event that he confessed this 'supercherie poétique' (poetic hoax) to Le Rouge, who took it in good spirit and gave the poet his blessing.[27]

While Cendrars greatly admired *Le Mystérieux Docteur Cornélius*, this section of *L'Homme foudroyé* suggests that he was even more interested in Le Rouge's life than in his literary activity; indeed, repeatedly the book articulates the message that living is much more important than being a mere writer. After a passage recounting the commission from Jacques Doucet to write *L'Eubage*, Cendrars's narrator comments on just how important it is for a writer to have lived and seen the world. Paradoxically, one needs life experience in order to become a writer; yet, on his admission, writing is a form of evasion that requires the individual to retreat from life:

> Je ne trempe pas ma plume dans un encrier, mais dans la vie. Ecrire, ce n'est pas vivre. C'est peut-être se survivre. Mais rien n'est moins garanti. En tout cas, dans la vie courante et neuf fois sur dix, écrire . . . c'est peut-être abdiquer. J'ai dit.
>
> (I do not dip my pen into an ink-well, but into life. Writing is not living. It is perhaps survival. But nothing is less guaranteed. In any case, in everyday life, nine times out of ten, writing is . . . perhaps it is an abdication. I have spoken.)[28]

This is a recurrent trope that punctuates Cendrars's writings throughout his entire career. And yet his oft-professed disregard for the writer's task is hard to believe in light of his extraordinary productivity and the sheer originality of his literary output. If the writing of this book was an abdication from life, then this is not at all the impression left on the reader, since the entire book is brimming with energy and an irresistible sense of the myriad wonders of everyday life.

Of the many prominent artists who belonged to his social circle, we learn next to nothing, with the exception of Fernand Léger, who does figure, albeit relatively briefly; as Jeff Bursey has observed, the book tells us nothing about the author's parents, siblings, first wife or children.[29] The characters who do figure prominently in the book are neither well known nor closely related to each other or to the author. Instead, the book constructs a mosaic of anecdotes involving various characters including his erstwhile camera operator Jicky and his wife; a woman who cleans the house in which he stays in the south of France, and her jealous husband; and various assorted members of the Roma community in the 'Zone' of Kremlin-Bicêtre on the southern outskirts of Paris. That is where the 'Rhapsodies gitanes' begin, on a day in 1923 when Cendrars's narrator agrees to introduce Léger to his Roma friends. Their visit coincides with a moment of extreme tension between two opposing clans: Scarface, a senior figure of the 'Spaniards', has been murdered by a member of the rival 'Transylvanians' shortly after being elected leader of the South Zone, or 'King of Sicily'. One of the victim's sons is Sawo, Cendrars's friend and erstwhile comrade from the French Foreign Legion. Sawo will in turn exact bloody revenge; some two hundred pages later, the book concludes with Sawo's first-person account of how he killed his father's murderer. The sheer importance of this figure in the narrative makes it tempting to agree with Philippe Gervais-Lambony's assertion that Sawo can be thought of alongside Moravagine as an alter ego of Cendrars.[30] The intervening sections of the 'Rhapsodies gitanes' take us to different times and places, but the individuals and communities living on the margins of society are at the forefront of this part and the book as a whole.

The short opening section, 'Dans le silence de la nuit', also announces the role that the theme of writing will play in the book. The letter addressed to Edouard Peisson alludes to the book as 'this first piece of writing', as if to suggest that Cendrars already knew that this would be merely the start of a much longer literary project. Later in the same letter, Cendrars writes a memorable passage in which he reflects on what it means to write. It is striking, both in the light it sheds on the text that follows and also in the specific terminology it adopts, 'braise' and 'cendres' evoking his chosen name:

> L'écriture est un incendie qui embrace un grand remue-ménage d'idées et qui fait flamboyer des associations d'images avant de les réduire en braises crépitantes et en cendres retombantes. Mais si la flamme déclenche l'alerte, la spontanéité du feu reste mystérieuse. Car écrire c'est brûler vif, mais c'est aussi renaître de ses cendres.

> (Writing sets ablaze a whole commotion of ideas, causing a chain of images to flare up before reducing them to crackling embers and crumbling ash. But though the flames set off the alarm, the spontaneous nature of the fire remains a mystery. For to write is to be burned alive, but it is also to be reborn from the ashes.)[31]

The implications of these lines are numerous and far-reaching. First, the highly evocative contention that writing is a fire is not only a striking figurative image, but one that must have had powerful personal associations for Cendrars as he wrote *L'Homme foudroyé*. Inevitably the invocation of fire reminds us of his first love, Hélène, who lost her life in a fire. It is also a bleakly appropriate metaphor for war – the First World War, memories of which are recalled in the first part of the book, as well as the Second World War that was ongoing during its writing. But the wording of this passage also very deliberately calls to mind another fire, the mythical one from whose ashes the phoenix is reborn. The presence of the word *braise* and the repetition of *cendres*, which occurs twice in this short passage, makes it clear that Cendrars was only too aware of the relevance of this mythological creature to his own situation and the new name and persona he invented for himself in 1912. The subtle allusion to his own pen name alerts us to the close parallels that the book will establish between the characters depicted and the writer himself. It prompts us to ask whether all the episodes that constitute this narrative are essentially intended to illustrate different aspects of Cendrars's own character. Whatever the case, it is clear that the various events that occur throughout the narrative reflect to a large extent the author's own life experiences and attitudes.

In the second section of the book, 'Le vieux port', Cendrars recalls his stay at the village of La Redonne near Aix-en-Provence in 1927. At that time, he had written all but the final chapter of his first Dan Yack novel, *Le Plan de l'Aiguille*, and needed to finish it. He took lodgings in the Château de l'Escayrol, a house in reality much less grand than its name suggested, in which he had the use of two adjacent rooms. He prepared for the task at hand, choosing to use the smaller room as his bedroom and the larger one as his study. He set up his typewriter in front of the double window and wrote three lines.[32] Despite this auspicious start, Cendrars is forced to admit that he did not write another word of the book during his entire stay in La Redonne. He concludes:

> Un écrivain ne doit jamais s'installer devant un panorama, aussi grandiose soit-il. J'avais oublié la règle. Comme saint Jérôme, un écrivain doit travailler dans sa cellule. Tourner le dos. On a une page blanche à noircir. Ecrire est une vue de l'esprit. C'est un travail ingrat qui mène à la solitude. On apprend cela à ses dépens et aujourd'hui je le remarque. Aujourd'hui, je n'ai que faire d'un paysage, j'en ai trop vu! '*Le monde est ma représentation*.'
>
> (A writer must never sit in front of a view, however magnificent it may be. I had forgotten that rule. Like St Jerome, a writer must work in his cell. Turn his back. We have a blank page to blacken. Writing is a vision inside the mind. It is thankless work that leads to loneliness. We learn this to our cost and today, I notice it. Nowadays, I could not care less about scenery, as I've seen too much! '*The world is my representation*.')[33]

These words are revealing, and not least the last sentence, quoted from Schopenhauer, to whom he returns repeatedly in this and other books.[34] Elsewhere, Cendrars thanks Schopenhauer for warning him against the pitfalls of overly intellectual writing *à la* Sartre: he writes, 'Les pièces philosophiques sont un ennui au théâtre, et Sartre monte ses thèses au théâtre. Les romans sont bien ou mal écrits, mais ceux de Sartre sont quelconques.' (Philosophical plays are boring in the theatre, and Sartre shows off his theses in the theatre. Novels are well or badly written, but Sartre's are mediocre.)[35] In *L'Homme foudroyé*, Cendrars suggests that writing is primarily concerned with opening up a view that is imagined rather than seen, and in so doing he sheds valuable light on his authorial intentions behind this book and the tetralogy as a whole. Yet whatever subject an author attempts to write about, the self inexorably enters the frame, and once again, Cendrars reaches for Nerval's words to explain his views. 'On n'écrit que "soi". C'est peut-être immoral. Je vis penché sur moi-même. "Je suis l'autre."' (One writes only 'oneself'. It may be immoral. I live hunched over myself. 'I am the other.')[36] The implications of this imbrication of self and other are far-reaching. The extract as a whole has wider ramifications, since it expresses the idea that the very process of documenting a self inevitably imposes a distance, making it different from the narrating voice that writes 'I'. This, too, is the implicit message behind the quotation marks that Cendrars has placed around 'soi' (oneself): even the most scrupulously detailed self-portrait that appears on the page can never be the same as the living being, since the subjective nature of writing, and the need to select, omit, edit and structure events at some remove from their occurrence, conspire to insert a space between the experience and its representation.

It seems fitting, too, that Cendrars should allude to Jerome, the fifth-century saint whose translation of the Bible into Latin entailed a careful negotiation of that most delicate of source texts, the holy Scripture. As the Latin origin of the word, *translatio*, reminds us, all translation entails a 'carrying over' of meaning from one entity to another. In this original sense, *translatio* also signified a shift from a literal to a figurative meaning, bringing it close to the sense of the ancient Greek term μετἄφορᾱ from which metaphor derives. Translation enacts a transfer, but so too does all writing to a greater or lesser degree, since it must renounce all claims to be a wholly objective representation of the truth. For this reason, writing that purports to have a factual basis is especially vulnerable to claims of distortion, inauthenticity and falsification. Cendrars is alert to this risk, and even questions the ethical implications of writing about himself: 'It may be immoral.'

The ethics of self-writing are all the more complex when they engage with significant historical events. Cendrars's tetralogy deals with aspects of the Occupation, which was ongoing during the writing process, but Laurence Guyon contends that the post-war tetralogy (to which Guyon adds *La Banlieue de Paris*) sees Cendrars affirming the specific historicity of the event, but only in order to annul it by means of his digressions, repetitions and manipulations of chronology. This, Guyon argues, serves as a means to transcend the historical singularity of the event and reinscribe it into the narrative in terms of a Nietzschean Eternal Return of war.[37]

The Volatilized Body

The book's richly suggestive title is itself a symptom of this complex, multilayered treatment of time. The title's eponymous man struck down was a soldier named Van Lees who fought in the First World War as a sergeant in the French Foreign Legion alongside Cendrars. As the opening pages of the book reveal, Van Lees suffered the most horrible death that the writer-turned-soldier would ever witness on a battlefield. Hit by a shell, he was blasted high into the air, causing his entire body to disintegrate immediately. As Cendrars notes, 'j'ai vu son pantalon ensanglanté retomber *vide* sur le sol' (I saw his blood-stained trousers fall to the ground *empty*).[38] This passage conveys with horrific directness the incomprehensible inhumanity of modern warfare and its monstrous capacity to kill with a force hitherto unseen. The scene is all the more shocking because of the invisibility of the enemy; as Paul Virilio has noted, the First World War was the first large-scale conflict in which the enemy was 'more or less invisible save for the flash and glow of his own guns'.[39] The sheer anonymity of the war, and its devastating effects on the humanity of those who lived through it, is a theme that returns later in Cendrars's tetralogy. Van Lees sums up the terrifying, almost otherworldly atrociousness of this new era of combat: he is 'cet homme assassiné en l'air par une goule invisible dans sa nuée jaune' (that man assassinated in mid-air by an invisible ghoul in a yellow cloud).[40] Cendrars's narrative recounts how he heard the victim's cry continuing to ring out for a long moment after the volatilized body had ceased to exist.[41]

Lurking beneath the account of Van Lees's fatal injury, but not evoked, is another injury, not mortal, but certainly life-changing: that of the book's author. The sheer proximity of the events narrated makes them relate all too closely to Cendrars's own life: the account of the sudden, violent death of Van Lees has obvious parallels with Cendrars's experience as a soldier and foreshadows the serious wounds that he sustained on the battlefield as well as the impact the war must have had on his psyche, aspects of his experience about which this often loquacious writer is uncharacteristically reticent. Van Lees died during the attack on the Navarin Farm in September 1915, the very same site and the same phase as the hostilities in which Cendrars sustained his own serious wound. As Bozon-Scalzitti notes, the fact that Cendrars personally witnessed the events narrated, and thus recounts them in the first person, makes it all the more difficult to avoid comparisons with his own situation. The story of Van Lees is thus ultimately also the story of Cendrars: 'The narcissistic insistance of "I have seen" underlines that Cendrars is contemplating, as in a mirror, his own death in the striking down of the other.'[42] Such a reading takes on even more weight when we consider that the explosion that kills Van Lees turns his body to embers and ash – *braise*, *cendres*.

In a literal sense, then, Van Lees is the 'homme foudroyé' of the title, struck down as if by a flash of lightning; and Cendrars, the ocular and auditory witness of the scene, is metaphorically struck down by this experience that foreshadows his own mutilation. We will consider the implications of this for the narrative strategies adopted in the book; but first, it is worth taking stock of how the narration of Van Lees's death relates to Cendrars's own account of the First World War.

Van Lees deserves to be understood as a reflection of Cendrars himself or at least as an extension of his persona; such an interpretation lends weight to the theory that the act of reliving Van Lees's death in writing is a displacement of Cendrars's deeply suppressed war injury, and perhaps also a form of therapy. If Cendrars is unable to write about his own experience – and the absence of a single detailed account of those events in his entire oeuvre suggests that this was indeed the case – then Van Lees can be seen as a narrative vehicle for the author's own trauma and an outlet for a pain so great that it must remain unspoken other than through indirect allusions.

Thomas Elsaesser notes that it is difficult to recognize trauma in literary and filmic representations precisely because trauma has a tendency to evade representation: 'If trauma is experienced through its forgetting, its repeated forgetting, then, paradoxically, one of the signs of the presence of trauma is the absence of all signs of it.'[43] Building on these words in a discussion of what he terms 'traumatic hermeneutics', Colin Davis writes of the challenges facing the interpretation of narratives of trauma, since they often avoid confronting the very subject that we might expect them to tackle: 'Trauma *isn't there*. This is not to say that it is not real, that it does not exist; but its sources and signs are not always immediately manifest.'[44] This leads to the question of how to interpret this absence; as Davis puts it, 'How do we distinguish between signs which are absent because there is nothing for them to signify and signs which are absent because what they signify is too dark, repressed and unknowable to be given manifest form?'[45]

In 'Dans le silence de la nuit', after the episode of Van Lees, Cendrars recounts the fate of Faval, another legionnaire in the company. Like Van Lees, Faval was to lose his life in combat at Navarin Farm in September 1915. Ever fearful of dying, Faval was clinging on to Corporal Cendrars when a fatal shot hit him between the eyes and caused him to fall on top of his corporal and putative protector. Cendrars recounts how he had to cut off a part of his own greatcoat in order to liberate himself from the dead weight of his fallen comrade.[46] Perhaps even more strikingly than the account of Van Lees's death, this episode of cutting something away in order to survive deserves to be interpreted as symbolic of Cendrars's own injury.

The published English edition of this book, in Nina Rootes's translation, bears the title *The Astonished Man*, which is ill-equipped to convey the different layers of meaning and the fundamental ambiguity of the original French. The translation does transmit the figurative sense of *foudroyer* (the expression 'foudroyer quelqu'un du regard' has the sense of looking daggers at someone); but in the passive form, *être foudroyé* literally means to be struck by lightning, a sense that is entirely absent from the title *The Astonished Man*. For this reason it is more meaningful, and truer to the multiple allusions in the original French title, to think of the book as being about *The Man Struck Down*; this captures both the literal and figurative senses of the term *foudroyé* as well as the ambiguity of the 'man', who could stand for Van Lees, the narrator, Cendrars himself, or indeed humankind. Unlike *The Astonished Man*, this title would convey the unprecedented violence of the war as well as its shocking impact on those who witnessed it at first hand and survived.

The uncanny disjuncture of sight and sound in the passage narrating the death of van Lees anticipates the many other spatio-temporal disruptions that we will encounter throughout this book and the three broadly autobiographical narratives that follow it. The refusal to follow a sequential chronology is just one of many features that distance these works from standard memoirs. Van Lees's dying cry, echoing in the air even after his body has been reduced to dust, disrupts the natural order in a macabre way as the physical manifestation of a body that no longer exists. Cendrars describes the short passage dedicated to the man's death as an ex-voto which should serve as his funeral oration.[47] Like Van Lees's final cry, Cendrars's words will continue to vouch for his existence long after his death.

In *The End*, the sixth and final volume of his series of autobiographical novels *My Struggle*, Norwegian author Karl-Ove Knausgaard considers the role of naming and identity. In a lengthy discussion of poems by Rainer Maria Rilke and Paul Celan, he muses on the relationship between the 'I', the name and society, invoking Scriptures of the Old Testament, the written fragments of Heraclitus, Rimbaud's declaration 'Je est un autre' and Joyce's experimental novels as notable instances of texts that interrogate the relationship between words and experience, and explore the boundaries of language, yet bring the reader in contact with an implied social other.[48] Reflecting at length on Celan's 1959 poem 'Engführung' (Straitening), he writes that upon death, we lose the capacity to be 'I', but our name lives on – for example, as an inscription on a headstone – as a reminder that we were once there. In this way, the name inscribes our identity in the social realm even after our death:

> The I is what is left of the person when the name is gone, the I is what dies when the person dies and the name lives on. The I is not erased in ecstasy, filled with the meaning of life, but in its opposite, being erased in the shadow of death, filled with its non-meaning.[49]

More speculatively, the account of Van Lees's body disintegrating in a split second may relate to Cendrars's writing practices in other ways. For instance, the sudden, inexplicable, brutal disappearance of his body can come to signify the complex, multiform, evasive nature of the writing self. Cendrars is implicitly present as the autobiographical subject and first-person narrator of the events depicted, yet if we look for the real Blaise Cendrars in the book, he disappears into thin air, to be replaced by the narrating presence called 'Blaise' that we encounter in the text. We have seen that a relation of near-identicality and identification between author and narrating presence has been a constant throughout Cendrars's oeuvre, and this is the case irrespective of whether or not he chooses to narrate from a first-person perspective or call his narrator 'Blaise'. While the author's identity is invoked most overtly in those writings that feature a protagonist called Blaise, we must be wary of interpreting these works as straightforwardly autobiographical; to some extent all of his main protagonists, from Johann August Suter to Moravagine and Dan Yack, reflect aspects of his own character without being synonymous with it.

If *L'Homme foudroyé* confirms the imbrication of the self and the act of writing, then it also suggests that words have a redemptive power that can overcome even the most entrenched hostility. The section 'Dans le silence de la nuit' begins with entertaining, light-hearted accounts of nocturnal sorties, initiated by Van Lees, in which the *poilus* would pilfer wine from the stocks of their fellow troops. By the end of this section, the mood has shifted, and we find Corporal Cendrars on a night-time mission of a different sort: he has come to a part of no man's land from which it is possible to glimpse the enemy lines. He is convinced that a German attack, should one be launched, will begin here. As the section nears its end, we find him lying prostrate outside the trenches, terrified and listening intently to the quiet movements of what he believes to be two or more enemy soldiers. He eventually realizes that the brushing sound he has been hearing is caused by his own bayonet in his shaking hands rubbing blades of grass. To calm his nerves, he begins to recite a poem by Rilke; he then recalls an altercation he had had with the German poet in

Paris before the war. According to Cendrars this confrontation, which is not documented in biographies of Rilke, had arisen over a French woman whom Rilke had been mistreating. The recollection prompts Cendrars to wonder where Rilke is at this moment, speculating that he may have deserted and sought refuge in neutral Switzerland, a decision about which Cendrars expresses undisguised scorn: 'Comme si la place d'un poète n'est pas parmi les hommes, ses frères, quand cela va mal et que tout croule, l'humanité, la civilisation et le reste.' (As if a poet's place were not among men, among his brothers, when things were going badly and everything collapsing, humanity, civilization and all the rest of it.)[50]

The poem by Rilke that Cendrars recited was written in 1901 and published in *Das Stundenbuch* (The Book of Hours). Cendrars cites its opening line in the original German no fewer than four times in the final section of 'Dans le silence de la nuit'; even if he cites it imperfectly,[51] he does correctly recall the note of isolation sounded by its opening line and which develops throughout the remainder of the poem:

In diesem Dorfe steht das letzte Haus
so einsam wie das letzte Haus der Welt.

Die Straße, die das kleine Dorf nicht hält,
geht langsam weiter in die Nacht hinaus.

Das kleine Dorf ist nur ein Übergang
zwischen zwei Weiten, ahnungsvoll und bang,
ein Weg an Häusern hin statt eines Stegs.

Und die das Dorf verlassen, wandern lang,
und viele sterben vielleicht unterwegs.

(In this hamlet is the last house
lonely as the last house in the world.

The road, loosing the village from its hold,
lengthens its slow wander into the night.

The little settlement is just a bridge
between two plains, timid, fearful of either,
with only a track along its built-up edge.

And those who leave the village wander a long time
and perhaps many will die along the way.)[52]

The poem recalls the conflation of nature and human experience in the opening lines of Dante's *Inferno*, in which the speaker finds himself midway through the journey of life in a dark forest. Rilke's poem, too, evokes life as a passage, and the solitary house emerges as a final place of transitory respite on a route that leads ineluctably to death. As we read the poem, we realize that Cendrars's chosen title for this section of the book has taken on a more sinister set of associations: 'Dans le silence de la nuit' now refers not only to Cendrars's risky nocturnal outings at the front, but to the eternal darkness that came to take Van Lees and Faval and very nearly him, too.

Rilke as an individual emerges from this anecdote in an extremely unflattering light, but the fact that Cendrars, against the background of the hostilities and in that moment of abject fear, should have chosen to recite not just a poem, but specifically a German one, is significant. His repeated invocation of the poem as a way of keeping terror at bay conveys a positive, life-affirming message: he seems to place his faith in the power of community and poetry as a means to prevail over brutality and enable us to assert our humanity even in the most barbaric circumstances.

As the opening section of *L'Homme foudroyé* has already hinted, a strong network of intertextual references underpins Cendrars's narrative and stresses the connection between literature and life. A curious feature of the book is its heavy reliance on a significant scholarly apparatus of endnotes and footnotes which throws the question of its literary genre into further confusion. The second of its three sections, 'Le vieux port', contains various borrowings from literary sources, including a short extract from a book by Edouard Peisson, to whom Cendrars addressed the letter at the start of his narrative. Each of the seven numbered chapters of 'Le vieux port' ends with a series of 'Notes pour le lecteur inconnu' (Notes for the Unknown Reader), in which Cendrars provides bibliographical information on some of the sources consulted or further comments on aspects of his text. The notes that conclude the opening section of 'Le vieux port' are typical of this attention to bibliographical detail: apart from the publisher's details relating to Peisson's 1943 novel *A Destination d'Anvers*, the notes contain extracts in Latin from manuscripts in the collection of the historic Bibliothèque du Roi housed in the French national library, as well as a reference taken from writings about

St Mary Magdalen held in the archives of the Bouches-du-Rhône and an unpublished document in the Imperial Library of St Petersburg. A further series of notes conclude the final section of 'Le vieux port'; here we find a reference to Cendrars's novel *D'Oultremer à Indigo*, an explanation of two colloquial Spanish terms used in the text and a detailed description of a boat journey undertaken in 1939. Such close attention to bibliographical detail prompts us to reflect on Cendrars's authorial intentions in this book. Does he merely wish to impress us with his wider reading? Or is his intention to persuade his reader that s/he is reading a factual account based on reliable textual sources? Whatever the case, it is clear that we are not dealing with any straightforward autobiography but with a literary approach that is much more complex and multiform.

Spatio-Temporal Disjunction in *L'Homme foudroyé*

L'Homme foudroyé is a mosaic of digressions, recollections, recurrent refrains and temporal shifts; in this respect, and also in its peripatetic character, jumping abruptly from one location to another without obvious connections or motives, it recalls the early poems. In what will prove to be characteristic of his post-war writing, Cendrars shifts rapidly from the present moment of narration to the past, only to bring the account once again into the present. The book begins against the background of the ongoing Second World War, and this triggers a series of recollections of the First World War and anecdotes primarily situated in the interwar years and occasionally the pre-war period. These are not ordered in any explicitly sequential way but do nevertheless have an underlying order that works by processes of association and allusion. The Route Nationale 10 provides a geographical and literary link to some of the 'Rhapsodies gitanes', giving Cendrars the opportunity to muse on the pleasures and attendant risks of driving fast. On a figurative level, this route can also be seen to symbolize his writing, with its rapid displacements and the sense it offers of the reader being hurtled from one narrated event to another. For Jay Bochner, the Nationale 10 'represents Cendrars himself, a passage to the whole world'.[53]

In a sense, the theme of travelling by car marks a development from the pre-war poetry, which celebrated other modes of transport such as boat and train; but the early poems and the mature prose both convey a sense that the act of travelling stimulates a certain kind of creativity that stems from a state of alertness to one's immediate environment.

As we saw, the *Prose du Transsibérien* conveys the impression of being assailed by images so numerous and disparate that they resist the poet's efforts to structure them: 'Autant d'images-associations que je ne peux pas développer dans mes vers/ Car je suis encore fort mauvais poète/ Car l'univers me déborde' (So many image-associations/ I can't get into my poem/ Because I'm still such a really bad poet/ Because the universe rushes over me).[54]

The impetus of the *Prose* is the moving train, whose jolting rhythm propels one image after another into the poet-narrator's consciousness. The resultant poem, with its digressions and abrupt spatio-temporal shifts, is the proof of his struggle to shape this material into a semblance of order. *L'Homme foudroyé* appears to follow a similarly random process, whereby one idea or recollection sparks another, allowing the narration to unfold seemingly at the whim of the narrator's memory.

Cendrars describes the exhilaration of witnessing the landscape distorted by a car driven at speed. He suggests that moving fast affects not only our perspective but our thought process:

> Ce n'est que petit à petit et par une longue pratique de l'automobile [...] que je compris que je me dépouillais insensiblement de tout en fonçant dans l'inconnu car à quoi peut-on comparer la vitesse sinon à la poussée lente de la pensée qui progresse sur un plan métaphysique, pénétrant, isolant, analysant, decomposant tout, réduisant le monde à un petit tas de cendres aérodynamisées (les angles s'usent au vent de l'esprit!) et reconstruisant magiquement l'univers par une formule fulgurante qui claque entre deux guillemets (comme on bat un record entre deux mises au point), cette illumination qui redonne vie: '*Le monde est ma représentation*.'
>
> (It was only gradually, and after a long experience of driving [...] that I realized I was insensibly stripping myself bare of everything by forging ahead into the unknown, for to what can one compare speed if not to the slow thrust of thought, which progresses on a metaphysical plane, penetrating, isolating, analysing, dissecting everything, reducing the world to a small pile of aerodynamized ashes (the corners worn away by the wind of the mind!) and magically reconstructing the universe by a fulgurating formula which claps between inverted commas (or the two

> points between which a record is broken) this enlightenment which restores life: '*All the world's my stage.*')[55]

Especially revealing here is the analogy that Cendrars makes out of the distorting yet powerfully intense experience of the world seen at speed: for him, the physical velocity of the hurtling car is akin to that of neural networks. And the specific terms in which he frames this are striking: his vision of the world, reduced to a small heap of aerodynamic ash (*cendres*) only to be rebuilt anew, sees him once again cite the trope of rebirth and recreation. If fast motion is the catalyst for this, then the process itself is not only recounted, but actually takes place in words: in reprising Schopenhauer's words, 'The world is my representation,' cited in the opening pages of the book, Cendrars returns to the idea that any given object requires a perceiving subject in order to take form and become meaningful.[56] Cendrars suggests that words are a means not merely to record the world, but to (re)create it; the world and its expression become coterminous. The terms he uses are significant: he writes of himself as 'fonçant dans l'inconnu' (rushing into the unknown), a phrase that could apply equally well to the experience of driving or of writing. The same can be said of 'mises au point', an expression that can refer to the tuning of a car engine but also relates to the editing practice of revising a text; the fact that this expression in enclosed in quotation marks suggests that he intended to preserve both associations.

The sheer accumulation of events and anecdotes that populate the book should not distract the reader from the quality and particular texture of the writing. In a passage of the third rhapsody devoted to his experiences in Brazil, the narrator observes the night sky: 'La nuit se doublait d'une buée humide, poisseuse qui suintait du sol, mais au-dessus de nos têtes le ciel grouillait d'étoiles. On eût dit une grande ville inversée.' (The darkness was intensified by a humid, sticky vapour that seeped out of the ground, but above our heads the sky was teeming with stars. It looked like a great inverted city.)[57] Such moments of intense beauty punctuate the narration here and there, reminding us that Cendrars was first and foremost a poet.

La Main coupée

This second volume in the post-war tetralogy appeared in print in 1946, only one year after *L'Homme foudroyé*. Compared with its predecessor, the subject-matter of *La Main coupée* prompts us to expect something much darker in character, focusing as it does on Cendrars's experiences as a soldier in the First World War. Unsurprisingly, given the bleakness of this setting, the book recounts the reality of life at the front: it offers myriad details of the everyday conditions with which the *poilus* had to contend. These included waterlogged trenches, the constant threat of injury or death affecting them, and the narrow-mindedness, vanity and stupidity of the highest-ranking military commanders. The book also provides details of some tricks to which the troops resorted in order to pilfer food, alcohol and tobacco from supply stores, and describes the excessive punishments meted out for wayward behaviour. Cendrars was incarcerated for thirty days for taking an unauthorized photograph of a damaged crucifix on the battlefield.

We also learn of the elaborate and deadly trap that Cendrars and a group of his fellow troops devised for the enemy on Christmas Eve 1914. This modern-day Trojan horse incorporated a gramophone player equipped with explosives which Cendrars and his accomplices placed close to the German front line in a daring and risky manoeuvre.[58] This episode is recounted with brio, and indeed, the tone of the book alternates between moments of high dramatic tension, mournfulness and comedy of a frequently bawdy tone. Unspeakably grim as it was, life at the front provided Cendrars with the basis of many entertaining anecdotes that find their way into the pages of this and other books penned by him.

The title leads the reader to assume that the author will finally broach the subject that he has evaded in his work for so long, namely, the loss of his right arm; the narrative thwarts any such expectations, however, and instead recounts the stories of various soldiers with whom the young Cendrars became acquainted during the Great War. The anecdotes that constitute the book range in tone from the serious and reflective to the humorous, and above all, they convey a vivid sense of the companionship and camaraderie that made the experience not only tolerable for Cendrars, but at times even amusing. In spite of its thematic focus on the darkest aspects of human behaviour, this work celebrates the power of the spirit to overcome adversity and find solace in the interactions with other humans. The book is prefaced by a poignant dedication to the author's sons. Dated 1944, it reads: 'Pour mes fils Odilon et Rémy quand ils rentreront de captivité et de guerre et pour leurs fils quand ces petits auront vingt ans hélas!' (For my sons Odilon andRémy, when they return from captivity and from the war and for their sons when, alas! these young men reach the age of twenty!)[59] Beneath it is another dedication, written after a telegram dated 26 November 1945 had brought the news that his son Rémy had been killed in an aeroplane accident during a training mission in North Africa.

The main part of the book is divided into chapters, each one devoted to a different main character. A connecting thread linking many of these portraits is that the figures in question lost their lives in the war. And so we encounter 'Rossi, tué à Tilloloy' (Rossi, killed at Tilloloy), 'Lang, tué à Bus' (Lang, killed at Bus), 'Robert Belessort, mort en Angleterre et Ségouâna, tué à la ferme de Navarin' (Robert Belessort, who died in England and Ségouâna, killed at Navarin Farm). The last of these rings particularly true, as Navarin Farm was the site of Cendrars's mutilation in September 1915. He had already alluded to this battle in *L'Homme foudroyé* in his textual 'ex-voto' devoted to Van Lees. This chapter of *La Main coupée* focuses on the two soldiers' friendship and on Ségouâna's relationship with Belessort's sister Claire. The narrative relays Ségouâna's death, and the author's own injury, in a remarkably deadpan way: 'Un mois plus tard, fin septembre, Ségouâna était tué lors de l'attaque de la ferme de Navarin où, moi-même, je perdis mon bras.' (A month later, at the end of September, Ségouâna was killed during the attack on the Navarin farm, where I myself lost an arm.)[60] We then discover that the letter of condolence that Cendrars wrote to the victim's fiancée was one of the first letters he had ever written with his left hand.[61] This is all he reveals on the subject of his own 'main coupée'; we learn nothing whatsoever about the author's state of mind, the process of recuperation or even the basic facts concerning the incident. Once again, then, Cendrars frustrates our expectations and denies us the account of his injury that we had hoped for.

The book builds up powerful momentum in its closing chapters, some of which offer its most poignant and memorable moments. In the twenty-first chapter, entitled 'Le Lys rouge' (The Red Lily), we encounter one of the best-known passages of Cendrars's entire post-war output, its notoriety due to the fact that it brings us close to 'the primal scene of his memoirs', as Richard Sieburth terms Cendrars's injury.[62] Yet it does so in a surreal, mythologized form and therefore seems to inhabit the realm of literature as much as it does life itself. The chapter, a mere two pages long, recounts an event that takes place one sunny morning in June in the normally peaceful commune of Tilloloy, southeast of Amiens. The atmosphere is calm; troops are waiting for lunch to be served and look forward to comparing the culinary skills of the new cook with those of his predecessor, Garnéro, who had been killed some time before. Suddenly, the young legionnaire Faval startles them all by shouting and pointing to an object that he has seen falling from the sky. As they rush towards it, the other soldiers realize to their horror what they are looking at:

> Nous avions bondi et regardions avec stupeur, à trois pas de Faval, planté dans l'herbe comme une grande fleur épanouie, un lys rouge, un bras humain tout ruisselant de sang, un bras droit sectionné au-dessus du coude et dont la main encore vivante fouissait le sol des doigts comme pour y prendre racine et dont la tige sanglante se balançait doucement avant de tenir son équilibre.
>
> (We had jumped up and were looking in stupefaction at something only three steps away from where Faval was standing: planted in the grass like a huge flower in full bloom, was a scarlet lily, a human arm streaming with blood, a right arm severed just above the elbow. The still-living fingers were digging into the soil, as if trying to take root there, and the bleeding stem was waving gently in the air to balance itself.)[63]

The men are struck dumb by this sight and cannot understand how the arm came to be there. There have been no aerial bombardments and no gunfire or bombings in the vicinity; and various telephone calls to the entire sector and even to the ambulance stations ascertain that no amputations have taken place. The distressed troops retire to their shelters in the trenches, leaving their lunch untouched. The narrative explains simply, 'Jamais nous n'eûmes la clef de l'énigme.' (We never discovered any clue to the enigma.)[64]

The elements of this scene are so uncanny, and so extraordinarily close to Cendrars's own injury, that it is extremely difficult to see it as anything other than a premonition of that experience, either dreamt or imagined. The unexplained appearance of the disembodied arm, its supernaturally animated character, still active in spite of the obvious physical impossibility of such a situation, and the fact that it is a right arm, severed above the elbow, all point towards the assumption that it must be a fictionalized transposition of Cendrars's experience. The inclusion of such a dreamlike chapter, with no apparent distinction between it and the more prosaic ones that surround it, poses questions relating to the narrative strategies at work. It is difficult to reconcile this incident with the book's more strictly autobiographical passages, unless we conclude that Cendrars deliberately encompasses the entire gamut of narrative modes, from the prosaically factual to the fanciful, the imagined or the oneiric.

The chapter that follows this one adopts a very different tone. It reflects on the sheer ordinariness of the individuals caught up in these extreme circumstances. We are reminded at this point of Henri Barbusse's combat novel *Le Feu* (Under Fire), in which the troops reject out of hand any notion of heroism. Rather than criticizing the German army, they reserve their fury for the senior ranks of the military and political establishments who they see as the real enemy and rightly blame for having caused this war in the first place.[65] Cendrars is similarly cynical towards the suggestion that he and his peers have behaved heroically. As the narrator states, what they have in common is their sheer ordinariness. He reflects on the fact that with one possible exception (Sawo the Roma, who deserted after he was denied leave when the passes failed to materialize), not one member of his unit had the makings of a hero. He reflects that their acts of sacrifice were made in self-defence and those who survived did so as the result of sheer luck rather than exceptional human qualities. Of the two hundred or so individuals he encountered in his commando detachment in just under a year, he notes:

> la majorité était en vérité des pauvres bougres qui sont tombés sans savoir pourquoi ni comment et dont, s'ils m'apparaissent encore dans mes songes avec leur corps meurtri et tout sanglant, et poussant des cris horribles, moi-même j'ai oublié leur nom et leur figure, leur comportement et les circonstances de leur mort exemplaire.
>
> (the majority of them were indeed poor buggers who fell without knowing the why or the wherefore, and even though they still appear to me in dreams, yelling horribly and with their shattered bodies streaming blood, in many cases I myself have forgotten their names and their faces, their behaviour and the circumstances of their exemplary deaths.)[66]

This last adjective throws into sharp relief the ironic gap that separates the genuinely remarkable nature of each death from its sheer forgettability, a fact that can be explained simply by the inconceivably high number of casualties, a volume so significant that it ceases to be meaningful on any comprehensible human level.

Towards the end of the book, Cendrars recalls two of his erstwhile fellow soldiers, Kohn and Bouffe-Tout (Dustbin), who are connected in his memory by nothing other than their shared love of singing.[67] This leads Cendrars's narrator to compile another list, but now he is at a loss as to the names of the victims. In the absence of their identities, then, he recites a litany of the various modern methods of annihilation employed to kill them. By this stage, it is clear that his patience has run out and that his overwhelming feeling is fury towards the sheer inhumanity and anonymity of this modern war: 'MACHIN, TRUC, CHOSE, tous morts, tous tués, crevés, écrabouillés, anéantis, disloqués, oubliés, pulvérisés, réduits à zéro, et pour rien' (WHO'S-IT, WHAT'S-HIS-NAME and THINGUMABOB: all dead, all killed, slain, crushed, annihilated, dismembered, forgotten, pulverized, reduced to zero, and for nothing).[68] These last three words are telling; throughout much of the book, Cendrars is more interested in recounting anecdotes about his fellow legionnaires, but at this moment, he directs his fury and frustration at the political and military leaders who had brought about this war in the first place.

As we have seen, the first two volumes of memoirs, written in the immediate aftermath of the Second World War, are deeply rooted in Cendrars's experience of the First World War. That war was waged at a distance, and at times hand-to-hand, by men who dug themselves into the ground and fought a largely invisible enemy; the fields of France were transformed into a featureless, mud-filled landscape that Apollinaire named an 'Ocean of Earth'.[69] In 1917, one of the 'journaux des tranchées', newspapers created by and for French troops serving in the Great War, reported the words of one soldier: 'L'Enfer ce n'est pas le feu, c'est la boue' (Hell isn't fire, it's mud).[70] While the third and fourth volumes of memoirs do not completely leave the war behind, they are primarily preoccupied with the elements of water and air: *Bourlinguer* is based on port cities, whereas *Le Lotissement du ciel* overtly and consistently raises its gaze skywards. These books will be the subject of the next chapter.

nine

Memoirs of Sea and Sky: *Bourlinguer* and *Le Lotissement du ciel*

In *L'Homme foudroyé*, Cendrars admits that his *Petit Larousse* is the one book that he takes everywhere with him. He must, then, have taken considerable pleasure in popularizing the word *bourlinguer* and seeing it enter the French lexicon.[1] The term did exist before him, but it was relatively obscure until he published his novel. Alongside Cendrars, the *Trésor de la langue française* cites three further literary sources, all of which date from 1936: these are Céline's *Mort à credit*, Louis Aragon's *Les Beaux Quartiers* and a third book by French-Flemish author Maxence van der Meersch called *L'Empreinte du dieu*. Yet it is unquestionably thanks to Cendrars that the word has acquired much greater currency in the French language and culture, largely because of the sustained nature of his undertaking as a writer-cum-nomad.

In turn, the concept of *bourlinguer* and its correlate *bourlingueur* have become synonymous with Cendrars himself. This image of him as a free spirit, travelling across the world, is one to which he himself contributed both in his writing and in a public image with which he became associated. Regarding the first of these, his writing, we have already witnessed his tendency to present himself as an explorer, whether hunting elephants in the poems of *Documentaires*, embracing the spirit of adventure that permeates the *Prose du Transsibérien*, or in the accounts of his escape from the family home as a teenager in *Vol à voiles* and other writings. A similar tendency has prevailed in the photographic portraits of him, typically taken outdoors, that have disseminated a particular visual image of him as a worldly-wise traveller. As Jérôme Meizoz observes in a highly perceptive article, Cendrars's entire oeuvre can be seen as a struggle between external and internal realms, in which the adventurer of the great outdoors tries to get the upper hand over the scholar sitting in a library.[2]

While *La Main coupée* was primarily concerned with producing portraits of different individuals whom Cendrars had encountered in his life as a soldier, *Bourlinguer*, by contrast, seems at first glance to be essentially about places and travel. Indeed, it grew out of a commission to write about port cities. Art publisher René Kieffer contacted Cendrars in the summer of 1946 inviting him to write captions to accompany a series of eighteen etchings by the Swiss artist Louis Valdo-Barbey, each depicting a different port. The concept was simple and its demands modest: Cendrars was given the choice of writing one or two pages to accompany each image, or producing a single text encompassing them all. Neither of these planned formats was even remotely similar to the lengthy narrative that Cendrars produced the following year. Flückiger reports that Cendrars already had various publishing projects underway at the time; the decisive moment to accept this commission seems to have been when he saw the list of ports and realized that almost all eighteen of them were meaningful to him on a personal level.[3]

Cendrars's enthusiastic immersion in this project caused his research and writing to grow so much that he missed a series of deadlines agreed with Kieffer.[4] By July 1947, he admitted to the editor that his book had amassed 272 pages but had only reached halfway through the list of ports. The reaction of the publisher, who had already spent money on the book's design, is not known but can be guessed. Cendrars, meanwhile, carried on regardless, racking up a substantial word count and writing enthusiastically about his progress to friends such as Jacques-Henri Lévesque.[5] Unsurprisingly, then, the project never saw the light of day in the anticipated form or with the intended publisher, but Cendrars found willing collaborators in the editorial team at Denoël; having published *La Main coupée* and issued him a contract for the book that would become *Le Lotissement du ciel*, they were working on the new edition of his complete poems. In early January 1948, Cendrars delivered the complete typescript of *Bourlinguer*, and it appeared in print in May of the same year. It became one of Cendrars's best-known books.

Ten of its eleven sections take us to working ports in different European countries: Italy (Venice, Naples, Genoa), Spain (La Coruña), France (Bordeaux, Brest, Toulon), Belgium (Antwerp), the Netherlands (Rotterdam) and Germany (Hamburg); in addition, the book features a port that preoccupied imaginations for centuries but never developed beyond the planning stage: Paris Port-de-mer. Place, then, is the common denominator that links the various narratives of this book. And as much as being in any given location, Cendrars clearly relishes the experience of travelling between places. As he puts it in *Le Lotissement du ciel*, 'il ne faudrait jamais arriver' (it would be better never to arrive). But arguably the real focus of the eleven chapters lies elsewhere: the book is a study of humanity, since all of its sections, and all of its locations, bring us back to relationships between people.

This is already in evidence in the opening chapter of *Bourlinguer*, which begins in the most famous library in Venice. The first-person voice that we encounter at the start of the book seems familiar enough after *L'Homme foudroyé* and *La Main coupée*: the unsuspecting reader could be forgiven for assuming initially that the 'je' in question is more or less synonymous with Cendrars again. Only when we reach the final words of the paragraph does it become clear that we are dealing with another person, and another time:

> Je ne souffle mot, je regarde par la fenêtre Venise. Venise. Reflets insolites dans l'eau de la lagune. Micassures et reflets glissants dans les vitrines et sur le parquet en mosaïque de la bibliothèque Saint-Marc. Le soleil est comme une perle baroque dans la brume plombagine qui se lève derrière les façades des palais du front de l'eau et annonce du mauvais temps au large, crachin, pluies, vents et tempête. Je ne souffle mot. A la place du *vaporetto* qui passe devant la *Dogana di Mari*, appareille une tartane. C'est le 11 novembre 1653 . . .
>
> (I do not breathe a word. I look out the window at Venice. Venice. Unusual reflections in the water of the lagoon. Slippery crystalline reflections in the windows and on the mosaic floor of the Library of Saint Mark's. The sun is like a baroque pearl in the carbon mist that rises behind the facades of the palaces on the waterfront and announces bad weather, drizzle, rain, wind and storms. I do not breathe a word. In place of the *vaporetto* that passes in front of the Dogana Da Mar, a tartane sets sail. It's the 11th of November 1653 . . .)[6]

While the first-person voice is thus not synonymous with the author, it is easy to see why Cendrars was drawn to this material. The second paragraph explains the significance of this date in 1653: it marks the day on which a fourteen-year-old stowaway was discovered aboard the vessel and was on the point of being thrown off the boat when he was rescued by an Englishman travelling incognito aboard. It transpires that this man was Henry Bard, Viscount of Belloment, extraordinary ambassador under King Charles II to the Shah of Persia and the Mughal emperor, with whom he was to forge an alliance with a view to helping Charles regain his throne. Shortly after this, Cendrars's narrative alludes to an elderly Venetian adventurer whose travels had taken him via Persia to India, where he had roamed European colonial outposts on the Eastern and Western coasts. His various activities included working as a negotiator, an interpreter, a correspondent, an intermediary in royal disputes and William Pitt's secret envoy in India.[7]

By now Cendrars's narrative strategy is clear: these vignettes set the scene for a depiction of a certain type of traveller and a vision of the world as a terrain to be explored. The reference to the narrative as a mirror image, a recognizable but distorted vision of the self, hoves into view. We go on to read a passage from the traveller's memoirs:

> Quand j'étais gosse, j'avais envie d'aller faire le tour du monde, mais comme mon père ne voulait pas en entendre parler, j'avais décidé de quitter Venise, ma ville natale, à la première occasion et de partir par n'importe quelle voie ou moyen. Un jour, ayant appris qu'une tartane appareillait sur le port pour je ne savais quelle destination, je réussis à me glisser à bord. J'avais quatorze ans . . .

> (When I was a lad, I wanted to travel the world, but as my father would not hear of it, I decided to leave Venice, my hometown, at the first opportunity and leave by any way or means. One day, having learned that a tartane was in the harbour preparing to sail for I knew not where, I managed to slip on board. I was fourteen . . .)[8]

Only some four pages into the text do we learn the identity of the Venetian voyager, who also turns out to be the protagonist of the story that we are reading: it is the seventeenth-century traveller and writer

Niccolao Manucci, whose memoirs, *Storia do Mogor*, were published in French in 1715 by the Jesuit priest François Catrou under the title *Histoire Générale de l'Empire du Mogol* (General History of the Mughal Empire) and were instrumental in popularizing orientalism in eighteenth-century Europe.[9] Cendrars's fascination with this source makes perfect sense in light of his own life story and the many poems and other works in which he expresses the desire to travel or simply to flee; the wanderlust that Manucci embodies makes him an antecedent of Cendrars.

The book thus sets up a series of tropes that relate very directly to Cendrars's self-portrayal as a *bourlingueur*. But it also makes an important point regarding the act of narrating one's own life experiences, and in this sense too, the bibliographical afterlife of Manucci's text sheds important light on Cendrars's stance towards literature of a broadly autobiographical nature. At the end of this short opening section, Cendrars appends brief notes for his 'unknown reader', in which he criticizes the neglect that Manucci suffered at the hands of two important nineteenth-century biographical resources: he bemoans Manucci's absence from Louis-Gabriel Michaud's *Biographie universelle*; and he corrects some important bibliographical errors that had found their way into Ferdinand Hoefer's *Nouvelle Biographie générale* published in 1860.[10]

The opening section of *Bourlinguer* thus presents itself to the reader in terms of certain key tropes that relate very directly to the post-war tetralogy, but also to Cendrars's literary oeuvre as a whole. These include travelling around the world and documenting it in writing, but also the history of literature and of scholarship: the fact that the narrative begins in a library, and engages with different conflicting versions of Manucci's life and work, already points to the perils of all literary endeavours that purport to tell the truth.

As Meizoz has observed, Cendrars here is creating an entire metatextual and intertextual infrastructure that frames and announces his own literary undertaking and its contradictions. Contrary to the opening paragraph, Cendrars's reading of Manucci cannot have taken place in the library of St Mark's – indeed, he never set foot in Venice – but he must have read the Venetian's account in the translation by William Irvine, which he re-translates into French in this section of the book. While he acknowledges Irvine's contribution to scholarship in disseminating the work of the otherwise unknown figure Manucci, he reprimands the Scotsman for denying the reader access to Manucci's words in their original languages, offering instead approximations in English, since Irvine on his own admission did not speak Manucci's languages and therefore had relied on the versions of the Venetian's writings provided by other scholars, works that, while earnest, lacked the authenticity of Manucci's voice.

Through meticulous close readings, Meizoz demonstrates how Cendrars constructs a posture of the writer-as-free-spirit. Cendrars aligns himself with the 'chroniqueurs' rather than scholars whose worthy but lifeless renditions merely flatten and deaden the original text. (The version written by the French priest François Catrou is 'the most brilliant, but also the least alive'.)[11] Symptomatic of this positioning of himself as being on the side of spontaneity and authenticity rather than academic scrupulousness, Cendrars writes the name as he claims to see it in front of him, in its handwritten form, 'Nicolao Manuci', continuing the fiction that he is reading in the library in Venice.

This short inaugural section, then, alerts us to the unreliability of texts, starting with the one the narrator is recounting. But it also prompts us to be aware of the complexities and limitations of all accounts that purport to be factual. It does so intertextually, through the different versions of Manucci's memoirs that are cited, but also metatextually, since Manucci is clearly an alter ego of the young Blaise Cendrars who, as we have seen, left the paternal home as a teenager to work in St Petersburg.

The specificity of place should not be neglected. Venice as a cosmopolitan trading city, a mercantile crossroads and a city whose nationality changed over the course of history offers an exemplary instance of international commerce and multilingual exchange, so it seems fitting that Cendrars should choose to begin his book there. Given the importance of specific places in the themes and structure of the book, its English translation is frustrating for anglophone readers, since the one published edition, *Planus*, translated by Nina Rootes, is also heavily abridged and modified, and the eleven chapters/ports of the original French book are reduced to a mere seven. The entire opening chapter in Venice is lost, its lengthiest one, 'Gênes' (Genoa), is renamed 'Naples', and the only other surviving chapters are those focusing on Antwerp, Corunna, Rotterdam, Hamburg and Paris, Seaport. The translator justifies these changes as being driven by the aim of appealing to readers 'who perhaps would have been deterred by a longer and more discursive book'.[12] This, however, creates an imbalance, with the Naples chapter now accounting for almost half of the book's entire length, and curtails the wide-ranging discussions that give the original text its rhythm and its complexity.

One further point deserves to be made about the obscure title of the English translation, *Planus*. Its meaning is explained in the chapter 'Gênes', which the English translation relocates to Naples, a puzzling editorial decision given that the original French text already has a separate chapter called 'Naples'. The narrator is reading the writings that the fourth-century monk and theologian Jean Cassien produced on his return from Egypt. In one text, Cassien explores the identity of demons and possessed spirits.[13] Cendrars's narrator describes encountering Cassien's work in the St Petersburg library in the winter of 1945. At the time, Cendrars's narrator was deeply immersed in the reading of the *Patrologie*, a series of theological works edited by the nineteenth-century French pastor Jacques-Paul Migne.[14] The room was silent, but for the scarcely audible sound of the librarian creeping around 'like a phantom'.[15] In this atmosphere, the narrator has an intense and surprising experience: 'Et c'est moi! Je me reconnais. On me tend un miroir.' (And there I was! I recognized myself. A mirror was held up to me.)[16] The reason for this sudden revelation was that he had chanced upon the definition of a particular category of daemons, found among impious spirits, known as 'les Vagabonds – *Planos* – et qui sont avant tout des séducteurs et des bouffons' (Vagabonds – *Planos* – who are, above all, beguilers and clowns).[17] A footnote added by Canon Léon Cristiani clarifies that this word, *planus* in the singular form, occurs in Pliny and also refers to a vagabond or adventurer.[18] *Planus*, then, is an apt term to describe Cendrars, even if the highly obscure and rarefied nature of the word makes it poorly qualified to capture the spontaneity and active character of the original French verb *bourlinguer*. The figure of a vagabond or adventurer is also a fitting label for the narrative itself, which is full of temporal and geographic digressions, circuitous routes and excurses: these take us on a non-linear journey through discrete chapters of the author's past. The lengthy chapter entitled 'Gênes' is exemplary of this: early on, we learn of the death of the narrator's beloved dog, Leone, knocked over by a mule-drawn tramcar.[19] Only a few pages afterwards, the text recounts the death of the narrator's childhood friend Elena, who is the victim of a freak accident, killed outright by the stray bullet of a huntsman's rifle as she and the narrator were playing.[20] Like *Prose du Transsibérien*, in which the motion of the fast-moving train dictates the rhythm of the protagonist's memory, here too we have a narrative strategy that eschews linearity in favour of a peripatetic, nomadic voice capable of making leaps across time and space. As Cendrars's narrator puts it in 'Gênes', the appearance of disorder that some may identify in his style in fact relies on consciously applied techniques of dislocation and disarticulation that, in the wake of Einstein, may be understood in the context of relativity.[21]

Elena is a lightly fictionalized cipher for Hélène, Cendrars's first love, who died in a fire in St Petersburg; she thus embodies the combination of 'Dichtung und Wahrheit' (poetry and truth) that Cendrars adopts from Goethe as the guiding principle of his own literary undertaking.[22] In places, the narrator is more straightforwardly autobiographical; an instance of this occurs later in the same chapter, when the narrator, aged sixty (Cendrars's age at the time of writing *Bourlinguer*), reflects on the retreat from physical life into the sedentary and solitary activity of writing. He acknowledges that he has three or four long novels to write, in addition to his personal memoirs, and anticipates that the task will take a full decade to complete. His description of the writing process is intriguing, especially in terms of how it relates to reality: he describes his practice as 'intercalant dans la vision directe celle, réfléchie, qui ne peut se déchiffrer qu'à l'envers comme dans un miroir' (intercalating the direct image with the reflection, which can be deciphered only in reverse, mirror-wise).[23]

Besides meditating on what Gaston Bachelard would call 'le génie du lieu' (the genius loci, or spirit of place), the book ultimately has another purpose, arguably its most important one, namely, to articulate a series of reflections on the act of writing and representing. Like Venice and the other ports that appear in it, this book is a melting pot, a heterogeneous place of encounter for different narrative voices, different places and different ways of seeing the world; the narrative is also a site of intertextual transit, since it is built on a history of literature and openly acknowledges its reliance on previous accounts. As much as it is about voyaging around the world, *Bourlinguer* expresses the pleasures and challenges of travelling through literature.

Le Lotissement du ciel

The fourth and final part of the tetralogy, perhaps more than any other work in Cendrars's oeuvre, is a barometer of how he not only reflects but anticipates changing views and understandings of literary practice. When the book was published in 1949, its complexity and its somewhat disjointed structure meant that it met with resistance and incomprehension from a readership expecting another *Bourlinguer*. As Claude Leroy notes, *Le Lotissement du ciel* is one of its author's least visited and least understood books (he refers to it as the 'black sheep' of his memoirs).[24] But over time its reception has evolved very significantly as readers have become more accustomed to innovative literary techniques and structuring devices, and also to the permeable boundaries between fact and fiction. Responses to this book have evolved to such an extent that French author Philippe Forest in 2011 judged it to be the most significant novel of the twentieth century.[25]

From the start, *Le Lotissement du ciel* (which literally translates as *The Allotment of the Sky*) raises questions that do not accommodate straightforward answers; the first of these relates to its literary genre, which seems intriguingly indeterminate. Presented as the fourth and final book in the post-war series of loosely autobiographical works, it invites expectations of stylistic and structural continuity with the preceding three volumes. Yet, while this final tome does share the ambitious length and first-person narrative voice of the preceding tomes, it may well come across as a somewhat inaccessible book, even to readers familiar with the author's earlier work. It is divided into three parts, the first of which, 'Le Jugement dernier' (The Last Judgement), runs to a mere fifteen pages; by contrast, the second, entitled 'Le Nouveau patron de l'aviation' (The New Patron Saint of Aviation), occupies nearly three hundred pages and discusses numerous occurrences of levitating saints. The challenge that this poses to the unsuspecting reader is intensified by the fact that some of these accounts, borrowed from various other sources, are left in their original Latin. The final section, entitled 'La Tour Eiffel sidérale (Rhapsodie de la nuit)' (The Sidereal Eiffel Tower (Rhapsody of the Night)), is over two hundred pages long and combines accounts of historical figures alongside anecdotes about fictitious characters.

Like the three preceding volumes of memoirs, *Le Lotissement du ciel* does at least partially fulfil our expectations of this genre by recounting numerous episodes from Cendrars's life, albeit without respecting chronological sequence. The events narrated allude to the various locations of his childhood, adolescence and early adulthood (Naples, Egypt, St Petersburg, New York) as well as his discovery of Brazil in the 1920s. It also takes in his experience as a soldier in the Foreign Legion during the First World War and as war correspondent for the British army in the Second. Remarking on the more melancholy tone of this book compared to the previous three, Claude Leroy notes its double preoccupation, with origins and with endings; he describes it as a final stocktaking before liquidation.[26] Here Leroy echoes Perloff, who refers to it as 'first and foremost a *death* book, specifically the death associated with twentieth-century warfare'.[27] Written when Europe was slowly beginning to recover from the devastating impact of another war, the book expresses its author's profound uncertainty about the state of the world. Even literature and the creative arts seem to him riddled with hypocrisy and opportunism as writers jump on the latest political bandwagon to promote their high-minded Literature. And this is not new; Cendrars admits that the posturing of the Parisian literary scene had prompted him to leave for Brazil in 1924.[28]

The titles of all three sections are telling. They reflect a recurrent tendency of this book to drift towards the immaterial, the metaphysical and the transcendental. This is offset and punctuated by many episodes that return to earthly matters; among the most captivating chapters are those where these two realms are present. One of the most powerful instances of this can be found in the sections dealing with war, where the terrifying reality of imminent danger and the tedium of the lulls between bouts of action are overlaid by reminiscences and reverie. The second section, 'Le nouveau patron de l'aviation' (The New Patron Saint of Aviation), derives from a factual situation whereby, at the time of writing, the world of aviation lacked a suitable patron saint. This part of the book proposes Joseph of Cupertino, the seventeenth-century Franciscan mystic and Christian saint, as a deserving holder of this role; but it also invites us to reflect on myth, its relationship to reality and the possibility of creating new realities through the act of writing. The third section, 'La Tour Eiffel sidérale' (The Sidereal Eiffel Tower), also deals with a real phenomenon, the constellations and the long-standing human urge to identify, chart and name them. This is also an important trope of poetry through the ages, and one that Cendrars knowingly exploits; indeed, in *L'Eubage*, that tale of a voyage into the hinterland of the sky, he himself had devoted an entire book to the movements of planets and stars.[29] In *Le Lotissement du ciel*, the epithet 'sidérale' refers to the ambition of one of its characters, Oswald Padroso, who aspires to have a new constellation named after the great Parisian landmark.

All three of the book's sections hint at a celestial theme, also perceptible in the book's overarching title, that runs throughout the entire book; accompanying this is a recurrent trope of elevation, which appears in many forms, natural and supernational alike. The kinds of flight that the narrative enumerates and explores range from the elevations of St Joseph

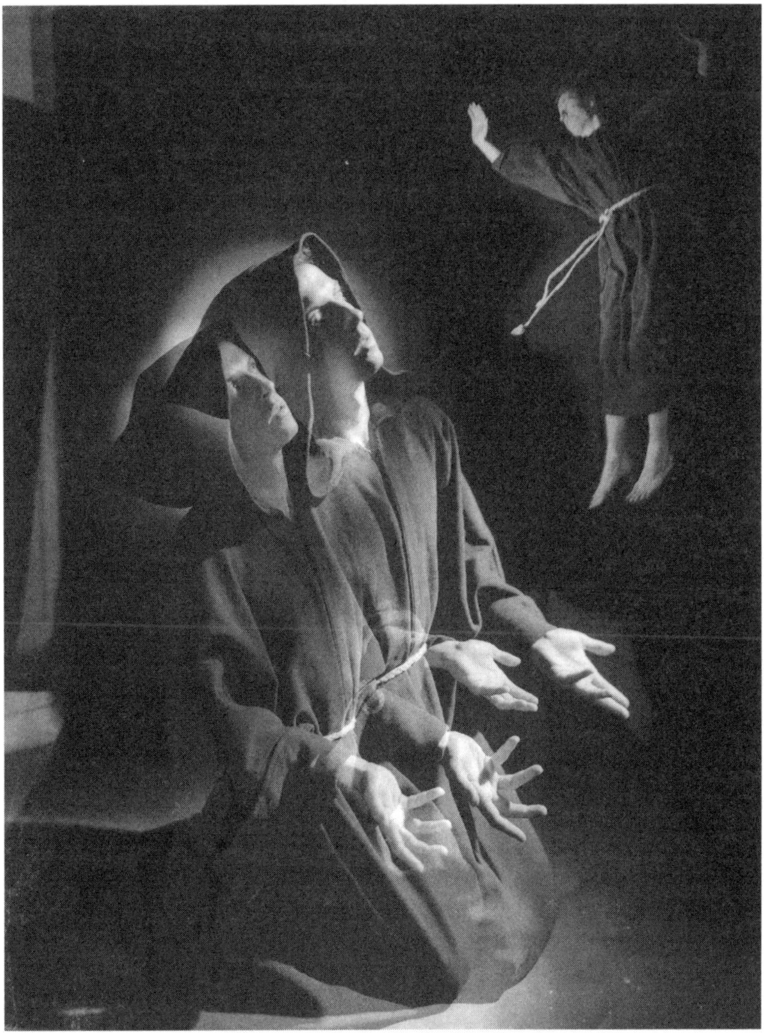

Lucien Lorelle, photograph from Blaise Cendrars, *Le Lotissement du ciel* (1949).

of Cupertino to the flight of angels, and from exotic birds to aeroplanes, such as the one in which Cendrars's son Rémy was flying when he lost his life. The theme of flying, then, provides a measure of continuity and thematic homogeneity that is much needed in a book whose structure might otherwise come across as somewhat disjointed.

One of the book's most profoundly personal allusions to elevation occurs roughly halfway through it, in the seventh chapter of 'The Sidereal Eiffel Tower', which is entitled 'Des Ombres dans le noir' (Shadows in the Darkness).[30] The incident in question takes us back to the First World

War and to Cendrars's experience of serving in the Foreign Legion. The chapter does that all-too-rare thing in Cendrars's oeuvre: it alludes, albeit briefly and opaquely, to the trauma of losing his right arm. In 1924, he had depicted a strikingly similar vision in the poem 'Orion' in *Feuilles de route*, which opens with the lines: 'C'est mon étoile/ Elle a la forme d'une main/ C'est ma main montée au ciel' (It's my star/ It has the shape of a hand/ It's my hand ascended to heaven).[31] Unsurprisingly, given his long-standing reluctance to discuss this experience, he deals with the aftermath of the injury rather than the incident itself. In this part of 'The Sidereal Eiffel Tower', before he alludes to his right arm, the narrator recalls how, whenever he looked up at the sky from his trench on the battlefield, he would see the constellation of Orion. For him, Orion represents a stellar hand. As he reflects upon seeing it in the night sky, it reminds him of an advertising sign that could be seen above the shops in Paris topped by a large neon sign in the shape of a red glove. Cendrars's narrator then relates his conviction that the severed arm had floated skywards, like one of the saints who fascinate him so much, only to find its way into the constellation of Orion. Like the incident of the red lily in *La Main coupée*, this anecdote seems to bring us closer to the unspeakable wound sustained on the fields of Champagne in September 1915.[32] Once again, metaphor and metonymy prove to be the only viable means by which he can deal with this trauma.

Before we leave this chapter behind, it is worth dwelling on the route that the narrative takes in order to arrive at the anecdote of the celestial arm, since it is illustrative of Cendrars's masterful but deceptive writing style, which on first sight appears loosely structured and circuitous yet proves to be brilliantly and subtly constructed. The shadows in the dark to which the title refers emerge as having numerous associations, both literal and figurative, that shed fascinating light on Cendrars's literary engagement with his own past and his strategies of coping with the trauma of mutilation. The chapter begins with a recollection of the many nights spent at the front during the First World War. The opening sentence, which lasts an entire page, begins by musing on the lookout post that Cendrars occupied for hours at night whenever he was not on patrol duty. As this first paragraph makes clear, Cendrars was still a young man, fresh out of studies, his head filled with Kantian terms and his heart awash with what he presents as metaphysical love fuelled by Schopenhauer's philosophy. He knew little about life, less still about humanity and virtually nothing about himself. Confrontation with the dizzying spectacle of mass destruction and the constant threat of death fuelled his youthful nihilism and seemed to bear out his most negative views of the world:

> Je me méprisais en particulier et méprisais avec une joie sadique la condition humaine en général que je voyais foulée aux pieds, pilonnée, asphyxiée, saignée, offerte en holocauste sur l'autel féroce et vorace des patries, le pavillon couvrant l'ignoble marchandise offerte à l'encan, sacrifiée pour rien, jetée à la vidange, les tranchées refaisant le plein.
>
> (I had nothing but contempt for myself, as an individual, and, in general, took a sadistic joy in despising the human condition as I saw men trampled underfoot, pounded, asphyxiated, bleeding, offered up as a holocaust on the greedy and violent altar of the nations, the flag unfurled to cover the ignoble merchandise offered up to auction, sacrificed to no purpose, thrown out with the garbage, for there were always plenty of replacements to fill the trenches.)[33]

As his narrative reveals, he became transfixed by the nocturnal spectacle visible from the vantage point of the lookout post. Here, the choice of words is revealing: into the narrow vertical opening of the niche, he writes, 'l'univers venait s'inscrire' (the universe came pouring through). This expression describes how that small space seemed to encapsulate the entire phenomenal world in natural as well as figurative senses: light filtered into it through the narrow gap, and all sorts of widely divergent thoughts tumbled pell-mell into the legionnaire's mind by a process of free association. The reflexive verb used here, 's'inscrire' (to be inscribed; literally, to inscribe itself), seems especially significant, since it relates to Cendrars's chosen vocation and to the act of writing more generally. 'Shadows in the Darkness' conveys the overwhelming spectacle of the new form of warfare that the First World War inaugurated and expresses the difficulty of describing a situation that defies any straightforward narration.

One of the reasons why the Great War proved so challenging to describe with accuracy was the sheer scale on which it was waged. This is the focus of the second paragraph of 'Shadows in the Darkness'; in shifting the focus to the inconceivably vast, anonymous mass of humanity involved in that war, it also, by implication, makes a similar observation about the war that followed it a little over two decades later, in 1939–45, in whose wake Cendrars wrote *Le Lotissement du ciel*: he alludes to what he terms an entire generation of living dead on the edge of no man's land. His first-hand experience of not one but two world wars must have strengthened his conviction that war is by definition disastrous and that millions of lives had been lost needlessly in the name of imperial ambition. The paragraphs that follow bombard the reader with a litany of arguments, so many reminders that the war has fundamentally, catastrophically damaged the entire Western world, dragging humanity into a moral no man's land and exposing an emptiness at the heart of humankind: 'c'est le monde entier qui s'est mis à suivre les clairons et les tambours de la Légion étrangère dans le *no man's land*, le pays qui n'est à personne, cette sombre, cette unique réalité, ce noir absolu' (it's the whole world that has followed the bugle calls and drums of the Foreign Legion into no man's land, the land that belongs to nobody, that sombre, unique reality, that absolute darkness).[34]

Cendrars's narrative returns to the image of the narrow slit in the wall of the lookout post. He describes it as an 'étroite fissure par laquelle mon esprit pouvait se risquer pour saisir [. . .] la vieillesse de la Terre, ses rides profondes, son visage, ses balafres' (a narrow gap through which my mind could risk a quick glance and capture [. . .] the age of the Earth, its deep wrinkles, its face, its scars).[35] This passage is just a small part of a much longer paragraph, almost all of which takes the form of a single, lengthy, intense sentence. In it, and throughout the remainder of the paragraph, the reader is invited to witness the verbalization of a visual phenomenon in which we join the narrator in looking through the narrow slit at an unfolding scene of extraordinary vividness. This could be read as an account of the experience of cinema, and particularly the close-up, that distinguishing feature of early experimental film's *photogénie*, in which the spectator is granted a privileged, almost supernaturally acute view of the filmed subject or action. Of course, the scene that Cendrars is describing here is no fiction but a very real situation, one that he and countless other *poilus* had experienced in person. But it seems telling that he reaches to the example of cinema as a means to convey what he is otherwise unable to express in its full magnitude, namely, the sheer otherworldly horror and intensity of being directly implicated in this modern kind of warfare. The paragraph ends with a description that is so overwhelmingly cinematographic, so much larger than life, that it becomes hard to tell whether we are witnessing the battlefield with the naked eye or on a cinema screen:

> un bout de route donnant sur des chevaux de frise, une pancarte, un sillon, une haie, un village en ruine, une porte de grange défoncée, un coin de paysage tout chahuté, des barbelés à l'infini, un macchabée en gros plan étranglé dans une chicane, chaque détail illuminé et enregistré au *flashlight*, au magnésium.
>
> (a stretch of road leading to some chevaux-de-frise,[36] a signpost, a furrow, a hedge, a ruined village, a broken barn door, a ransacked area of ground, barbed wire stretching as far as the eye could see, a corpse in close-up strangled in a chicane, every detail illuminated and captured in flashlight, in magnesium).[37]

The long series of isolated observations reads like a sequence of brief shots as each object in turn falls under the gaze of the camera eye. And like the cinematographic approach that it emulates, the sequence derives meaning from the implied connections between the various sights that come into the film-maker's field of vision – or, in this case, the writer's imagination. Thus, as we read the passage, we piece together each of these sights and take stock of the shifts in perspective and points of view one by one, as if watching them appear on screen in sequence. These set the scene and lead us around it, familiarizing us with its elements: a view of a road leading to some defence structures suggests an establishing shot; this gives way to a series of general shots of specific objects – a signpost, a furrow, a hedge – before we are presented with a panoramic view of a ruined village, presumably in the distance. The vision of lines of barbed wire vanishing into the distance calls to mind some of the vast panoramic shots that Abel Gance filmed during the First World War for his 1919 classic *J'Accuse* in which, as discussed earlier, Cendrars appeared in a minor role. The camera-narrative finally settles on the vivid sight of a hanging corpse, not only in close-up, but illuminated and recorded in the bright magnesium glare of a flashlight (ironically, a German invention). This sight is not followed by any further description or commentary, and nor are we told the nationality of the dead soldier. Cendrars's chapter began by reflecting upon the sheer anonymity of this war, so it is fitting that even this close-up does not afford us any further insight other than to bring into horrific, graphic focus the grotesque reality of warfare.

What the reader takes from this passage of cinematic writing is neither a heightened sensibility nor a superior understanding of the meaning and purpose of this war. From his lookout post, Cendrars's narrator gains an enhanced view of the action, but far from affording him any clearer sense of what is happening around him, it seems on the contrary, in its overwhelming intensity, to overload his conceptual faculties. We are reminded of the narrating voice of *Prose du Transsibérien* looking out of the window of the fast-moving train, who is forced to admit to being overwhelmed by more associations and images than he is capable of cramming into his poem.[38] Here again, we are left with the impression that the writing self has been reduced to a camera of sorts, registering scenes mechanically but unable to process them. This theme recurs throughout the chapter: it also resonates with many of Cendrars's other texts, including *L'Eubage*, an extract of which he includes as the fifth chapter of 'The Sidereal Eiffel Tower'. In it, and indeed in this portion of *Le Lotissement du ciel*, the natural world and the narrator's seeing eye become part of an extended metaphor for cinema. As a result, the reader's perception too takes on a quasi-filmic intensity, and it becomes difficult to distinguish between the unfolding of real time, the construction of narrated time and the cinematographic rhythm of the implied camera shots. All three modes, it seems, become imbricated, and together they offer us a multilayered, simultaneous experience of the scene unfolding incrementally. Seen from this perspective, the passage begins to make sense cinematographically, and this is reflected at a syntactic level. The commas between individual observations do not offer any explanations or attempt to construct any explicit links or causal connections; they merely allow each element under the spotlight or in the camera eye to exist momentarily in our consciousness. These brief glimpses create a pulse, a rhythm that begins to resemble the flickering of the arc light used in early film projectors or the brief, almost imperceptible moments of darkness that would have separated each frame passing through an early twentieth-century film projector at a rate of sixteen frames per second. The shadows in the darkness to which the chapter title alludes are without doubt partly those of the cinema.

The passage conveys lucidly and subtly Cendrars's sensibility, a product of literature in the era of cinema, and a direct consequence of this new form of mechanized war. His writing style, shaped and modulated by the mechanics of film-making, and profoundly affected by the emotional impact of modern warfare, reflects his own first-hand experience of the film medium, but also offers a means to capture the reality of war, if not understand it. Indeed, he seems to suggest that the camera-narrator is the only viable framework through which to recount something as profoundly traumatic and incomprehensible as this slaughter on a massive scale. The literary trope of the camera offers Cendrars a narrative device that signals a measure of detachment from the events narrated. His approach bears out the observations of Christophe Wall-Romana, who argues convincingly that Cendrars's writing is deeply marked by the aesthetics of cinema.[39]

After the first allusion to no man's land, the narrator reflects on the incomprehensible clash between the human striving for knowledge and reason and the world's failure to offer any such meaning. He twice refers to Schopenhauer, and once specifically mentions his 1813 book, *On the Fourfold Root of the Principle of Sufficient Reason*, whose maxims he used to recite at the front as a means of trying to make sense of the madness.[40] We have seen how Cendrars frequently cites Schopenhauer's defining statement, 'The world is my representation'; but even the German philosopher's belief in causality and his principle of sufficient reason cannot explain what has happened to the world. Cendrars's narrator repeatedly stresses the impossibility of conveying the enormity of the war or the gravity of its consequences:

> peut-on concevoir un tableau synthétique plus absurde et plus logique de cette grande fadaise qu'est la vie humaine sur terre, une meilleure illustration du néant de la vie spirituelle de l'homme, une preuve plus manifeste de l'impuissance, de l'inutilité de son activité intellectuelle ?
>
> (can we conceive of a more absurd and logical overall picture of this great nonsense that is human life on Earth, a better illustration of the nothingness of the spiritual life of man, a more manifest proof of the powerlessness, the uselessness of his intellectual activity?)[41]

This view that the world simply has no meaning, and evades all attempts to make sense of it, recurs at intervals throughout the chapter: later on, the narrator hints that this war has brought humanity face-to-face with its mute, chillingly inhuman other: 'Le silence n'est pas humain' (Silence is not human).

Another point worth mentioning in the chapter's opening paragraph relates to the specific choice of words used. The narrow slit of light, mentioned in the opening lines of the chapter and again two pages further on, is described as 'un créneau découpé dans une plaque blindée, une meurtrière, un judas' (a niche cut into an armoured plate, a murder hole, a peephole).[42] In its first definition, the noun 'meurtrière' literally denotes a murderess, but in the specific context of fortresses and military architecture it was used to describe the narrow openings through which arrows could be fired. In English it is sometimes known as an arrow hole or murder hole. The term 'judas' has a specific usage in military contexts, where it signifies a gap or opening; but the word itself is identical to the biblical figure of that name, and it seems that etymologically it derives from the implicit treachery of being in a position to see one's adversary while remaining unseen.[43] In previous centuries, war was governed by a heroic ethos according to which soldiers were expected to be visible to their adversary; from this perspective, a judas would indeed infringe this moral code. Given Cendrars's sensitivity to nuance, and his masterful command of the well-turned *mot juste*, it seems significant that both of these words, *meurtrière* and *judas*, are used twice in short succession. Moreover, they precede lengthy discussions of betrayals; the chapter goes on to recount the stories of Cendrars's peers and acquaintances who betrayed the French nation by avoiding conscription. The first of these is his erstwhile close friend Robert Delaunay, who had profoundly and definitively lost Cendrars's respect as a result of their very different decisions on the outbreak of war. He had let Cendrars down, first, by evading conscription under the false pretences of mental instability. Cendrars expresses a measure of understanding for this act in itself, although not without condescension: 'je comprends la peur des coups' (I understand the fear of being hit).[44] What sealed Delaunay's fate in Cendrars's eyes was the former's ostentatious, hypocritical and wholly unapologetic behaviour when he returned to Paris after a lucrative and peaceful period of artistic activity in Spain and Portugal during the war: he brought the certificate of insanity that he had obtained from the French embassy in Madrid and waved it gleefully in the faces of those around him, including the *mutilé de guerre* that Cendrars had become in the meantime.[45] While Cendrars does not provide any details on how this behaviour made him feel, it is fair to assume that he was deeply offended by such a shameless lack of tact on Delaunay's part. The fact that the two never again met, and that he never again collaborated on a work of art with Sonia Delaunay, suggests that the war years affected his relationship with the artist couple in profound and lasting ways. After 1918, Cendrars did, however, go on to work alongside other artists of his generation, including Fernand Léger, who had fought and sustained serious injuries in the Great War; he also collaborated with a younger generation of artists after 1945, including the photographer Robert Doisneau, whose career he helped to launch.

The second subject of treacherous behaviour cited in the chapter is the Swiss-born poet-boxer Arthur Cravan, who had frequented the same Parisian social circles as the Delaunays and Cendrars in the pre-war years. With unconcealed scorn, Cendrars's narrative recounts Cravan's many ostentatious but unsuccessful publicity stunts, including a farcical and prematurely terminated boxing match in Barcelona in which he was to face the world champion, Jack Johnson. This, like so many of Cravan's other stunts, was a non-event, and Cendrars narrates with some disdain the fury that the whole episode caused Johnson when he realized how damaging this would be to his reputation as a professional. With particular vehemence Cendrars condemns the decision taken by the physically robust Cravan, when war was declared in 1914, to swim to safety across the bay separating France and Spain and join that 'other big mouth' Robert Delaunay.[46] The account of Cravan's misadventures does not stop with the man himself, but provides Cendrars with an opportunity to snipe at the Dada group with which the poet was affiliated. Cendrars's account of this period shares with the reader in some detail his negative feelings towards both the Dadaists' refusal to fight in the war and what he implies is the hypocrisy of decrying the hostilities, and even deriving creative inspiration from them, but not openly engaging with them or seeking to put a stop to them.

The passage recalling the split with Robert Delaunay is revealing in terms of what it has to say about the respective fortunes of the visual artists of the avant-garde and their peers on the poetic scene since the early years of the twentieth century. As Cendrars must have been only too acutely aware, many painters and sculptors of his generation, some of whom had once frequented the low-rent studios of La Ruche, had gone on to make very considerable sums of money thanks to the agents representing them and a booming commercial market; the poets, meanwhile, remained in relative poverty even though their work was no less creative or innovative than that of the visual artists.

Alongside the real people who appear in *Le Lotissement du ciel* are some fictitious figures, one of whom is Dr Oswaldo Padroso. We encounter him towards the end of the book in the thirteenth section of 'La Tour Eiffel Sidérale', which is titled 'The Novel of Morro Azul'. Padroso nearly shares his first name with Cendrars's friend the Modernist writer Oswald de Andrade, who had hosted his first stay in Brazil in 1924. Padroso is a characteristic hybrid of reality and invention. His home is Morro Azul, a beautiful fazenda that not only genuinely exists, but which Cendrars had visited in 1924 in the company of Andrade. The choice of location is well suited to the book's symbolic layers: part of it is exposed to the sky, and so it provides a fitting backdrop for the various celestial narratives that unfold in the book. Padroso is also intriguingly apt as a figure through whom to end Cendrars's (non-)memoirs: the Brazilian is obsessed with Sarah Bernhardt, for whom he has developed a cult worship stemming from 1909, when he met her during her tour to São Paolo. He had protected her from the hordes of adoring fans whose fervent attentions could have put her in danger; in recognition of his courageous action, he received a single kiss from his heroine, accompanied by a scrap of lace, which the legendary actress tore from her undergarments and pushed into his hand as a token of gratitude. With this, Padroso had enough to fuel a lifetime of worship. As he explains to Cendrars: 'Ma religion est faite.' (My religion is made.)[47]

Padroso is in many respects a foil for Cendrars, whose long-standing love for Raymone was similarly idealized and, it seems, largely unrequited. The relationship between character and author is perhaps better exemplified in terms of the way a mirror image resembles yet distorts the body. For Claude Leroy, Padroso is a reverse alter ego in that he acts as a counterpoint, an embodiment of the shadow that accompanies every illumination.[48] Of the various characters who make an appearance in the book, arguably Sarah Bernhardt too can be interpreted as an imperfect double of Cendrars in terms of her life experiences. By the time she visited Brazil, she was already an internationally renowned stage and screen actress; but she was no longer a young woman and no longer at the peak of her career or celebrity. Indeed, by the time of her world tour, she had several decades of high-profile acting behind her, and arguably her star had already begun to wane some time before then. In 1909, the year in which Padroso claims he met her, the actress was 65 years of age and suffering from severe leg pain. An injury sustained on stage exacerbated this to such an extent that she contracted gangrene and had to have her leg amputated close to the hip in February 1915. During the remainder of the First World War, she continued to tour and made motivational visits to the troops serving at Verdun and the Argonne. In this light, the figure of Bernhardt offers a parallel of Cendrars, who must have felt a considerable degree of compassion for her. At a time when he was enjoying a late blossoming of his writing career, he must have been more than usually sensitive to her own efforts to keep her acting career alive well into her mature years.

The book concludes with an intriguing conflation of political and personal events. Introduced as a 'Post-scriptum pour le pessimiste que je suis' (Post-Scriptum For the Pessimist That I Am), the final paragraphs recount the liberation of Aix-en-Provence in 1944, the news of which is brought to the author by a group of international war correspondents attached to the U.S. Army. Cendrars explains that this incident took place on 21 August 1944; as is often the case in his books, this date has symbolic value – it was exactly one year to the day since he had returned to writing after suffering a three-year-long period of writer's block. The conclusion of *Le Lotissement du ciel* thus takes us full circle by discreetly alluding to the date at which the post-war memoirs began, as his preface to *L'Homme foudroyé* confirmed.[49]

This overlapping of world events, personal experience and the writing process also marks the closing words of the book. Among the war correspondents is a Brazilian who reports that Oswaldo Padroso, prompted by France's capitulation to the Nazis in June 1940, had finally given up his forty-year-long 'hypnosis'. Cendrars's relief at hearing this news is tempered by the feeling that Padroso's renunciation is at the same time an abdication and 'humiliating for Poetry'. For Cendrars, idealized love and sacrifice was a deeply poetic act, and one to which he could relate only too easily. The final words of the book contain Cendrars's enumeration of the places and dates of its writing: Aix-en-Provence, 11 August 1946. Villefranche-sur-Mer, 1 September 1948. Saint-Segond, 9 March–1 May 1949. The first two of these dates are Raymone's and his birthdays. Only three months after completing this book, Cendrars married his idealized muse, almost exactly 32 years after they had first met.

The four volumes that constitute the post-war tetralogy are unreliable as autobiographical accounts, since they fail to provide a clear, linear account of his life and are replete with inventions and asides. Yet almost despite themselves they do still provide a wealth of information on events from Cendrars's life, his past and present opinions, his literary influences and peers, and his creative methods; they offer us an array of insights into how writing and living can feed, and feed off, each other. But the books do more than this; they also inaugurate a new literary genre. Whether we situate them within an 'automythobiography', to use Claude Louis-Combet's term, or describe them as prototypical examples of 'autofiction' written some decades before Serge Doubrovsky defined that genre, these four books constitute a radically innovative as well as prolific expansion of Cendrars's literary oeuvre.[50] Each of the four volumes is self-contained and has a totality of its own; each also has a distinctive narrative tone and a particular thematic focus that distinguishes it from the others. Yet seen as a whole, the tetralogy acquires another layer of meaning that derives from the relationships that its four constituent parts establish with one another. All four share a first-person narrative voice; they all strike a tone of complicity with the reader and enhance this in the various asides, bibliographical references and invitations to answer conundrums that the narrator cannot fathom, as well as in the 'notes to an unknown reader' that all four works contain.

Cendrars's four 'memoirs that are not memoirs' represent a very significant element of his literary oeuvre. Their considerable length speaks to their author's ambition, but so too does the first-person discourse that brings together expansive digressions, philosophical passages, entertaining anecdotes, asides to the reader and scholarly notes. Taken as a whole, the diverse and eclectic style of writing that we encounter in these four tomes resists definition. The refusal of these books to adopt any straightforward literary identity is unorthodox and for some readers doubtless difficult, but this is one of the features of the tetralogy that makes it so compelling to us today. In the twenty-first century, at a time when life writing has diversified and helped to erode simplistic distinctions between factual and fictional modes of writing, these books deserve a new readership.

As we have seen, Henry Miller was an early aficionado of Cendrars's distinctive writing style. Miller now seems prescient in recognizing the lengths to which Cendrars was prepared to go in order to break with narrative tradition and even with his own habitual practices:

> Oui, Cendrars is full of excrescences. There are passages which swell up out of the body of his text like rank tumours. There are detours, parentheses, asides, which are the embryonic pith and substance of books yet to come. There is a grand efflorescence and exfoliation, and there is also a grand wastage of material in his books. Cendrars neither cribs nor cabins, nor does he drain

> himself completely. When the moment comes to let go, he lets go. When it is expedient or efficacious to be brief, he is brief and to the point – like a dagger. To me his books reflect his lack of fixed habits, or better yet, his ability to break a habit. (A sign of real emancipation!) In those swollen paragraphs, which are like une mer houleuse and which some readers, apparently, are unable to cope with, Cendrars reveals his oceanic spirit.[51]

The form of these books is deceptive: beneath the appearance of a loose, occasionally rambling structure, they all establish networks of subtle connections and echoes that play out within each volume and across all four. The narration of the First World War is a notable instance of this, since incidents and characters appear and reappear across all four volumes, creating an effect of cumulative familiarization that brings the reader gradually closer to Cendrars's world. All four books make creative use of the uncertain boundaries between fact and fiction, mixing elements of both and levelling them out. As a result, we feel inclined to conclude that even when a given anecdote is embellished or even entirely invented, it is conveying a deeper truth about life. Conversely, some of the true stories that Cendrars narrates are so extraordinary that they prompt us to muse on the seemingly inexhaustible capacity of the world to surprise us. The complex ways in which the books manipulate and subvert chronology reflect the workings of memory and the imbrication of the narrated past, the present moment of their narration and the different present moment of our own reading. These are subtle works that all hint at the very essence of narrative and explore different ways in which the act of writing can not only reflect a given reality but create new realities of its own: 'le monde est ma représentation.' In these four volumes, Cendrars tells us much about his own life, but more than that, he invites us to reflect on our own life and on what it means to construct a life through writing.

ten

From the Suburbs of Paris to the End of the World

By the end of the 1940s, a measure of stability governed Cendrars's life. Having divorced Féla in 1937, he finally married Raymone in a civil ceremony in 1949; a decade later, they had a church wedding after Cendrars converted to Catholicism. The success of the post-war memoirs had helped create Cendrars's public image as an adventurous globetrotter. Yet the *génie du lieu*, the particular appeal of places near and far, had always been important to him, as too had the act of travelling; and both of these types of experience are vital elements of his literary oeuvre. In *L'Homme foudroyé*, Cendrars bemoans the lack of writings that focus on the banlieue of Paris.[1] His interest in the outskirts of the city was not new; even his poems written before 1914 end with a list of the places in which they had been written, and these often include several locations in and around the city. His fascination with the city's outermost edges is typical of his attitude to other subjects too; he is often to be found exploring the margins rather than the centre, and we have observed how his post-war autobiographical writings are more interested in documenting the lives of ordinary people than in charting the goings-on of the rich and famous.

La Banlieue de Paris

Robert Doisneau met Cendrars in 1945 when the director of *Le Figaro* sent the photographer on an assignment to coincide with the publication of *L'Homme foudroyé*. They enjoyed each other's company, and Cendrars was so impressed by Doisneau's work that he wrote to him proposing that they work together on a volume.[2] The result of that was the large-format book *La Banlieue de Paris* (The Suburbs of Paris), published in 1949 by Seghers. It consists of a text by Cendrars followed by Doisneau's photographs. Cendrars's essay is divided into four parts, each corresponding to a geographic area: South, West, East and North. The photographic section is divided into eight categories: 'Gosses' (Kids), 'Amour' (Love), 'Décors' (Scenery), 'Dimanches et fêtes' (Sundays and Holidays), 'Loisirs' (Leisure), 'Travail' (Work), 'Terminus' (Terminus) and 'Habitations' (Living Spaces).

The essay begins in characteristically peripatetic style, with Cendrars focusing his attention on Paris and its surroundings, recalling his experiences of engaging in flânerie. As we might expect of an offbeat writer like Cendrars, this wandering is not undertaken on the city's streets where Baudelaire, Benjamin and the Surrealists locate their peregrinations, but instead takes an unusual, underground form that is historical and literary as well as geographic. The text begins close to the author's home in a street that it introduces as the allée des Veuves, a place name that ceased to exist in the mid-nineteenth century, when it was renamed avenue Montaigne. It seems fitting that Cendrars should live in a street named after the sixteenth-century writer and pioneer of the philosophical *essai*, since this happy accident overlays Cendrars's autobiographical writing with a historical texture that taps into the rich French tradition of essay writing. *Bourlinguer* had begun with an epigraph taken from Montaigne, and this short essay has much in common with that book and the other heavily autobiographical writings of the immediate post-war period.

As Cendrars's essay confirms, he had made various forays beneath the streets of Paris in the company of friends who were employed as sewage workers. On several occasions he walked the 6 kilometres from the avenue Montaigne, just north of the Seine, emerging at the Porte d'Orléans on the southernmost edge of the city, and continued as far as Arcueil, where his friend the composer Erik Satie lived. Since Satie was rarely at home on those occasions, Cendrars would usually continue his walk through the still unfinished streets to Gentilly, from where he would catch a train back as far as the Gare du Luxembourg, confident of encountering his friend in one of the brasseries of the boulevard Saint-Michel or Montparnasse. On occasion, though, he would keep walking as far as Sceaux, 5 kilometres further south.

These journeys on foot and by train are opportunities for another, chronological kind of flânerie, since the places visited invoke different historic moments. His excursions are also literary, since each location triggers associations with writers and creators past and present: thus Satie's refusal to join the fashionable Paris set recalls Cézanne's resistance to being pigeonholed, while Arcueil prompts Cendrars's narrative to reflect upon the first publicized sexual abuse scandal involving the Marquis de Sade, which took place in his château there in 1768. These places and occurrences also bring us back ineluctably to Cendrars himself: the fact that Sade's crime was committed on Easter Sunday implicitly recalls *Les Pâques à New York* and its portrayal of modern-day city life. And Cendrars muses on the fact that it was impossible to predict which one of the Paris stations his train would return to after his nocturnal sorties, 'probably following the whim of the train conductor who is playing chess or the station masters who are playing cup-and-ball'.[3] Here both the idea of trains choosing their own route and the specific wording remind us of lines from *Prose du Transsibérien* that refer to station masters playing chess and 'bilboquets diaboliques' (infernal toys).[4] By the end of the paragraph, the narrative has returned to the avenue Montaigne, not before crossing paths with Sade's fellow pornographer and rival Restif de la Bretonne.

As is already clear from the opening pages, Cendrars's text itself is a masterful act of *bourlingage* that works across different temporal and spatial layers. A single sentence stretches out over an entire page, its words flowing seamlessly between sights, recollections and anecdotes. Like the train wending its way back to Paris in the early hours 'par des banlieues lointaines qui allaient se multipliant' (through distant suburbs that kept multiplying),[5] the text follows a sinuous trajectory that skilfully unites the present moment of writing with the narrator's own reminiscences and the more distant past of previous centuries to which he alludes.

The first section goes on to consider social housing; the growth of the petite bourgeoisie; city planning and its failure to provide adequate housing for the masses; refuse collections; the Communist Party and the rise of the Front Populaire in 1937; the Spanish Civil War; the attitudes of wealthy business owners; the misery of life in Montrouge; the ubiquity of bistros, and some forms of popular entertainment these establishments hosted, including a performer whose act entailed him sticking his head into a cage of rats and allowing them to sink their teeth into his ear lobes and forehead before he would take revenge by biting off their heads with a flourish.

Towards the end of the first section, Cendrars turns to Doisneau, his work and photography more generally. He also considers its distinctive qualities compared with literature: for Cendrars, photography is a more

Constantin Brancusi, photograph of Erik Satie's apartment house on rue Cauchy in Arcueil, nicknamed 'the four chimneys', taken shortly after Satie's death in 1925.

effective means of capturing the humanity of its subject.[6] He reflects on his own writing:

> Je suis un déclassé, un transplanté, et la déformation professionnelle et aussi la fatigue de l'écrivain qui exerce un métier esquintant, me poussent au noir pour ne pas dire à un pessimisme systématique. Sur le plan social, je n'ai pas la foi, j'en ai trop vu, et non de l'autre côté du monde en des peuplements invraisemblables improvisés d'urgence, rushes des chercheurs d'or, et, aujourd'hui, campements des chercheurs d'uranium, mais justement ici, dans cette banlieue parisienne où la misère imprègne tout et pue comme la première fois que j'y ai mis les pieds.
>
> (I'm classless, transplanted, and my professional conditioning, along with the exhaustion of the writer whose job wrecks him, drive me towards darkness, not to say towards a systematic pessimism. On the social front I've got no faith left; I've seen too much, and not on the other side of the world in implausible improvised population movements, gold rushes, and, these days, camps of uranium prospectors, but right here in these Parisian suburbs where poverty impregnates everything and stinks just like the first time I set foot there.)[7]

He goes on to reflect on how little the banlieue has changed since previous centuries; once more, this prompts him to allude to literature, citing the case of François Villon, who was banished from the city of Paris and took refuge in the suburbs, where he lived in abject poverty, spending his days drinking, womanizing and fighting: 'Telle qu'elle est, la banlieue d'aujourd'hui est restée ce qu'elle était déjà au moyen âge, c'est-à-dire un monde à part, et, pour beaucoup, un maquis, une planque.' (The suburbs of Paris are still the same today as they were in the Middle Ages, that is to say a world apart, and for many, a maquis, a hideout.)[8]

The first section closes as it began, by considering the connections between modern-day society and earlier times. Cendrars returns to the medieval era and the construction of cathedrals, noting that Doisneau's photographs are redolent of that historical period. Commenting on one of Doisneau's photographs depicting a manual worker, he likens the photographer's actions to those of a thief, intent on pursuing his target. Here, too, he is doubtless reflecting on Villon.

The second section, 'Ouest' (West), expresses some fierce criticism of the superficial values and the obsession with property ownership that characterize the bourgeoisie. The narrator challenges the reader not to feel alienated by the behaviour of those whose only ambition is 'l'épargne faite de sordides économies pour arriver enfin à l'épanouissement d'un rêve longtemps refoulé: avoir "sa" villa!' (to amass a nest-egg from sordid penny-pinching in order finally to realize a long-repressed dream: a 'villa' of one's own!)[9]

As someone who had spent most of his adult life shunning the trappings of bourgeois life, Cendrars must have felt particular dismay in contemplating the lack of ambition and imagination in the lives of the *banlieusards*. He narrates with palpable scorn the superficiality and banality of petty-bourgeois values and above all the lack of ambition in their lives. While writing fondly about the railway networks on which so many suburb-dwellers rely for their commute to work, he is scornful of the lack of interest that they take in their surroundings or the every-day activities that could be rewarding but have become meaningless and lifeless. Modern work with its frenetic rhythm and incessant schedules has distanced people from their own humanity: 'Ils peuvent courir pour attraper leur métro en se bousculant et même sauter dans leur train en marche, mais ils ne savent plus marcher, flâner, s'arrêter, respirer. Trop de hâte. Ils ne s'appartiennent plus.' (They can run to catch their metro, jostling each other out of the way, and even jump on the train once it's moving, but they no longer know how to walk, wander, pause, breathe. Too much haste. They don't belong to themselves any more.)[10] Cendrars reserves particular disdain for office work, which has pushed people away from the important things in life: 'Les femmes ne sont pas nées pour être dactylos ni les hommes ne sont au monde pour être dans un bureau. L'homme à la bêche n'a pas de faux col.' (Women weren't born to be typists, and men didn't come into this world to work in an office. A man who wields a spade doesn't need a detachable collar.)[11]

The third section, 'Est' (East), is the shortest, but it manipulates chronology, skilfully interweaving the moment of writing with earlier periods. It begins with the exclamation 'Vive les congés payés du mois d'août qui vident les ateliers!' (Long live the paid holidays in August that empty the workshops!)[12] and celebrates the leisure activities made possible for working people since 1936 when the Front Populaire government had introduced paid holidays for the month of August.[13] Three times this heading is repeated, and the pleasures of summertime are enumerated; on the fourth occurence, the mood of the section changes dramatically as the author reminds us that the first time a paid national holiday was introduced had been in 1914 and coincided with the start of the First World War. The text charts the gradual shift in mood as the summer of peacetime reached its conclusion, and many of those who would soon lose their lives did their best to avoid contemplating the future.[14] Young men who were drafted into the French army or, like the author, the Foreign Legion, unaware of what awaited them, lingered as long as possible in civilian society and exploited as many opportunities as possible to enjoy themselves while they could, even if this meant taking leave without permission. As the author states: 'Que cela simplifie l'existence que de vivre au jour le jour. C'est une vérité. Bientôt nous allions mourir au jour le jour. C'est une autre vérité et une simplification encore plus grande.' (How simple life becomes when you live from day to day. That's one truth. Soon we were going to die day to day. That's another truth and an even greater simplification.)[15]

Cendrars recalls how his batallion spent the first few weeks of the war in the suburbs to the east of Paris. As he describes it, many of his fellow legionnaires had not fully taken cognizance of the prevailing events and adopted a state of wilful self-delusion, as if subconsciously they knew the fate that awaited them and had decided to live to the full while they could: 'pour la plupart de mes camarades qui allaient tomber anonymement dans cette longue guerre des tranchées, les corvées auxquelles on nous affectait se terminaient en parties de plaisir, beuveries ou gueuletons' (for most of my comrades who would fall anonymously in this long trench warfare, the chores we were assigned to ended in parties of pleasure, drinking bouts or nosh ups).[16] The text draws a parallel with the Second World War, and particularly with France's capitulation to the Nazis in 1940.

The fourth and final section, 'Nord' (North), engages critically with factory life and its perpetuation of harsh and dehumanizing working conditions in the mid-twentieth century. Likening these institutions to prisons, the narrative argues that whether they are in public or private hands, the end result for the worker is forced labour.[17] Cendrars relates these observations to his own experience and acknowledges that he has never undertaken a conventional job. As he makes clear, he is staunchly opposed to the tyranny of alienated labour: 'je n'ai pas honte de le dire, j'ai fui, j'ai déserté la grande peine des hommes, le travail industriel, le travail maudit.' (I'm not ashamed to say it, I fled, I deserted the great struggle of men, industrial work, accursed work.)[18] Adopting the non-conformist stance of a bohemian, he argues controversially that even the freedom of destitution is better than the enslavement of factory work.[19] The implication here is that he aspires to a kind of bohemian anarchism or anti-capitalism, though he shies away from any consistent political agenda.

After such a negative portrayal of industrialized manual labour, the book takes a surprising turn as Cendrars narrates in much more positive terms a visit he made to the Royal Arsenal in London in March 1940 in his capacity as war correspondent for the British Army. He recalls being struck by the extraordinary cleanliness of the site and the calm atmosphere that prevailed, confounding all his expectations of the appearance of a factory. He finds that the workers resemble clerical employees rather than manual labourers.[20] A significant feature of what makes this workplace tolerable is the pride that the workers take in their job; another is that each of them has assigned a place for personal mementos such as family photographs as a means of bringing touches of humanity into the factory.[21]

The final pages find Cendrars at the airfield in Le Bourget; as he watches aeroplanes landing and taking off, he speculates on their destinations and origins. This association of thoughts takes him from London with its underworld to New York's Bowery and from there to the cities on the Pacific Coast, onwards to Shanghai with its enormous, densely populated floating shanty towns, and to Moscow with its modern-day abandoned children. He reflects on the developmental process that leads from childhood to adulthood, and, having just mused on war, he wonders whether the deaths inflicted by Napoleon, Hitler, Stalin and Genghis Khan could have been predicted by studying them when they were children.

The short final paragraph relates to childhood and focuses on one of Doisneau's photographs in the album depicting a little boy walking along the muddy edge of a road in Aubervilliers. Facing the camera, the boy seems cheerful; his hands are loosely clenched and convey a sense of resolve as he walks away from the bleak backdrop of nondescript houses, seemingly oblivious to the danger of walking on a road used by motor vehicles. Naming the boy '[le] fils d'Israël d'Aubervilliers' (the son of Israel from Aubervilliers), Cendrars speculates on the boy's thoughts and wonders if he is thinking of Goliath, whom he will kill one day with a stone between the eyes fired from a slingshot.[22] Cendrars's choice of this photograph expresses hope for the resilience of humans, particularly in the aftermath of the Holocaust, but it is also a fitting image in light of the author's own identity: not only the solitary boy, but the tyre tracks on the

Robert Doisneau, photograph that appears with the title *Le fils d'Israël d'Aubervilliers*, in Blaise Cendrars, *La Banlieue de Paris* (1949).

road, to which Cendrars draws the reader's attention, embody the free spirit of the *bourlingueur* and the insatiable desire to explore the world, even if that world is fundamentally hostile.

Emmene-moi au bout du monde!

The series of radio interviews conducted with Michel Manoll in 1950 confirmed Cendrars's status as a raconteur of the highest order and as a popular writer. The years up to his death in 1961 were the antithesis of a gentle retirement, as he continued to plan new books and adaptations of his earlier publications. In 1956, he suffered a stroke from which he never fully recovered. In the third of his interviews, he announced that he was planning to write a new novel – not, this time, another thinly veiled autobiography, but 'un roman-roman' (a novel-novel). As he observes, 'on ne voit plus qu'un seul personnage dans mes livres: Cendrars! [. . .] Le plus gros danger pour un écrivain c'est d'être victime de sa légende, de se prendre à son propre piège.' (everybody sees just one character in my books: Cendrars! [. . .] The greatest danger for a writer is to fall victim to his own legend, to be caught in his own trap.)[23] He insists, however, that his characters are not simply mirrors of himself, citing the case of Flaubert, who, for all his protestations of assuming the identity of his character Madame Bovary, remained a sturdy man from Normandy.[24] Asked by Manoll about his planned journeys to China and India, Cendrars voices his hope that these unfamiliar settings will stimulate him to write, and write differently: 'Un écrivain vivant doit se renouveler. Et le dépaysement y est favorable.' (A living writer has to renew himself. And estrangement is helpful in that regard.)[25] Not only would the novel be purely a work of fiction, but its main protagonist would be a woman. Moreover, even though he never again moved away from Paris, the novel would, in more than one sense, take him to the end of the world. In late 1950, he had found a working title for it, *Emporte-moi au bout du monde* (Bring Me to the End of the World), although for the next three years he could not decide whether it would be a work of detective fiction or a love story.[26] The book he finally wrote is neither, at least not in any conventional sense. It is, however, a *roman à clef*, a fact that somewhat undermines Cendrars's pledge to write an entirely fictional work. The action centres on Thérèse Eglantine, a stage actress in her 79th year; she is based on Marguerite Moreno, whose fading career was revived when she played the lead role in Louis Jouvet's hugely successful production of Jean Giraudoux's *La Folle de Chaillot*.[27] The book opens with a long and graphic scene detailing Thérèse's vigorous tryst with Jean-Jean, her young legionnaire lover. Thérèse is a week away from the dress rehearsal for her part in *Madame l'Arsouille*, the latest play by the fashionable Guy de Montauriol. Much of the novel adheres to the dramatic unity of time, the first ten chapters unfolding in a mere 24 hours. In Chapter Five, a man is shot dead, and we never find out who killed him or why. But to dwell on this would be to miss the point; the book is above all about life in its messy, multiform totality. Bochner, comparing the novel to the films of Antonioni, suggests that Cendrars has 'purposely created an elaborate red herring which turns out to be precisely the point, an unsolvable mystery'.[28] The book reflects upon what it means to act, both in the theatrical sense and in life more generally. Thérèse's reaction to the murder is to incorporate it into the action of the play. As the title of Chapter Two states, 'Living Is a Magic Act', and the book asserts this wholeheartedly. One of Thérèse's most dramatic acts happens in the theatre, but it is real: when she arrives very late for a rehearsal, she lets all her clothes fall to the floor and recites a ballad by Villon that decries the ageing process. The other outstanding moment takes place outside the theatre, but acquires the status of a great theatrical coup: when she is called to the office of the chief of police for questioning, she smashes its window with her elbow on entering and launches into an extraordinary monologue, a tour de force of improvisation that sets out the various reasons why she might have been suspected of shooting the victim, before dismissing them one by one. Her speech ranges widely, not to say wildly, encompassing anecdotes about Paris and citing a host of characters including Schiller, Baudelaire, the Symbolist poet Jean Lorrain, Marcel Proust, Sarah Bernhardt, Pablo Picasso, Helena Rubinstein and Cendrars himself.[29] Thérèse's scattershot speech is characteristic of the book as a whole, which encompasses the gamut of literary registers from quasi-philosophical passages to whodunnit dialogues, bawdy descriptions of sex and scatological jokes. The eighth chapter is called 'Le cul n'a pas d'âme' (The Arse Has No Soul). In *Emmene-moi au bout du monde!*, Cendrars has interwoven fact and fiction, comedy and suspense, and once again he has succeeded in taking his literary oeuvre in a bold new direction.

The book was published in January of 1956 to a mixed reception. The stroke he suffered that summer left him partially paralysed. He recovered enough to work on a collection of previously published short stories, *Trop c'est trop* (Too Much Is Too Much), seeing it into print at the start of 1957. But he ended that decade in a dramatically weakened state. The erstwhile globetrotter was immobilized, and his only outings now entailed sitting on the pavement outside his flat in Paris. On 17 January 1961, he received his first ever literary award, the Grand Prix Littéraire de la Ville de Paris, but was too ill to attend the ceremony. He was at home when he died four days later, on 21 January 1961, aged 73.

Conclusion

An Enduring Modernity

Take Me to the End of the World, then, finds Cendrars reinventing himself and his literary oeuvre right up to the last few years of his life. Extremely diverse and wide-ranging as it is, his output from the early years through to the 1950s is united by a spirit of innovation and an irrepressible energy. One defining characteristic of his profile as a writer is that he was enriched by his experience of the world but kept himself at a distance from the literary groups, movements and -isms that proliferated throughout the twentieth century. It seems clear that he preferred to create by himself. Another factor that made it easier for Cendrars to plough his furrow on his own was that he was uninterested in abstract theory; for him, the act of writing should be unfettered and should not pin its colours to any rigid political, literary, aesthetic or ideological mast. Replying to a letter from a young Belgian academic, Robert Guiette, in 1920, he writes: 'Non, je n'ai jamais publié de manifeste. Ni aucun article d'ordre esthétique poétique.' (No, I have never published a manifesto. Nor any article on poetic aesthetics.)[1] At a time when poetry continued to be the focal point of much literary experimentation, he proposed an alternative form of innovation, one that did not depend on belonging to a collective, or even necessarily on writing. Perhaps this is the distinguishing characteristic of Cendrars's particular form of modernity: it stems from the belief that living is as important as writing and much more valuable than theorizing. In the same letter to Guiette, he makes this clear: 'Moi, je ne puis pas vous parler de moi. Je n'ai pas le temps et vivre intensément est plus beau que d'écrire.' (I can't tell you about myself. I don't have the time and living intensely is more beautiful than writing.)[2] An aversion to 'writing by numbers' characterizes

Cendrars's particular identity as a writer. Interviewed by Michel Manoll in 1950, he describes work as 'une malédiction' (a curse) and states this is why he has no desire to stick to the disciplined method that enabled him to write his post-war tetralogy. 'On a autre chose à faire dans la vie que d'écrire des livres.' (There are other things to do in life than write books.)[3]

His attachment to life, to everyday life, helps us to understand his resistance to academicism, especially of the sort that regards popular literature and entertainment as less worthy than canonical texts. A refusal of Literature with a capital L is one of the abiding characteristics that ultimately define Cendrars, yet it does so alongside and in insouciant contrast to his extraordinary erudition. A voracious consumer of books – he referred to reading as his 'drug'[4] – his writing displays an impressive breadth of references, making no qualitative distinction between fifteenth-century poetry, ancient religious writings and popular serial novels sold in kiosks. As befits the son of an inventor, his career as a whole can be seen as a series of experiments, which met with varying degrees of commercial and literary success. As François Bon observes, 'Il n'y a d'écrivains que ceux qui ont raté. Beckett parlait de *rater mieux*. Avec Cendrars il faudrait parler de rater en grand.' (The only kind of writers are those who have failed. Beckett spoke about *failing better*. With Cendrars we should talk about failing bigger.)[5] Without doubt, failure plays an important part in his life and his work alike: the real and invented protagonists of his books, from Johann August Suter to Jean Galmot, Moravagine to Dan Yack, are all glorious failures, but what interests Cendrars is not so much their lack of success as the vital energy that compels them to take on the world against all odds. Perhaps Thérèse Eglantine, the heroine of *Take Me to the End of the World*, is the closest we come in his work to a literary heroine in her refusal to let other people, her failing body or the evils of the world get the better of her as she approaches her eightieth year.

Even if his attempts to break into the world of film directing ended in 'divorce',[6] the medium of film did shape his oeuvre in various ways, and he continued to explore innovative forms of writing that encompass the technologies of his day. In 1952, he wrote a 'sound poem' for Radio France, weaving his lines around recordings of voices, songs, sounds and snippets of life from around the world that were stored in the radio station's sound archives.[7] He wrote a series of radio plays in the 1950s, and when they were published in 1959, he gave them the collective title *Films sans images* (Films Without Images), as if to assert his new affiliation with the auditory alongside the textual and visual. In the foreword to this volume, he makes a statement that reiterates the very same populist intentions that lie behind his poems, his prose writing and his myriad interactions with artists and film-makers:

> la poésie de notre temps (et des autres) se nourrit aussi de légendes et de voix: on peut la découvrir en tournant le bouton d'un appareil de radio.
> Mettons qu'il s'agisse de poésie populaire, et tout le monde sera content, y compris les auteurs.
>
> (the poetry of our time (and others) feeds on legends and voices: you can discover it by turning the dial on a radio.
> Let's call it popular poetry, and everyone will be happy, including the authors.)[8]

Another of Cendrars's enduring traits is a persistant reluctance to assume the role of man of letters; a palpable hostility towards the literary establishment comes across in his writing and in the testimonies of those who knew him. His absence from many of his own book launches, his distancing from the more scholarly tendencies in the Parisian avant-garde and his critical remarks about other writers point towards the insecurity of a literary autodidact who never completed his own schooling. Fellow novelist and lifelong friend Albert t'Serstevens wrote *L'Homme que fut Blaise Cendrars* in the wake of his friend's death.[9] t'Serstevens is disarmingly unromantic in his recollection of the nature and extent of his friend's motivation to fulfil the role of writer; indeed, he has no compunction in accusing him of a degree of laziness matched only by his own. He recalls how the two of them used to while away hours playing boules and expresses puzzlement at the fact that this lifestyle did not prevent them from being prolific writers. He even confesses that he hardly ever saw Cendrars sitting in front of his typewriter and that they hardly spoke about their work at all, concluding that they must both have felt ashamed of that 'enslavement'.[10]

Claude Leroy too has commented on the 'pudeur de créateur' (creator's shame) that prevented Cendrars from wishing to be seen at his writing desk.[11] One reason that t'Serstevens posits for Cendrars's reluctance to sit at his typewriter and work is, quite simply, that he was not naturally disposed to enduring such sedentary activity for sustained

Robert Doisneau, photograph of Cendrars in Aix-en-Provence, 1945.

periods. Cendrars himself says as much in one of his interviews with Michel Manoll, echoing almost verbatim a passage from *L'Homme foudroyé*.[12] He states that, for him, writing is not really living, since it is not the life of the body. He describes it as a vice that disgusts him. Questioned by Manoll on the fact that he has nevertheless managed to write prolifically, he replies:

> Oui, il y en a une quarantaine, une cinquantaine, je ne sais pas, mais qui sont plutôt les produits de ma paresse que de mon activité. Car jamais je n'ai été un monsieur qui écrit dans un cabinet dix, onze heures par jour etc. J'ai essayé de le faire ces dernières années pour rattraper le temps perdu durant l'Occupation, mais bien, au bout du troisième, du quatrième, du cinquième volume – je crois que j'en ai fait cinq – j'en ai marre. Et je ne souhaite qu'une seule chose, c'est de m'arrêter.

> (Yes, I've done around forty, fifty [books], I don't know, but they are more the products of my laziness than of my activity, because I've never been a man who writes in a study for ten, eleven hours a day, etc. I've tried to do this in recent years to make up for lost time during the Occupation, but well, by the end of the third, fourth, fifth volume – I think I've done five [since then] – I've had enough and the only thing I want is to stop.)[13]

The series of photographic portraits that Robert Doisneau took of him in 1945 depict him out of doors, surrounded by nature or chatting with manual workers in his local bar, and in the street joking with a group of young Gypsies. When Doisneau manages to depict the writer at work, it is not at a writing desk in a study, but at the kitchen table of his home in Aix-en-Provence.[14] This is where we will leave him, sitting at his typewriter. On the table are piles of newspapers, a few books and sheaves of notes annotated in his distinctive left-hand scrawl. We imagine his coat is hanging just out of view, and perhaps the door is ajar, letting the sounds of the street filter inside. We sense it is only a matter of time before Monsieur Cendrars gets up again and goes out into the world.

REFERENCES

Notes on works are made using the following abbreviations:

CP *Blaise Cendrars: Complete Poems*, trans. Ron Padgett, with an introduction by Jay Bochner (Berkeley, Los Angeles and London, 1992)
OAC, I *Oeuvres autobiographiques complètes*, I, ed. Claude Leroy, with the collaboration of Michèle Touret (Paris, 2013)
OAC, II *Oeuvres autobiographiques complètes*, II, ed. Claude Leroy, with the collaboration of Jean-Carlo Flückiger and Christine Le Quellec Cottier (Paris, 2013)
OR, I *Oeuvres romanesques*, I, *précédé des Poésies complètes*, ed. Claude Leroy, with the collaboration of Jean-Carlo Flückiger and Christine Le Quellec Cottier (Paris, 2017)
OR, II *Oeuvres romanesques*, II, ed. Claude Leroy, with the collaboration of Marie-Paule Berranger, Myriam Boucharenc, Jean-Carlo Flückiger and Christine Le Quellec Cottier (Paris, 2017)
TADA *Oeuvres complètes*, ed. Claude Leroy et al., *Tout Autour d'Aujourd'hui*, 15 vols (Paris, 2001–6)

Where printed English translations are used, these are indicated. All other translations are my own.

Introduction

1 Henry Miller, *The Books in My Life* (New York, 1969), p. 60.
2 Richard Sieburth, 'Blaise Cendrars in the Sky', *Times Literary Supplement*, 24 September 2014, www.the-tls.co.uk.
3 Philippe Forest, 'Blaise Cendrars, ou, L'Art de léviter parmi les désastres', in *Le Roman du XX siècle*, ed. Jean Rouaud (Paris, 2011).
4 The term '(auto)mythobiographie' derives from Claude Louis-Combet, *Ecrire de langue morte* (Rennes, 1985), p. 41; Claude Leroy, 'Préface', in OAC, I, p. xvi. Philippe Forest also refers to a 'mythobiographie' in discussing Cendrars with Mathieu Garrigou-Lagrange on *La Compagnie des auteurs: Blaise Cendrars*, Episode 4: 'Le monde est ma représentation', Radio France Culture, 2017.
5 The photographs are reproduced in *Doisneau rencontre Cendrars*, exh. cat., Archives littéraires suisses, Bibliothèque Nationale, Bern (2006).

6 'Blaise Cendrars: en bourlinguant . . .', radio interview with Michel Manoll as part of the series *Les Grandes Heures*, Radio France, 1950.
7 Miller, *The Books in My Life*, p. 60.
8 L. A. Vigneras, 'Blaise Cendrars', *French Review*, XIV/4 (February 1941), pp. 311–18; here, p. 311.
9 Miriam Cendrars, *Blaise Cendrars: l'or d'un poète* (Paris, 1996), back cover.
10 Christine Le Quellec Cottier, *Blaise Cendrars: un homme en partance* (Lausanne, 2010).
11 Georgiana Colvile, *Blaise Cendrars, écrivain protéiforme* (Amsterdam and Atlanta, GA, 1994).
12 Francis Boder, *La Phrase poétique de Blaise Cendrars* (Paris, 2000).
13 Maria Teresa de Freitas and Claude Leroy, ed., *Brésil: L'Utopialand de Blaise Cendrars* (Paris, 1998); Claude Leroy, ed., *Blaise Cendrars et la guerre* (Paris, 1995); Claude Leroy and Jean-Carlo Flückiger, ed., *Blaise Cendrars, bourlingueur des deux rives* (Paris, 1995); Gabriel Umstätter, *Blaise Cendrars au coeur des arts*, exh. cat., Musée des Beaux Arts, La Chaux-de-Fonds (2014).
14 Blaise Cendrars, *Oeuvres complètes*, ed. Claude Leroy et al., 15 vols (Paris, 2000–2006). The series as a whole bears the collective title *Tout autour d'aujourd'hui* (henceforth *TADA*).
15 Blaise Cendrars, *Oeuvres autobiographiques complètes*, ed. Claude Leroy et al., 2 vols (Paris, 2013). Henceforth *OAC*.
16 See, for example, 'Titres' in *Dix-neuf poèmes élastiques*, written in 1914 and almost entirely consisting of sentences from a newspaper article, or the volume *Kodak* (*Documentaire*) (1924), almost all of which is copied and pasted from other sources.

1 Birth of a Poet: From Sauser to Cendrars

1 Miriam Cendrars, *Blaise Cendrars: la vie, le verbe, l'écriture* (Paris, 2006), pp. 82–3.
2 See Erkki Huhtamo, *Illusions in Motion: Media Archeology of the Moving Panorama and Related Spectacles* (Cambridge, MA, 2013), p. 376.
3 Claude Leroy, 'Chronologie', in *OAC*, II, p. xi.
4 *OR*, I, p. 19; *CP*, p. 17.
5 Martin Sixsmith, *Russia: A 1,000-Year Chronicle of the Wild East* (London, 2012).
6 Miriam Cendrars, *Blaise Cendrars: l'or d'un poète* (Paris, 1996), p. 25.
7 Leroy cites Tolstoy, Dostoevsky, Turgenev, Gorky and Gogol in 'Chronologie', p. xii. Miriam Cendrars cites additionally Taine, Michelet, Dante, Darwin, La Bruyère, Maupassant, George Sand and Malebranche. Miriam Cendrars, *Blaise Cendrars: l'or d'un poète*, p. 27.
8 Leroy, 'Chronologie', p. xii.
9 Letter from Freddy Sauser to Hélène dated 11 April 1907, in Miriam Cendrars, *Blaise Cendrars: la vie, le verbe, l'écriture*, p. 135.
10 Miriam Cendrars, *Blaise Cendrars: la vie, le verbe, l'écriture*, p. 136.
11 Dany Savelli, 'Examen du paratexte de la *Légende de Novgorode* découverte à Sofia et attribuée à Blaise Cendrars', *Revue de littérature comparée*, 313 (2005), pp. 21–33.

12 Leroy, 'Chronologie', p. xiii.
13 Ibid.; Miriam Cendrars, *Blaise Cendrars: la vie, le verbe, l'écriture*, p. 150.
14 See, for example, David Martens, 'D'un Gourmont l'autre. Le premier des masques de Blaise Cendrars', *Fabula-LhT*, 'L'Écrivain préféré' (March 2008), www.fabula.org.
15 Jay Bochner, *Blaise Cendrars: Discovery and Re-Creation* (Toronto, Buffalo, NY, and London, 1978), p. 31. The article appeared in *Les Hommes nouveaux*, the journal that Cendrars had set up with Emil Szittya and Marius Hanot.
16 The biographical information cited here and elsewhere in the book is indebted to Claude Leroy's invaluable 'Chronologie', pp. ix–lii.
17 Blaise Cendrars in conversation with Joël Curchod, 2 July 1954, in *Sous le signe du depart. Entretiens de Blaise Cendrars*, vol. I. Radio Télévision Suisse. Audio recording.
18 Miriam Cendrars, *Blaise Cendrars: l'or d'un poète*, p. 34.
19 See interview between Cendrars and Michel Manoll in *Blaise Cendrars vous parle . . .*, *TADA*, XV, pp. 157–60.
20 See, for example, Claude Leroy, 'Dossier', in Blaise Cendrars, *Poésies complètes avec 41 poèmes inédits*, *TADA*, I, p. 340.
21 *Blaise Cendrars vous parle . . .*, *TADA*, XV, pp. 159–60.
22 Ibid., p. 160.
23 Charles E. Walters, 'Russians to the Rescue: The Icefield Described', *Daily Telegraph*, 25 April 1912. Reproduced in *Encyclopedia Titanica*, www.encyclopedia-titanica.org, accessed 14 September 2019.
24 *Congressional Record: Containing the Proceedings and Debates of the Sixty-Third Congress, Second Session*, vol. LI, Part 5, 13 March 1914 (Washington, DC, 1914), p. 4787.
25 Bochner, *Discovery and Re-Creation*, p. 39.
26 Leroy, 'Chronologie', p. xvii.
27 *Blaise Cendrars vous parle . . .*, *TADA*, XV, p. 6.
28 See ibid.
29 *OR*, I, p. 10; *CP*, p. 6, translation amended. I am grateful to Adam Watt for his insights on this passage.
30 Remy de Gourmont, *Une Nuit au Luxembourg* (Paris, 1906). See especially pp. 21–9. Text readable online at https://gallica.bnf.fr.
31 *OR*, I, p. 9; *CP*, p. 5.
32 Ibid.
33 *OR*, I, p. 8; *CP*, p. 4.
34 Guillaume Apollinaire, 'Zone', *Alcools* (Paris, 1925), in *Selected Poems*, trans. Martin Sorrell (Oxford, 2015), pp. 14–15.
35 *OR*, I, p. 53; *CP*, p. 53.
36 *OR*, I, p. 17; *CP*, p. 15.
37 *OR*, I, p. 8; *CP*, p. 4.
38 *OR*, I, p. 53; *CP*, p. 53.
39 Leroy, 'Chronologie', p. xvii.
40 Henri-François Rey, 'Ainsi parlait Cendrars de son copain Léger', *Arts*, 10 November 1954, reproduced in Claude Leroy, ed., *Rencontres avec Blaise Cendrars* (Paris, 2007), p. 176.

41 Sonia Delaunay, radio interview, in *La Compagnie des auteurs: Blaise Cendrars*, Episode 3: 'Ecrire la guerre', by Matthieu Garrigou-Lagrange, Radio France Culture, 22 November 2017, at www.franceculture.fr.
42 Däubler also describes the Tower as 'der erste Expressionist' (the first Expressionist). Theodor Däubler, *Der neue Standpunkt* (Leipzig, 1919), p. 182. His allusion to it as Delaunay's father is cited in John J. White, *Literary Futurism: Aspects of the First Avant-Garde* (Oxford, 1990), p. 156, n. 36.
43 Virginia Spate, *Orphism: The Evolution of Non-Figurative Painting in Paris, 1910–1914* (Oxford, 1979), p. 172.
44 Blaise Cendrars, 'La Tour Eiffel', in 'Peintres', part 7 of *Aujourd'hui*, in *Oeuvres*, IV (Paris, 1962), p. 196.
45 Blaise Cendrars, 'La Tour Eiffel', pp. 195–200; here, pp. 195–6. For the accurate dates, see Leroy, 'Chronologie', p. lxii.
46 *Trésor de la langue française informatisé*, http://atilf.atilf.fr, accessed 13 September 2021.
47 Robert Delaunay, *Du Cubisme à l'art abstrait* (Paris, 1957), p. 61.
48 Sonia Delaunay, radio interview, in *La Compagnie des auteurs: Blaise Cendrars*, Episode 3: 'Ecrire la guerre'.
49 Miriam Cendrars, *Blaise Cendrars: la vie, le verbe, l'écriture*, pp. 310–11.
50 Cendrars, letter in *Der Sturm*, CLXXXIV/5 (November 1913), p. 127, in *OR*, I, p. 209. Also viewable online at Princeton University Library's Blue Mountain Project: http://bluemountain.princeton.edu.
51 Sonia Delaunay, *Nous irons jusqu'au soleil* (Paris, 1978), cited in Claude Leroy, 'Notice', in *OR*, I, p. 1210.
52 A. Sidoti, *Genèse et dossier d'une polémique: La Prose du Transsibérien et de la Petite Jehanne de France. Blaise Cendrars–Sonia Delaunay novembre–décembre 1912–juin 1914* (Paris, 1987).
53 *Le Testament de Françoys Villon de Paris, orné de figures du temps* (Paris, 1918). The 'h' in Jehanne's name was dropped in editions of *Prose du Transsibérien* published after 1919.
54 Cited in Sidoti, *Genèse et dossier d'une polémique*, pp. 107–8.
55 Letter to Georges Sauser-Hall, 22 December 1913, cited in Leroy, 'Notice', p. 1209.
56 *OR*, I, p. 19; *CP*, p. 17.
57 Ibid.
58 *OR*, I, p. 20; *CP*, p. 17.
59 *OR*, I, pp. 22–5; *CP*, pp. 20–23.
60 *OR*, I, p. 24; *CP*, p. 21.
61 *OR*, I, p. 17; *CP*, p. 15.
62 Variants of these lines occur at different points in the poem: *OR*, I, pp. 17, 18, 28; *CP*, pp. 15, 26.
63 Cendrars, letter in *Der Sturm*, p. 127, in *OR*, I, p. 209. It is thought that fewer than the planned 150 copies were actually produced.
64 I am grateful to the staff of the Beinecke Rare Books and Manuscripts Library at Yale University for kindly granting me access to one of the few remaining original copies of the *Prose*. The practical difficulty of unfolding the paper is accentuated by the size of the object, the frailty of the material and an awareness of the extremely high value that these command today. The facsimile copies published by Yale University Press (2008) and Presses

universitaires de France (2011) offered valuable access to the poem in its original form. The facsimiles also gave readers the opportunity to handle this precious artefact without fear of damaging it – in other words, in a manner more in keeping with the author's and artist's probable intentions. But these too are now out of print, hard to find and considered collector's items in their own right.

65 *OR*, I, p. 209.
66 Sidoti, *Genèse et dossier d'une polémique*, pp. 15–23.
67 *OR*, I, p. 22; *CP*, p. 20.
68 *OR*, I, p. 28; *CP*, p. 26. Cendrars misspells the surname of Pyotr Kropotkin, an anarcho-communist polymath whose *Memoirs of a Revolutionist* appeared in English in 1899 and in French as *Autour d'une vie: mémoires* in 1902.
69 *OR*, I, p. 30; *CP*, p. 28.
70 *OR*, I, p. 31; *CP*, p. 29.
71 See Esther Cohen, *The Crossroads of Justice: Law and Culture in Late Medieval France* (Leiden, New York and Cologne, 1993).
72 The big wheel appears in numerous paintings by Robert Delaunay slightly pre-dating *Prose du Transsibérien*, such as *Les trois Fenêtres, la Tour et la Roue* (1912–13), or his different versions of *L'Equipe de Cardiff FC* (1912–13).
73 John Harding, 'Blaise Cendrars et la Roue', in *Cendrars, l'aventurier du texte*, ed. Jaqueline Bernard (Grenoble, 1992), pp. 73–85.
74 José Ortega y Gasset, *La Deshumanización del Arte y otros ensayos de estética* [1925] (Madrid, 1987), p. 73.
75 Robert Delaunay, letter to August Macke, in *Du Cubisme à l'art abstrait*, p. 181.
76 Henri Bergson, *L'Evolution créatrice* (Paris, 1907), pp. 236–7. *Creative Evolution* (New York, 1911), p. 249.
77 *OR*, I, p. 56; *CP*, p. 58.
78 This will be discussed in more detail in Chapter Nine.
79 Leroy, 'Notice', p. 1225.
80 Charles-Ferdinand Sunier, 'Les quatre manuscrits du Panama', in *Continent Cendrars*, 1 (Neuchâtel, 1986), pp. 24–31.
81 Leroy, 'Notice', p. 1225.
82 *OR*, I, p. 33; *CP*, p. 33.
83 *OR*, I, p. 36; *CP*, p. 36.
84 *OR*, I, p. 38; *CP*, p. 38.
85 Cendrars, *Le Panama*, in *OR*, I, p. 38. The insight about Perlberg is provided by Claude Leroy. See his n. 18 on p. 1235. *CP*, p. 38.
86 *OC*, I, p. 38; *CP*, p. 38.
87 *OC*, I, p. 46; *CP*, p. 47.
88 This and other facts relating to the history of the Bouillon Kub are available on the Maggi website: http://concourskubor.fr/kubor.html, accessed 13 September 2021.
89 *OC*, I, p. 49; *CP*, p. 49.
90 *OC*, I, p. 35; *CP*, p. 35.
91 Jay Bochner, 'Introduction', in *CP*, p. xxv.
92 It was thanks to his contacts with Jean Cocteau that Cendrars obtained his position at Editions de la Sirène in February 1917.

93 Cendrars, 'Les Poètes d'aujourd'hui devant la science de la linguistique moderne'. Conference given on 21 February 1924 in São Paolo, Brazil. In *Aujourd'hui*, TADA, XI, pp. 98–114; here, p. 114.
94 The Cendrars archives at the Bibliothèque nationale suisse in Bern have two ink drawings that Cendrars produced as preliminary drafts of the cover design that Raoul Dufy would adapt for the published version. See Marius Michaud, *Cahiers Blaise Cendrars No. 1: Catalogue du Fonds Blaise Cendrars* (Boudry-Neuchâtel and Bern, 1989), p. 53.
95 Bochner, 'Introduction', *CP*, p. xxv.
96 *OR*, I, pp. 33–5; *CP*, pp. 33–4.
97 Roland Barthes, *La Chambre Claire: notes sur la photographie* (Paris, 1980).
98 *OR*, I, p. 44; *CP*, p. 44.
99 *OR*, I, pp. 37, 42; *CP*, pp. 37, 42.
100 *OR*, I, p. 44; *CP*, p. 44.
101 The advertisement falls at this point, on p. 30 of the original edition published in 1918 under Cendrars's auspices by Editions de la Sirène. Subsequent editions, including the Pléiade volume, have placed it as close to these lines as typography allows.
102 *OR*, I, p. 49; *CP*, p. 50.
103 *OR*, I, p. 31; *CP*, p. 29.
104 Ibid.
105 *OR*, I, p. 49; *CP*, p. 50.
106 Ibid.
107 Gilles Deleuze and Félix Guattari, *A Thousand Plateaus: Capitalism and Schizophrenia* (Minneapolis, MN, 1987), p. 25.
108 Leroy, 'Notice', p. 1183.

2 Profound Today: Poetry Before and After the Great War

1 These poems appeared in the journals *Montjoie!*, *Der Sturm* and *Les Soirées de Paris*, and would be published as a collection in 1919 as *Dix-neuf poèmes élastiques*.
2 Miriam Cendrars, *Blaise Cendrars: la vie, le verbe, l'écriture* (Paris, 2006), p. 323.
3 Ibid., p. 324.
4 Text cited in Jean-Jacques Becker, 'La Vision de la guerre chez Cendrars', in *Blaise Cendrars et la guerre*, ed. Claude Leroy (Paris, 1995), p. 14.
5 Giselle Bienne in conversation with Matthieu Garrigou-Lagrange, *La Compagnie des auteurs*: *Blaise Cendrars*, Episode 3: 'Ecrire la guerre', Radio France Culture, 2017, at www.franceculture.fr.
6 Cendrars and Rubiner wrote admiringly about each other's work, and Cendrars planned but never completed a translation of his German friend's novel *Das himmlische Licht* (Leipzig, 1916). Cendrars refers to Rubiner in 'Une nuit dans la forêt' (1929). See *OAC*, I, p. 102.
7 Miriam Cendrars, *Blaise Cendrars: la vie, le verbe, l'écriture*, pp. 329–30.
8 Ibid., p. 328.
9 Giselle Bienne, *La Ferme de Navarin* (Paris, 2008), p. 42.
10 Blaise Cendrars, *La Main coupée*, in *OAC*, I , pp. 525–801.

11 Miriam Cendrars, *Blaise Cendrars: la vie, le verbe, l'écriture*, p. 342.
12 Ibid., p. 437.
13 *Blaise Cendrars vous parle . . .*, TADA, XV, p. 154.
14 Blaise Cendrars, *Dix-neuf poèmes élastiques* (Paris, 1919).
15 See Claude Leroy, 'Notice', in *OR*, I, p. 1238.
16 Cendrars, letter in *Der Sturm*, CLXXXIV/5 (November 1913), p. 127, in *OR*, I, p. 209.
17 Ibid.
18 Clive Scott, *Reading the Rhythm: The Poetics of French Free Verse, 1910–1930* (Oxford, 1993), p. 135.
19 *OR*, I, p. 60; *CP*, p. 63.
20 *OR*, I, pp. 56, 59, 69; *CP*, pp. 56, 61, 77.
21 Raoul Hausmann's 'Phonemes' emerged around 1919 and had an influence on Schwitters, who wrote versions of his *Ursonate* between 1924 and 1932. See, for example, Timothy O. Benson, *Raoul Hausmann and Berlin Dada* (Ann Arbor, MI, 1987); Roger Cardinal and Gwendolen Webster, *Kurt Schwitters: A Journey through Art* (Berlin, 2010).
22 *OR*, I, p. 57; *CP*, p. 59.
23 The fact that Pierre Reverdy chose *Nord-Sud* as the title of the avant-garde revue he directed from 1917 to 1919 adds a further layer of referentiality to this line.
24 Louis Figuier's *Merveilles de la science, ou descriptions populaires des inventions modernes* (Paris, 1867) contains an illustration of a steamboat on p. 256 with the caption 'Bateau à vapeur faisant le service d'Omnibus sur la Seine' (Steamboat providing an omnibus service on the Seine).
25 Gilles Deleuze, *Cinéma 1: L'Image-mouvement* (Paris, 1983), p. 65.
26 *OR*, I, p. 57; *CP*, p. 59.
27 Cendrars's involvement with cinema and its impact on his writing will be discussed in Chapter Three.
28 *OR*, I, p. 70; *CP*, p. 79.
29 Theo van Doesburg, 'Abstract Expression in Film', *De Stijl*, IV (1921), p. 112.
30 See Chapter Nine.
31 *OR*, I, p. 71; *CP*, p. 80.
32 *OR*, I, pp. 71–2; *CP*, p. 80.
33 Garrett White, 'Translator's Introduction', in Blaise Cendrars, *Hollywood: Mecca of the Movies* (Berkeley, Los Angeles, CA, and London, 1995), p. xxxi.
34 Cendrars, *La Main coupée*.
35 *Blaise Cendrars vous parle . . .*, TADA, XV, p. 154.
36 *OR*, I, p. 75; *CP*, p. 83.
37 *OR*, I, p. 76; *CP*, p. 84.
38 Sigmund Freud, 'Beyond the Pleasure Principle', in *On Metapsychology* (Harmondsworth, 1987, The Penguin Freud Library, vol. XI), pp. 282–3.
39 Cathy Caruth, *Unclaimed Experience: Trauma, Narrative and History* [1996] (Baltimore, MD, and London, 2016), p. 3.
40 *OR*, I, p. 77; *CP*, p. 86. See, for example, 'Orion', in *OR*, I, pp. 144–5; *La Main coupée*, pp. 785–6; *Le Lotissement du ciel*, in *OAC*, II, pp. 680–94.
41 See Miriam Cendrars, *Blaise Cendrars: la vie, le verbe, l'écriture*, p. 344. In 2013, Christie's auction house advertised a pencil portrait of Gabrielle by Modigliani with the handwritten dedication 'à Cendrdrars' [*sic*]. The

notes add that it was a gift from the artist in 1918. See www.christies.com, accessed 14 September 2021.

42 Raymone Duchâteau, cited in Miriam Cendrars, *Blaise Cendrars: la vie, le verbe, l'écriture*, p. 385.

43 Miriam Cendrars, *Blaise Cendrars: la vie, le verbe, l'écriture*, p. 353.

44 Claude Leroy, 'Chronologie', in *OR*, I, p. lix.

45 This will be discussed in Chapter Seven.

46 The text is reproduced without the illustrations in *OR*, I, pp. 337–42.

47 *OR*, I, p. 339. English translation in Blaise Cendrars, *Modernities and Other Writings*, ed. with an introduction by Monique Chefdor, trans. Esther Allen (Lincoln, NE, and London, 1992), p. 3.

48 Claude Leroy, 'Dossier', in Blaise Cendrars, *Poésies complètes avec 41 poèmes inédits*, *TADA*, I, p. 475.

49 Henri Bergson, *L'Evolution créatrice* (Paris, 1907), p. 89; *Creative Evolution* (London, 1911), p. 93.

50 *OR*, I, p. 339; *Modernities*, p. 3.

51 Guillaume Apollinaire, 'Il pleut', in *Calligrammes: poèmes de la paix et de la guerre 1913–1916* (Paris, 1918), p. 62; 'It's Raining', in *Calligrammes: Poems of Peace and War, 1913–1916* [1980], trans. Anne Hyde Greet and I. S. Lockerbie (Berkeley and Los Angeles, CA, and London, 2004), pp. 100–101.

52 'Profound Today', in *OR*, I, p. 339; *Modernities*, p. 3.

53 *OR*, I, p. 340; *Modernities*, p. 4.

54 *391*, 14 (November 1920), ed. Francis Picabia.

55 Guillaume Apollinaire, 'Zone', *Alcools* (Paris, 1925), in *Selected Poems*, trans. Martin Sorrell (Oxford, 2015), pp. 7–15; here p. 8.

56 *OR*, I, p. 340; *Modernities*, p. 4.

57 Ibid.

58 Ibid.

59 Walter Benjamin, 'Paris, the Capital of the Nineteenth Century' [1935], in *The Arcades Project*, trans. Howard Eiland and Kevin McLaughlin (Cambridge, MA, and London, 2002), pp. 3–13.

60 *OR*, I, p. 340; *Modernities*, p. 5.

61 Guillaume Apollinaire, 'Lundi rue Christine', in *Calligrammes*, pp. 35–7; 'Monday Christine Street', in *Calligrammes: Poems of Peace and War*, pp. 53–7.

62 Bergson, *L'Evolution créatrice*, p. 302; *Creative Evolution*, p. 287.

63 *OR*, I, p. 339; *Modernities*, p. 3.

64 Bergson, *L'Evolution créatrice*, p. 2; *Creative Evolution*, p. 2.

65 *OR*, I, p. 340; *Modernities*, pp. 4–5.

66 In the era of oil lamps, railway semaphore signals used a blue lens, which combined with the lamp's yellow glow to create a green light. I am grateful to Andrew Rothwell for this insight.

67 Ken Beauchamp, *History of Telegraphy* [2001] (London, 2008), p. 219.

68 *OR*, I, p. 341; *Modernities*, p. 5.

69 Ibid.

70 Ibid.

71 Ibid.

72 *OR*, I, pp. 341–2; *Modernities*, pp. 5–6.

73 Benjamin writes: 'Aus einem lockenden Augenschein oder einem überredenden Klanggebilde wurde das Kunstwerk bei den Dadaisten zu einem Geschoß.' Walter Benjamin, *Das Kunstwerk im Zeitalter seiner technischen Reproduzierbarkeit* (Frankfurt am Main, 1963), p. 38.
74 *OR*, I, p. 341; *Modernities*, p. 5.
75 The *Trésor de la Langue Française* confirms that Gautier used the verb 'virguler' as early as 1868, but it remains a highly rare form.
76 Guillaume Apollinaire, 'L'Antitradition futuriste' (Milan, 1913).
77 *OR*, I, p. 342; *Modernities*, p. 6.
78 The metonymic visualization of poetry as a stock cube is the inspiration behind Pierre Alferi's volume *Kub or* (Paris, 1994). The book was published in English as *Oxo*, trans. Cole Swensen (Providence, RI, 2004).
79 Henri Poincaré, *Théorie des tourbillons* (Paris, 1893).
80 See Bergson, *L'Evolution créatrice* and *Creative Evolution*, especially Chapter 1.
81 Pierre Reverdy, *Les Ardoises du toit* (Paris, 1918); *Roof Tiles and Other Poems of Pierre Reverdy*, trans. Mary Ann Caws and Patricia Terry (Lincoln, NE, 1981); Pierre Albert-Birot, *Trente-et-un poèmes de poche* (Paris, 1917).

3 Through the Lens: Writing, Photography, Cinema

1 *OAC*, I, p. 316. *The Astonished Man*, trans. Nina Rootes (London and Chester Springs, PA, 2004), p. 122.
2 Cendrars, interviewed in *Le Figaro* in 1957, cited in Richard Hughes, *Dites-nous, Monsieur Blaise Cendrars . . .* (Lausanne, 1969), p. 176.
3 *Blaise Cendrars vous parle . . .*, *TADA*, XV, p. 39.
4 Ibid., pp. 57–8.
5 *OR*, I, p. 744; Blaise Cendrars, *Modernities and Other Writings*, ed. with an introduction by Monique Chefdor, trans. Esther Allen (Lincoln, NE, and London, 1992), p. 26.
6 Fernand Léger, 'Autour du *Ballet mécanique*', in *Fonctions de la peinture* (Paris, 1965), p. 134.
7 Richard Abel, *French Cinema: The First Wave, 1915–1929* (Princeton, NJ, 1984), p. 300.
8 Ricciotto Canudo, 'Préface: Paris, décembre 1922', in *La Roue, après le film d'Abel Gance*, p. 4, cited ibid.
9 *OR*, I, p. 347; *Modernities*, p. 11.
10 *OR*, I, p. 348; *Modernities*, p. 12.
11 *OR*, I, p. 350; *Modernities*, p. 14.
12 *OR*, I, p. 746; *Modernities*, p. 28.
13 *OR*, I, p. 747; *Modernities*, p. 29.
14 *OR*, I, p. 746; *Modernities*, p. 28.
15 Carrie Noland, *Poetry at Stake: Lyric Aesthetics and the Challenge of Technology* (Princeton, NJ, 1999), p. 92.
16 Jay Bochner, 'Blaise without War: The War on Anarchy in Blaise Cendrars's *Moravagine*', trans. Rima Canaan Lee, *Modernism/Modernity*, II/2 (1995), pp. 49–62. See especially p. 56.

17 Blaise Cendrars, *La Fin du monde filmée par l'Ange N.-D.* (Paris, 1919); *OR*, I, pp. 351–72.
18 The term is taken from Paul Virilio, *La Machine de vision* (Paris, 1988).
19 *L'Eubage* and its connections to art and science are examined in detail in Eric Robertson, '"Space and Time, Sublimated": Science in Balla, Boccioni, Cendrars and Survage', in *Art and Science in Word and Image: Exploration and Discovery*, ed. Keith Williams et al. (Leiden and New York, 2019), pp. 115–30.
20 *OR*, I, p. 770; *Modernities*, p. 87.
21 *OR*, I, pp. 743–4; *Modernities*, pp. 25–6.
22 The text appeared in four successive numbers of the journal *Signaux de France et de Belgique.*
23 Blaise Cendrars, *Oeuvres complètes*, vol. IV (Paris, 1960), p. 17.
24 The theme of the creation of the world runs in parallel in Cendrars's literary oeuvre to that of the end of the world, which is central to the scenario *La Fin du monde filmée par l'ange N.-D.* (1919) and the novel *Moravagine* (1926). On the links between Carl Einstein's *Negerplastik* and Léger's costume designs, see Mikel Bilbao Salsidua, 'The Creation of the World: A Tapestry by Fernand Léger at the Bilbao Fine Arts Museum', *Buletina: Museo de Bellas Artes de Bilbao*, 8 (2014), pp. 185–217.
25 The essay originally appeared on the front page of the magazine *Chantecler* on 26 February 1927. *OAC*, I, pp. 311–14; here p. 314.
26 *OR*, I, p. 314. Cassandre, whose real name was Adolphe Mouron, produced other highly iconic designs, including those for the French railways.
27 Blaise Cendrars and Cassandre, *Le Spectacle est dans la rue* (Montrouge, 1935).
28 Garrett White, 'Translator's Introduction', in Blaise Cendrars, *Hollywood: Mecca of the Movies*, trans. and introduction by Garrett White (Berkeley and Los Angeles, CA, 1995), p. xlix.
29 On this subject, see Noland, *Poetry at Stake.*
30 Blaise Cendrars, *Poésies complètes avec 41 poèmes inédits* (Paris, 2001), *TADA*, I, pp. 275–7; *CP*, p. 212.
31 Cendrars, 'Les Poètes modernes dans l'ensemble de la vie contemporaine', in *Aujourd'hui, Jéroboam et la sirène, Sous le signe de François Villon, Le Brésil, Trop c'est trop* (Paris, 2005), *TADA*, II, p. 92.
32 *OR*, I, p. 314.
33 Ibid.
34 *OR*, I, p. 312.
35 Ibid.
36 *Aujourd'hui 1917–1929, suivi de Essais et réflexions 1910–1916* (Paris, 1987), p. 89.
37 *OAC*, I, pp. 328–9.
38 Francis Lacassin, 'Gustave Le Rouge, le gourou secret de Cendrars', in *Europe*, 566 (June–July 1976), pp. 71–101.
39 Yvette Bozon-Scalzitti, *Blaise Cendrars, ou, La Passion de l'écriture* (Lausanne, 1977).
40 Walter Benjamin, 'Kleine Geschichte der Photographie' [1931], in Walter Benjamin, *Das Kunstwerk im Zeitalter seiner technischen*

Reproduzierbarkeit: Drei Studien zur Kunstsoziologie (Frankfurt am Main, 1963), pp. 45–64; here, p. 50.
41 Walter Benjamin, 'The Work of Art in the Age of Mechanical Reproduction', in *Illuminations*, ed. Hannah Arendt, trans. Harry Zorn (London, 1999), p. 227.
42 Ibid., p. 230.
43 Jacques Lacan, *Ecrits*, I (Paris, 1966), pp. 93–4.
44 Tim Armstrong, *Modernism, Technology and the Body: A Cultural Study* (Cambridge, 1998), p. 100.
45 Richard Abel, 'Exploring the Discursive Field of the Surrealist Film Scenario Text', in *Dada and Surrealist Cinema*, ed. Rudolf Kuenzli (Cambridge, MA, and London, 1996); Abel, *French Cinema: The First Wave*.
46 Gilles Deleuze, *Cinéma 1: L'Image-mouvement* (Paris, 1983), p. 72, n. 74.
47 Philippe Pilard, 'Cendrars: cinéma de rêve, rêve de cinéma', *SUD: Blaise Cendrars. Colloques poésie Cerisy 18e année* (1988), pp. 123–32.
48 Peter Nicholls, *Modernisms: A Literary Guide* (London, 1995), pp. 122–3.
49 Henri Béhar, 'Débris, collage et invention poétique', *Blaise Cendrars: Europe*, 566 (June–July 1976), pp. 102–14.
50 Clive Scott, *Reading the Rhythm: The Poetics of French Free Verse, 1910–1930* (Oxford, 1993), pp. 154–83; here, p. 160.
51 *OR*, I, p. 120; *CP*, p. 132.
52 Jean Epstein, 'Bonjour cinéma', in *Ecrits sur le cinéma* (Paris, 1974), vol. I, p. 92.
53 *OR*, I, p. 120; *CP*, p. 132.
54 *OR*, I, p. 118; *CP*, p. 130.
55 According to Cendrars, this opportunity took place shortly before he left to direct *La Venere nera* in Rome. *OAC*, I, p. 324.
56 *OR*, I, p. 92.
57 Blaise Cendrars, 'Lettre à [Alexander] Smirnoff', in Blaise Cendrars, *Aujourd'hui 1917–1929 suivi de Essais et réflexions 1910–1916* (Paris, 1987), p. 194; Blaise Cendrars, 'Poètes', in *Aujourd'hui*, p. 96.
58 Cendrars, 'Titres', in *OR*, I, p. 69; 'Titles', *CP*, p. 77.
59 Thierry de Duve, *Résonances du Readymade: Duchamp entre avant-garde et tradition* (Nîmes, 1989), p. 159.
60 Marcel Duchamp, *Duchamp du signe* [1975] (Paris, 1994), p. 49.
61 Blaise Cendrars, 'Les Poètes modernes dans l'ensemble de la vie contemporaine', lecture presented on 12 February 1924 in São Paulo, in Cendrars, *Aujourd'hui*, p. 98.
62 Marcel Duchamp, 'A propos des *Ready-Mades*', in *Duchamp du signe*, p. 191.
63 Ibid.
64 Thierry de Duve, *Au Nom de l'art: pour une archéologie de la modernité* (Paris, 1989), pp. 107–44.
65 José Ortega y Gasset, *La Deshumanización del Arte y otros ensayos de estética* [1925] (Madrid, 1987).
66 Ibid., p. 59.
67 Benjamin, 'The Work of Art in the Age of Mechanical Reproduction', p. 227.

68 Ibid.
69 *OR*, I, p. 118; *CP*, p. 130.
70 *OR*, I, p. 121; *CP*, p. 133.
71 Blaise Cendrars, 'Roof Garden', in *OR*, I, p. 121; *CP*, p. 101.
72 Ibid.
73 *Prose du Transsibérien et de la petite Jeanne de France*, in *Du Monde entier*, pp. 27–45; here, p. 41.
74 Philippe Bonnefis, *Dan Yack: Blaise Cendrars phonographe* (Paris, 1992).
75 Michel Foucault, 'La Peinture photogénique', in Gilles Deleuze and Michel Foucault, *Gérard Fromanger: Photogenic Painting/La Peinture photogénique* (London, 1999), p. 95.
76 Francis Lacassin, 'Gustave Le Rouge le gourou secret de Cendrars', *Europe*, 566 (June–July 1976), pp. 71–101.
77 Jean-Pierre Goldenstein, *19 Poèmes élastiques de Blaise Cendrars* (Paris, 1986), p. 138.
78 Scott, *Reading the Rhythm*, p. 164.
79 Benjamin, 'Kleine Geschichte der Photographie', p. 50.
80 Francis Lacassin, 'Préface', in Gustave Le Rouge, *Le Mystérieux Docteur Cornélius* (Paris, 1975), p. 13.

4 Crossing the Line: Cendrars's American Odysseys

1 Claude Leroy, in *La Compagnie des auteurs: Blaise Cendrars*, Episode 2: 'Moderne comme Cendrars', presented by Matthieu Garrigou-Lagrange, Radio France Culture (2017).
2 Armand Lanoux, radio interview, cited ibid.
3 Christine Le Quellec Cottier, 'Notice', in *OR*, I, p. 1367.
4 *Blaise Cendrars vous parle . . .*, *TADA*, XV, pp. 35–6.
5 John Dos Passos, *The Best Times: An Informal Memoir* (New York, 1966).
6 Jay Bochner, *Blaise Cendrars: Discovery and Re-Creation* (Toronto, Buffalo, NY, and London, 1978), p. 77.
7 See the discussions of *La Prose du Transsibérien*, *Kodak* (*Documentaire*), *Le Plan de l'aiguille* and *Dan Yack*.
8 *Feuilles de route*, in *OR*, I, pp. 125–80.
9 Claude Leroy, 'Notice', in *OR*, I, pp. 1279–81.
10 Leroy, *La Compagnie des auteurs: Blaise Cendrars*, Episode 2.
11 *OR*, I, p. 167; *CP*, p. 140.
12 Leroy, 'Notice', p. 1282.
13 Blaise Cendrars, *Feuilles de route I. Le Formose*, with eight drawings by Tarsila (Paris, 1924).
14 *OR*, I, p. 128; *CP*, p. 140.
15 Ibid.
16 *OR*, I, p. 128; *CP*, p. 141.
17 Guillaume Apollinaire, *Calligrammes: poèmes de la paix et de la guerre 1913–1916* (Paris, 1918), p. 18; *Calligrammes: Poems of Peace and War*, pp. 26–9. The place names Hyères and Maintenon, virtual homophones of 'hier' (here) and 'maintenant' (now), create a neat elision of spatial and temporal imagery.

18 *OR*, I, p. 129; *CP*, p. 141.
19 Ibid.
20 *OR*, I, p. 131; *CP*, p. 143.
21 *OR*, I, p. 131; *CP*, p. 144.
22 As Leroy observes, Cendrars's friend Elisabeth Prévost provided him with detailed accounts of hunting for elephants in Africa. These, rather than any first-hand experience, found their way into Cendrars's poems on the subject.
23 *OR*, I, pp. 144–5; *CP*, p. 159.
24 *OR*, I, p. 145; *CP*, p. 159.
25 See Claude Leroy, Préface', in *OAC*, I, p. 1; and 'Notice', p. 1509.
26 *La Main coupée*, in *OAC*, I, pp. 785–6. The story of Oswaldo Padroso is recounted in 'Le Roman du Morro Azul', in *Le Lotissement du ciel*, in *OR*, II, pp. 680–94. These books will be examined in Chapters Eight and Nine.
27 Bochner, *Discovery and Re-Creation*, p. 67.
28 See Claude Leroy's n. 18 on *Feuilles de route*, in *OR*, I, pp. 1287–8.
29 Carole Maccotta, 'Stratégies racialistes de l'adaptation: *L'Anthologie Nègre* de Blaise Cendrars et le ballet *La Création du monde*', PhD thesis, University of North Carolina at Chapel Hill, 2011.
30 *OR*, I, p. 163; *CP*, p. 180.
31 *OR*, I, p. 166; *CP*, p. 183.
32 The SS *Gelria* was operated by the Royal Holland Lloyd Line, and travelled between Buenos Aires and Southampton. See https://discovery.nationalarchives.gov.uk/details/r/C9364710, accessed 14 September 2021.
33 *OR*, I, p. 137; *CP*, p. 150.
34 The poem contains the lines: 'San Francisco/ That's where you read the story of General Sutter who conquered California/ And who, a multimillionaire, lost all his money when gold was discovered on his land'. *Le Panama, ou, Les Aventures de mes sept oncles*, in *OR*, I, p. 37; *CP*, p. 37.
35 Le Quellec Cottier, 'Notice', in *OR*, I, pp. 1365–84; here, p. 1369.
36 *OR*, I, p. 387; Blaise Cendrars, *Gold: The Marvellous History of General John Augustus Sutter*, trans. Nina Rootes (London and Chester Springs, PA, 1982), p. 15.
37 *OR*, I, p. 394; *Gold*, p. 26.
38 In an interview recorded in 1954 for Radio Télévision Suisse, Cendrars tells of his short-lived jobs in New York in 1911: he worked as a butcher in an abattoir and a hopeful but underqualified designer of women's fashion. Some poems in *Feuilles de route* describe the sights of port cities including Le Havre viewed from aboard a transatlantic liner.
39 Yvette Bozon-Scalzitti, *Blaise Cendrars, ou, La Passion de l'écriture* (Lausanne, 1977), p. 37.
40 Cited by Le Quellec Cottier in 'Notice', in *OR*, I, p. 1375. Cendrars's open letter to American booksellers is reproduced in its entirety ibid., pp. 484–6. Another open letter addressed to his North American publishers, Harper & Brothers, is reprinted on pp. 481–3.
41 *OR*, I, p. 389; *Gold*, pp. 19–20. Translation modified.
42 Andrew Rothwell, '*L'Or*: Cendrars between Realism and Post-Modernism', *Essays in French Literature*, XXXII–XXXIII (1995/6), pp. 81–115.

43 *OR*, I, p. 387; *Gold*, p. 15.
44 *OR*, I, p. 401; *Gold*, p. 37.
45 *OR*, I, p. 387; *Gold*, p. 16.
46 *OR*, I, p. 415; *Gold*, p. 57.
47 'Autour de L'Or', in *OR*, I, pp. 471–96, especially pp. 475–80 and pp. 488–94.
48 'Interview de Blaise Cendrars sur le cinema par François et André Berge', *Les Cahiers du mois* (October 1925), in *OR*, I, pp. 472–5.
49 'Suggestions pour une intrigue feminine à intercaler dans l'adaptation cinématographique de "Sutter's Gold", Roman de Blaise Cendrars. Dactylogramme, 1926', in *OR*, I, pp. 475–80.
50 Myriam Boucharenc, in *La Compagnie des auteurs: Blaise Cendrars*, Episode 4: 'Le Monde est ma représentation', presented by Matthieu Garrigou-Lagrange. Radio France Culture (2017).

5 A Dangerous Mind: *Moravagine*

1 The letter to Cocteau is reproduced in Jean-Carlo Flückiger, 'Dossier', in *Moravagine*, *TADA*, VII, pp. 358–9.
2 See Christine Le Quellec Cottier, 'Transparence de *Moravagine*', in *Blaise Cendrars 6: sous le signe de Moravagine*, ed. Jean-Carlo Flückiger and Claude Leroy (Caen, 2006), pp. 113–28.
3 See, for example, 'Pro Domo', in *OR*, I, p. 687; *L'Homme foudroyé*, in *OAC*, I, p. 242. *The Astonished Man*, trans. Nina Rootes (London and Chester Springs, PA, 2004), p. 67.
4 'Autour de *Moravagine*', in *OR*, I, pp. 705–9.
5 'Pro Domo', pp. 688–9, and 'Notice', ibid., p. 1415.
6 Franz Blazek, *La Philosophie de Golgotha (extraits)*, in *OR*, I, pp. 709–19. See also Le Quellec Cottier, 'Transparence de *Moravagine*', pp. 113–28.
7 Cendrars, letter to Jacques-Henri Lévesque, in *Blaise Cendrars – Jacques-Henri Lévesque Correspondance 1922–1959: 'Et maintenant veillez au grain!'*, ed. Michèle Touret (Carouge-Geneva, 2017).
8 Jay Bochner, 'Blaise without War: The War on Anarchy in Blaise Cendrars's *Moravagine*', trans. Rima Canaan Lee, *Modernism/Modernity*, II/2 (1995), pp. 49–62; here, pp. 49–50.
9 Ibid., p. 50.
10 Cendrars, letter to Robert Delaunay, 1916. Bibliothèque Nationale, Paris, Fonds Delaunay. Cited in Jean-Carlo Flückiger, 'Histoire d'un livre', in *Blaise Cendrars 6: sous le signe de Moravagine*, pp. 15–41 (p. 25).
11 Blaise Cendrars, *Vol à voile*, in *OAC*, I, p. 35. *Sous le signe de François Villon*, written in 1939, is reproduced for the first time in the same volume. On the reasons why it was never published in Cendrars's lifetime, see *OAC*, I, pp. 837–8.
12 Oxana Khlopina, 'Blaise Cendrars, une rhapsodie russe', PhD thesis, Université Paris X-Nanterre, 2007, cited in *OAC*, I, p. 865, n. 2.
13 Blaise Cendrars, *Moravagine suivi de La Fin du monde filmée par l'Ange N.-D et de L'Eubage.* Textes présentés et annotés', ed. Jean-Carlo Flückiger (Paris, 2003), *TADA*, VII, pp. 3–251.

14 Stephen K. Bellstrom, 'The Beckoning Void in *Moravagine*', *Studies in 20th-Century Literature*, III/2 (1979), pp. 173–85.
15 *Moravagine*, in OR, I, p. 546.
16 Ibid., p. 547.
17 Bellstrom, 'The Beckoning Void', p. 173.
18 *Moravagine*, in OR, I, pp. 674–5.
19 Remy de Gourmont, *Sixtine: roman de la vie cérébrale* (Paris, 1890); available online at http://gallica.bnf.fr. *Very Woman (Sixtine): A Cerebral Novel*, trans. J. L. Barrets (New York, 1922), available online at www.gutenberg.org.
20 Arthur Schopenhauer, *Über die vierfache Wurzel des Satzes des zureichenden Grundes* (Leipzig, 1818–19).
21 OR, I, p. 502; *Moravagine*, trans. Alan Brown (New York, 2004), p. 10.
22 Ibid.
23 OR, I, p. 509; *Moravagine*, p. 19.
24 OR, I, p. 525.
25 See Flückiger, 'Dossier', in *Moravagine*, TADA, VII, p. 358, n. 163.
26 See Jean-Carlo Flückiger, 'Dossier', in Blaise Cendrars, *Moravagine, suivie de La Fin du monde filmée par l'Ange N.-D.* (Paris, 2003), p. 346, n. 3; and OR, I, p. 1439.
27 OR, I, p. 544; *Moravagine*, p. 62.
28 OR, I, p. 540; *Moravagine*, p. 59.
29 *Profond aujourd'hui*, in OR, I, p. 339.
30 OR, I, p. 653; *Moravagine*, p. 175.
31 OR, I, p. 659; *Moravagine*, p. 181.
32 Jay Bochner, *Blaise Cendrars: Discovery and Re-Creation* (Toronto, Buffalo, NY, and London, 1978), p. 168.
33 OR, I, p. 660; *Moravagine*, p. 182, translation slightly amended.
34 Bochner, *Discovery and Re-Creation*, p. 161.
35 Ibid., p. 162.
36 Kenneth Goldsmith, *Uncreative Writing: Managing Language in the Digital Age* (New York, 2011). See also Marjorie Perloff, *Unoriginal Genius: Poetry by Other Means in the New Century* (Chicago, IL, and London, 2010).
37 Cendrars, 'Pro Domo', in OR, I, pp. 688–9; *Moravagine*, p. 218.
38 Cendrars, 'Pro Domo', in OR, I, p. 688; *Moravagine*, p. 218.
39 Cendrars, 'Pro Domo', in OR, I, p. 688; *Moravagine*, p. 218, translation amended.
40 See Claude Leroy, *La Main de Cendrars* (Paris, 1996).

6 Polar Extremes: *Le Plan de l'Aiguille* and *Les Confessions de Dan Yack*

1 OAC, I, pp. 276–9. Gaillard had a near-fatal fall on to rocks at La Redonne one night while Cendrars was living there. Cendrars discovered him by chance and carried him on his back to a local bistro, where a doctor was called. *L'Homme foudroyé* reprints a letter Cendrars had written on this subject to the editors of *Les Cahiers du sud*, for which Gaillard had played a key role. See OAC, I, pp. 284–5.
2 Claude Leroy, 'Chronologie', in OR, I, p. lxx.
3 Claude Leroy, 'Notice', in OR, I, p. 1510.

4 Ibid.
5 Diogène 19 April 1946, p. 5. Cited in Leroy, 'Notice', p. 1502.
6 Jay Bochner, *Blaise Cendrars: Discovery and Re-Creation* (Toronto, Buffalo, NY, and London, 1978), p. 182.
7 This place name clearly derives from the former seat of the whaling industry, Deception Island, which was one of the destinations of Charcot's expedition.
8 See Leroy, 'Notice', p. 1505. Jean-Baptiste Charcot, *Autour du Pôle Sud*, 2 vols (Paris, 1910). Volume I, *Expédition du Français (1903–1905)*, was reprinted by Tohu-Bohu éditions in 2018 followed by volume II, *Expédition du Pourquoi Pas? (1908–1910)*, in 2019.
9 See, for example, *OR*, I, p. 913.
10 *OR*, I, p. 901; *Dan Yack*, trans. Nina Rootes (London and Chester Springs, PA, 2002), p. 94, translation slightly amended.
11 *OR*, I, p. 889; *Dan Yack*, p. 81.
12 *OR*, I, pp. 923–4; *Dan Yack*, p. 116.
13 *OR*, I, p. 924; *Dan Yack*, p. 118.
14 Thomas Edison in *North American Review*, June 1878.
15 *OR*, I, p. 947. English translation: *Confessions of Dan Yack* [1990], trans. Nina Rootes (London and Chester Springs, PA, 2002), p. 8. On the radio adaptation, see Leroy, 'Notice', p. 1527.
16 *OR*, I, p. 891.
17 *OR*, I, p. 925; *Dan Yack*, p. 117.
18 Ibid.
19 The experiments of Hugo Ball, Kurt Schwitters, Antonin Artaud, François Dufrêne and others break words down into pure sound.
20 See Roger Icart, *Abel Gance, ou, Le Prométhé foudroyé* (Lausanne, 1983), pp. 129–30, 448.
21 Ibid., p. 129.
22 For fascinating theoretical insights into the relationship between technology and the prosthesis, see David Wills, *Prosthesis* (Stanford, CA, 1995).
23 *OR*, I, pp. 1003–4; *Confessions of Dan Yack*, pp. 73–4. This intertext is particularly interesting in light of the role played by voice, ventriloquism and electricity in *Eve future*.
24 *OR*, I, p. 1003; *Confessions of Dan Yack*, p. 73.
25 *OR*, I, p. 1005; *Confessions of Dan Yack*, p. 76.
26 *OR*, I, p. 881; *Dan Yack*, p. 73.
27 Ibid.
28 *OR*, I, p. 890; *Dan Yack*, p. 80.
29 *OR*, I, p. 881; *Dan Yack*, p. 73.
30 *OR*, I, p. 882; *Dan Yack*, p. 73.
31 *OR*, I, p. 882; *Dan Yack*, p. 74.
32 *OR*, I, p. 1017; *Dan Yack*, pp. 88–9.
33 *OR*, I, p. 1017; *Dan Yack*, p. 89.
34 *OR*, I, p. 1006; *Confessions of Dan Yack*, p. 77.
35 *OR*, I, pp. 1040–41; *Confessions of Dan Yack*, pp. 113–14.
36 *OR*, I, p. 1004; *Confessions of Dan Yack*, p. 74.

7 Extraordinary Lives: From Homer to Hollywood

1 John F. Pile, *A History of Interior Design* (London, 2005), pp. 351–2.
2 See Jean-Carlo Flückiger, 'Notice', in *OR*, II, pp. 1310–18.
3 Fred D. Pasley, *Al Capone: The Biography of a Self-Made Man* (New York, 1930).
4 Flückiger, 'Notice', in *OR*, II, p. 1311.
5 Henry Miller, *The Books in My Life* (New York, 1969), pp. 42–3.
6 John Paul Jones, 'Extracts from the Journals of My Campaigns' [1785], at www.americanrevolution.org.
7 Jean-Carlo Flückiger, 'Note sur le texte', in *OR*, II, p. 1318.
8 *John Paul Jones, ou, L'Ambition*, in *OR*, II, p. 893.
9 Ibid., p. 894.
10 Ibid.
11 Ibid., pp. 895–6.
12 Gilles Deleuze, *Cinéma 1: L'Image-mouvement* (Paris, 1983), p. 125.
13 Jean Epstein, *La Poésie d'aujourd'hui. Un Nouvel état d'intelligence. Lettre de Blaise Cendrars* (Paris, 1921). For the essays on cinema, see Jean Epstein, *Ecrits sur le cinéma 1921–1953*, vol. I: *1921–1947* (Paris, 1974).
14 Jean Epstein, 'De quelques conditions de la photogénie', in *Le Cinématographe vu de l'Etna* [1926], in *Ecrits sur le cinéma*, vol. I, pp. 131–52. See also Richard Abel, *French Film Theory and Criticism* (Princeton, NJ, 1988), p. 314.
15 Christophe Wall-Romana, *Jean Epstein: Corporeal Cinema and Film Philosophy* (Oxford, 2016), p. 27. See also Wall-Romana, 'Epstein's Photogénie as Corporeal Vison: Inner Sensation, Queer Embodiment, and Ethics', in *Jean Epstein: Critical Essays and New Translations*, ed. Sarah Keller and Jason N. Paul (Amsterdam, 2012), pp. 51–72.
16 Epstein, *Bonjour cinéma*, p. 94, cited in Wall-Romana, 'Epstein's Photogénie as Corporeal Vision', p. 53.
17 Laura U. Marks, *The Skin of the Film: Intercultural Cinema, Embodiment and the Senses* (Durham, NC, and London, 2000), p. 2.
18 *OR*, I, p. 341; *Modernities*, p. 5.
19 *John Paul Jones, ou, L'Ambition*, in *OR*, II, p. 900.
20 Ibid.
21 On exofiction, see, for example, Frédérique Roussel, 'Philippe Vasset. De Passage secret', *Libération*, 22 August 2013.
22 *John Paul Jones, ou, L'Ambition*, in *OR*, II, p. 900.
23 Miller, *The Books in My Life*, p. 60.
24 Ibid.
25 *L'Homme foudroyé*, in *OAC*, I. See also Flückiger, 'Notice', p. 1315.
26 See Graciela Mann and Hans Mann, *The Twelve Prophets of Aleijadinho* (Austin, TX, 1967).
27 The manuscript of *L'Argent* is reproduced in *OR*, II, pp. 1031–44. See also 'Autour de *L'Argent*', *OR*, II, pp. 1045–7.
28 *L'Argent*, in *OR*, II, 1038.
29 Myriam Boucharenc, 'Notice', in *OR*, II, p. 1092.
30 *La Vie secrète de Jean Galmot (Rhum)*, in *OR*, II, p. 10.
31 Boucharenc, 'Notice', p. 1095.

32 *La Vie secrète de Jean Galmot (Rhum)*, in *OR*, II, p. 5.
33 Claude Leroy, 'Chronologie', in *OR*, II, p. xv.
34 'Vol à voile', in *OAC*, I, p. 41.
35 'Lettre dédicatoire à mon premier éditeur', in *OAC*, I, p. 5.
36 *Le Testament de Françoys Villon de Paris, orné de figures du temps* (Paris, 1918). On Cendrars's recollection of the price of the book, see *OAC*, I, p. 7.
37 'Lettre dédicatoire à mon premier éditeur', in *OAC*, I, p. 6.
38 Ibid., p. 11.
39 Ibid., p. 12.
40 Ibid., pp. 12, 13, 16–17.
41 Ibid., pp. 20–22.
42 Ibid., p. 17.
43 Ibid., p. 25.
44 'Vol à voile', in *OAC*, I, p. 75.
45 Claude Leroy, 'Notice', in *OAC*, I, p. 850.
46 Ibid.
47 *OAC*, I, p. 84.
48 *OAC*, I, p. 85.
49 *OAC*, I, p. 86.
50 Ibid.
51 Ibid.
52 Leroy, 'Notice', p. 852.
53 *OAC*, I, p. 99.
54 Ibid.
55 *OAC*, I, p. 115.
56 *OAC*, I, p. 136.
57 Built by William Hamilton and Company in Port Glasgow in 1904, the *Moshulu* is still in use as a floating restaurant in Philadelphia.
58 'Mes Chasses', in *D'Oultremer à indigo*, in *OR*, II, pp. 401–43.
59 Leroy, 'Notice', p. 838.
60 Walter Benjamin, 'The Work of Art in the Age of Mechanical Reproduction' [1936], in *Illuminations: Essays and Reflections*, trans. Harry Zohn (New York, 1968), pp. 217–51.
61 *OAC*, I, p. 133.
62 Ibid.
63 Samuel Beckett, *Krapp's Last Tape and Other Shorter Plays* (London, 2009).
64 Ivor Montagu, *With Eisenstein in Hollywood: A Chapter of Autobiography. Including the Scenarios of 'Sutter's Gold' and 'An American Tragedy'* (Berlin, 1968); Christine Le Quellec Cottier, 'Notice', in *OR*, I, p. 1381.
65 Daniel Winkler, 'Empereurs de Californie? Blaise Cendrars et Luis Trenker à la recherche de l'Or', in *BlaiseMédia. Blaise Cendrars et les médias*, ed. Birgit Wagner and Claude Leroy (Paris, 2006), p. 85.
66 Le Quellec Cottier, 'Notice', p. 1382.
67 Cendrars, 'Hollywood', *TADA*, III, pp. 74–6.
68 *OR*, II, p. 137.
69 Ibid., p. 136.
70 Ibid., p. 160.

71 Ibid., p. 177.
72 Al Jennings, *Hors la loi! . . . La vie d'un outlaw américain racontée par lui-même. Traduction et adaptation de l'américain et du slang par Blaise Cendrars* (Paris, 1936).
73 *OR*, II, p. 182.
74 Ibid., p. 242.
75 Ibid., p. 279.
76 Ibid., p. 401.
77 *Blaise Cendrars vous parle . . .*, *TADA*, XV, p. 72. See also 'Chasse à l'éléphant' (Elephant Hunt), in *OR*, I, p. 121; *CP*, p. 133.
78 Elisabeth Prévost, 'Blaise Cendrars: deux années dans les Ardennes', in *Madame mon copain: Blaise Cendrars, Elisabeth Prévost, une amitié rarissime*, ed. Monique Chefdor (Nantes, 1997), p. 40.
79 Ibid. See also Claude Leroy, 'Notes et variantes', in *OR*, II, p. 1193.
80 Prévost, 'Blaise Cendrars: deux années dans les Ardennes', pp. 44–5. Aspects of Prévost appear in the fictional character Diane de la Panne. See 'Une drôle de vierge', in *L'Homme foudroyé*, *OAC*, I, pp. 213–35.

8 Memoirs Without Being Memoirs: Reinventing the Self

1 Sonia Delaunay, in *La Compagnie des auteurs: Blaise Cendrars,* Episode 3: 'Ecrire la guere' presented by Matthieu Garrigou-Lagrange, Radio France Culture, 22 November 2017.
2 Blaise Cendrars, *Chez l'armée anglaise* (Paris, 1940).
3 Claude Leroy, 'Notice', in *OAC*, I, p. 881.
4 Ibid., p. 1005.
5 Edouard Peisson, *L'Homme couvert de dollars* (Paris, 1946).
6 Leroy, 'Notice', p. 881.
7 Jay Bochner, *Blaise Cendrars: Discovery and Re-Creation* (Toronto, Buffalo, NY, and London, 1978), p. 81.
8 *Blaise Cendrars vous parle . . .*, *TADA*, XV, p. 55.
9 Jean-Jacques Rousseau, *Les Confessions* [1782, 1789], p. 17; see, for example, Laurent Nunez, *L'Enigme des premières phrases* (Paris, 2017).
10 Gérard Genette, *Nous. Essai d'autobiographie* (Paris, 1972), pp. 33–9.
11 Philippe Lejeune, *Le Pacte autobiographique* (Paris, 1975).
12 'Identity is a fact immediately grasped – accepted or rejected, at the level of the enunciation; resemblance is a relation, subject to infinite discussions and nuances, established from the utterance.' Ibid., p. 35.
13 Michael Sheringham, *French Autobiography: Devices and Desires, Rousseau to Perec* (Oxford and New York, 1993).
14 Max Saunders, *Self-Impression: Life-Writing, Autobiografiction, and the Forms of Modern Literature* (Oxford and New York, 2010), p. 145.
15 Christine Le Quellec Cottier, *Blaise Cendrars: un homme en partance* (Lausanne, 2010), p. 90. On the word 'prochronisme', she cites the 1915 edition of the *Dictionnaire Larousse*.
16 See the discussion of *Sous le signe de François Villon* in Chapter Seven.
17 See the discussion of the *Prose du Transsibérien* in Chapter One.
18 Serge Doubrovsky, *Fils* (Paris, 1977).

19 Lee Rourke, 'The Hazy World of Blaise Cendrars', *The Guardian*, 23 July 2007, at www.theguardian.com.
20 Marjorie Perloff, 'Introduction', in Blaise Cendrars, *Sky: Memoirs*, trans. Nina Rootes (New York, 1992), p. 1.
21 Bruno Frank, radio interview recorded by Fabrice Pinte, cited in 'Blaise Cendrars', *L'Atelier de la creation*, 14–15, Radio France Culture, December 2012.
22 OAC, I, pp. 169–71.
23 Ibid., p. 170.
24 *L'Homme foudroyé*, inside cover; OAC, I, p. 165.
25 On Radiguet and Cingria, see OAC, I, pp. 370–71. Le Rouge (whose name Cendrars writes as Lerouge, the author's birth name) is discussed extensively throughout the 'Première Rhapsodie: le fouet'. OAC, I, pp. 313–51; *The Astonished Man*, trans. Nina Rootes (London and Chester Springs, PA, 2004), pp. 121–50.
26 See the discussion of *Documentaires* in Chapter Three.
27 OAC, I, p. 329; *The Astonished Man*, p. 133.
28 OAC, I, p. 370; *The Astonished Man*, p. 166.
29 Jeff Bursey, 'Preface', in *The Astonished Man*, p. iii.
30 Philippe Gervais-Lambony, 'Temps maîtrisé, espace refondé: l'expérience humaine de l'espace selon Blaise Cendrars. Étude des *Rhapsodies gitanes* (*L'homme foudroyé*, 1945)', *Cybergeo: European Journal of Geography*, Political, Cultural and Cognitive Geography, document 817, accessed 25 February 2021, at http://journals.openedition.org/cybergeo/28071; DOI: https://doi.org/10.4000/cybergeo.28071.
31 OAC, I, p. 171; *The Astonished Man*, p. 14.
32 OAC, I, p. 241; *The Astonished Man*, p. 67.
33 Ibid.
34 'The world is my representation' is taken from Schopenhauer's 1813 essay *Über die vierfache Wurzel des Satzes des zureichenden Grundes* (*On the Fourfold Root of the Principle of Sufficient Reason*).
35 *Blaise Cendrars vous parle . . .*, TADA, XV, p. 37.
36 OAC, I, p. 242; *The Astonished Man*, p. 68.
37 Laurence Guyon, 'Événement, répétition, annulation dans les Mémoires de Blaise Cendrars', in *Que m'arrive-t-il?*, ed. Philippe Corno and Emmanuel Boisset (Rennes, 2009), pp. 95–106.
38 OAC, I, p. 176; *The Astonished Man*, p. 19.
39 Paul Virilio, *Guerre et cinéma: logistique de la perception* (Paris, 1984); *War and Cinema: The Logistics of Perception*, trans. Patrick Camiller (London and New York, 2009), p. 70.
40 OAC, I, p. 176; *The Astonished Man*, p. 19.
41 Ibid.
42 Yvette Bozon-Scalzitti, *Blaise Cendrars, ou, La Passion de l'écriture* (Lausanne, 1977), pp. 138–9.
43 Thomas Elsaesser, 'Postmodernism as Mourning Work', p. 199. Cited in Colin Davis, *Traces of War: Interpreting Ethics and Trauma in Twentieth-Century French Writing* (Liverpool, 2018), p. 30.
44 Davis, *Traces of War*, p. 30.
45 Ibid.
46 OAC, I, pp. 187–9; *The Astonished Man*, pp. 28–9.

47 *OAC*, I, p. 176; *The Astonished Man*, p. 19.
48 Karl-Ove Knausgaard, *The End*, trans. Martin Aitken and Don Bartlett (London, 2018), pp. 397–477. The discussion of Celan begins on p. 424.
49 Ibid., p. 447.
50 *OAC*, I, pp. 192–3; *The Astonished Man*, pp. 32–3.
51 Cendrars's version reads: 'Dies Haus ist das letzte Haus der Welt . . .'.
52 Rainer Maria Rilke, *The Book of Hours: A New Translation with Commentary*, trans. Susan Ranson, ed. with an introduction and notes by Ben Hutchinson (Rochester, NY, 2008), pp. 26–7.
53 Bochner, *Discovery and Re-Creation*, p. 200.
54 'Prose du Transsibérien', in *OR*, I, p. 28; *CP*, p. 26.
55 *OAC*, I, pp. 456–7; *The Astonished Man*, p. 220.
56 Schopenhauer's original words are 'Die Welt ist meine Vorstellung', in *Die Welt als Wille und Vorstellung* (Leipzig, 1818–19).
57 *OAC*, I, p. 457; *The Astonished Man*, p. 220.
58 *La Main coupée*, in *OAC*, I, pp. 630–37; *Lice*, translator not credited (London, 1973), pp. 81–7.
59 *OAC*, I, p. 529; *Lice*, p. 5.
60 *OAC*, I, p. 564; *Lice*, p. 33.
61 Ibid.
62 'Le Lys rouge', in *OAC*, I, pp. 785–6; *Lice*, pp. 182–3; Richard Sieburth, 'Blaise Cendrars in the Sky', *Times Literary Supplement*, 24 September 2014.
63 *OAC*, I, p. 785; *Lice*, p. 182.
64 *OAC*, I, p. 786; *Lice*, p. 183.
65 Henri Barbusse, *Le Feu: journal d'une escouade* (Paris, 1916); *Under Fire*, trans. Robin Buss (London, 2003).
66 *OAC*, I, p. 787; *Lice*, pp. 181–2.
67 *OAC*, I, p. 791; *Lice*, p. 187.
68 *OAC*, I, p. 792; *Lice*, p. 188.
69 Guillaume Apollinaire, 'Océan de terre', in *Calligrammes: poèmes de la paix et de la guerre* (Paris, 1918), pp. 142–3.
70 Words of a French soldier, cited in *Le Bochofage*, 26 March 1917. See Stéphane Audoin-Rouzeau, 'L'Enfer, c'est la boue!', in *14–18: Mourir pour la patrie* (Paris, 1992), p. 147.

9 Memoirs of Sea and Sky: *Bourlinguer* and *Le Lotissement du ciel*

1 Cendrars kept a cutting of a newspaper article on the inclusion of the word 'bourlinguer' in the *Dictionnaire de l'Académie*. Jean-Carlo Flückiger, 'Notice', in *OAC*, II, p. 974.
2 Jérôme Meizoz, 'Posture et poétique d'un bourlingueur: Cendrars', in *Poétique*, III/147 (2006) pp. 297–315.
3 Flückiger, 'Notice', p. 961.
4 Ibid., p. 962.
5 Ibid., p. 963.
6 *Bourlinguer*, in *OAC*, II, p. 5. My translation. A tartane was a small boat used for fishing and trading in the Mediterranean from the late sixteenth to the late nineteenth century.

7 *OAC*, II, pp. 6–7.
8 Ibid., p. 8.
9 The two versions to which Cendrars refers are François Catrou, *Histoire générale de l'empire du Mogol depuis sa fondation jusqu'à présent*, vol. III: *Sur les mémoires portugais de M. Manouchi, vénitien* (Paris, 1715), available online at https://gallica.bnf.fr; and Niccolao Manucci, *Storia do Mogor; or, Mogol India, 1653–1708*, trans. with an introduction and notes by William Irvine (London, 1907), available online at http://asi.nic.in/asi_books/34977.pdf.
10 Louis-Gabriel Michaud, ed., *Biographie Universelle ancienne et moderne*, 52 vols (Paris and Leipzig, 1811–28); Ferdinand Hoefer, ed., *Nouvelle Biographie Universelle*, 48 vols (Paris, 1856–62).
11 *OAC*, II, p. 13.
12 Nina Rootes, 'Translator's Note', in Blaise Cendrars, *Planus* (London, 1972), n.p.
13 *OAC*, II, pp. 79–84; *Planus*, pp. 41–5.
14 The texts, printed in Latin, are available at http://patristica.net/latina.
15 *OAC*, II, p. 83; *Planus*, p. 45.
16 Ibid.
17 Ibid.
18 Ibid. Cendrars cites his source as Léon Cristiani, *Jean Cassien, la spiritualité du désert*, 2 vols (Saint-Wandrille, 1946); *OAC*, II, p. 220, note A.
19 *OAC*, II, p. 98; *Planus*, p. 56.
20 *OAC*, II, p. 105; *Planus*, p. 66.
21 *OAC*, II, p. 164; *Planus*, p. 100.
22 Johann Wolfgang von Goethe's autobiography, *Dichtung und Wahrheit*, was first published in 1811.
23 *OAC*, II, pp. 163–4; *Planus*, pp. 99–100.
24 Claude Leroy, 'Préface', in Cendrars, *Le Lotissement du ciel* (Paris, 1996), p. 8.
25 Philippe Forest, 'Blaise Cendrars, ou, L'Art de léviter parmi les désastres', in *Le Roman du XX siècle*, ed. Jean Rouaud (Paris, 2011).
26 Claude Leroy, 'Notice', in *OAC*, II, p. 1005.
27 Marjorie Perloff, 'Introduction', in Blaise Cendrars, *Sky: Memoirs*, trans. Nina Rootes (New York, 1992), p. 2.
28 *OAC*, II, pp. 571–2.
29 *L'Eubage: aux antipodes de l'unité*, in *OR*, I, pp. 751–70.
30 *OAC*, II, pp. 595–614; *Sky*, pp. 191–207.
31 See *Feuilles de route*, in *OR*, I, pp. 144–5.
32 *La Main coupée*, in *OAC*, I, pp. 785–6.
33 *OAC*, II, p. 596; *Sky*, p. 191.
34 *OAC*, II, pp. 596–7; *Sky*, pp. 192–3.
35 *OAC*, II, p. 597; *Sky*, p. 193.
36 A cheval-de-frise, literally, a Friesian horse, was a term used to describe a form of anti-cavalry deterrent used in warfare since the medieval era, and was still employed in the First World War.
37 *OAC*, II, p. 597.
38 *OR*, I, p. 28; *CP*, p. 26. This poem is discussed in Chapter One.
39 Christophe Wall-Romana, *Cinepoetry: Imaginary Poetries in French Cinema* (New York, 2013). See especially p. 177.

40 Arthur Schopenhauer, *Über die vierfache Wurzel des Satzes vom zureichenden Grunde / Über den Willen. Kleinere Schriften*, I (Zürich, 2007). English translation: *On the Fourfold Root of the Principle of Sufficient Reason and On the Will in Nature*, trans. Karl Hillebrand (London, 1907).
41 OAC, II, p. 596.
42 Ibid., p. 595.
43 *Trésor de la langue française*, at http://stella.atilf.fr, accessed 16 September 2021.
44 OAC, II, p. 602.
45 Ibid.
46 OAC, II, p. 605.
47 Ibid., p. 683.
48 Claude Leroy, *La Main de Cendrars* (Paris, 1996), p. 159.
49 OAC, I, p. 171.
50 Claude Louis-Combet explains his term 'automythobiographie' in *L'Homme du texte* (Paris, 2002).
51 Henry Miller, *The Books in My Life* (New York, 1969), p. 67.

10 From the Suburbs of Paris to the End of the World

1 OAC, I, p. 407.
2 Cendrars, undated letter to Doisneau, reproduced in *Doisneau rencontre Cendrars* (Paris, 2006), pp. 63 and 99.
3 *La Banlieue de Paris* (Paris, 1949), p. 6.
4 OR, I, p. 27; CP, p. 25.
5 *La Banlieue de Paris*, p. 6.
6 Ibid., pp. 16–17.
7 Ibid., p. 16.
8 Ibid.
9 Ibid., p. 21.
10 Ibid., p. 26.
11 Ibid.
12 *La Banlieue de Paris*, p. 36.
13 Nicholas Atkin, *The French at War, 1934–1944* (London and New York, 2001), p. 24.
14 *La Banlieue de Paris*, p. 37.
15 Ibid., p. 37.
16 Ibid.
17 Ibid., p. 47.
18 Ibid.
19 Ibid., p. 48.
20 Ibid., p. 49.
21 Ibid., pp. 49–50.
22 Ibid., p. 55.
23 *Blaise Cendrars vous parle . . .*, TADA, XV, pp. 58–9.
24 Ibid., p. 58.
25 Ibid., p. 59.

26 Claude Leroy, 'Notice', in *OR*, II, pp. 1206–7. The book, with its definitive title *Emmene-moi au bout du monde!* (literally, Take Me to the End of the World!), appeared in Alan Brown's English translation as *To the End of the World* (London, 1966).
27 *Blaise Cendrars vous parle . . .*, p. 150, and n. 111, p. 346.
28 Jay Bochner, *Blaise Cendrars: Discovery and Re-Creation* (Toronto, Buffalo, NY, and London, 1978), p. 225.
29 *OR*, II, pp. 638–54; *To the End of the World*, pp. 163–81.

Conclusion: An Enduring Modernity

1 Michèle Touret, ed., *Blaise Cendrars – Robert Guiette: Lettres 1920–1959. 'Ne m'appelez plus . . . maître'* (Carouge-Geneva, 2013), p. 29. Cendrars mentions the writings on art that he had published in the short-lived review *La Rose rouge*.
2 Ibid., p. 30.
3 *Blaise Cendrars vous parle . . .*, *TADA*, XV, p. 6.
4 Ibid., p. 7.
5 François Bon, 'L'Alfa Roméo de Blaise Cendrars' (December 2012), available online at https://flaneriequotidienne.wordpress.com.
6 *Blaise Cendrars vous parle . . .*, p. 135.
7 'Archives sonores', in *OR*, I, pp. 325–6. The radio broadcast can be found on the Radio France Culture website: www.franceculture.fr/emissions/les-nuits-de-france-culture/rythmes-et-bruits-du-monde-1ere-diffusion-28061952, accessed 17 September 2021.
8 'Avertissement', in *Films sans images*, *OC*, 8, pp. 311–484; here p. 312.
9 Albert t'Serstevens, *L'Homme que fut Blaise Cendrars* (Paris, 2004).
10 Ibid., p. 131.
11 Leroy discussed Cendrars's work in *La Compagnie des auteurs: Blaise Cendrars*, Episode 2: 'Moderne comme Cendrars', presented by Matthieu Garrigou-Lagrange, Radio France Culture (2017).
12 *OAC*, I, p. 370.
13 Cendrars, interview with Michel Manoll, 1950. Recording reproduced in *La Compagnie des auteurs: Blaise Cendrars*, Episode 1: 'Vivre est un acte magique', presented by Matthieu Garrigou-Lagrange, Radio France Culture (2017).
14 For the photographs of Cendrars, see *Doisneau rencontre Cendrars* (Paris, 2006), pp. 28, 30, 33, 35.

SELECT BIBLIOGRAPHY

Writings by Blaise Cendrars in French

The complete poems, novels and autobiographical works of Blaise Cendrars are available in the authoritative Gallimard (Pléiade) edition:

Oeuvres autobiographiques complètes, ed. Claude Leroy et al., 2 vols (Paris, 2013)

Oeuvres complètes, ed. Claude Leroy et al., 15 vols (Paris, 2000–2006). The series as a whole bears the collective title *Tout autour d'aujourd'hui*.

Oeuvres romanesques, ed. Claude Leroy et al., 2 vols (Paris, 2017)

A Selection of Works by Blaise Cendrars in English Translation

The Astonished Man, trans. Nina Rootes (London and Chester Springs, PA, 2004)

Complete Poems, trans. Ron Padgett, with an introduction by Jay Bochner (Berkeley and Los Angeles, CA, and London, 1992)

Complete Postcards from the Americas: Poems of Road and Sea, trans. with an introduction by Monique Chefdor (Berkeley and Los Angeles, CA, and London, 1976)

Confessions of Dan Yack [1990], trans. Nina Rootes (London and Chester Springs, PA, 2002)

Dan Yack [1990], trans. Nina Rootes (London and Chester Springs, PA, 2002)

Gold: The Marvellous History of General John Augustus Sutter, trans. Nina Rootes (London and Chester Springs, PA, 1982)

Hollywood, Mecca of the Movies, translated and with an introduction by Garrett White (Berkeley and Los Angeles, CA, and London, 1995)

Modernities and Other Writings, edited and introduced by Monique Chefdor, trans. Esther Allen in collaboration with Monique Chefdor (Lincoln, NE, and London, 1992)

Moravagine, trans. Alan Brown, with an introduction by Paul La Farge (New York, 2004)

Planus, trans. Nina Rootes (London, 1972)

Sky: Memoirs, trans. Nina Rootes (New York, 1992)

To the End of the World [1991], trans. Alan Brown, with an introduction by Margaret Crosland (London and Chester Springs, PA, 2002)

Blaise Cendrars: Correspondence

Berranger, Marie-Paule, ed., *Blaise Cendrars – Jacques-Henri Lévesque. Correspondance 1922–1959: 'Et maintenant veillez au grain!'* (Carouge-Geneva, 2017)

Bochner, Jay, et al., ed., *Blaise Cendrars – Henry Miller. Correspondance 1934–1959: 'Je travaille à pic pour descendre en profondeur'* (Carouge-Geneva, 2013)

Boucharenc, Myriam, ed., *Blaise Cendrars – Raymone Duchâteau. Correspondance 1937–1954: 'Sans ta carte je pourrais me croire sur une autre planète'* (Carouge-Geneva, 2015)

Chefdor, Monique, ed., *Madame mon copain: Blaise Cendrars, Elisabeth Prévost, une amitié rarissime* (Nantes, 1997)

Le Quellec Cottier, Christine, ed., *Blaise Cendrars – Henry Poulaille. Correspondance 1925–1961: 'Je travaille et commence à en avoir marre'* (Carouge-Geneva, 2014)

Touret, Michèle, ed., *Blaise Cendrars – Robert Guiette. Lettres 1920–1959: 'Ne m'appelez plus . . . maître'* (Carouge-Geneva, 2013)

Biographical Works on Blaise Cendrars

Bienne, Giselle, *La Ferme de Navarin* (Paris, 2008)

Cendrars, Miriam, *Blaise Cendrars: la vie, le verbe, l'écriture* (Paris, 2006)

——, *Blaise Cendrars: l'or d'un poète* (Paris, 1996)

Dos Passos, John, *The Best Times: An Informal Memoir* (New York, 1966)

t'Serstevens, Albert, *L'Homme que fut Blaise Cendrars* (Paris, 2004)

Select Bibliography of Works on Blaise Cendrars

Bernard, Jaqueline, ed., *Cendrars, l'aventurier du texte* (Grenoble, 1992)

Blaise Cendrars. Europe, 566 (June–July 1976)

Bochner, Jay, *Blaise Cendrars: Discovery and Re-creation* (Toronto, Buffalo, NY, and London, 1978)

Boder, Francis, *La Phrase poétique de Blaise Cendrars* (Paris, 2000)

Bonnefis, Philippe, *Dan Yack: Blaise Cendrars phonographe* (Paris, 1992)

Bozon-Scalzitti, Yvette, *Blaise Cendrars, ou, la Passion de l'écriture* (Lausanne, 1977)

Briche, Luce, *Blaise Cendrars et le livre* (Paris, 2005)

Campa, Laurence, ed., *Album Cendrars* (Paris, 2013)

Caws, Mary Ann, *Manifesto: A Century of Isms* (Lincoln, NE, 2000)

Colvile, Georgiana, *Blaise Cendrars, écrivain protéiforme* (Amsterdam and Atlanta, GA, 1994)

Dow, William, 'John Dos Passos, Blaise Cendrars, and the "Other" Modernism', *Twentieth Century Literature*, XLII/3 (Autumn 1996), pp. 396–415

Flückiger, Jean-Carlo, and Claude Leroy, ed., *Continent Cendrars, 6: Sous le signe de Moravagine* (Caen, 2006)

de Freitas, Maria Teresa, and Claude Leroy, ed., *Brésil: L'Utopialand de Blaise Cendrars* (Paris, 1998)
Goldenstein, Jean-Pierre, *19 Poèmes élastiques de Blaise Cendrars* (Paris, 1986)
Le Quellec Cottier, Christine, *Blaise Cendrars: un homme en partance* (Lausanne, 2010)
Leroy, Claude, *Dans l'atelier de Cendrars* (Paris, 2011)
——, ed., *Blaise Cendrars et la guerre* (Paris, 1995)
——, ed., *Rencontres avec Blaise Cendrars* (Paris, 2007)
——, and Jean-Carlo Flückiger, eds, *Blaise Cendrars, bourlingueur des deux rives* (Paris, 1995)
Martens, David, *L'Invention de Blaise Cendrars. Une poétique de la pseudonymie* (Paris, 2010)
Michaud, Marius, *Cahiers Blaise Cendrars No. 1: Catalogue du Fonds Blaise Cendrars* (Boudry-Neuchâtel and Bern, 1989)
Miller, Henry, *The Books in My Life* (New York, 1969)
Perloff, Marjorie, *The Futurist Moment: Avant-Guerre, Avant-Garde and the Language of Rupture* (Chicago, IL, and London, 1986)
Poizat-Amar, Mathilde, *L'Eclat du voyage: Blaise Cendrars, Victor Segalen, Albert Londres* (Oxford, Bern, Berlin, Brussels, Frankfurt am Main, New York and Vienna, 2017)
Robertson, Eric, 'Painting Windows: Robert Delaunay, Blaise Cendrars, and the Search for Simultaneity', *Modern Language Review*, XL/4 (1995), pp. 883–96
——, '"Space and Time, Sublimated": Science in Balla, Boccioni, Cendrars and Survage', in *Art and Science in Word and Image: Exploration and Discovery*, ed. Keith Williams et al. (Leiden, 2019), pp. 115–30
——, 'Writing the Alphabet of Cinema: Blaise Cendrars', in *Literature and Visual Technologies: Writing After Cinema*, ed. Julian Murphet and Lydia Rainford (London, 2003), pp. 137–54
Rothwell, Andrew, '*L'Or*: Cendrars between Realism and Post-Modernism', *Essays in French Literature*, XXXII/33 (1995/96), pp. 81–115
Scott, Clive, *Reading the Rhythm: The Poetics of French Free Verse, 1910–1930* (Oxford, 1993)
Shingler, Katherine, 'An Art Novel for the Age of Mechanical Reproduction: Blaise Cendrars's *Dan Yack*', in *French Studies*, LXVII/1 (2013), pp. 47–60
SUD: Blaise Cendrars. Colloques poésie Cerisy 18e année (1988)
Wagner, Birgit, and Claude Leroy, ed., *BlaiseMédia. Blaise Cendrars et les médias* (Paris, 2006)
Wall-Romana, Christophe, *Cinepoetry: Imaginary Cinemas in French Poetry* (New York, 2013)

Exhibition Catalogues

Blaise Cendrars au cœur des arts, exh. cat., Musée des Beaux Arts, La Chaux-de-Fonds (2014)

Dis-moi, Blaise. Léger, Chagall, Picasso et Blaise Cendrars, exh. cat., Musée National Fernand Léger, Biot/ Musée National Marc Chagall, Nice/ Musée National Picasso la Guerre et la Paix, Vallauris (2009)

Doisneau rencontre Cendrars, exh. cat., Archives littéraires suisses, Bibliothèque nationale suisse, Bern (2006)

General Critical Reading

Abel, Richard, *French Cinema: The First Wave, 1915–1929* (Princeton, NJ, 1984)

Armstrong, Tim, *Modernism, Technology and the Body: A Cultural Study* (Cambridge, 1998)

Atkin, Nicholas, *The French at War, 1934–1944* (London and New York, 2001)

Barbusse, Henri, *Le Feu: journal d'une escouade* (Paris, 1916)

——, *Under Fire*, trans. Robin Buss (London, 2003)

Barthes, Roland, *La Chambre Claire: notes sur la photographie* (Paris, 1980)

Beauchamp, Ken, *History of Telegraphy* [2001] (London, 2008)

Benjamin, Walter, *The Arcades Project*, trans. Howard Eiland and Kevin McLaughlin (Cambridge, MA, and London, 2002)

——, *Illuminations*, ed. Hannah Arendt, trans. Harry Zorn (London, 1999)

——, *Das Kunstwerk im Zeitalter seiner technischen Reproduzierbarkeit* (Frankfurt am Main, 1963)

Bergson, Henri, *L'Evolution créatrice* (Paris, 1907)

Caruth, Cathy, *Unclaimed Experience: Trauma, Narrative and History* [1996] (Baltimore, MD, and London, 2016)

Corno, Philippe, and Emmanuel Boisset, ed., *Que m'arrive-t-il?* (Rennes, 2009)

Davis, Colin, *Traces of War: Interpreting Ethics and Trauma in Twentieth-Century French Writing* (Liverpool, 2018)

Deleuze, Gilles, *Cinéma 1: L'Image-mouvement* (Paris, 1983)

——, and Félix Guattari, *A Thousand Plateaus: Capitalism and Schizophrenia* (Minneapolis, MN, 1987)

——, and Michel Foucault, *Gérard Fromanger: Photogenic Painting/La Peinture photogénique* (London, 1999)

De Duve, Thierry, *Au Nom de l'art: pour une archéologie de la modernité* (Paris, 1989)

——, *Résonances du Readymade* (Nîmes, 1989)

Doubrovsky, Serge, *Fils* (Paris, 1977)

Duchamp, Marcel, *Duchamp du signe* [1975] (Paris, 1994)

Freud, Sigmund, *On Metapsychology*, The Penguin Freud Library, vol. XI (Harmondsworth, 1987)

Genette, Gérard, *Nous. Essai d'autobiographie* (Paris, 1972)

Goldsmith, Kenneth, *Uncreative Writing: Managing Language in the Digital Age* (New York, 2011)

Hughes, Edward, *Egalitarian Strangeness: On Class Disturbance and Levelling in Modern and Contemporary French Narrative* (Liverpool, 2021)
——, *Writing Marginality in Modern French Literature: From Loti to Genet* (Cambridge, 2001)
Icart, Roger, *Abel Gance ou le Prométhé foudroyé* (Lausanne, 1983)
Lacan, Jacques, *Ecrits*, I (Paris, 1966)
Léger, Fernand, *Fonctions de la peinture* (Paris, 2005)
Le Rouge, Gustave, *Le Mystérieux Docteur Cornélius* (Paris, 1975)
Lejeune, Philippe, *Le Pacte autobiographique* (Paris, 1975)
Marks, Laura U., *The Skin of the Film: Intercultural Cinema, Embodiment and the Senses* (Durham, NC, and London, 2000)
Montagu, Ivor, *With Eisenstein in Hollywood: A Chapter of Autobiography. Including the Scenarios of 'Sutter's Gold' and 'An American Tragedy'* (Berlin, 1968)
Nicholls, Peter, *Modernisms: A Literary Guide* (London, 1995)
Ortega y Gasset, José, *La Deshumanización del Arte y otros ensayos de estética* [1925] (Madrid, 1987)
Peisson, Edouard, *L'Homme couvert de dollars* (Paris, 1946)
Perloff, Marjorie, *Unoriginal Genius: Poetry by Other Means in the New Century* (Chicago, IL, and London, 2010)
Poincaré, Henri, *Théorie des tourbillons* (Paris, 1893)
Saunders, Max, *Self-Impression: Life-Writing, Autobiografiction, and the Forms of Modern Literature* (Oxford and New York, 2010)
Schopenhauer, Arthur, *Die Welt als Wille und Vorstellung* (Leipzig, 1818–19)
Sheringham, Michael, *French Autobiography: Devices and Desires, Rousseau to Perec* (Oxford and New York, 1993)
Virilio, Paul, *Guerre et cinéma: logistique de la perception* (Paris, 1984)
——, *La Machine de vision* (Paris, 1988)
——, *War and Cinema: The Logistics of Perception*, trans. Patrick Camiller (London and New York, 2009)
Wall-Romana, Christophe, *Jean Epstein: Corporeal Cinema and Film Philosophy* (Oxford, 2016)
Williams, Keith, et al., eds, *Art and Science in Word and Image: Exploration and Discovery* (Leiden, 2019)
Wills, David, *Prosthesis* (Stanford, CA, 1995)

Video and Audio Materials

'Blaise Cendrars', *L'Atelier de la creation*, 14–15. Radio France Culture, December 2012
'Blaise Cendrars: en bourlinguant . . .'. Radio interview by Blaise Cendrars with Michel Manoll as part of the series *Les Grandes Heures*, Radio France, 1950
La Compagnie des auteurs: Blaise Cendrars. Four-part radio transmission, presented by Matthieu Garrigou-Lagrange. Radio France Culture
Episode 1: 'Vivre est un acte magique', with Patrice Delbourg

Episode 2: 'Moderne comme Cendrars', with Claude Leroy
Episode 3: 'Ecrire la guerre', with Gisèle Bienne
Episode 4: 'Le monde est ma représentation', with Philippe Forest and Myriam Boucharenc

'Rythmes et bruits du monde'. Radio recording by Blaise Cendrars, 1952. Radio France Culture.

Archival Sources

The Fonds Blaise Cendrars (Blaise Cendrars Archive) is located in the Archives littéraires suisses, overseen by the Bibliothèque nationale suisse, Bern. It contains the extensive archives that Cendrars compiled during his lifetime, which were supplemented after his death by his daughter Miriam Cendrars. The holdings of the Fonds were augmented by the collections of Raymone Cendrars and Mme Jacques-Henri Lévesque and by further material from Miriam Cendrars. The Fonds contains a vast array of published books, manuscripts, photographs, correspondence and other materials produced by and pertaining to Cendrars.

ACKNOWLEDGEMENTS

This book has been a long time in the making and has grown in ways that I had not envisaged at the beginning. It has been shaped by many productive exchanges for which I am indebted to those mentioned here. The late Miriam Cendrars gave me valuable advice when I first visited her father's archives at the Bibliothèque nationale suisse in Bern. The staff who run the Fonds Cendrars there have been a tremendous help: Marius Michaud and, more recently, Fabien Dubosson assisted by Vincent Yersin, were generous with their time and expertise, as too was Fabian Scherler. I am grateful to the Department of Languages, Literatures and Cultures and the Humanities and Arts Research Institute at Royal Holloway, University of London, for help towards the cost of image rights. Thanks are also due to the rights holders for their generous assistance.

At Reaktion Books, publisher Michael Leaman encouraged me to write the book that this has become and waited patiently for the manuscript to materialize. His keen interest in Cendrars made it clear that Reaktion was the right publisher for the book. Alex Ciobanu as assistant to the publisher offered valuable help throughout the editing and design processes. It was also a pleasure to work with the supremely efficient editor Phoebe Colley. The anonymous readers appointed by Reaktion provided encouraging feedback and insightful suggestions that I have tried my best to incorporate. Any omissions are of course my own.

The book incorporates work first presented as papers hosted by organizations including the University of Oxford's Modern French Research Seminar, The Scottish Word and Image Group (SWIG) at the University of Dundee, the International Association of Word and Image Studies (IAWIS/AIERTI) and the Northeast Modern Language Association (NeMLA). My thinking about Cendrars has also benefitted from conversations with colleagues, family members and friends including Elza Adamowicz, Jonathan Black, Kate Conley, Marja Härmänmaa, Gary Harris, Susan Harrow, Hope Margetts, Tim Mathews, Peter Read, Alex Robertson, Isabel Robertson, Nigel Saint, the late Michael Sheringham, Paola Sica, Robert Vilain, Adam Watt and James S. Williams. Andrew Rothwell's writings on Cendrars and his close reading of mine have been extremely valuable. Francis Edeline has shared generous insights into how poetry works. Eddie Hughes introduced me to the Prose du Transsibérien many years ago and remains a great mentor and friend. Johanna Malt read my manuscript, made insightful suggestions, helped generously with translations and has supported me in countless other ways. Finally, I wish to thank my parents, Tom and Marion Robertson, who sparked my childhood curiosity about France on family holidays and continue to take an interest in my work nearly a half century later. This book is dedicated to them.

PHOTO ACKNOWLEDGEMENTS

The author and publishers wish to express their thanks to the below sources of illustrative material and/or permission to reproduce it:

All photos courtesy Fonds Blaise Cendrars, Archives littéraires suisses, Bibliothèque nationale suisse, Bern, unless otherwise specified.

© ADAGP, Paris and DACS, London 2021: pp. 99, 101, 128, 165 (top and bottom); akg-images/Lucien Lorelle: p. 259; from Jean Charcot, *Le 'Pourquoi-pas?' dans l'Antarctique: journal de la deuxième expédition au Pôle sud, 1908–1910* (Paris, 1910), photo Bibliothèque nationale de France, Paris: p. 175; © Collection D. Wallard/ADAGP, Paris, all rights reserved: pp. 224, 225; © DACS, London 2021: pp. 24, 168; © Robert Doisneau/Gamma-Rapho: pp. 280, 286; © Raoul Dufy, ADAGP, Paris and DACS, London 2021: p. 49; © Estate of John Dos Passos: p. 164; © Pracusa20210329: pp. 162–3 (© Succession Miriam Cendrars for the poem by Blaise Cendrars); private collection: p. 219; photo courtesy Railroad Archives: p. 50; photo Roger Schall, © Collection Schall: p. 192; © Succession Brancusi, all rights reserved, ADAGP, Paris and DACS, London 2021, photo © Centre Pompidou, MNAM-CCI, Paris, RMN-Grand Palais/Dist. Photo Scala, Florence: p. 275; © Succession Miriam Cendrars: pp. 25, 48, 53, 79 (all rights reserved); © Tarsila do Amaral: p. 130; © & TM. MOURON – AM.CASSANDRE. Lic 2021-07-01-02 www.cassandre.fr: pp. 106–7, 110–11, 166–7.

INDEX

Page numbers in *italics* indicate illustrations